Foundations of
Early Childhood
Education

Bernard Spodek
University of Illinois

Olivia N. Saracho
University of Maryland

Michael D. Davis
Virginia Commonwealth University

Foundations of Early Childhood Education

Teaching Three-, Four-,
and Five-Year-Old Children

Second Edition

Prentice Hall, Englewood Cliffs, New Jersey 07632

Library of Congress Cataloging-in-Publication Data

Spodek, Bernard.
    Foundations of early childhood education : teaching three-, four-,
and five-year-old children / Bernard Spodek, Olivia N. Saracho,
Michael D. Davis. -- 2nd ed.
        p.   cm.
    Includes bibliographical references.
    ISBN 0-13-326737-7
    1. Education, Preschool. 2. Education, Preschool--United States.
3. Education, Preschool--Curricula.   I. Saracho, Olivia N.
II. Davis, Michael D. III. Title.
LB1140.2.S733 1991
372.21--dc20   90-33898
                                                          CIP

Cover: "Mother Playing with Her Child," by Mary Cassatt.
The Metropolitan Museum of Art, from the Collection
of James Stillman. Gift of Dr. Ernest G. Stillman,
1922. (22.16.23)

Editorial/production supervision: Mary McDonald
Interior design: Karen Buck
Cover design: Patricia Kelly
Prepress buyer: Debbie Kesar
Manufacturing buyer: Mary Anne Gloriande
Photo research: Page Poore

© 1991, 1987 by Prentice-Hall, Inc.
A Division of Simon & Schuster
Englewood Cliffs, New Jersey 07632

Printed in the United States of America
10 9 8 7 6 5 4 3 2 1

ISBN   0-13-326737-7

Prentice-Hall International (UK) Limited, *London*
Prentice-Hall of Australia Pty. Limited, *Sydney*
Prentice-Hall Canada Inc., *Toronto*
Prentice-Hall Hispanoamericana, S.A., *Mexico*
Prentice-Hall of India Private Limited, *New Delhi*
Prentice-Hall of Japan, Inc., *Tokyo*
Simon & Schuster Asia Pte. Ltd., *Singapore*
Editora Prentice-Hall do Brasil, Ltda., *Rio de Janeiro*

Contents

PREFACE   xv

1. INTRODUCTION   1

OBJECTIVES   1

Early Childhood Education   2
  Nursery Schools   3
  Child Care Centers   4
  Head Start   5
  Kindergarten   6
Forces That Affect the Field   7
  Long-Term Effects   8
Trends in Early Childhood Education   9
  Early Education of the Handicapped   10
  Expansion of Kindergarten   11
  Extending School Downward   11
A Look Ahead   12

REFERENCES   12

SUGGESTED ACTIVITIES   13

2. HISTORICAL TRADITIONS   15

OBJECTIVES   15

Educating Young Children in Colonial America   16
Development of Early Childhood Education   17
    The Oberlin School   17
    Robert Owen Creates the Infant School   17
    The Beginning of the Kindergarten   19
    Reform in the Kindergarten   22
    The Child Care Center Develops   23
    The Montessori Method   24
    The Nursery School   27
Federal Involvement in Early Childhood Education   28
Contemporary Developments   29

REFERENCES   30

SUGGESTED ACTIVITIES   31

3. EARLY CHILDHOOD INSTITUTIONS AND PROGRAMS   32

OBJECTIVES   32

Institutions in Early Childhood Education   34
    Child Care Centers   34
    Family Day Care Homes   35
    Kindergarten   38
    Programs for At-Risk Children   39
    Preschool Handicapped   39
    Head Start   40
    Programs for Four-Year-Old Children   41
Institutional Sponsorship   42
    Public vs. Private Programs   43
    For-Profit vs. Not-for-Profit Programs   43
    Church-Related vs. Secular Programs   43
    Fee-Supported vs. Tax-Supported Programs   44
    Employer-Supported Child Care   44
    Purchase of Service   45
Relationships with Social Service Agencies   45
Issues Related to Early Childhood Institutions   46
    Licensing   46
    Accreditation   48
    Making Child Care More Accessible   49
Summary   49

REFERENCES   50

SUGGESTED ACTIVITIES   51

4. BECOMING AN EARLY CHILDHOOD PRACTITIONER   52

OBJECTIVES   52

Roles   54
    Center Director   54
    Teacher   54
    Caregiver   56
    Assistant Teacher   56
    Teacher Aide   56
Professionalizing the Field   56
    Early Childhood Professional Path   59
    Alternative Careers Related to Young Children   62
Preparing to Be an Early Childhood Practitioner   64
    Programs That Prepare Practitioners   64
    Credentialing and Certification   65
    Ethical Considerations   68
    Males in Early Childhood Education   68
    Issues and Concerns   70
Summary   71

REFERENCES   71

SUGGESTED ACTIVITIES   73

5. THE CHILD IN THE EARLY CHILDHOOD PROGRAM   74

OBJECTIVES   74

Developmental Theories and Theorists   75
    G. Stanley Hall (1844–1924): The Child Study Movement   75
    Arnold Gesell (1880–1961): Developmental Ages and Stages   76
    Sigmund Freud (1856–1939): Personality Development   77
    Erik Erikson (1902–   ): Psychosocial Development   79
    B. F. Skinner (1904–1990): Operant Conditioning   81
    Jean Piaget (1896–1980): Intellectual Development   82
Nature and Nurture in Children's Development   84
Developmental Areas   84
    Physical Development   84
    Cognitive Development   87
    Language Development   88
    Emotional Development   90
    Social Development   91
    Development of Values   92
Regularities and Irregularities in Young Children's Development   92
    Cultural Differences   92
    Language Differences   93
    Social Class Differences   95
    Exceptional Children   96

Summary 96

REFERENCES 97

SUGGESTED ACTIVITIES 98

6. **PLANNING AND ORGANIZING THE PHYSICAL ENVIRONMENT 100**

OBJECTIVES 100

Setting the Stage 101
Organizing for Instruction 106
    Activity Centers 109
    Furniture and Equipment 111
    Free and Inexpensive Materials 113
Designing Outdoor Play Areas 114
    Selecting Outdoor Materials and Equipment 115
Scheduling Activities 116
Summary 120

REFERENCES 121

SUGGESTED ACTIVITIES 121

7. **PLANNING AND ORGANIZING THE SOCIAL ENVIRONMENT 122**

OBJECTIVES 122

Organizing Children 123
    Grouping 123
    One-to-One Interactions 125
    Using Children to Extend Teaching 126
Classroom Management 126
    Setting Limits 126
    Behavior Modification 127
    Kounin's Model of Classroom Management 128
    Dreikurs' Model of Discipline 129
    Redirection 130
    Guiding Children's Behavior 130
    Managing Problem Behavior 131
    Teaching Positive Social Interactions 133
    Supporting Children's Prosocial Behavior 134
    Play Intervention 134

Organizing Adults   136
    Working with Paraprofessionals   137
    Working with Volunteers   137
    Working with Community Resources   138
Summary   139

REFERENCES   140

SUGGESTED ACTIVITIES   140

8. WORKING WITH PARENTS   142

OBJECTIVES   142

Families   143
Working with Parents   145
    Parent Involvement   146
    Parent Advisory Groups   149
    Parent Education   149
Communicating with Parents   153
    Informal Communication Techniques   154
    Formal Communication Techniques   154
Working Successfully with Parents   158
Summary   159

REFERENCES   159

SUGGESTED ACTIVITIES   160

9. EVALUATION IN EARLY CHILDHOOD PROGRAMS   161

OBJECTIVES   161

Ways of Gathering Information   162
    Observations   162
    Standardized Tests   167
    Informal Tests   169
Program Evaluation   171
Evaluating Classroom Settings   172
Screening Exceptional Children   176
Recording and Communicating the Results of the Evaluation   177
    Reporting to Parents   178
Summary   179

REFERENCES   180

SUGGESTED ACTIVITIES   181

10. PLAY IN EARLY CHILDHOOD EDUCATION   183

OBJECTIVES   183

Defining Play   184
  Understanding Play   185
  Gender Differences in Play   188
  Stages in Play Development   188
  Using Play to Achieve Educational Goals   189
Developing Play Activities   190
  Outdoor Play   191
  Indoor Play   192
  Initiating Play Activities   192
  Moving Children's Play Along   192
Supporting Outdoor Play   194
  Large-Motor Activity   194
  Wheel Toys   195
  Building Structures   195
  Sand and Water   196
  Dramatic Play   197
  Games   198
Supporting Indoor Play   200
  Block Building   200
  Dramatic Play   204
  Table Activities   206
Play and the Early Childhood Curriculum   208
Summary   210

REFERENCES   211

SUGGESTED ACTIVITIES   212

11. CREATIVE ACTIVITIES   213

OBJECTIVES   213

Self-Expression   214
  Creativity   215
Art Experiences   216
  Two-Dimensional Art   216
  Three-Dimensional Art   221
  Craft Activities   226
Music Activities   228
  Rhythmic Activities   229
  Singing with Young Children   231
  Using Musical Instruments   234

Movement Education   237
    Creative Movement   240
    Movement Activities for Physical Development   240
Summary   244

REFERENCES   *245*

SUGGESTED ACTIVITIES   *245*

12. **LANGUAGE AND LITERACY**   **247**

OBJECTIVES   *247*

Language Arts Programs for Young Children   248
    Goals of a Language Arts Program   248
    Children's Literature   249
    Dealing with Stereotypes in Children's Literature   256
    Poetry   257
    Storytelling   260
    Professional Materials for Storytelling   262
    Puppetry   262
    Creative Dramatics   266
    Finger Plays   267
    Action Stories   269
Teaching Reading and Writing   270
    Designing a Reading Readiness Program   270
    Emergent Literacy   272
    Schema Theory   274
    The Relationship Between Reading and Writing   275
    Teaching about the Written Language   277
Summary   280

REFERENCES   *281*

SUGGESTED ACTIVITIES   *283*

13. **COGNITIVELY ORIENTED LEARNING:**
    SCIENCE AND MATHEMATICS   **284**

OBJECTIVES   *284*

Cognitive Theory   285
Science for Young Children   286
Topics for Early Childhood Science   288
    Physics   288
    Animals   289
    Plants   291
    Weather   293
    Nutrition   296

Ecology and the Environment   298
Materials and Experiences for Early Childhood Science   300
Mathematics for Young Children   301
Topics for Early Childhood Mathematics   302
    Counting   303
    Number   303
    Seriation   304
    Sets   305
Materials for Early Childhood Mathematics   305
Using Everyday Events to Teach about Mathematics   308
Summary   310

REFERENCES   310

SUGGESTED ACTIVITIES   311

**14. SOCIAL-PERSONAL LEARNING:
THE SOCIAL STUDIES AND BEYOND   312**

OBJECTIVES   312

Developing and Understanding the Social World   313
A Social Studies Program for Young Children: Content   315
    Concepts   316
    Field Trips   317
    Resource Persons   319
    Artifacts   320
    Audiovisual Materials   320
    Acting on Acquired Knowledge   321
    Mapping   322
A Social Studies Program for Young Children: Socialization   323
    Learning School and Community Roles   324
    Developing School-Appropriate Behavior   324
    Building Self-Awareness   326
    Young Children and Values   327
    Levels of Moral Thought   328
    Developing Cultural Awareness: Multicultural Education   330
Summary   332

REFERENCES   333

SUGGESTED ACTIVITIES   334

15. TOWARD PROFESSIONALISM   335

OBJECTIVES   335

Teachers' Personal Development   336

Teachers' Professional Development   337
    In-Service Programs   338
    Professional Organizations   342
    Organizations Concerned with Children and Families   343
    ERIC Clearinghouses   344
    Journals   345
    Position Statements   346
Summary   347

REFERENCES   *348*

SUGGESTED ACTIVITIES   *348*

INDEX   351

Preface

Early childhood education has always been an exciting and dynamic field. It has continued to maintain its dynamism in the four years since the first edition of this book was published. The knowledge we have gained in the recent past about how children learn and develop, our awareness of the positive results of enrolling young children in early childhood education programs, and the increased acceptance of early childhood education by the American public make this a particularly opportune time to study early childhood education and to prepare to become an early childhood education professional.

Foundations of Early Childhood Education is an introductory text for students preparing to teach children ages three through five. It is intended to provide basic knowledge about the field of early childhood education, about the work that practitioners do with young children, and about the ideas that underlie that work. It can be used in undergraduate courses in four-year colleges and universities as well as in community colleges. Because of the wealth of resources included in this book, students will wish to keep it as a reference as they begin their teaching.

This book presents a realistic view of the field of early childhood education. It integrates theory with practice so that the reader can understand not only what things happen in schools for young children, but why they happen as well. The book is written in a clear, concise style using understandable language. Concepts are carefully explained. Practical examples and appropriate illustrations are provided throughout so that even the most complicated ideas can be understood.

The book describes the historical traditions of the field of early childhood education as well as contemporary early childhood institutions and programs, the types of practitioners in the field, and the requirements for different practitioner roles. It also presents basic theories and knowledge of child develop-ment that are so vital to teaching young children. The text provides the basis for planning the physical and social environment for teaching, for using different forms of educational evaluation, and for working with parents. A separate chap-ter is included for each curriculum area to help the reader focus on the specifics of program planning and implementation.

Within each topic, basic theory and research are related and integrated with practical knowledge gained from classroom teaching. Careful attention is given to provide the most up-to-date research and to address emerging issues in the field. Examples, practical applications, and guidelines for practice as well as verbal and visual illustrations are generously used to help students explore the implications of the concepts, ideas, and theories presented throughout the book.

The material throughout this textbook has been expanded and updated. More current facts, illustrations, and references have been provided as appropri-ate. New topics have been added, including a discussion of public school pro-grams for four-year-olds, child advocacy, and the emergence of literacy in young children.

We wish to acknowledge our debt to the many persons who have contrib-uted to the development of this text. Much of the knowledge we have gained over the years and that is reflected in this book comes from the many contacts we have had with others in the field: teachers, undergraduate and graduate students, and parents and children. We wish especially to thank those who reviewed our manu-script at various stages and provided helpful suggestions, criticism, and com-ments. These include Professors Nita H. Barbour of the University of Maryland (Baltimore County), Judy Campbell of Parkland College (Illinois), Jacqueline Blackwell of Indiana University (Indianapolis), and John Cryan of the University of Toledo.

We also wish to thank the staff, parents, and children of Martin Luther King Jr., George Washington, and Thomas Paine Elementary Schools in Urbana, Illinois, especially those in Sandra Beak's, Melanie Turnspeed's, and Jane Maehr's kindergarten classes, of the Garza Elementary School in Brownsville, Texas, and of Early Learning Children's Center in Champaign, Illinois. The bulk of the pho-tographs of children in school were taken in these classes by Bernard Spodek.

Most important, we wish to acknowledge the support and encourage-ment we have received from our families during the period we were writing this book. Without the love and support of Connie, Meg, and Sally Davis, of Francisca S., Pablo J., Saul Villareal, and Lydia Gonzales, and of Prudence Spodek, this book would not have been possible.

1

Introduction

OBJECTIVES

After completing this introductory chapter, the student will be able to:

1. Define early childhood education.
2. Describe early childhood programs in different settings for children ages three to five, including: nursery school, child care center, Head Start program, prekindergarten, private kindergarten, and public kindergarten.
3. Identify the social forces that influence the field of early childhood education.
4. Specify the educational effects of preschool programs on children.
5. Describe recent trends in early childhood education.

The early years in children's lives have long been considered among the most important. Children learn a great deal at this age, and what they learn has long-term, significant consequences.

From infancy on, children develop physically, mentally, socially, and emotionally. Much of this development is related to maturation. The ability of young children to walk, to talk, to think logically and to function as part of a group is dependent upon maturation, but it is also influenced by their experiences. Education begins at this early stage. Parents teach children to walk and to talk. They teach children self-caring skills, manners, values, and a host of other things. Parents and other family members become the children's first teachers, stimulating children's physical and mental growth. Parents generally do not study how to teach their children. They naturally and spontaneously interact with children. Their teaching skills grow out of living with their children throughout the day. Although it is informal, the instructional role of parents is critical in the lives of young children.

The child's home provides an important context for learning. In many ways, the school supplements the home. Young children's experiences in school are no less natural then their experiences in their home child-rearing environment, although often they can be planned with greater care. It is the integration of education in and out of school that is important.

We generally assume that children will be raised in a good home—one that will provide for all the needs of the young child. This is not always the case, however. Many families lack adequate resources to provide all the complex requirements of rearing children within our society. Families are not always able to provide the best conditions for the development of their children. Poverty, isolation, and the demands of earning a living can limit what may be available. Early childhood programs work hand in hand with families to provide the necessary basis for the children's development, supplementing parents' child-rearing efforts and increasing the support to allow children to assume their role in society successfully. Many of the programs offered in schools or centers function in isolation from the home. But educational programs can be brought into the home as well. Such home-based educational programs, involving parents as well as children, are especially effective for very young children.

EARLY CHILDHOOD EDUCATION

Early childhood education is generally defined as the education of children from birth to age eight. It includes programs for infants and toddlers, nursery school, child care, and preschool programs, as well as kindergarten and primary grades. Sometimes the term *early childhood education* is used to refer to those programs serving children under the age of six. Sometimes it is used to refer just to programs for children below kindergarten age. The material in this text will focus only on three- through five-year-old children who are educated and cared for in kindergarten and prekindergarten settings, such as nursery schools and child care centers.

Children in their early childhood years are served by many kinds of institutions. The majority of children from ages five through eight are educated in the kindergarten and primary grades of the public schools. Some are educated in private institutions: religious and parochial schools as well as private secular schools. Most programs for children below age five are in private institutions, and are operated either for-profit or not-for-profit. These institutions serve fewer children than do the public schools, and often enroll groups that are alike in economic status, ethnicity, or some other group trait. Child care centers differ from nursery schools. They have longer daily hours and are concerned with caring for as well as educating children. No one program or setting can meet all the needs of all young children and their families.

Public schooling in the United States usually begins at age five or six, with enrollment in public school kindergarten or first grade. This situation, however, is changing. A number of states are beginning to include four-year-olds in public education. Also, while compulsory school attendance is not required in most states until the age of seven, some states are beginning to require attendance as early as age five. Other states are requiring kindergarten attendance for admission to first grade.

As kindergarten became part of the public school system, it was often considered as something different that was grafted on to the elementary grades. Public school educators often seemed unsure as to whether kindergarten really belonged. Early childhood education has now become more widely accepted as part of public education. Increasingly, public schools are accepting responsibilities for educating children below the typical kindergarten entrance age of five. Four-year-olds are being enrolled in public school prekindergarten programs in many communities, and schools are beginning to educate children even younger than age four. Still, most children below age five are not in the public schools. They are educated in nursery schools, day care centers, and Head Start programs, as well as private kindergartens. These institutions are similar in many ways. They also differ in some ways, including varied institutional settings, services offered, program goals, and even psychological theories that underlie the programs.

Nursery Schools

The original nursery school, described in Chapter 2, was based on a philosophy of nurturance: a concern for the child's social, physical, emotional, and intellectual needs. The nursery school teacher bathed children, dressed them in clean outfits, provided them with food and rest, saw that they received sufficient fresh air, and also educated them. The children were taught self-caring skills (such as washing oneself and tying one's shoelaces) and taking care of plants, animals, and the school environment. They were involved in music, language, reading readiness, writing, mathematics, and science activities. Play was an important part of the program, which flowed freely indoors and outdoors. The children were provided with opportunities for art construction, water play, playing with sand, and other nonstructured activities.

Nursery schools provide a broad-base education to children below kindergarten age.

Most nursery schools today are concerned *primarily* with children's education. Most colleges and universities also use the nursery school as a laboratory to prepare early childhood teachers and to conduct research. Departments of child and family studies (or their equivalent) may use nursery schools as laboratories and demonstration centers for child development, education for parenthood, and instruction on home management. Parent-cooperative nursery schools, in which parents own the school and often participate in the children's programs, offer nursery school education at a reasonable cost and often focus on parent education. This may include child observations, discussions, and meetings on topics such as child development, nutrition, and child-rearing practices.

Presently the emphasis in nursery school is to provide a broad-based education to children below kindergarten age. Nursery educators are concerned with intellectual learning, but important emphasis is also placed on expression and creativity.

Child Care Centers

The history of child care in the United States consists of sporadic attempts to provide care for workers' children and patchwork legislation to regulate children's centers. A unique feature of a child care center is that it serves the children of parents who cannot be at home full-time to take care of their children. These parents may be raising children in a single-parent home, working, ill, hospitalized, or not able to care for their children during the day for some other reason.

Presently child care is offered in a variety of settings. Young children are cared for in homes, either by relatives or neighbors, or in child care centers. Licensed or unlicensed family day care homes are run on a small scale in private residences. Child care centers offer care and education on a larger scale. These centers serve three-, four-, and five-year-old children as well as infants and toddlers. Often, they also serve school-age children before and after school and when public schools are closed. The child care center is open for a long period every day, often from 6:00 A.M. until 6:00 P.M. Its hours depend on the needs of the children's parents. The child care center assumes a unique responsibility, supplementing the care of parents who are not available to their children during some part of the day.

Ideally, a good child care center is staffed by teachers who are well prepared in the education and care of young children, contains an adequate amount of equipment and material, and offers a high-quality program of education responsive to the needs of young children. Child care programs can and should be as good as the best nursery school, kindergarten, or Head Start program.

Traditionally, child care has been an individual family's concern. States are involved in child care primarily by establishing minimum licensing standards that protect children from harm. The federal government presently provides limited support for child care through the Social Security Act and through limited tax credits. There are presently bills before Congress to provide greater support for child care. Business and industry are also becoming increasingly involved in child care as a worker's benefit or a means to insure continuity in the work force.

Head Start

It became evident in the 1960s that children from economically impoverished families were failing in school at an alarming rate. Available evidence suggested that early intervention could make a critical difference (e.g., Bloom, 1964; Hunt, 1961). After a variety of research programs were launched, the Department of Health, Education and Welfare funded Project Head Start as part of the war on poverty. Head Start represented a national commitment to provide comprehensive services for children under age six who came from low-income families. When Head Start was conceived, there was a lack of strong research evidence on the effects of early intervention. Significant research to date, however, provides evidence to support Head Start programs.

Head Start is currently administered by the Administration for Children, Youth and Families in the Department of Health and Human Services. It is a compensatory program; 90 percent of the Head Start children come from families with low incomes; 10 percent of the children are handicapped. The purpose of the program is to improve the health and physical ability of poor children, to develop their physical and intellectual skills, to involve parents in their children's program, and to provide appropriate social services for the family. Eighty percent of the funds flow from the federal government, and 20 percent are expected to come from local sources. Sometimes this local support is provided as an in-kind contribution, for example, providing space and maintenance. A community action agency can run the Head Start program directly or can contract for services from public or private nonprofit agencies.

Head Start was created as a unique program for young children. The underlying assumption is that success in school and in life is based on the child's complete growth: what a child knows, how a child feels, how well the child's body functions, the child's social skills, and the child's view of him or herself. Parents play a major role in the Head Start program, attending meetings, participating in the program, and serving on Policy Advisory Committees. Head Start teachers strive to work with parents as a team, to have parents supplement them, support them, and work in the same direction. The teachers work intensively with children and their parents; the parents are included in and feel part of the program.

Head Start has demonstrated its success with children during the past twenty-five years. Unfortunately, limits on federal appropriations have kept the program from serving the majority of the children who need the service. Presently, only about 25 percent of those children who are eligible are enrolled in Head Start.

Kindergarten

Kindergarten programs in the United States primarily serve five-year-old children, although more four-year-old kindergartens are coming into existence, and kindergartens in many other countries enroll children ages three through six. Kindergarten programs include crafts and art activities, and different types of play activities. The child's present life and its context is often used as a source of learning and is reflected in play. Thus, blocks, dolls, and miniature housekeeping materials are provided to represent the child's life context.

The kindergarten movement began in America as an agent of social and educational reform. As kindergartens were established in public schools, they provided an opportunity for greater numbers of children to attend kindergarten.

Kindergarten programs provide a wide range of educational activities.

In earlier kindergartens the teaching of reading was carefully avoided. It is still a major issue, as academic skills are being taught in many kindergartens today. Whereas in the past, kindergartens influenced and modified the primary grades, currently the primary grades seem to be influencing kindergartens in the public school (Spodek, 1982).

The kindergarten program has had strong and lasting effects on American education. It has focused on educational issues in a democratic society: the relationship of teachers, parents, and children; whether the kindergarten should be used primarily to prepare children for the primary grades; whether it's more important to develop children's social skills and creativity or train children in academics; and the need to assist low-income children to achieve social mobility. These are all critical issues in early childhood education today, and they are being debated by educators, psychologists, philosophers, sociologists, and politicians.

FORCES THAT AFFECT THE FIELD

In its development, early childhood education has always been responsive to social forces, and these forces continue to shape programs today. One such force has been the increasing number of mothers working outside the home. This has had a strong impact on American family life. Women work for a variety of reasons: to raise their standard of living, to adapt to different lifestyles, or to seek greater personal satisfaction. Both home and work had to change as mothers of young children went to work. We have become aware that raising children is a family responsibility rather than only the woman's responsibility. High-quality child care is essential to allow women to achieve career goals outside the home.

A number of employers provide work-site child care centers for their employees as well as for children in the surrounding communities. Others offer a referral service or purchase child care services from existing centers. This development reflects a number of social changes: strides in the education of women; changes in lifestyles and family structure; technological developments in the economy; less time consumed in the management of the household; and the encouragement given to women to employ their strengths and talents in a variety of ways.

Another reason for the need for child care centers is that the increased number of working women has also led to a decline in the availability of traditional baby-sitters. Grandparents and unmarried relatives are no longer at home, known and trusted servants are no longer employed, and neighbors are no longer old family friends. To replace these, child care agencies have expanded.

There are other social conditions that have created a shortage of child care services. Some mothers are returning to college or vocational school to acquire the necessary skills and knowledge to gain meaningful employment. These women need quality care for their children while they attend school. Mothers of young children with handicapping conditions also need special services, as do children of mothers who are ill or themselves handicapped. For these families quality child care may be unavailable or beyond their means.

Another social force affecting young children is the reduced space available for children's play. High-rise apartments, townhouses, and other multiple-family dwellings tend not to have trees, rocks, or large grassy areas. Some homes (rural, urban, affluent, poor) have become simpler and more automated, leaving children with limited opportunities to explore and create. Finally, family planning has reduced the size of families, making it more difficult to find playmates for young children. Previously, children were able to play with their brothers and sisters or with neighbors.

These forces have had an impact on our society so that child care services cannot be provided by families alone. Other social institutions, private industries, and government and community agencies are becoming increasingly involved in the need to find or create needed child care services.

Long-Term Effects

While early childhood programs are used to respond to social problems, they also have pervasive and long-lasting educational effects. The Consortium on Longitudinal Studies report, *Persistence of preschool effects* (Lazar, Hubbell, Murray, Rosche, & Royce, 1977), demonstrates that early intervention programs can provide significant long-term educational benefits to children. Early intervention can help reduce the number of children who are assigned to classes for the handicapped and who are retained in a grade because of low achievement. Early childhood programs have also produced significant increases in IQ and achievement in the early primary grades. Children in these programs are also more likely to give achievement-related reasons for feeling good about themselves.

The High/Scope report, *Changed Lives* (Berrueta-Clement, Schweinhart, Barnett, Epstein, & Weikart, 1984), also demonstrated the long-term effects of early childhood education. The authors suggest that, in terms of both social and economic costs, early childhood education more than pays for itself in relation to money that need not be spent later. Their cost-benefit analysis shows a 7-to-1 return on investment.

It is not enough just to provide programs for young children; the programs must be of high quality. Benjamin Bloom (1964), J. McVicker Hunt (1961), and Robert Hess and Virginia Shipman (1965) all support the importance of environmental factors in the development and education of young children. A study by Jean V. Carew (1980) examined home-reared and day care children in their second and third years of life to record their everyday experiences. She then compared the relationship of these experiences to the children's test performance. Effective caregivers, whether parents or teachers, were successful in integrating a variety of strategies to develop children's intellectual competence. Young children seemed to master important cognitive and social skills and develop positive attitudes about people and situations when they worked alone or interacted with others in a child care setting. The quality of the interactions and the learning experiences were a central factor in the children's cognitive development.

The attributes of effective caregivers found in Carew's study were also found by Marlis Mann (1970), who studied lower socioeconomic parents' use of elaboration and extension to assist their children in describing, labeling, predicting, and defining relationships, as well as making associations. The amount and diversity of the mothers' verbal stimulation were important factors in improving children's concept development. Phyllis Levenstein (1970) in her parent education program focused on improving verbal interaction skills in parents of low-income children. She found that when they were improved, intellectual functioning improved significantly. These studies and one by Ann P. Streissguth and Helen L. Bee (1972) show a relationship between verbal stimulation and the development of intelligence. They suggest that improving the quality of the interactions of caregivers and children can enhance the learning and intellectual development of young children.

The programs described have been designed for low-income children. The impact of early education on the lives of middle-class children is not as clear. One study, by Jean M. Larson and Clyde C. Robinson (1989), has demonstrated positive effects on school achievement for low-risk, advantaged boys, though not for girls. Perhaps early childhood programs have emphasized the same types of skills that parents of middle-class children already emphasize, and thus the influence of the educational program is masked for these children.

James Macdonald (1969) describes early childhood education as a form of deliberate social intervention. The need for such intervention has grown out of society's need to prepare children to adjust to the existing social order. School experiences can help children conform to this order or prepare them for a new emerging society. Whatever its purpose, however, effective early childhood education programs help children change. The important thing for teachers is to ensure that the change is in a direction we value.

TRENDS IN EARLY CHILDHOOD EDUCATION

Early childhood education has changed significantly since the 1960s. A number of trends have become evident in recent years. One trend is the move to decrease the size of children's groups. In some public schools there may be more than 30 children in a kindergarten class. School personnel are now attempting to make them smaller. In Indiana, for example, the Prime Time program helped to bring first grades down to an average of 18 children per class in its first year, and similar reductions are being made in second and third grades and in kindergarten.

Another trend has been toward greater parent involvement. As a result of Head Start and various programs for the handicapped, more and more early childhood educators are seeking to include parents in the educational endeavor. Parents can help in identifying children's needs and in advising about program elements. They can also be involved in program design decisions and may have the right to approve or reject program changes as well as make suggestions for its improvement.

Other issues that have recently emerged relate to the education of young handicapped children, especially in classes with normal children, and the expansion of public school kindergarten.

Early Education of the Handicapped

In the past, programs for handicapped children, when available, were provided only for children of school age, often not until they were seven years old. Early intervention programs, however, have shown pervasive and long-lasting effects on children who have educational deficits. Although not all children's disabilities are cured, often children are able to learn to utilize their personal resources and capacities at an early age.

In the past, when handicapped children were educated, they were usually provided separate programs in separate settings. These segregated programs were not necessarily more successful, however, and in many cases they reduced the educational opportunities for children. Handicapped children did not learn to interact with nonhandicapped people in a normal environment. What they did learn was often difficult to transfer to everyday situations. Furthermore, handicapped children who were educated in normal settings were shown to achieve at an equal or better level than those in separate programs. As a result, a movement developed to educate children in the least restrictive educational setting and in as normal a situation as possible. Many handicapped children have been integrated with nonhandicapped children in "mainstreamed" classes (Spodek, Saracho, & Lee, 1983).

Unfortunately, this integration of handicapped children into a regular classroom, when appropriate, does not often happen to preschool children. Many public schools do not offer programs for children below age five except for handicapped children. Head Start does provide for the integration of handicapped and nonhandicapped children, since 10 percent of the children enrolled must be handicapped. This number represents a small percentage of those who might be served, however.

This situation may change. As public schools enroll more children in kindergarten and prekindergarten programs, the prospect of mainstreaming young children increases. In addition, there is a movement developing for the public schools to educate even young handicapped children.

In 1976, Public Law 94–142, the Education of All Handicapped Children Act, required all schools receiving federal aid to provide education for handicapped children, ages three to twenty-one, in the least restrictive educational setting. While young handicapped children were included in this act, schools only needed to provide education for them if comparable age nonhandicapped children were enrolled. Public Law 99–457, the Education of the Handicapped Act Amendments of 1986, extended the requirement to educate handicapped children to infants and toddlers as well as preschool children. While states are still in the process of planning for the services to be offered under this act, it is likely that most services for infants and toddlers will be home-based, while services for preschoolers will be predominately school-based.

Expansion of Kindergarten

Kindergartens have been included in public elementary schools for over one hundred years. However, most kindergartens differ from the rest of the grades in many ways. This is partly the result of the kindergarten children being younger as well as differences in the traditions of kindergarten education and elementary education. Age-grade standards and existing testing procedures for older children place many restrictions on kindergarten teachers and children.

Many early childhood educators believe that the children's classroom should be a miniature society. They focus on the relationship between the children's out-of-school and in-school experiences and value children's active participation as learners. These teachers serve to guide the learning experiences rather than instruct directly.

As kindergartens have been integrated into elementary schools, however, the primary grade curriculum has been imposed on the kindergarten. In many kindergarten classrooms, the educational programs look very much like first-grade programs. Preschools have also been pressured to push for early literacy by parents' anxiety and zeal for their children to learn to read early.

Extending Schooling Downward

Over the past decade, public schools have significantly expanded their early childhood education programs, not only by increasing kindergarten enrollments and creating all-day kindergartens, but by extending their programs downward and enrolling younger children. At present, twenty-seven states support prekindergarten programs in public schools (Mitchell, Seligson, & Marx, 1989). Some of these programs serve children as young as age three.

While some school systems have offered prekindergarten education for all four-year-old children, others have offered programs only to special populations of children. Most of these prekindergarten programs are designed for children who are considered to be at-risk of educational failure later in their school career. This judgment may be made based on demographics, with children who are poor, from bilingual backgrounds, in single-parent families, with teen-age mothers, or come from another background that may indicate a greater potential for failure in school than the norm. Sometimes these children are identified as being at-risk because they have siblings who are having difficulty in school. In addition, children may be identified through preschool screening as having some developmental delay, but not to the extent that they are considered handicapped.

Programs for at-risk children generally provide some educational enrichment to foster language and intellectual development. Often there is a parent education component to such programs, so that children are not served in isolation. Whether such programs should be available to all children or just for targeted populations remains at issue. There are also some educators who believe that public schools should provide comprehensive extended day programs that serve child care needs rather than just part-day programs of education.

A LOOK AHEAD

These and other issues will be explored in the rest of the book, along with some information about the context of these issues and the implications for teachers. First, several chapters present the historical traditions of early childhood education, a look at early childhood institutions and programs, and a review of the kinds of practitioners found in early childhood education and the preparation necessary to become a practitioner. A brief review of child development concepts and theories is also provided. These represent the foundations of knowledge of early childhood education.

Succeeding chapters discuss the physical and social environment, covering the immediate context in which early childhood education takes place. Following the environment are chapters concerned with ways of working with parents and ways of evaluating programs.

Next are chapters that deal directly with program content: play, creative activities, language and literacy, science and mathematics, and social-personal learning. Since any textbook, course, or program to prepare early childhood practitioners represents only the beginning of professional preparation—a process that continues throughout one's career—the final chapter looks at how early childhood educators can continue to extend their knowledge.

Thus, this book represents a beginning step—a foundation—for those interested in learning about early childhood education. Only by continuously reflecting about practice, seeking additional sources of knowledge, and working together with other early childhood educators can we achieve the level of professional competence necessary for all early childhood teachers.

REFERENCES

BERRUETA-CLEMENT, J. R., L. J. SCHWEINHART, W. S. BARNETT, A. S. EPSTEIN, AND D. P. WEIKART (1984). Changed lives: The effects of the Perry Preschool Program on youths through age 19. *Monographs of the High/Scope Education Research Foundation, 8.*

BLOOM, B. (1964). *Stability and change in human characteristics.* New York: John Wiley & Sons.

BREDEKAMP, S. (Ed.). (1987). *Developmentally appropriate practice in early childhood programs serving children from birth through age 8.* (exp. ed.) Washington, DC: National Association for the Education of Young Children.

BRICKER, D. D., AND W. A. BRICKER (1971). *Toddler research and intervention project report: Year I.* IMRID Behavioral Science Monograph 10. Institute of Mental Retardation and Intellectual Development. Nashville, TN: George Peabody College.

BUREAU OF THE CENSUS (1978). *Population characteristics: School enrollment . . . social and economic characteristics of students: October 1977* (Advance report). Washington, DC: U.S. Government Printing Office.

CAREW, J. V. (1980). Experience and the development of intelligence in young children at home and in day care. *Monographs of the Society for Research in Child Development, 45,* Serial No. 187.

COHEN, S., M. SEMMES, AND M. J. GURALNICK (1979). Public Law 94-142 and the education of preschool handicapped children. *Exceptional Children, 45,* 270–285.

CONSORTIUM ON DEVELOPMENTAL CONTINUITY (1977). *The persistence of preschool effects.* Department of Health, Education and Welfare Publication #(OHD) 78-30130.

HESS, R., AND V. SHIPMAN, (1965). Early experience and the socialization of cognitive modes in children. *Child Development, 36,* 869–886.

HUNT, J. M. (1961). *Intelligence and experience.* New York: Ronald.

KEYSERLING, M. (1972). *Windows on day care.* New York: National Council of Jewish Women.

LARSON, J. M. AND C. C. ROBINSON (1989). Later effects of preschool on low-risk children. *Early Childhood Research Quarterly, 4*(1), 133–144.

LAZAR, I., V. R. HUBBELL, H. MURRAY, M. ROSCHE, AND J. ROYCE (1977). *Summary report: The persistence of preschool effects: A long-term follow-up of fourteen infant and preschool experiments.* Washington, DC: U.S. Department of Health, Education and Welfare, Administration of Children, Youth and Families, OHDS, #OHDS 78-30129.

LEVENSTEIN, P. (1970). Cognitive growth in preschoolers through verbal interaction with mothers. *American Journal of Orthopsychiatry, 40,* 426–429.

MACDONALD, J. (1969). A proper curriculum for young children. *Phi Delta Kappan, 50*(7), 406–409.

MAGID, R. Y. (1983). *Child care initiatives for working parents: Why employers get involved.* New York: AMA Membership Publications Division, American Management Association.

MANN, M. (1970). *The effect of a preschool language program on two-year-old children and their mothers.* Final Report. ERIC Document No. ED 045 224.

MITCHELL, A., M. SELIGSON, AND F. MARX (1989). *Early childhood programs and the public schools: Beyond promise and practice.* Dover, MA: Auburn House.

SPODEK B. (1982). The kindergarten: A retrospective and contemporary look. In L. Katz (Ed.), *Current topics in early childhood education,* Vol. 4, pp. 173–191. Norwood, NJ: Ablex Publishing Co.

—— (1988). Conceptualizing today's kindergarten curriculum. *Elementary School Journal, 89*(2), 203–212.

SPODEK, B., O. N. SARACHO, AND R. C. LEE (1983). Mainstreaming handicapped children in the preschool. In S. Kilmer (Ed.), *Advances in early education and day care,* Vol. 3, pp. 107–132. Greenwich, CT: JAI Press.

STREISSGUTH, A. P., AND H. L. BEE (1972). Mother–child interactions and cognitive development in children. In W. W. Hartup (Ed.), *The young child: Reviews of research,* Vol. 2. Washington, DC: National Association for the Education of Young Children.

UNITED STATES DEPARTMENT OF HEALTH, EDUCATION AND WELFARE, ADMINISTRATION FOR CHILDREN, YOUTH AND FAMILIES (1977). *Day care centers in the United States.* Washington, DC: U.S. Government Printing Office.

UNITED STATES DEPARTMENT OF HEALTH, EDUCATION AND WELFARE (1976). *Statistical highlights from the national childcare consumer study.* Washington, DC: The Department, #OHD 76–31096.

UNITED STATES DEPARTMENT OF LABOR (1977). *Working mothers and their children.* Washington, DC: Women's Bureau, Employment Standards Administration, The Department.

WEBER, E. (1984). *Ideas influencing early childhood education: A theoretical analysis.* New York: Teachers College Press.

WESTHOFF, C. R., AND R. PARKE, JR. (Eds.) (1972). *Demographic and social aspects of population growth and the American future.* U.S. Government Printing Office.

ZIGLER, E. (1972). Paper presented at the Education Commission of the States Meeting, Denver, December 7.

SUGGESTED ACTIVITIES

1. Discuss the value of good child care, nursery school, Head Start, and kindergarten programs for young children.

2. Visit different early childhood programs as a part of a small group (e.g., child care center, nursery school, Head Start, kindergarten). Compare the similarities and differences in educational setting, educational purposes, goals, philosophy, and types of experiences provided. Allow each group to share its report.

3. Interview an early childhood program director. Inquire about the purpose of the program, community served, and other related information.

4. Describe an ideal early childhood school for young children. Include descriptions of the building, classrooms, playground, eating facilities, and rest rooms. Use photographs or drawings if possible.

5. Develop a chart comparing the various schedules used in a child care center, Head Start program, nursery school and kindergarten program.

6. Develop a directory of early childhood schools. For each school include a brief description of the settings, fees, requirements for admission, program services, hours, meals (if any), teacher/child ratio, and special services offered.

2

Historical Traditions

OBJECTIVES

After completing this chapter on historical traditions, the student will be able to:

1. Describe the beginning of early childhood education.
2. Identify the pioneers in the field, including Jean Frederick Oberlin, Robert Owen, Freidrich Froebel, Maria Montessori, and Margaret McMillan.
3. Discuss the philosophy of Owen's infant school, Froebel's kindergarten, Montessori's *Casa dei Bambini*, and McMillan's nursery school.
4. Describe the beginning of Head Start.
5. Explain the relationship between current programs and historical programs.

Young children have always been educated, but only within relatively recent history has this education taken place outside of the home—and only in the last two hundred years have special institutions been designed to educate young children. If we are to understand the field of early childhood education, then we must know something of its historical roots and its development.

This chapter describes the beginnings of early childhood education in the United States and its roots in European institutions. It discusses the history of the kindergarten, nursery school, child care center, and Montessori school in relation to the development of contemporary institutions and issues.

EDUCATING YOUNG CHILDREN IN COLONIAL AMERICA

With the establishment of the first colonies in America, even before there was a United States of America, many communities began to provide schools for their children. The American colonies were essentially Protestant. Some were established as religious communities, often to escape religious oppression that particular sects had felt in Europe. In many of these communities each family was responsible for ensuring that their children would learn to read. Since only by reading the Bible could each individual achieve salvation, reading ability became a religious imperative. Often the father was the one to teach reading to his young child. In communities with a sizable number of families living close together, the church operated a primary school so that each child would learn to read. In the Massachusetts colony, by 1647 the law required that towns establish schools for young children.

These early schools were not graded by age as our present schools are. All children were educated in the same class and there was no minimum age for school attendance. Often children as young as three and four were enrolled in these schools, spending their day sitting on backless benches, trying to learn to read along with their older brothers and sisters. It was only toward the middle of the nineteenth century that school attendance laws were passed establishing minimum age levels for children to attend school. It was felt that very young children would be better off spending their days at home with their mothers rather than in the primary school. There was also a fear that the pressure of intellectual activity, including learning to read, could cause insanity for younger children who were not quite ready for such learning. In addition, schools would be simpler to manage if the very young were excluded (May & Vinovskis, 1977).

The lack of special forms of education in colonial America reflected what was happening with education in Europe. No special arrangements were made for the education of young children. For one thing, schooling as we know it today was limited to a minority. Education for most meant learning basic literacy skills. Most children were prepared for their adult roles by being educated at home or apprenticed in a shop. In addition, there was less of a distinction made between childhood and adulthood than is found today.

DEVELOPMENT OF EARLY CHILDHOOD EDUCATION

If we wish to find the beginnings of the development of schools for young children, we must look to Europe for these roots.

The Oberlin School

The earliest reported schools designed especially for young children were developed about 1767 by Jean Frederick Oberlin, a Protestant minister who lived in Alsace, an eastern province in France. Although Oberlin was responsible for founding the school, he did not teach in it. That responsibility rested with his wife, Madame Madeleine Oberlin, until her death in 1784, and with Sarah Banzet and Louise Scheppler, who also managed the Oberlin household.

The Oberlin school enrolled children as young as age two or three. The school program included teaching handicrafts as well as exercise and play. The children gathered in a circle around Louise Scheppler, who would talk to the children as she knitted. Later, older children took on some of her responsibilities. Pictures of subjects taken from nature and history were shown to the children. At first they were shown the pictures alone. When the children were familiar with the pictures, they were told the names of the objects in their regional dialect. Later, the names of the objects were spoken in proper French while the picture was shown. Thus, the children learned to speak and read French as well as the dialect spoken in their home, while they learned about the world (Deasey, 1978).

This "knitting school" was so popular that it expanded to five neighboring village centers before Oberlin's death. Oberlin's methods were not adopted more generally in other sections of France, however. With the coming of the French Revolution, religious clerics and their work became suspect. Since Oberlin was a minister, French citizens were concerned that his teaching would be both religious and anti-revolutionary. Although Oberlin was respected both during and after the revolution, the "knitting school" remained an isolated phenomenon in France and the idea never expanded into Europe. Perhaps the time was not yet ripe for a major effort in support of education for young children.

Robert Owen Creates the Infant School

Another early childhood institution that began in Europe was the *infant school*, established by Robert Owen in 1816. Owen was an English industrialist and social reformer. When he took over the management of a textile mill in New Lanark, Scotland, he became concerned about the working and living conditions of his employees. Children as young as age six worked in the mills, where conditions were poor. The conditions under which the workers lived were like those described in Charles Dickens' novels; working people all over England at that time lived poorly. This situation led Owen to seek social reforms, at least in his mill community. He raised the minimum working age in his mill from six to ten

Robert Owen, father of the infant school.

years and provided better housing for his workers. He also started a company store where merchandise was sold to the workers at lower prices. He worked at making the town cleaner and at persuading the people who lived there to remain sober. In addition, he started schools for both children and adults. All these reforms were to prepare for the creation of a newer society that would improve the lives of all people.

Owen called his school the *Institute for the Formation of Character*. The part of the school set aside for the youngest was called the *infant school*. The children enrolled in this school were taught reading, writing, arithmetic, sewing, geography, natural history, modern and ancient history, dance, and music. Often children were taken on field trips to observe things as they existed in the real world. Objects and models were also brought into class for children to observe. The youngest children spent a great deal of time out-of-doors and were not forced to attend to lessons. Most important, children were not physically punished and were not restrained more than was necessary. Children were taught only what they could understand. The teachers wanted to help the children, as a result of instruction, to form good habits and learn to treat each other with kindness.

Owen's ideas about a school for poor and working-class children spread well beyond his mill town in Scotland. Owen's books about his new view of society and the schools that would prepare children for it were read throughout Europe and the United States. Infant schools were established in many American cities in the 1820s. Robert Owen himself came to the United States during this time to lecture and to establish a community based upon his new view of society. He purchased a town, New Harmony, Indiana, from a religious group as a base for establishing his new society. The settlement at New Harmony lasted for only two years, and by the mid–1830s the infant school movement had faded in the United States (Harrison, 1968).

Although they did not last a long time, the infant schools served an important function. They represented a movement to provide a humane form of education for young children. They also represented a type of social reform through education. Many of these infant schools served poor children. While the children were given moral instruction and taught to read, their mothers were freed from child care so that they could find work outside their homes.

The Beginning of the Kindergarten

Freidrich Froebel established the first *kindergarten* in Blankenburg, Germany, in 1837. In its view of children and in its educational purpose, it was different from any school that had been designed before. It had an influence on the education of young children throughout the world.

Froebel viewed education as an extension of his view of the world and his understanding of the relationship between the individual, God, and nature. Each individual, he felt, reflects the whole of his or her culture, just as each tree reflects the whole of nature. Froebel saw education as fostering the natural development of children. He used the garden as a symbol of childhood education. Just as young plants and animals grow naturally according to their own laws if cared for properly, so would children grow according to their laws. Thus, kindergarten education would follow the nature of the child. Play was seen as a method of education and a way for children to copy the natural life of man.

Froebel thought of education as knowledge being transmitted through symbols. He developed a set of activities and materials that would teach young children the important concepts of the unity of the individual, God, and nature.

Freidrich Froebel, creator of the kindergarten.

The *gifts* that he designed included ten sets of manipulative materials. The first gift consisted of six woolen balls, each symbolizing unity. The second gift consisted of a wooden ball, cube, and cylinder, representing unity, diversity, and the combination of the two ideas. The next four gifts were sets of small wooden blocks made up of different shaped elements that formed a cube when put together. The seventh gift consisted of sets of wooden tablets, one of squares and the other of triangles. The eighth gift included lines made of wooden strips. The ninth gift was circles or parts of circles. The tenth and final gift was soft peas or wax pellets and sharpened sticks or straws. Each gift was to be used to make specific constructions according to specific instructions given by the kindergarten teacher.

The curriculum also included *occupations*, or arts and craft activities and constructions. These included work with clay, wood, and cardboard, as well as paper cutting, paper weaving, paper folding, and paper pricking. Bead stringing, drawing, embroidering, and weaving were also included. The games and songs used in the Froebelian kindergarten were taken from Froebel's *Mutter and Kose-Leider*. In addition to these, the kindergarten program also included nature study and work in language and arithmetic (Lilley, 1967).

5. Embroidering.
— For Girls and Boys —
Worsted, of 12 different colors, and 3 Worsted-Needles, 1 Perforating-Needle, 10 pieces of Bristol Board, 1 piece of Blotting Paper, 10 leaves of white paper, 136 Designs on 12 plates, and Instructions.   Price $0.75.

Designed to teach the elements of fancy-work, to convey correct ideas as to number and form, and to still further educate the eye in the selection and combination of colors. — The objects produced (like those of most of the other Occupations) look pretty, and may be used as presents.

6. Cork- (or Peas-) Work.
— For Boys and Girls —
60 Cork Cubes, 60 pieces of Wire, 1, 2, 3, and 4 inches long, respectively, 1 Piercing-Pin, 108 Designs on 12 plates, and Instructions.   Price $0.75.

Designed to instruct in the proportions of geometrical figures and in the production of outlines of solids and of real objects, while teaching also accuracy of measurement and the elements of perspective, etc.

7. Plaiting (Slat-interlacing).
— For Girls and Boys —
30 Wooden Slats, 9 inches long by ½ inch wide, and 30 Slats, 6 inches long by ¼ inch wide, 93 Designs on 12 plates, and Instructions.   Price $0.75.

Designed to teach precision and nicety of adjustment, to instruct in geometrical form, and to stimulate the invention of fancy figures.

Children's occupations in a Froebelian kindergarten.

FIGURE 2-1 Abstract from: Syllabus of Froebel's *Education of Man*

Education defined by the law of divine unity.

Free self-activity: the essential method in education.

Unity, individuality, and diversity: the phases of human development.

The several stages of childhood, boyhood, and manhood to be duly respected in their order.

The various powers of the human being to be developed by means of suitable external work.

Nature and value of the child's play.

The family is the type of true life and the source of active interest in all surroundings.

The games of boyhood educate for life by awakening and cultivating many civil and moral virtues.

The true remedy for any evil is to find the original good quality that has been repressed or misled, and then to foster and guide it aright.

The purpose of the school and of its work is to give to the child the inner relations and meanings of what was before merely external and unrelated.

The essential work of the school is to associate facts into principles, not to teach isolated facts.

Mathematics should be treated physically, and mathematical forms and figures should be considered as the necessary outcome of an inner force acting from a center.

Writing and reading grow out of the self-active desire for expression and should be taught with special reference to this fact.

In the study of plants, animals, etc., the work proceeds from particulars to generals, and again from generals to particulars in varied succession.

From natural objects and the products of man's effort, the study should proceed to include the relations of mankind.

The prime purpose throughout is not to impart knowledge to the child, but to lead the child to observe and to think.

The general purpose of family and school instruction is to advance the all-sided development of the child and the complete unfolding of his nature.

F. Froebel, *The Education of Man,* W. H. Hailmann, Trans. (New York: D. Appleton, 1887).

Froebel's kindergarten program soon became popular in Germany. The kindergarten concept expanded as young women were trained to be kindergarten teachers by Froebel and his followers. With the wave of German migration to the United States in the mid- nineteenth century, which brought many of these trained women into the country, the kindergarten idea came to America just as it had come to other countries. The first American kindergarten was established in Watertown, Wisconsin, in 1856 by Margarethe Schurz. She invited the children of her relatives into the kindergarten she had created in her home for her own children. Other German language kindergartens were established at about this time in various cities throughout the United States.

The first English-speaking kindergarten was founded in Boston in 1860 by Elizabeth Peabody. For many years she traveled throughout the United States, speaking about the purpose of kindergartens and their benefits to children. She helped establish kindergartens wherever she went. The first public school kindergarten was established in 1873 in St. Louis. Susan Blow, the teacher, lectured and taught kindergarten education, continuing to be a champion of Froebelian kindergarten education throughout her life.

During the rest of the nineteenth century, kindergartens were sponsored by many different agencies. Churches, settlement houses, factories, and trade unions all sponsored kindergartens. A number of private kindergartens, for which fees were charged, were also established. Kindergartens were seen as particularly important for the children of the poor. They served to make life better for those children growing up in a slum, providing them with food, clothing, and education. By reaching poor children at an early age, it was hoped that the kindergarten could eliminate the problems of urban poverty (Shapiro, 1983). In each case, kindergarten teachers did not work just with the young children in their classes: parents were also served by the programs. Mother's clubs were organized so that the kindergarten program could be brought into the homes of children as well.

Reform in the Kindergarten

By the beginning of the twentieth century, ideas about kindergarten were beginning to change. A liberal group of kindergarten educators, who continued to support Froebel's views of the importance of childhood, suggested that we were learning things about the nature of childhood that were making Froebelian kindergarten education obsolete. Kindergartens were paying too much attention to symbols and not enough to the child's life. The child study movement had emerged. The study of children through observation suggested new ideas about what was considered educational for children. In addition, the progressive education movement was developing. This movement emphasized freedom and activity in the classroom and suggested a form of kindergarten education that would reflect the everyday life of the child. Under the leadership of younger kindergarten educators like Patty Smith Hill and Alice Temple, the kindergarten program was modernized and Americanized. The *occupations* of Froebel were considered too tedious for children, and different arts and crafts activities were substituted. The *gifts* were supplanted by building blocks and dramatic play areas. American songs and games were included in the program as the kindergarten was transformed.

In the progressive kindergarten, the child's life experience became the focus of the curriculum. Kindergarten activities helped children reconstruct their experiences, to abstract meaning from them and move their thinking to higher levels (Weber, 1984).

By the middle of the 1920s the reform of the kindergarten that had begun at the turn of the century was essentially completed. Kindergarten education was still not available to all children. There were some public schools that supported kindergartens, but not a great many. Even as late as the mid 1960s fewer than half of the five-year-olds in the United States were attending kindergarten (Spodek, 1982).

Today the picture is quite different. By the beginning of the 1980s, almost 90 percent of five-year-olds were in kindergarten, and by 1986 all states were providing support for public kindergartens within the elementary schools.

The Child Care Center Develops

There seems to be some disagreement as to when child care centers first appeared in the United States. Some say the first day nursery, as these centers were called, was established in Philadelphia during the Civil War, to free women for work in war factories and as nurses in hospitals for the war wounded (Whipple, 1929). Others say that the first day nursery was established some years earlier, in 1854, in the New York Nursery and Child's Hospital (Forest, 1927). In any event, the American day nurseries were modeled after the French *crèche*, which translates into English as "crib." These crèches were established in Paris as early as 1844 to care for children of working mothers, to fight infant mortality, and to teach hygiene to parents.

The day nurseries were primarily custodial agencies. They were more concerned with *caring* for children than with educating them. When the factory system was established in the 1800s, women were forced to look for work outside of their homes. Handicraft activities that could be done at home were becoming obsolete. Goods began to be manufactured by large machines that needed to be tended by relatively unskilled workers, and women and children were often hired. Women tending to the machines for long periods of time during the day could not care for their young at the same time, and day nurseries were established to serve the needs of the children of these women.

In the first day nurseries, children were cared for, cleaned, and fed by matrons who might also cook and clean in the centers. In the better day nurseries, trained kindergarten teachers might be hired to provide educational activities during part of the day. It was not until the 1920s, however, that day nurseries began to offer early educational programs on a regular basis. The image of the day nursery as a purely custodial agency gave way to that of a child care center in which children were cared for and educated by formally prepared nursery school teachers and child care workers, as well as by more informally prepared caregivers.

The Montessori Method

Maria Montessori was the first woman to graduate as a physician from an Italian medical school. After her graduation at the turn of the century, she worked at the psychiatric clinic of the University of Rome, and came in contact with "idiot children." She grew to believe that it was possible to train these mentally defective children to be more competent and to lead fuller lives rather than simply to keep them safe. Dr. Montessori sought out the ideas of others to find the key to an appropriate education program for handicapped children. She read the works of Froebel as well as those of Edouard Sequin, a French physician who had developed innovative methods of working with handicapped children. Building on what she found, she experimented with new methods and materials that proved successful in the education of these children.

When Maria Montessori was asked by the Rome Association for Good Building to establish a school, she was able to transfer her success from handicapped to nonhandicapped children. This association was creating new housing for poor families in a slum neighborhood, and wished to provide for the children. For two years Maria Montessori worked to develop her innovative program in the *Casa Dei Bambini*, or children's house, as she called her school. To help her, she hired a young woman who had not been trained as a teacher. Montessori brought materials she developed into the school and observed how the children used them. On the basis of these observations, Montessori then modified the materials as needed and established procedures for their use.

Maria Montessori with a child studying shapes.

News of the success of the program spread. People from all over Italy and throughout the world came to observe her work and report on it. Many came to be trained by Dr. Montessori in the new method. As word spread, her method became popular and soon Montessori schools were established worldwide.

Montessori, like Froebel, saw the development of the young child as a process of unfolding. She also conceived of education as self-activity, leading to self-discipline, independence, and self-direction. Unlike Froebel, who was interested in abstract ideas, Montessori viewed children's perceptions of the world as the basis for knowledge. Their senses had to be trained for them to become more knowledgeable. Thus, she developed a set of materials and procedures that allowed each sensory element to be separated out. With the use of these self-correcting materials, children learned to become aware of different sensations and organize them in their minds.

To help children learn about sounds, Maria Montessori created a set of boxes. All the boxes looked alike, but each contained a different kind of material. By shaking each box, a child would produce a unique sound. The sound made by one box could be compared with the sounds made by other boxes. The boxes could be ordered on the basis of the loudness of the sound. They could also be matched with boxes in another set. Similar activities were devised to train the other senses: touch, sight, smell, and taste. Each activity was matched with a set of special materials to be used by children in specific ways. Children could use the self-corrective materials independently.

Muscular education, gardening, and nature study were also included in the Montessori program. Emphasis was placed upon teaching academic skills through the Montessori materials as well. Materials used for counting led the children to learn arithmetic. Reading and writing were taught simultaneously,

Children in a Montessori class in sensory activities and exercises in practical life.

with children first feeling sandpaper letters against a smooth background, form-ing letters with a finger in a basin of sand, then placing wooden or cardboard letters together to form words. The reading method taught was a phonetic one, since in Italian each letter form corresponds to a specific sound. Montessori was concerned that reading be taught early. She felt there was a sensitive period for learning to read between the ages of two and six. Instruction before that period would not be effective and children would have a more difficult time learning to read once the sensitive period was past (Montessori, 1965).

The Montessori program also included Exercises in Practical Life. These were activities that would help children function independently. They include dressing oneself, as well as cleaning and caring for oneself and one's surround-ings. Each practical skill was taught with a prescribed sequence of activities.

The Montessori method arrived in the United States before World War I. Montessori education continued to grow from that time until about 1930. Each year during this period saw more Montessori schools established, primarily pri-vate ones that depended upon tuition payments for survival. With the stock mar-ket crash of 1929 and the depression that followed, many of these schools were forced to close. The Montessori movement faded in the United States during this time, even though it continued to survive in other countries. Maria Montessori helped establish new schools in Spain, Italy, and other European countries dur-ing the 1920s and 1930s. She spent the World War II years in India, where she trained teachers and helped to create new Montessori schools. After World War II she returned to Europe, where she remained active professionally until her death. Not only did she train Montessori Directresses, as these teachers are called, but she also worked to maintain the integrity of the Montessori method.

There was a resurgence of interest in Montessori education in the United States in the late 1950s. Montessori education has again become popular in our country, though differences have surfaced among Montessori educators. There are two groups that currently support Montessori education. One, the Associa-tion Montessori Internationale (AMI), strives to maintain the purity of the Mon-tessori method. The other group, the American Montessori Society (AMS), is less concerned with preserving the purity of the method. This group recognizes that other child development specialists have had insights about the education of chil-dren similar to those of Maria Montessori. They also feel that new knowledge has been created about children and about education since Montessori's time. The AMS schools are willing to modify the Montessori method and to include activi-ties that were not a part of the original *Casa Dei Bambini*.

While the Montessori method has been an alternative to traditional early childhood programs for most of this century, there are few well-designed studies that have tested its effectiveness. One of the problems is that, as in all approaches to early childhood education, the ways in which theories are put into action are as varied as the theories themselves. Thus, research actually assesses a particular concrete example of a theory as placed in action, rather than the theory itself. In reviewing the research on Montessori education, Shelly L. K. Lindauer (1987) suggests that some aspects of Montessori education—possibly the individualized attention and slow paced, structured sequencing of instruction—is at least benefi-cial for disadvantaged boys.

The Nursery School

Rachel and Margaret McMillan created the first nursery school in London in 1911. Although they were both born in the United States, the McMillan sisters came to Britain during childhood, after their father had died and their mother returned to her family home. Margaret was the speaker and writer for the two sisters. She had studied music and acting during her formative years. While spending much of her young adult life as a governess and companion, she gained personal satisfaction by pursuing social causes and engaging in political activities. In 1894 she was elected to the school board of Bradford, England, and became an advocate for the needs of poor children in school. She fought to provide children with medical examinations, school lunches, and school baths. She became convinced that the medical and social problems she saw in these children could be corrected or prevented by proper care before the children's entrance to school.

In 1902 Margaret left Bradford and joined her sister in London, where the two sisters opened a medical clinic for children. Soon they expanded the clinic's activities, and an open air children's camp was established. A daytime nursery was a logical extension of these activities, and the entire operation was moved to the Depthford area of London, which was then a slum. There, a college to prepare nursery school personnel soon took its place alongside the nursery school.

Rachel McMillan died in 1917, but her sister continued the work until her own death in 1931. Together they conceived of the nursery school as an institution for the education and nurturance of children from two to seven years of age. The nursery school was to provide to children of the poor the same advan-

Margaret McMillan, founder of the nursery school.

tages in growing up that were available to children in wealthier homes. Good health practices, medical examinations, adequate nutrition, cleanliness, fresh air, and proper exercise were all elements of the nursery school. These, combined with a worthwhile educational program, would support the total development of the child.

Unlike the Montessori school, the nursery school placed a high value on creativity and play. It was felt that imagination grows naturally in young children and could help the children advance in all areas of human development. Creativity would serve the needs of workers as well as managers, scientists, and artists. School programs could support the development of creativity in children by providing expressive activity, play, art, and movement. Along with these, the nursery school provided activities to teach self-caring skills and to support perceptual-motor learning. Gardening and nature study were also a part of the program, as were academically oriented readiness activities (McMillan, 1919).

The work of the McMillans and of others who joined in the nursery school movement drew considerable attention in England. The government there passed the Fisher Act of 1918, which allowed for the establishment of nursery schools within the public school system of England. Unfortunately, adequate funds to make them universal were never forthcoming. In the 1920s English-trained nursery school educators came to the United States to demonstrate their program, while a number of Americans went to England to study nursery school education. Nursery schools were established in many colleges and universities throughout our country. A number of private and welfare-oriented independent nursery schools were also established during this decade.

FEDERAL INVOLVEMENT IN EARLY CHILDHOOD EDUCATION

The 1930s depression had its impact on early childhood education as it had on other forms of human services. The nation's economy was in trouble. Tax collections slowed dramatically and many public school systems had to limit their activities because they lacked funds. Some kindergartens that had become part of public schools were closed. Other classes at various levels were also closed, and class sizes were increased. Teachers were released by school boards who could no longer pay their salaries. The federal government, under the New Deal policies of President Franklin D. Roosevelt, established a number of work relief programs. Nursery schools were established to provide work for unemployed teachers. Training workshops were established to orient teachers who came from many grade levels to work in these nursery schools. These workshops would provide them with an understanding of child development and early childhood education.

Thus nursery schools were introduced into many communities in the United States, not primarily as a service to children, but as a service to adults. However, the children were well served by these programs, which continued until work relief was no longer needed.

The end of the depression saw the beginning of World War II. Whereas there had not been enough jobs for those seeking work during the depression, the country soon felt a need for increased numbers of workers. Young people were going into the armed forces, and war-related industries were expanding. As in past emergencies, the call went out for women to join the war effort by joining the work force. To accommodate the needs of children of war workers, the federal government, under the Lanham Act, established child care centers in war industry areas. Education and care were provided for young children in these centers, which sometimes operated on a 24-hour basis while their mothers were at work. Unfortunately, the Lanham Act called for the withdrawal of these day care funds shortly after the end of the war. With peace came the withdrawal of government involvement in early childhood education.

In was not until the mid-1960s that the government again became involved in early childhood education. At this time there developed an increased concern for the status of poor people. There was also a belief that poverty was a social problem that could be solved. It was felt that the federal government should use its resources to aid in the solution of these problems. Working along with foundations, the government funded research studies on the effects of early experience on the development and academic achievement of poor children. A number of experimental programs in preschool education were established and a variety of educational programs tested. Growing out of this effort came the Head Start program, which has offered massive support of early childhood education. Although only about 25 percent of the eligible preschool children have been served by Head Start, it still remains one of the largest and most popular programs of early childhood education in existence.

CONTEMPORARY DEVELOPMENTS

The institutions described in this chapter have all influenced early childhood education as it exists today. Those still in existence have changed in some way from the original, since all must respond to contemporary concerns. The kindergarten is no longer a separate institution. In America it is a class serving five-year-olds primarily as part of an elementary school. Kindergartens are part of public education in all states, although not all five-year-old children attend kindergarten. In addition, a number of states are adding classes for four-year-olds to the public schools.

Nursery schools are no longer designed to serve children of the poor. They have become half-day programs and are primarily educational in their orientation. Child care programs have become the fastest growing element in the early childhood education field. To a great extent this development reflects the changing family structure and the changing role of women in our society. As more women work, there is a greater need for child care services. As nuclear families become more dominant and single-parent families increase, that care must be provided outside the home. Day care for the youngest is often provided in individual homes, with child care centers serving children from the age of three up.

Montessori schools still exist and seem to be thriving. They are not all as pure in their adherence to the Montessori method as they once were. There is still a search for what is essentially Montessorian in the method. While still predominantly a form of private education, Montessori education is an alternative program in some public schools. Head Start continues to survive and it remains a popular government program for young children. In 1972 the Head Start concept was expanded to include services for handicapped children. In addition, special programs for preschool handicapped children have been evolving over the past fifteen years.

In the last several years we have seen an increase in the acceptance of early childhood education as an essential service for our society. Positive long-term effects have been shown for both Head Start and other programs for poor children (Collins, 1983; Consortium for Longitudinal Studies, 1983). In addition, positive effects of good day care programs for young children have been demonstrated (Caldwell & Freyer, 1982). There was an effort to develop and identify distinctive approaches to early childhood curriculum, often called "program models," during the 1960s and 1970s. Early childhood education tends to be an eclectic field, however, borrowing ideas from a variety of sources and integrating new ideas with older ones. Thus today, with the exception of Montessori Education, it is hard to find a school that contains an approach to early childhood education that is distinctly different from others.

Early childhood programs do vary in relation to the ages of the children served. They also vary in relation to the institutional arrangements through which they are offered and the kinds of services provided by each. These are discussed in greater detail in the next chapter.

REFERENCES

CALDWELL, B. M., AND M. FREYER (1982). Day care and early education. In B. Spodek (Ed.), *Handbook of research in early childhood education*, pp. 341–374. New York: Free Press.

COLLINS, R. C. (1983). Headstart: An update on program effects. *Newsletter of the Society for Research in Child Development*, Summer.

CONSORTIUM FOR LONGITUDINAL STUDIES (1983). Lasting effects of early education. *Monographs of the Society for Research in Child Development*.

DEASEY, D. (1978). *Education under six.* New York: St. Martin's Press.

FOREST, I. (1927). *Preschool education: A historical and critical analysis.* New York: Macmillan.

HARRISON, J. F. C. (1968). *Utopianism and education: Robert Owen and the Owenites.* New York: Teachers College Press.

LILLEY, I. (1967). *Freidrich Froebel: A selection from his writing.* Cambridge, England: Cambridge University Press.

LINDAUER, S. L. K. (1987). Montessori education for young children. In J. L. Roopnarine and J. E. Johnson (Eds.), *Approaches to early childhood education*, pp. 109–126. Columbus, OH: Merrill Publishing Co.

MAY, D., AND M. A. VINOVSKIS (1977). A ray of millenial light: Early education and social reform in the infant school movement in Massachusetts, 1826–1840. In T. Harevan (Ed.). *Family and kin in urban communities 1700–1930.* New York: New Viewpoints.

MCMILLAN, M. (1919). *The nursery school.* London: J. M. Dent and Sons.

MONTESSORI, M. (1965). *Dr. Montessori's own handbook.* New York: Schocken Books.
SHAPIRO, M. S. (1983). *Child's garden: The kindergarten movement from Froebel to Dewey.* University Park, PA: Pennsylvania State University Press.
SPODEK, B. (1982). The kindergarten: A retrospective and contemporary view. In L. Katz (Ed.), *Current topics in early childhood education, Vol. IV*, pp. 173–191. Norwood, NJ: Ablex.
STEINFELS, M. O. (1973). *Who's minding the children? The history and politics of day care in America.* New York: Simon & Schuster.
WEBER, E. (1984). *Ideas influencing early childhood education.* New York: Teachers College Press.
WHIPPLE, G. (1929). *Preschool and parental education.* 28th Yearbook of the National Society for the Study of Education.

SUGGESTED ACTIVITIES

1. Talk to directors of local nursery schools and child care centers in the community. Find out which is the oldest nursery school and the oldest child care center. Learn why and how these programs were originally established. Compare the original goals of the center with their current goals. Prepare a report to share with the class.

2. Interview the curriculum director of a local school district. Find out when kindergartens were first offered in the public schools. See if they have some of the original curriculum guides or photographs of early classes to share with the class.

3. Visit a Montessori program. Observe there for a morning. Compare the activities and equipment you observe with those originally suggested by Dr. Montessori.

4. Search through your college and local libraries. See if you can find books written before 1900 on kindergarten education. Compare these books with current early childhood textbooks you know.

3

Early Childhood Institutions and Programs

OBJECTIVES

After completing this chapter on early childhood institutions and programs, you should be able to:

1. Define child care center and family day care home.
2. Distinguish between licensing and accreditation of centers.
3. Describe Head Start, Home Start, and kindergarten programs.
4. Compare public with private centers; profit with not-for-profit centers; church-related with secular; and fee-oriented with tax-supported centers.
5. Explain the relationship of early childhood centers to social services agencies.
6. Describe the use of "purchase of service" to provide child care services.
7. Explain why employer supported child care services are considered an important employee benefit.
8. Describe some of the ways that an employer can provide child care support.
9. Explain why parents and professionals are interested in programs for four-year-olds.

If you were to walk into ten different early childhood programs at 9:30 A.M. on a Wednesday morning, there's a good possibility that you would see children participating in very similar activities. Whether they are in large groups with the teacher, in small groups, or working individually, they may be using similar materials.

If you stayed awhile, however, differences among the programs would become apparent. Some programs have half-day sessions; others last a full day. Some programs provide meals; others do not. Some involve parents as volunteers in the classroom or may even be owned and operated by parents; others provide no role for parents. Some have teachers who act as guides for learning; others have teachers who use direct instruction throughout the day. You would also notice differences in class size, adult/child ratio, and physical settings.

Even though all early childhood programs provide similar experiences for children, there are differences among programs. Some differences are more apparent than others. Programs may differ in philosophy, goals, and purposes, but they all exist to meet the needs of children and their families.

Early childhood programs have been gaining more acceptance in the United States in recent years. Kindergarten programs have expanded, Head Start remains a strongly supported federal program, and income tax credits for child care have become a reality.

The proportion of children under age six with mothers in the work force has increased from 29 percent in 1970 to 51 percent in 1988. Sixty percent of all women of working age will have jobs by the year 2000. If the trend continues, by 1995 there will be approximately 15 million preschool children with mothers working (Hofferth, 1989). Child care now represents a substantial amount of a family's budget, with middle income families spending about 10 percent and lower income families spending as much as 26 percent of their budget for child care (Hofferth, 1989).

When Mississippi began to provide kindergarten classes for children in 1986, all fifty states offered kindergarten as part of the public school experience. However, only ten states require kindergarten attendance.

As was noted in the previous chapter, programs for young children have a long and varied history. However, it was not until the mid 1960s, with the advent of President Lyndon Johnson's "Great Society" initiative, that early childhood programs were seen as relevant to our economic and social needs (Decker & Decker, 1988). Head Start began in the summer of 1965 as a way to help break the cycle of poverty for children, provide comprehensive support for their development, and improve their chances for success in public schools. The Head Start movement was only one of a number of catalysts that hastened the growth of early childhood education programs in the United States. Changes in the roles of women, in family structures, and in the economy all have influenced the development of the field.

In this chapter we explore the various types of early childhood programs that are available and the ways in which they differ from one another. Institutional sponsorship, relationships with social service agencies, and important issues such as day care standards and licensing are also discussed. It may be interesting to compare some of the historical forerunners of these programs as described in Chapter 2 with those that exist today.

INSTITUTIONS IN EARLY CHILDHOOD EDUCATION

Many different institutions provide programs for young children. Federal, state, and local governments, as well as industry, religious groups, parent groups, and private entrepreneurs all sponsor early childhood programs. However, these programs are not all offered for the same reasons. Governments have attempted to improve the quality of life for families; industry has provided child care for workers to lower worker absenteeism, to keep them on the job longer, or as a fringe benefit; religious groups often wish to provide a service to parishioners and increase church membership; and so on. Regardless of the sponsorship or the purpose, the quality of care and the appropriateness of the educational component to the developmental level of the child should be the most important concern for everyone involved.

The high level of interest in early childhood programs comes from at least five different sources: (1) the increased demand for child care from working mothers in all income groups; (2) a concern about productivity, international competitiveness, and the changing nature of the nation's work force, which includes more women and has greater ethnic and cultural diversity; (3) a view of child care as a central force in helping mothers move off of Aid for Dependent Children (AFDC) and into the job market; (4) a desire to provide a better start in life for poor children; and (5) the accumulating body of evidence that high-quality early childhood programs have long-term positive effects for disadvantaged children (Mitchell, 1989). These reasons suggest that programs for young children are an issue not just for working women or for low-income families.

According to Bettye M. Caldwell (1984), a former president of the National Association for the Education of Young Children:

> Professional child care is a comprehensive service to children and families which functions as a sub-system of the child rearing system and which supplements the care children receive from their families. . . . Professional child care is not a substitute or a competitor for parental care. . . . Professional child care programs vary in quality, just as family experiences vary in quality. Program quality depends upon the characteristics and training of the staff, the physical setting, and the support for such service provided by the society at large. (p. 4)

Caldwell's statement can be applied to *all* early childhood programs regardless of sponsorship or philosophy.

Child Care Centers

Child care is usually an extended day program with children being cared for up to 12 hours daily. It may take place in the child's home, in another person's home, or in a child care center. Child care is aimed at three different age groups:

(1) infants and toddlers, (2) children ages three to five and (3) children from ages five to twelve in before- and after-school care. The programs fall into one of three categories: (1) *custodial care,* where care is primary; (2) *developmental care,* where psychomotor development, cognitive development, language, self-concept, and social development are primary concerns; and (3) *comprehensive child care,* where developmental care is provided along with a full range of support services.

Contemporary child care centers have at least two components: child care and education. The two functions are bound together in any good early childhood program. Children cannot be well cared for without learning and they cannot learn well without being properly cared for (Mitchell, 1989).

The primary purpose of child care, however, is the *care* of the child. The care component can include providing hot meals, adequate rest, and a safe environment under the supervision of trained personnel. The education component may include large-group, small-group, and individual activities that teach children and are developmentally appropriate.

Child care is normally provided in one of two settings: a child care center or a family day care home. Child care centers may be housed in community buildings, public schools, factories, hospitals, and just about any place else where there is space available that can be modified to meet health and safety regulations and to serve the needs of children. Sunday school classrooms or church halls, for example, are used as child care centers during the week. Regardless of where programs are housed, there are a number of factors that seem to influence the quality of child care. Among these are staff/child ratio, group size, and staff qualifications.

Bettye M. Caldwell and Marjorie Freyer (1982), reporting on the National Day Care Study, stated that the highest quality programs were those that had a high staff/child ratio. The report suggests that a ratio of one adult for every seven children is optimal for three- to five-year-olds, 1:6 for two- to three-year-olds, and 1:4 for children under two. These ratios allow each child to be cared for as an individual and to be provided with quality care and educational experiences.

The second and most important variable that affects the quality of child care is group size. The group should be no larger than twice the number of children allowed per adult in the staff/child ratio (Caldwell & Freyer, 1982). In other words, in a center using a 1:7 adult/child ratio for three- to five-year-old children, the maximum size of the group should be fourteen children with two adults.

The third variable affecting the quality of child care is the qualifications of the teaching staff. Those centers that had staff members with child development or early childhood education training tended to have higher quality programs.

Family Day Care Homes

When caregivers open their homes to serve small groups of children, they create family day care homes. Many parents who are uncomfortable with having their children placed in a child care center value the warm, family atmosphere that may be available in a family day care home. Many people believe that a home

Early childhood programs can be found in many settings.

A public elementary school contains a kindergarten program.

This community child care center functions in a building specifically designed for young children.

This former elementary school houses the community's Head Start program.

A child care center operates in a private residence.

This church operates a weekday child care center.

is the proper place to care for young children. This attitude is reflected in the fact that care for very young children is more often provided in homes than in centers (Almy, 1975). In 1985, 22 percent of the children receiving care were provided for in family day care homes (U.S. Bureau of the Census, 1987).

Family day care homes tend to serve toddlers more than other age groups. However, infants, preschool, and school-age children are also served in this setting (Stevens, 1982). A day care home can be beneficial because of the small number of children served in each setting, the flexibility that parents have in dealing with one person, and the fact that parents can choose a home that has a value orientation similar to their own (Almy, 1975). Finally, day care homes serve a wide range of ages, and children can benefit from playing with those both older and younger.

One problem is that a great number of family day care homes are unregulated. Thus, there are no legal controls over the environment or the caregiver. The National Day Care Home Study found that, regardless of regulatory status, homes tended not to exceed the recommended group size limit of six children per home, but caregivers spend more time interacting with children in regulated homes than in unregulated homes (Stevens, 1982).

Often child care has been viewed as a need of low-income families. Actually, child care is used by families at all socioeconomic levels. In a study done in Shaker Heights, Ohio, an affluent suburban community, Davis and Solomon (1980) found that of the 423 families using child care, the most common arrangement was to have a baby-sitter come into their own home. Twenty-one percent of those surveyed reported that their child care needs were not met, and 40 percent felt that the cost of child care was a problem. The major reason that people used child care was employment related, and centers were the least used or desired choice of care.

Regardless of the type of center or program that a child participates in, it is important to note that no consistent negative effects of out-of-home child care have been found in over a dozen child development investigations (O'Connell, 1983). Good child care is not harmful to children. Since in many cases it allows people to improve their standard of living and to provide more effectively for their children, it is a benefit to both families and society.

Kindergarten

Most adults who attended kindergarten vaguely remember a time of circle games, sand, water, blocks, housekeeping centers, and other activities that were enjoyable while allowing for their interaction with teachers, children, and materials. They spent the day interacting with the teacher, other children, and a variety of interesting and stimulating materials. These memories reflect the importance of children having experiences that allow for social, emotional, physical and intellectual growth.

During the past decades, many schools have moved away from a child centered kindergarten approach. Rather than being concerned with the needs of individual children, these program chose to focus on the development of academic skills. The curriculum is based on specific objectives that all children are required to meet, and textbooks and workbooks are the primary source of instruction. David Elkind (1986) suggests that poorer kindergarten programs are "miseducating young children," and that this miseducation occurs because education decision makers ignore expert knowledge about how children learn and develop.

Professionals, responding to the increased pressure for academically oriented kindergartens, have focused on the importance of "developmentally appropriate practices." Developmentally appropriate kindergarten programs are those that reflect children's learning abilities and interests at particular times in their lives. Such programs are based on knowledge of how children learn at particular stages of development and are designed by experienced, well-trained, early childhood professionals (Davis, 1989; Bredekamp, 1987).

Another concern has been whether children should attend all-day or half-day kindergartens. Current research studies, though neither consistent nor conclusive, suggest that all-day kindergarten programs have some advantage in regard to increasing children's academic achievement. Too little evidence is available to draw any conclusions regarding children's socioemotional development (Stinard, 1982). Although only a minority of children attend all-day kindergarten at present, the number is growing as states move to provide funding for kindergartens on the same basis as for other elementary grades.

No matter what the structure and focus of kindergarten programs, teachers must recognize that for most children today kindergarten is not their first experience with schools. More than half the children who come to kindergarten have had prior experience in a nursery school or child care center, and that percentage will continue to rise.

Programs for At-Risk Children

At-risk children are those who have a high probability of educational problems in the future. There are two populations of at-risk young children: those who have developmental problems and those who come from homes that may not provide adequate support for children's learning and development. This latter group may include children from low-income homes, children of migrant workers, children for whom English is not a primary language, children of single parents and children of teen-age parents. Special programs have been designed to meet the needs of both groups.

Preschool Handicapped

Public Law 99–457, the Education of the Handicapped Act, Amendments, 1986, provides for the education of two groups of young handicapped children, from birth through age two and from ages three to five. Individual states have the responsibility to provide services to children and their families in each group.

The program for infants and toddlers is to be a multidisciplinary approach involving a number of agencies. Services are to be provided for children who are experiencing developmental delays in cognitive development, physical development, language and speech development, psycho-social development and self-help skills. Children who are diagnosed as having a high probability of developmental delay in the future may also be served (Parsons, 1987).

Services must be provided at no cost and include, but are not limited to, the following:

family training	psychological services
counseling	case management services
home visits	medical services necessary for diagnostic or evaluation purposes
speech instruction	
occupational therapy	health services necessary to enable child to benefit from other intervention
physical therapy	
screening and assessment services	

All of the above must be delivered by qualified personnel (Parsons, 1987).

An important part of the services to infants and toddlers is the Individualized Family Service Plan, developed by a multidisciplinary team and the parents, and describing the services that are to be provided to both the handicapped child and the family (Lowenthal, 1987).

By the 1990–91 school year, every state is expected to provide a free, appropriate public education for all handicapped children ages three to five. States that fail to comply with the law will lose funding for other federal programs designed to serve the needs of young handicapped children. States are not required to label children categorically, but may use a general category of developmental delay instead.

Programs may follow a variety of models; they may be part-day or full-day, and center-based or home-based. The importance of the role of the family is emphasized in the law and, whenever appropriate, a child's Individualized Educational Program will include instruction for parents (Lowenthal, 1987).

Head Start

Head Start began in 1965 as an eight-week summer program for children from low socioeconomic-status families. The intent was to give children an early experience that would help them prepare for their school careers. During the first summer, 500,000 children were enrolled in 11,000 centers (Hodges & Cooper, 1981). More than nine million children have since been enrolled in Head Start and more than 400,000 children are currently being served (Decker & Decker, 1988).

In the beginning, Head Start had seven objectives: (1) improving the child's physical health and abilities, (2) helping the social and emotional development of the child, (3) improving the child's mental process and skills, (4) establishing patterns and expectations of success, (5) increasing the child's capacity to relate positively to family members while at the same time strengthening the family's stability and capacity to relate positively to the child, (6) developing a positive attitude toward society in the child and his or her family and fostering constructive opportunities for society to work together with the poor in solving their problems, and (7) increasing the sense of dignity and self-worth within the child and his or her family (Hodges & Cooper, 1981). The program was child and family oriented and was seen as both an educational and a social endeavor.

Head Start soon grew into a full-year program, and in the years of its existence it has been responsible for many educational innovations. Although the initial program was similar to that of a good traditional nursery school, later modifications incorporated many contemporary theories and practices.

Head Start is a good example of a comprehensive program that meets young children's social, emotional, physical, and intellectual needs. It provides health care, meals, parent education, and a variety of appropriate learning experiences so that children can be successful in school and at home. Since

1972, Head Start has been required to provide services to handicapped children. Ten percent of Head Start's enrollment capacity is designated for the handicapped.

Home Start was developed as an offshoot of the Head Start program, and was designed to take place within the child's home. It was primarily for poor children and their families. Its objective was to strengthen the parents' ability to facilitate their children's development. Home Start made use of personnel who visited homes regularly and trained parents in appropriate ways of working with children (Almy, 1975).

Head Start has been one of the most studied early childhood programs, and the results have been encouraging. Lawrence Schweinhart and David Weikart (1986) reported on the results of the Head Start program. They concluded that

1. Short-, mid- and long-term positive effects are possible.
2. Adequately funded Head Start programs run by well trained, competent teachers can achieve the level of quality operation that will lead to positive effects.
3. Equal educational opportunity for all people is a fundamental goal of the great American experiment and good Head Start programs can make a sound contribution to the achievement of this goal. (p. 50)

Researchers have also found an improvement in parenting abilities and an enhancement of positive reactions between mothers and their children as a consequence of Head Start enrollment (Calhoun & Collins, 1981). Over 95 percent of Head Start parents have favorably endorsed it and a large percentage of parents have actually participated in the program (Zigler & Lang, 1983).

Edward F. Zigler and Mary E. Lang (1983) feel that Head Start should begin expanding into (1) full-day child care for children of working parents, (2) programs to fight child abuse and neglect, (3) parent education and teenage pregnancy programs, and (4) childhood injury-prevention programs. These are critical needs in our society and Head Start may be the proper place to address them.

Programs for Four-Year-Old Children

The issue of whether programs for four-year-old children should be provided as a part of state-funded education initiatives is one that is receiving support from many groups. Organizations such as the American Federation of Teachers and the National Association of State Boards of Education have gone on record in support of programs for four-year-olds as part of public schooling. At present, 28 states provide early childhood programs for at least some four-year-olds (Lubeck, 1989; Morado, 1989; Schultz & Lombardi, 1989).

The concern for four-year-olds is based primarily on the number of children in this age group who are at risk for school failure. Current state programs focus only on children who have been identified as potentially having problems in school or have been limited to locations where there are large numbers of at-risk children.

Anne Mitchell, Michelle Seligson and Fern Marx (1989) reported the results of the *Public School Early Childhood Study*. The study looked at public school involvement in prekindergarten programs and assessed how different states and school districts addressed the needs of prekindergarten children. They found that school districts operate a variety of programs that are funded from a single source or through a combination of federal, state, and local sources. Teachers in these programs are generally required to have an appropriate educational background and usually are state certified. Regardless of their credentials, teachers earn lower salaries in Head Start and child care programs in these public school programs.

Most of the programs are half-day and are provided to limited populations. Class sizes are reasonable when compared to accepted standards of one adult to ten children, with group size not exceeding twenty for four-year-old children. The best of the programs were characterized by strong leadership. The administrator was someone who understood early childhood education and child development and had the respect of the teachers.

The Early Childhood Task Force of the National Association of State Boards of Education (1988) released a report, *Right from the Start,* that recommended the development of early childhood units as part of elementary schools. The units would provide a new way of teaching children ages four to eight and would serve as a focal point for providing services to preschool children and their parents. One of the goals of the early childhood unit would be a commitment to include parental involvement in decision making about their own child and the program.

A primary concern of many professionals is to ensure that the programs will provide children with developmentally appropriate experiences and not with a curriculum built around pencil and paper tasks, memorization, and other academic activities. The interest in programs for four-year-olds will continue to rise as the need for child care increases. It remains to be seen how states will respond when parents want to extend programs to serve all four-year-old children.

INSTITUTIONAL SPONSORSHIP

Early childhood programs are sponsored by many different institutions. Social agencies, parent groups, school districts, corporations, and private individuals may each assume the responsibility for providing programs to young children and families. It is helpful to understand the distinctions among the various types of institutional sponsorships.

Public vs. Private Programs

One of the major distinctions made between programs is whether they are publicly owned or privately owned. Public programs are those that are operated by governmental bodies such as school districts or departments of social services. Sometimes programs are sponsored by nongovernmental agencies but are funded through public monies. Many Head Start and Home Start programs are examples of such sponsorship.

Private programs are those that are offered by an individual, a group, or a corporation. They do not receive public funding directly. Such programs rely on fees, contributions, or purchases of service by government agencies to generate operating income. Most nursery schools, parent cooperatives, United Way-sponsored programs, and owner-operated day care centers are examples of private sponsorship. Even privately operated centers may receive some public support, since about 20 percent of the children in private centers receive some public subsidy.

For-Profit vs. Not-for-Profit Programs

A second distinction that can be made is between programs that are operated "for profit" and those that are "not for profit." Those that are for profit are run as businesses with the purpose of making money, providing their owners with a return or profit on their financial investment. According to Roger Neugebauer (1989), the majority of day care centers in the United States are privately owned and operated for profit. Those centers are also called *proprietary centers*.

All public centers operate on a not-for-profit basis. They operate within a fixed budget. Their income usually contains a combination of funds from an agency or foundation, along with fees paid by parents, and they hope that the income generated by such a center will equal its expenses. Most church-sponsored and agency-sponsored programs are in the private, not-for-profit category.

Church-Related vs. Secular Programs

Early childhood programs in the United States have always made use of church-owned facilities. Sometimes the space for the center is rented or it may be donated by the church. Often early childhood programs make use on Monday through Friday of Sunday school classrooms, kitchens, and meeting halls. Programs that operate in church facilities are not necessarily religious but may be independent of the churches in which they are housed. A study done by the National Council of Churches found that of 14,589 church-housed programs, 56 percent were operated by the church and 44 percent were operated independently. Only 9.3 percent of the centers used the preschool program to further Christian education (Lindner, 1983). Ninety-nine percent of the programs surveyed did not restrict enrollment in the center to church members.

Secular programs do not represent any religious orientation. All programs with public sponsorship are secular even when such a program is housed in a church facility. In fact, many government-sponsored programs make use of church buildings.

Fee-Supported vs. Tax-Supported Programs

Fee-supported programs are those that depend on fees charged for services. Some centers require fees but also receive funds from sources such as the United Way or a private foundation to supplement their income. Often these centers base tuition upon parents' ability to pay for services. In other centers the fees charged are the only revenue available to the operators. The fees in these programs tend to be higher than in subsidized programs unless the cost of the program is deliberately kept low. Child care costs range from $30–$45 per week for family day care to $60–$90 per week for care in a center. It is not unusual, however, for costs to run as high as $100–$150 a week in certain areas (NAEYC, 1986).

Tax-supported programs are those that receive financial support from state, local, or federal governments. They may or may not charge fees to their clients, depending on the level of funding received from government sources and upon the program's policy.

Employer-Supported Child Care

Employer-supported child care has been one of the fastest growing employee benefits of the 1980s. Nationwide, more than 2,500 employers are now providing some form of child care assistance for their employees (Friedman, 1986). According to an American Society of Personnel Administration survey, only 10 percent of U.S. corporations currently offer child care support as a benefit, but almost half of them are considering doing so (Hickox, 1988).

Employer interest in day care has been generated as a consequence of a changing labor force. There are a great many more women with families working today, and women tend to return to work sooner after having a child (Burud, Collins, & Devine-Hawkins, 1983). Employers are sometimes interested in sponsoring child care to (1) reduce employee turnover, (2) reduce absenteeism, (3) increase worker productivity and concentration on the job, (4) improve employee recruitment, (5) enhance worker morale, and (6) enhance company image (Burud, Collins, & Devine-Hawkins, 1983; Hicks & Powell, 1983). Employer-sponsored day care can increase the opportunity for families to spend time together, since parents can spend lunch, breaks, and travel time with their children. Employees also benefit financially when child care is offered as a fringe benefit. Parents may save time by bringing their children to a center at work rather than having to drop them off at a different destination (Hicks & Powell, 1983).

Companies that provide child care assistance seem to have a number of common characteristics (Galinsky, 1989). They tend to have a high percentage of female employees; they are more likely to be involved if high quality child care is available in the immediate area; and they have used child care as an incentive to attract new workers in areas where there is a labor shortage. To date, businesses such as banks, insurance companies, hospitals, and high-tech firms are those most likely to be involved in providing child care assistance to employees.

Employer support for child care can take many different forms, including sponsoring a child care center in the work place, purchasing space in an existing center to guarantee that employees have access to child care, or working with community service agencies to support the development of new centers. The most important factor in determining a company's involvement seems to be that the employer recognizes that many workers have a pressing need for quality child care, and not meeting that need can affect the work place.

Corporations that do not wish to support child care services directly may choose to provide an information and /or referral service, or sponsor parent education programs, so that employees will become more knowledgeable about child care and early education. Another way to help employees with child care is by easing time constraints through creative scheduling. Approaches such as flextime, job sharing, and work-at-home allow the employee greater latitude when making child care decisions (Friedman, 1986).

As the number of parents in the work place continues to rise, the need for employer supported child care options will become even greater. Employers entering into child care should hire professional consultants who have the appropriate background, education, and experience to design and implement child care support services (Hicks & Powell, 1983).

Purchase of Service

Purchase of service refers to an agency's paying for services for a child in a child care center. The responsible agency, whether government, community, or corporate, contracts with an independent center to provide an appropriate early childhood program for particular children.

Some companies that provide day care for their employees are not large enough or are not willing to take the responsibility to sponsor their own child care center. These companies often purchase space for their employees' children in a setting that is convenient to the employees' home or work place. Service may also be purchased for handicapped children when a public-school-based program isn't available but an appropriate private center is; in this case the local school board assumes financial responsibility.

RELATIONSHIPS WITH SOCIAL SERVICE AGENCIES

As increasing numbers of children enroll in child care programs, there has been a corresponding increase in the number and range of services they require in order to have an optimal educational experience. While in many centers the staff is adequately trained to present educational programs, few centers can provide the comprehensive social, psychological, and medical services that may be needed. In many cases this need has led to preschool programs becoming closely affiliated with local social services agencies that can provide these services.

Medical assistance can take the form of free physical examinations, immunization, and general health care. Often physicians and nurses from a local clinic visit the center on a regular basis to provide services to children. Some centers have a nurse or doctor on call for emergencies, while others make use of local hospitals or medical and dental schools.

Psychological services may include counseling for children, parents, or families, and testing in the event of suspected handicapping conditions. In many cases, parents seek advice from the center staff for direct help or knowledge of where they can go for assistance. Knowing how to make referrals is a necessary part of the early childhood educator's skills.

Social service agencies may help parents obtain welfare or food stamps. They may also be involved in substance abuse counseling, and may have responsibility for handling child abuse and neglect cases.

Teachers of young children also have an obligation to know the signs of child abuse and neglect. In many states, a teacher who knows or suspects that a child is being abused or neglected is required by law to report that suspicion to authorities. Usually there is a statewide toll-free number that can be called. The information will be passed on to a government agency for investigation and action. The caller is protected from legal suit as long as there is no malice in the report.

People who work in early childhood programs cannot be all things to all people. Often teachers can help parents deal with simple family problems. However, it is important that teachers recognize the limits of their expertise and be aware of the community agencies that are available to serve the parents and children.

ISSUES RELATED TO EARLY CHILDHOOD INSTITUTIONS

In dealing with issues related to early childhood education, we always seem to come back to one set of questions: "What are reasonable standards for early childhood centers and for the people who work in them?" and "How can we ensure that these standards are met?" There are many views as to which standards would most likely result in quality programs. The important point to remember is that all standards are designed to protect children.

Licensing

Licensing is a way for a government agency to protect children by ensuring that a center has met minimum standards. While each state establishes its own requirements, there are some common areas that seem to be a part of all licensing procedures.

Decker and Decker (1984) refer to the following components for licensing:

1. regulations for organization and administration
2. regulations for staffing
3. regulations for plant and equipment
4. health and safety regulations
5. program regulations, including content, scheduling, and planning and guidance of children

Regulations concerning content are generally minimal and do not specify objectives or goals for learning.

At one time licensing standards for day care were also established by the federal government. The Federal Interagency Day Care Regulations were passed in 1968 and were incorporated into Title XX of the Social Security Act of 1975. These requirements applied only to centers receiving federal assistance. Presently, if a center is receiving federal funding, it must meet state and local licensing requirements, but there are no longer any federal requirements to be met (Collins, 1983).

NAEYC (1984) has taken the following position regarding child care licensing:

The National Association for the Education of Young Children affirms the importance of child care licensing as a vehicle for controlling the quality of care for children in settings outside their own homes. NAEYC supports licensing standards that:

- take into account the nature of the child care setting and the number of children to be served
- set standards for centers, group homes, and family homes
- include care of children from infancy through school age
- cover full-time, part-time, and drop-in care arrangements
- include facilities serving children with disabilities
- reflect current research demonstrating the relationship between the quality of care provided and such factors as group size, staff/child ratio, and staff knowledge and training in early childhood education or child development
- are clearly written, enforceable, and vigorously enforced
- are administered by agencies which are known about and accessible to parents and the individuals providing care for children
- include written policies describing processes for initial licensing, renewal inspections, revocation, and appeals

Because licensing requirements stipulate the basic necessary conditions for protecting children's well-being, NAEYC firmly believes that all forms of supplementary care for young children should be licensed and that exemptions from licensing standards should not be permitted. Whenever a single program or group of programs is exempted or given special treatment, the entire fabric of licensing is weakened.

It is a public responsibility to ensure that child care programs promote optimal development in a safe and healthy environment. All parents who need child care have the right to choose from settings which will protect and educate their children in a nurturing environment. (Passed by the NAEYC Governing Board, November 2, 1983.)

The National Day Care Study findings provide guidelines for selecting high-quality child care: small groups, supervised by caregivers with career preparation in child development and early childhood education (Collins, 1983). While there is much we still do not know about the relationship of program elements to young children's learning and development, there exists a good deal of accepted professional knowledge to guide regulators of early childhood programs.

Ninety to 95 percent of early childhood centers are licensed, and all states provide at least minimal standards. It has been estimated that anywhere from 50 percent to 90 percent of family day care homes are not licensed. In 1986, there were 165,000 regulated homes in the United States, with 105,000 of these actually operating. These homes could accommodate approximately 500,000 children. Comparing these figures with those from 1977, it appears that the number of licensed homes has increased by about one third in the last ten years (Hofferth, 1989).

In spite of the difficulty in locating and evaluating the thousands of family day care homes in the United States, the effort should be undertaken for the protection of children.

Accreditation

Because licensing addresses *minimum* standards for early childhood programs, a license does not provide a judgment of quality. In order to identify high-quality centers that meet standards beyond those of licensing, NAEYC has developed a program of center accreditation through the establishment of the National Academy of Early Childhood Programs. It is hoped that, through the Academy, the quality of programs serving young children will improve with the evaluation of these programs based upon the established criteria.

The NAEYC accreditation program is based upon a self-study by a center, using the accrediting criteria. These criteria are related to:

- interactions among staff and children
- curriculum
- staff-parent interactions
- staff qualifications and development
- administrative procedures
- staffing patterns
- physical environment
- provisions for health and safety
- provision of nutrition and food services
- assessment of program effectiveness

On the basis of the self-study, the center submits a written program description. If the Academy staff determines that the description is complete and that standards seem to have been met, it arranges for an on-site visit by an early childhood specialist to validate that the information provided is an accurate reflection of the center's program. On the basis of the center's and the validator's reports, a commission may accredit the center. This accreditation is valid for three years (NAEYC, 1984). Accreditation does not have the force of law, but it does carry the backing of an organization with more than 40,000 members who are interested in quality experiences for young children.

While the center accreditation program is new, 650 programs have already received accreditation. This figure represents programs from all 50 states (Smith, 1988). It has within it the potential for establishing and maintaining standards of quality in early childhood programs and of recognizing centers that meet these standards. It is hoped that this process will stimulate recognition of the need for high-quality programs in early childhood education and will, directly and indirectly, improve the education and care of young children in the United States.

Making Child Care More Accessible

Another continuing issue in the field of early childhood education relates to making high-quality programs accessible to the growing number of young children and families that require them. One way this might be done is through an expanded Head Start program, serving a wider population of children and including a full-day child care component. A second possibility that has been suggested is to include extended child care as part of public school programs (Morgan, 1980).

Still a third approach being considered is to increase federal funding for early childhood programs. The 101st Congress considered a variety of approaches, including tax credits and direct federal expenditures in support of child care. Increased funding may ease the child care burden for families while providing incentives for new and expanded centers.

Regardless of the setting, societal needs require more early childhood centers to educate and care for young children. The establishment of standards, licensing procedures, and accreditation will help determine whether or not they are good places for children and families. Our concern should be not only to make early childhood education programs more readily available, but to ensure that all programs are of the highest quality possible.

SUMMARY

Early childhood programs provide a wide range of services to families. Programs vary in purpose, philosophy, size, sponsorship, and standards. Within this diversity, however, there are certain elements such as adult/child ratio, group size, and staff qualifications that seem to be universal conditions for a high-quality program. These are embedded in licensing and accreditation standards.

People in the field of early childhood education and those anticipating entering it have the responsibility of ensuring that the concern for standards of quality programs will continue and that reasonable conditions and appropriate programs are available for all children.

REFERENCES

ALMY, M. (1975). *The early childhood educator at work.* New York: McGraw-Hill.

BREDEKAMP, S. (Ed.)(1987). *Developmentally appropriate practice in early childhood programs serving children from birth through age eight (expanded edition).* Washington, DC: National Association for the Education of Young Children.

BURUD, S. L., R. C. COLLINS, AND P. DEVINE-HAWKINS (1983). Employer supported child care: Everybody benefits. *Children Today, 12*(3), 2–7.

CALDWELL, B. M. (1984). What is quality child care? *Young Children, 39*(3), 3–12.

CALDWELL, B. M., AND M. FREYER (1982). Day care and early education. In B. Spodek (Ed.), *Handbook of research in early childhood education,* pp. 341–347. New York: Free Press.

CALHOUN, J. A., AND R. C. COLLINS (1981). A positive view of programs for early childhood intervention. *Theory into Practice, 20,* 135–140.

CHATLIN-MCNICHOLS, J. P. (1981). The effects of Montessori school experience. *Young Children, 36*(5), 49–66.

CHILD CARE LICENSING: POSITION OF THE NATIONAL ASSOCIATION FOR THE EDUCATION OF YOUNG CHILDREN (1984). *Young Children, 39*(2), 50–51.

CLASS, N., AND R. ORTON (1980). Day care regulations: The limits of licensing. *Young Children, 35*(6), 12–17.

COLLINS, R. C. (1983). Child care and the states: The comparative licensing study. *Young Children, 38*(5), 3–11.

DAVIS, M. D. (1989). Preparing teachers for developmentally appropriate kindergarten classrooms. *Dimensions, 17*(3), 4–7.

DAVIS, J., AND P. SOLOMON (1980). Day care needs among the upper middle classes. *Child Welfare, 59,* 497–499.

DECKER, C. A., AND J. R. DECKER (1988). *Planning and administering early childhood programs* (4th ed.). Columbus, OH: Merrill.

ELKIND, D. (1986). Formal education and early childhood education: An essential difference. *Kappan, 67,* 631–636.

FRIEDMAN, D. (1986). *Child care makes it work: A guide to employer support for child care.* Washington, DC: National Association for the Education of Young Children.

GALINSKY, E. (1989). Update on employer-sponsored child care. *Young Children, 44*(6), 2.

HICKOX, R. F. (1988). Child care benefit boost seen. *Employee Benefit News,* August, 3.

HICKS, M., AND J. POWELL (1983). Corporate day care, 1980's: A responsible choice. *Dimensions, 11*(4), 4–10.

HODGES, W., AND M. COOPER (1981). Head Start and follow through: Influences on intellectual development. *Journal of Special Education, 15*(2), 221–237.

HOFFERTH, S. L. (1989). Public policy report: What is the demand for and supply of child care in the United States? *Young Children, 44*(2), 28–33.

LINDNER, E. W. [LETTER TO THE EDITOR] (1983). *Young Children, 38*(6), 2.

LOWENTHAL, B. (1987). Public Law 99–457: *An ounce of prevention.* ERIC Document Reproduction Service ED 293300.

LUBECK, S. (1989). Four-year olds and public schooling? Framing the question. *Theory into Practice, 28*(1), 3–10.

MERRO, J., ET AL. (1976). Options in education, radio program #45 broadcast the week of September 20, ERIC Document Reproduction Service No. ED 133082.

MITCHELL, A. (1989). Old baggage, new visions: Shaping policy for early childhood programs. *Phi Delta Kappan, 70*(9), 664–672.

MITCHELL, A., M. SELIGSON, AND F. MARX, (1989). *Early childhood programs and the public schools.* Dover, MA: Auburn House.

MORADO, C. (1989). State government roles in schooling for 4-year olds. *Theory into Practice, 28*(1), 34–40.

MORGAN, G. (1980). The politics of day care. *Day Care and Early Education, 8*(1), 29–31.

NATIONAL ASSOCIATION FOR THE EDUCATION OF YOUNG CHILDREN. (1984). *Accreditation criteria* and procedures of the National Academy of Early Childhood Programs. Washington, DC: National Association for the Education of Young Children.

NATIONAL ASSOCIATION FOR THE EDUCATION OF YOUNG CHILDREN (1986). The child care market. Washington, DC: National Association for the Education of Young Children.

NATIONAL ASSOCIATION OF STATE BOARDS OF EDUCATION (1988). Right from the start: The report of the NASBE Task Force on Early Childhood Education. Alexandria, VA: National Association of State Boards of Education.

NEUGEBAUER, R. (1989). Surveying the landscape: A look at child care '89. Child Care Information Exchange, 66, 13–16.

O'CONNELL, J. C. (1983). Research in review. Children of working mothers: What the research tells us. Young Children, 38(2), 63–70.

PARSONS, S. A. (1987). Early intervention in rural states: The impact of P. L. 99–457. ERIC Document Reproduction Service No. ED 295396.

SCHWEINHART, L. J., AND D. P. WEIKART, (1986). What do we know so far? A review of the Head Start synthesis project. Young Children, 41(4), 49–55.

SCHULTZ, T., AND J. LOMBARDI, (1989). Right from the start: A report on the NASBE Task Force on Early Childhood Education. Young Children, 44(2), 6–10.

SMITH, M. M. (1988). NAEYC annual report October 1, 1987–September 30, 1988. Young Children, 44(1), 34–37.

STEVENS, J. H., JR. (1982). Research in review. The National Day Care homes Study: Family day care in the United States. Young Children, 37(4), 59–66.

STINARD, T. A. (1982). Synopsis of research on kindergarten scheduling: Half-day, everyday; full-day, alternate day; and full-day, everyday. ERIC Document Reproduction Service No. 219151

U. S. BUREAU OF THE CENSUS (1987). Who's minding the kids? Child care arrangements: Winter 1984–85. Current Publication Reports, Series P–20, No. 426. Washington, DC: U.S. Government Printing Office.

ZIGLER, E. F., AND M. E. LANG (1983). Head Start: Looking toward the future. Young Children, 38(6), 3–5.

SUGGESTED ACTIVITIES

1. Interview the personnel director of a local corporation. Find out if the corporation provides child care services. If not, do they have any plans to do so? Ask the director about the reasons for being involved (or not involved) in child care.

2. Locate and read your state's regulation for reporting child abuse and neglect. Identify your legal responsibility as an early childhood educator.

3. Interview a parent who has a child in a child care program. Find out why that parent enrolled the child in that program.

4. Obtain a copy of your state's licensing regulations for child care centers. Compare their requirements with NAEYC's center accreditation standards.

5. Observe a Head Start center for a day. Describe how the activities are related to the seven Head Start objectives.

6. Interview a child in a family day care home. Find out what he or she likes best and likes least in the center.

7. Interview the principal of a school that has a prekindergarten program. Try to determine how and why the program came into existence.

4

Becoming an Early Childhood Practitioner

OBJECTIVES

After completing this chapter on becoming an early childhood practitioner, the student should be able to:

1. Describe the roles and responsibilities of a center director, teacher, caregiver, assistant, and aide.
2. Compare certification with credentialing.
3. Discuss the qualifications and responsibilities related to early childhood educational careers.
4. Identify three reasons why early childhood teachers might leave the field to pursue other careers.
5. Discuss the role of males in early childhood education.
6. Identify ways to increase the social status of early childhood educators.
7. Discuss how the teacher education reform movement has affected the preparation of teachers of young children.

Saul began his career in early childhood education as an aide in a Head Start program. He had a high school degree and an interest in working with young children. Head Start sponsored him over a period of years to take continuing education classes that led to a two-year degree. He then continued through a Bachelor's degree in early childhood education. Saul is now beginning his fifth year as a first-grade teacher in a Follow-Through class.

Elise graduated from college in 1970 with a Bachelor's degree in elementary education. She began teaching second grade in a large urban city. After three years her husband was transferred to Europe. There she helped establish a parent cooperative nursery school. On returning to the United States, she completed a Master's degree in early childhood and became the director of a nursery school. From there Elise became director of a large community-supported day care center. Today she is affiliated with a junior college as a CDA trainer.

Mark graduated with a two-year degree in electronics. He quickly discovered he was more comfortable in a "people-oriented" setting. Since he had worked as a baby-sitter while in school, he decided to become a child care aide. Mark applied for and obtained a job at the center at his church. As his interest in children and in the field grew, he began taking courses at night for a degree in child development. After a year at the center he was promoted to teacher. He received his degree after five years of part-time study. He has now decided to begin work on a Master's degree in social work. He wants to continue working with children and families but not in the classroom. He felt that he was beginning to burn out after 6 years, 50 weeks a year, 9 hours a day of working with two- and three-year-old children.

Mary Jo graduated from a four-year teacher education program with a degree in early childhood education. She taught kindergarten for five years and earned a Master's degree in educational applications of computers. She now works for a computer company designing software for young children.

Susan received a Bachelor's degree and Master's degree in child development. She was a teacher and director in a franchised day care center for 15 years. She is now a licensing supervisor for her state's Department of Children and Family Services.

Martha received a vocational school certificate as a child care aide and went to work in a neighborhood center upon graduation. When Martha's first child was born she decided to give up her job in the center and care for a small group of children in her home. She now has two children of her own and cares for four other children in her home five days a week.

All of the people mentioned have a long-term relationship to the field of early childhood education, but only Saul has been working in a classroom with children for his entire career. This is a classic "good news/bad news" situation for early childhood education. The good news for people entering the field is that it is exciting to think of the large number of career possibilities that are available. The bad news is that as the field has developed, many fine teachers have been leaving the classroom to move into other positions.

Twenty years ago a degree in child development or early childhood education allowed you to spend your career as a classroom teacher of young children, possibly moving into a director's position after a period of time. Today, career opportunities for people who specialize in early childhood are available in hospitals, community centers, publishing houses, computer companies, retail businesses, and recreation. As the field continues to expand, the possibilities for people with early childhood backgrounds will be endless.

In this chapter we present issues related to becoming an early childhood practitioner and discuss how they may affect your career in early childhood education. We also provide information about the traditional careers and some of the newer career paths available to those interested in working with young children.

ROLES

The traditional careers in early childhood education have been in five job categories: director, teacher, caregiver, assistant and aide. Each of these positions requires different competencies; each may have a role in a quality program. Positions may differ from one another in the kinds of duties performed. There may also be different entry-level expectations for each. For example, a director needs all of the skill, knowledge, abilities, and experience that a teacher needs but must also have additional training in administration and supervision to run a center.

While the roles may be similar, titles and requirements may change from place to place. For example, a center director may be called a program director, senior teacher, or early childhood specialist. A brief description of each of the job categories may be useful to illustrate this point.

Center Director

A director has the ultimate responsibility for what happens in that center during the day. To be a successful director, one must have knowledge of children, curriculum, appropriate instructional methods, parent education, and staff training techniques, as well as knowledge of administrative methods.

Administering a center takes specialized skill and knowledge. It requires expertise in budgeting procedures, licensing regulations, payroll and benefit procedures, and hiring, due process, and firing procedures. Directors must also know about health, safety, and fire regulations, nutritional needs of children, and ways to evaluate both children and staff.

It is most important for the director to have previous first-hand experience as a teacher of young children in order to fully understand the dynamics of the classroom and of teacher/child interactions. Directors who have not had classroom experience may tend to focus on the administrative part of the position and to leave the critical aspects of development and learning to chance.

Teacher

Teachers of young children have an enormous responsibility to children and families because they provide both care and learning. What does it take to be a teacher of young children? Lillian Weber (1982) feels that teachers must

Teachers of young children must possess important personal qualities.

trust parents and that they have an obligation to know the content that is part of their teaching role. Millie Almy and Agnes Snyder (1947) suggest that teachers should have the personal characteristics of physical stamina, world mindedness, understanding of human development, and respect for personality, and that they should be imbued with scientific spirit. Sarah Lou Leeper (1968) adds the importance of a love of children, patience, kindness, warmth, outgoingness, and security.

The personal characteristics of a teacher become more meaningful when they are applied to the following tasks for which teachers are responsible each day. These include:

- establishing the learning environment
- selecting the developing goals
- managing a classroom
- communicating with children
- acting as go-between for parent and school
- choosing appropriate content
- choosing appropriate instructional materials
- evaluating children's progress
- reporting on the special needs of children to the appropriate authorities (e.g., suspected child abuse or neglect, suspected handicapping conditions)
- working as a faculty member and as part of an instructional team

In addition, in some centers teachers may be called upon to do other things. They might teach religious education, work as part of a child screening team, speak to parent groups, or help in the recruiting of new children.

Caregiver

Caregivers function in child care centers and day care homes. They are primarily responsible for the health, care, and safety of the children in their group. While there is no doubt that their interaction with children results in the children's intellectual, physical, emotional, and social growth, their primary concern is to see that the children are healthy, happy, and safe. Caregivers feed, change, protect, empathize with, and care for those in their charge. Giving children a sense of well-being, a sense of security, and a sense of trust are goals the caregiver strives to meet. Christine Cataldo (1983) feels that infant caregiving requires emotional responsiveness, a high level of initiative and energy, and skills in managing groups of babies. Other important traits for all caregivers include patience, sensitivity to changing needs, and good observational skills.

Assistant Teacher

Assistant teachers may do many of the things that a teacher or caregiver does. However, they are generally not responsible for planning or evaluating activities. Assistants take directions from the teacher and implement those directions to the best of their ability. The assistant teacher may work with large groups, small groups, or individual children and may supervise indoor or outdoor activities. However, the assistant is always working under the direction of the teacher or caregiver. The assistant teacher provides the teacher with daily reports of children's progress. This information can be invaluable as the teacher plans for future activities.

In many instances, assistant teachers are part-time people. Often they work as assistants while attending school to become teachers.

Teacher Aide

Teacher aides see that all of the little tasks that make a center or classroom run are done well and on time. They may be responsible for mixing paint, filing records, setting up activities, supervising nap time, fixing snacks, and any other of the hundreds of jobs that are necessary for a center to function. Aides also may have to assist in the kitchen, drive the bus to pick up children, or comfort children who become ill during the day. The aides make it possible for teachers and caregivers to spend most of their time with children.

PROFESSIONALIZING THE FIELD

Many early childhood practitioners are concerned about being seen as babysitters with no specialized training. In reality, teaching young children requires a core of skills and knowledge related to planning, implementing, and evaluating developmentally appropriate programs. However, since the field lacks a common set of requirements for teachers, those teaching young children do so with a variety of educational and experiential backgrounds. Some lack the skills, knowledge, and values necessary to be competent professionals.

One way to raise the level of respect given to teachers of young children is to "professionalize" the field by raising standards for those who work in early childhood education. As the period of training becomes longer and the content more rigorous, the status of those in the field should increase and salaries, benefits, and working conditions improve.

Bernard Spodek, Olivia N. Saracho and Donald L. Peters (1988) suggest that the initial idea of a profession came from the "learned professions" such as law, medicine, and the clergy. All three require the completion of a long training program in higher education and tend to involve mental activity. Human services fields such as teaching, social work, and counseling are often considered to be professions. However, since they require less preparation than law or medicine, they often have lower levels of status attached to them. Human-services professionals have moved to increase their status by raising standards for admission, monitoring the competence of those in practice, and by taking greater responsibility for the field.

The National Association for the Education of Young Children (1984) surveyed child care salaries and working conditions. The survey was distributed to 48,000 practitioners. Of the 5,000 surveys returned, 3,818 responses could be analyzed. Eight-seven percent of the respondents were female; 11 percent were members of a minority group. Of those responding, 1,025 had no permits or credentials for doing their job. Approximately one fourth of the practitioners (1,289) had been in the field fewer than five years and 34 percent of those in teacher, lead-teacher or head-teacher positions did not have even a bachelor's degree.

The problem with making job distinctions within the early childhood education field is that we have relatively little status in the eyes of society. Lana Hostetler and Edward Klugman (1982) state that while child care programs are expanding, the status of workers in those programs has not risen. They refer to the Department of Labor *Dictionary of Occupational Titles*, which assigned a low skill level rating to "day care workers and nursery school attendants" as recently as 1977.

One reason for low status is the lack of entry-level requirements for positions in the field. The fact that there is a general lack of certification or credential requirements for directors, teachers, caregivers, assistant teachers, and teacher aides in early childhood programs makes it possible for almost anyone to enter the field (Davis, 1982; Spodek & Saracho, 1982). When little is required of practitioners in a field, then little status is given to those practitioners.

Additionally, there may be a number of ways to qualify for a position. For example, Virginia's Child Care Center Standards (1988) require the following for program directors:

All program directors shall be 21 years of age and meet one of the following sets of qualifications:

a. A Bachelor's degree or Endorsement in Early Childhood Education, Child Development, Elementary Education, Psychology, or other related field from an accredited college or university.

b. Forty-eight semester hours or 72 quarter hours of college credit from an accredited college or university of which 12 semester hours or 18 quarter hours are in Early Childhood Education, Child Development, or other subjects relating to group care of children; and one year programmatic experience in a child care setting, nursery school, or elementary school.

c. A one year early childhood certificate from an accredited college or university, plus two years programmatic experience in a child care setting, nursery school, or elementary school. One year of this experience must be in a staff supervisory capacity. (p. 11)

A person qualifying under paragraph *a* could become a center director without having worked with children on a full-time, professional basis. When little is required of practitioners in a field, then little status is given to those practitioners.

Different levels of professional status may need to be established for different roles in the field. The highest levels of professional status and the highest set of requirements might be required of those who have the responsibility for planning and supervising programs. Lesser professional status can be sought for those trained personnel who assist the professionals and work under their guidance. This approach is represented in the NAEYC levels of professional status, where different expectations are appropriate for different positions.

Finally, professionalism in teaching has to do with doing the *right* thing at the *right* time for the *right* reasons. Arthur W. Combs (1982) feels that what distinguishes a profession like counseling, social work, medicine, law, pastoral care, or teaching from some mechanical operations is the necessity for the professional worker to act as an immediate problem solver. In the helping professions there are no cut-and-dried decisions about what acts to perform or words to say. What teachers do at any given moment is based on a judgment about what is appropriate to the hundreds of factors in any situation. These actions must be justified. It is the justification that separates the professional from the others.

It is hoped that we will come to a time when specific expectations will be established for each position and those applying will be screened to ensure that they are qualified. The field must be able to guarantee to the public that those working with young children have the necessary skills and are competent practitioners (Davis, 1982). We need to establish standards for the different levels of knowledge and skills necessary for aides, assistants, caregivers, teachers, and directors to perform their jobs well (Davis & Alexander, 1982).

This guarantee is particularly important since, as Donald L. Peters (1988) points out, early childhood teachers have a degree of autonomy that far exceeds that of most public school teachers. They must be able to plan and implement programs, choose appropriate methods, organize the environment, and meet the needs of diverse children. This ability to operate successfully as autonomous professionals is one key to increasing the status of the early childhood profession.

Professionalism means doing the right thing at the right time for the right reasons.

Early Childhood Professional Path

NAEYC has recommended an early childhood professional path that consists of four levels. The following is a description of the knowledge and skills required for each level and the ways in which these can be acquired:

Level 1. Early Childhood Teacher Assistant

Level 1 is an entry-level position. People at this level are preprofessionals who implement program activities under direct supervision of the professional staff. Such supervision occurs directly in the classroom by an Early Childhood Associate Teacher or Early Childhood Teacher who is in charge of the group of children and who models professional skills and contributes to the growth of the individual serving in the assistant role.

This level requires basic and minimal personal qualities which include a potential for and willingness to improve one's skills in working with young children, mental and physical health, a genuine liking of children, ability to get along with other adults, and general dependability.

The basic educational requirement for entry at this level is a high school diploma or equivalent. No specialized Early Childhood preparation is required for entry at this level, but once employed, the individual should participate in professional development programs.

Level 2. Early Childhood Associate Teacher

Level 2 consists of Early Childhood Associate Teachers, professionals who independently implement program activities and who may be responsible for the care and education of a group of children.

To be qualified as an Early Childhood Associate Teacher, the individual must be able to demonstrate competency in six basic areas as defined by the National Child Development Associate (CDA) Credentialing Program:

- to establish and maintain a safe, healthy learning environment

- to advance physical and intellectual competence of children

- to support social and emotional development and provide positive guidance and discipline

- to establish positive and productive relationships with families

- to ensure a well-run, purposeful program responsive to participant needs

- to maintain a commitment to professionalism

These qualifications can be achieved by successfully completing either a system of competency evaluation such as the one implemented by the CDA National Credentialing program or an associate degree in Early Childhood Education or Child Development. The attainment of these competencies requires supervised field experiences in appropriate settings with young children.

Level 3. Early Childhood Teacher

Level 3 consists of Early Childhood Teachers, professionals who are responsible for the care and education of a group of children. Individuals at Levels 2 and 3 may perform similar roles and functions. The different titles reflect the different patterns of formal education received and the extent of background knowledge of child development.

The qualifications of an Early Childhood Teacher are presented in NAEYC's *Teacher Education Guidelines for Four- and Five-Year Programs* (1982). To be qualified as an Early Childhood Teacher, the individual must demonstrate all Level 1 and 2 competencies and also possess theoretical knowledge and practical skills in:

- human development through the life span, with special emphasis on cognitive, language, physical, social, and emotional development, both typical and atypical, from birth through age eight

- historical, philosophical, psychological, and social foundations of Early Childhood Education

- curriculum for young children, including goal setting and developmentally appropriate content and methodology

- observation and recording of children's behavior for purposes of assistance in achieving goals, providing for individual needs, and appropriately guiding children

- preparation for working in settings that include atypical children: understanding the needs of developmentally diverse children, and recognizing conditions requiring assistance from other professionals

- communication and conference techniques, interpersonal and intergroup relations, and techniques for working with staff as an instructional team

- family and community relations, including communication with parents and parent involvement

- awareness of value issues and the existence of codes of ethics in professional life

- comprehension of cultural diversity and its implications

- legislation and public policy as it affects children, families, and programs for children

Completion of a baccalaureate degree in Early Childhood Education or Child Development from an accredited college or university is used to predict the existence of the competencies required of an Early Childhood Teacher. The attainment of these competencies requires supervised field experiences in appropriate settings with young children. The requirements specified for this level do not exclude people who wish to enter Level 3 primarily on the basis of experience in the field, as colleges are increasingly accepting relevant experience as evidence of partial fulfillment of degree requirements.

Level 4. Early Childhood Specialist

Level 4 consists of professionals who supervise and train staff, design curriculum and/or administer programs. Every Childhood program should have at least one qualified Early Childhood Specialist, who in small programs may also be the Director or Master Teacher. Larger programs should have more than one Early Childhood Specialist.

To qualify as an Early Childhood Specialist, an individual must be able to demonstrate all Level 1, Level 2, and Level 3 competencies as well as competency in the following areas:

- designing and supervising the implementation of developmentally appropriate program content and curriculum

- designing and implementing appropriate staff development activities and adequate supervision of personnel and volunteers

Completion of the following education and experience is used to predict the existence of the qualifications required of an Early Childhood Specialist: baccalaureate degree in Early Childhood Education or Child Development from an accredited college or university plus successful completion of at least three years of full-time teaching experience with young children, and/or an advanced degree.

The Early Childhood Specialist role requires expertise in the areas of curriculum design, supervision of adults, and staff development. This expertise may be obtained through specific administrative coursework within the baccalaureate program or may require additional training and experience beyond the baccalaureate degree.

National Association for the Education of Young Children (1984). NAEYC Position Statement on Nomenclature, Salaries, Benefits, and the Status of the Early Childhood Profession. Washington, D.C.: NAEYC.

NAEYC is presently refining the job descriptions and qualifications that correspond to these levels. One suggestion establishes the professional roles of Assistant, Teacher, Mentor, Coordinator, and Director. Each position would have specific educational requirements and job responsibilities.

Alternative Careers Related to Young Children

Most students going into early childhood education want to teach children and can see themselves doing it for a long time. A few students look beyond the classroom and think of becoming a center director, a parent counselor, a university teacher, or a supervisor.

However, as Lana Hostetler (1984) stated, "Not everyone can (or should) work with young children in group care. Although mothers and grandmothers have cared for children for generations without training, group care of young children is not the same as mothering, nor is it baby-sitting or substitute care" (p. 77). Some students who begin a program in early childhood education will find they are not suited as *teachers* of young children and may choose to work with children in other ways. Majoring in Early Childhood can provide a background for a career in a related field that can still provide contact with children and families.

Recently, the increased interest in early education, the increased need for child care, the continuing societal pressures on children and families, and the growing field of high-technology teaching tools have helped to open up a wide range of career opportunities for people with backgrounds in early childhood education or child development.

Publishers of children's books, learning materials, and computer software need people who can develop and present materials to teachers and who understand the specific learning and instructional needs of young children. It is important that professionally designed materials are developmentally appropriate as well as educationally worthwhile and that they reflect current knowledge about children's learning. Early childhood professionals can provide publishers and equipment manufacturers with knowledge to help ensure the appropriateness of new products.

New laws protecting the rights of children and laws against child abuse and neglect have fostered the development of a group of social workers who have an understanding of young children and who can assist both parents and children during difficult times. While such a position requires added preparation, a background in early childhood education can provide a solid base.

Managing toy stores, merchandising children's clothes, books, and furniture, and representing firms that sell school equipment and supplies are sales-oriented professions in which an early childhood background can be particularly helpful.

For those interested in staying within the field of education but not in a classroom, there are a number of career possibilities. School psychologists, visiting teachers, and school librarians are professionals who work with individuals or small groups of children. Each of these requires training beyond early childhood education. How many hours of preparation and what specific types of courses will be required will vary from state to state, depending on certification requirements. Most of these positions require some classroom experience as well.

Another area that has a growing number of opportunities is health care. Hospitals teachers, home teachers, and child-life specialists are three roles that enable early childhood majors to apply their expertise in health-related areas.

Judith Seaver, Carole A. Cartwright, Cecilia B. Ward, and C. Annette Heasley (1979) have organized careers with young children into five different patterns: those that serve children directly, those that serve families directly, those that organize services for children and families, those that provide information to professionals that work with or for children and families, and those that provide to the general public goods and services affecting children and families. Figure 4–1 lists available careers in each of the five patterns.

While the growth of career possibilities in early childhood education has been a positive development, it has also brought with it a number of concerns. These concerns for professionalism, certification or credentialing, entry requirements, and working conditions are all "growing pains" that the field is currently working through. It is to be hoped that they will be resolved in a manner that will be equitable for everyone and that will ensure quality programs for children.

If you find working with young children inspiring but feel you are not a match for day-to-day classroom contact, these alternatives may be worth pursuing. A visit to your college or university counseling center can provide further information about careers that require and value knowledge of young children.

FIGURE 4–1   Careers with Young Children

Pattern	**Examples of Careers**
1. Serving children directly	Teacher, child care worker, school nurse, physical therapist, hospital play aide
2. Serving families directly	Social worker, family therapist, parent educator, public health nurse
3. Organizing services for children and families	School administrator or supervisor, college teacher, recreation director
4. Providing information to professionals who work with children and families	Researcher, evaluation specialist, librarian, author, editor
5. Providing goods and services affecting children and families	Department store buyer, newspaper reporter, toy designer, children's book author, architect, legislative aide.

J. W. Seaver, C. A. Cartwright, C. B. Ward, and C. A. Heasley, *Careers with Young Children* (Washington, DC: NAEYC, 1979).

PREPARING TO BE AN EARLY CHILDHOOD PRACTITIONER

In 1982 James L. Hymes, Jr., stated that one major accomplishment of the past fifteen years in the field of early childhood education was an increase in junior college, four-year-college, and graduate programs and the advent of the Child Development Associate Credential to train people to work with young children. This means that more people are entering the field of early childhood education. It also means that those who do enter the field are more likely to have adequate preparation.

Programs That Prepare Practitioners

There are a number of programs that prepare early childhood practitioners. Some train aides, others educate teachers, but all are dedicated to improving the level of competence of those in the field.

The Council for Early Childhood Professional Recognition (1989) identified 1,488 post-secondary education programs in the 50 states, the District of Columbia, Guam, Puerto Rico, and the Virgin Islands that provide formal training in early childhood education or child development. The programs have been given a variety of titles, including Early Childhood Education, Child Development, Family and Child Development, Child Care Training, Child Study, Early Childhood Development, and Family Day Care Provider.

The students who are in these preparation programs are almost always people who are planning to enter the field. They have little or no experience with young children and are relying on their education to provide them with the expertise necessary to be successful. Preparation programs can be found in high schools, vocational-technical schools, community colleges, and four-year colleges and universities. High school and vocational-technical schools usually prepare students to be aides or caregivers in child care centers. Community college programs may prepare students to be teacher aides in elementary schools or teachers in child care centers or nursery schools. Most four-year programs enable students to become certified teachers. Students in these programs can complete all the requirements to receive state certification and become qualified to teach in kindergarten or the primary grades.

Most of the four-year programs are relatively young. They generally offer Bachelor's degrees and in many cases are closely related to elementary education programs (Spodek, Davis, & Saracho, 1983).

During the past decade a movement to reform teacher education has developed as a result of general dissatisfaction with public education. *A Nation Prepared: Teachers for the 21st Century* (Carnegie Forum on Education and the Economy, 1986) and *Tomorrow's Teachers: A Report of the Holmes Group* (1986), have both offered designs for restructuring teacher preparation programs. Additionally, some states have either done away with undergraduate education majors or have limited the number of education courses that can be offered within such an undergraduate major, forcing colleges to change the way they prepare teachers.

One approach to restructuring has been to require education students to complete an undergraduate major in liberal arts and sciences and a graduate major in education. This results in a five-year program. Students who complete such a program may earn both a bachelors degree in liberal arts and sciences and either a full masters degree in education or credits towards such a degree.

An important trend in teacher education is the addition of a testing requirement and the demonstration of competency before a candidate can be awarded a permanent certificate. Many states require teachers to complete a college program and take a standardized test such as the National Teacher Examination in order to receive a provisional teaching certificate. To qualify for a permanent certificate, the candidate then has to demonstrate mastery of specified teaching skills such as questioning, classroom management, and the evaluation of learning. The final judgment as to whether a teacher is competent may be made by a building administrator or by an outside evaluation team. In some cases, teachers receive feedback on their strengths and weaknesses and are provided with in-service assistance to help them improve before they are observed a second time.

All programs, those preparing aides as well as teachers, include some form of teaching practice or field experience. This practice gives students an opportunity to work with children in a realistic setting and allows them to gain a better understanding of what children are like. These experiences also allow students to discover if they are suited for teaching. Regardless of the purpose of the preparation program, the goal is to ensure that those who work with young children have the skills, knowledge, and ability to do it well.

Credentialing and Certification

A *teaching certificate* is a license to teach. It is granted by a state to everyone who has successfully completed the necessary requirements. Usually certification is based at least partly on the completion of a Bachelor's or Master's degree teacher education program, though there may be other requirements. Certification offers legal permission to teach a certain grade level or in a certain subject area. While certification is required to teach in public schools, it is often not required in private schools or in nursery schools or child care centers.

A *teaching credential* is usually offered by an agency or association upon completion of a specialized training program rather than by a state. Although some certified teachers take additional training to receive a specialized credential, normally one need not be certified to earn the credential.

Two of the best-known credentials in early childhood education are the Montessori Credential, offered by the Association Montessori Internationale (AMI) or the American Montessori Society (AMS), and the Child Development Associate (CDA) credential. It is not necessary to be a certified teacher to obtain these credentials. In fact, CDA was set up to offer a credential to people working in early childhood education who did not have a college degree or formal teacher preparation.

The Child Development Associate credential came into being in 1970. Dr. Edward Zigler, then director of the Office of Child Development, recognized a need for a system to ensure that those working with young children had the skills, knowledge, and values necessary to provide quality educational programs. A task force was commissioned to determine the scope of the program, and the Child Development Associate Consortium was funded in 1972 (Campbell & Reed, 1976). There are six CDA competency areas (see Figure 4–2).

A direct assessment model is utilized and each candidate's ability is evaluated by a team of early childhood professionals. The assessment takes place on-site and includes observations, interviews, and a portfolio review. A CDA candidate must demonstrate competence in each of these areas in order to qualify for the credential. Each candidate's ability is assessed by an evaluation team.

A second approach to earning a CDA credential began in 1990, and is known as the Child Development Associate Professional Preparation Program (CDA, 1989). In this model, students participate in a three-phase, year-long program leading to that credential. The phases are (1) field work, (2) course work, and (3) final evaluation. The program is designed to provide students with a variety of experiences to help them develop the skills necessary to be successful in their work with young children.

More than 30,000 people have earned the CDA credential since the first ones were awarded in 1975. Forty states plus the District of Columbia have accepted the CDA credential as a means of meeting staff qualification requirements (Powell & Dunn, 1990).

Whereas certification is necessary to teach in the public schools and the Montessori credential is necessary to teach in a Montessori school, the CDA credential is usually earned by people who have already entered the field and are

FIGURE 4-2 CDA Competencies and Related Functional Areas

Competency Area I:

Setting Up and Maintaining a Safe and Healthy Learning Environment.

Functional Areas:

1. *Safe:* Candidate provides a safe environment by taking necessary measures to reduce or prevent accidents.
2. *Healthy:* Candidate provides an environment that is free of factors which may contribute to or cause illness.
3. *Environment:* Candidate selects materials and equipment and arranges the room to the developmental level of the children.

Competency Area II:

Advancing Physical and Intellectual Competence of Children.

Functional Areas:

1. *Physical:* Candidate provides a variety of appropriate equipment, activities, and opportunities to promote the physical development of children.

2. *Cognitive:* Candidate provides activities and experiences which encourage questioning, probing, and problem-solving skills appropriate to the developmental level of the child.
3. *Language:* Candidate helps children acquire and use language as a means of communicating their thoughts, feelings, and understanding.
4. *Creative:* Candidate provides a variety of experiences and media that stimulate children to explore and express their creative abilities.

Competency Area III:

Building Positive Self-Concept and Individual Strength in Children.

Functional Areas:

1. *Self-Concept:* Candidate helps each child to know, accept, and appreciate him- or herself as an individual.
2. *Individual Strength:* Candidate helps each child develop a sense of independence and acquire the ability to express, understand, and control his or her feelings.

Competency Area IV:

Organizing and Sustaining the Positive Functioning of Children and Adults in a Group in a Learning Environment.

Functional Areas:

1. *Social:* Candidate helps the children learn to get along with others and encourages feelings of mutual respect among the children in the group.
2. *Group Management:* Candidate provides a positive routine and establishes simple rules with the group that are understood and accepted by children and adults.

Competency Area V:

Bringing About Optimal Coordination of Home and Center Child-Rearing Practices and Expectations.

Functional Areas:

1. *Home/Center:* Candidate establishes positive and productive relationships with parents and encourages them to participate in the center's activities.

Competency Area VI:

Carrying Out Supplementary Responsibilities Related to the Children's Programs.

Functional Area:

1. *Staff:* Candidate works cooperatively with other staff members concerning plans, activities, policies, and rules of the center.

Child Development Associate Consortium, *Competency Standards* (Washington, DC: The Consortium, 1977).

working with children. It is a requirement for employment for some roles in Head Start and in some child care programs.

Ethical Considerations

Ethics are guidelines that help early childhood educators to determine how they should conduct themselves. Such guidelines can assist us in distinguishing between good and bad practice. Lilian Katz (1977) feels that ethics help us to act in terms of what is right rather than merely on what is expedient. They keep us from taking shortcuts in the way we approach children.

One set of ethical guidelines, the *Code of Ethical Conduct,* has been developed by the National Association for the Education of Young Children (1989). The primary focus of the code is on professional practice with children and their families in preschools, child care centers, family day care homes, kindergartens, and primary classrooms.

There are four sections to the code, each containing ideals and principles to guide conduct and to assist in resolving ethical dilemmas that arise daily. Section I is concerned with ethical responsibilities to children. Ethical responsibilities to families are contained in section II, and section III contains ethical responsibilities to colleagues. The last section, section IV, focuses on ethical responsibilities to community and society. Figure 4–3 contains the "Statement of Commitment" of this *Code of Ethical Conduct.*

A code of ethics affirms to the public that there are standards of practice that all early childhood educators are expected to follow in their work with children. When a child is accepted into a center, the parent has the right to assume that the staff will serve the child's interests. Standards of ethics provide the caregiver with rules to ensure that only acceptable behavior is practiced.

Increasingly early childhood educators have been expected to deal with a wide range of social problems including child abuse and neglect, substance abuse (drugs or alcohol), and sex education. Whether or not sex education is included as part of the curriculum may depend on the value orientation of the parents. Substance abuse and child abuse, however, must be every practitioner's concern. Early childhood practitioners have an ethical responsibility to protect the children who are left in their care.

Males in Early Childhood Education

There are many more females than males in early childhood education. Most males who enter education tend toward the higher age levels; few work with young children. The field of early childhood education has been traditionally female oriented.

Recently, there has been an increase in the number of males entering the field. One cause of this trend is a better understanding of the qualities necessary to work successfully with young children. Many males have those qualities. Another

**FIGURE 4–3   The National Association for the Education of Young Children
Statement of Commitment**

As an individual who works with young children, I commit myself to furthering the values of early childhood education as they are reflected in the NAEYC Code of Ethical Conduct.

To the best of my ability I will:

• Ensure that programs for young children are based on current knowledge of child development and early childhood education.

• Respect and support families in their task of nurturing children.

_____

*The Statement of Commitment expresses those basic personal commitments that individuals must make in order to align themselves with the profession's responsibilities as set forth in the NAEYC Code of Ethical Conduct.

• Respect colleagues in early childhood education and support them in maintaining the NAEYC Code of Ethical Conduct.

• Serve as an advocate for children, their families, and their teachers in community and society.

• Maintain high standards of professional conduct.

• Recognize how personal values, opinions, and biases can affect professional judgment.

• Be open to new ideas and be willing to learn from the suggestions of others.

• Continue to learn, grow, and contribute as a professional.

• Honor the ideals and principles of the NAEYC Code of Ethical Conduct.

National Association for the Education of Young Children, "Code of Ethical Conduct and Statement of Commitment," *Young Children, 45* (1), pp. 24–29. Copyright 1989 by the National Association for the Education of Young Children, Washington, D.C. Reprinted with permission.

reason has been the blurring of boundaries between male and female roles in our society. It is acceptable for males to assume what were traditionally female roles just as it is acceptable for females to assume what were traditionally male roles. In addition, the growth of the field of early childhood education is providing numerous opportunities for well-trained males and females.

According to Seifert (1988), research on male teachers of young children has focused primarily on three issues: their personal and professional backgrounds, their classroom teaching styles, and their feelings about early childhood education as a career. Men differ substantially from women only in their feelings about early childhood education as a career. While relatively few of the men interviewed aspired to be administrators, many did look forward to leaving the classroom eventually and to pursuing other careers related to working with children.

Seifert (1983) reported a study with the following findings about the male teacher in early childhood education:

- He likes children as well as any other teacher who works with young children.
- He likes children enough to ignore the distractions of other careers.
- He may sometimes experience discrimination against males, but not necessarily.
- He sees relationships between his teaching and other related work.
- He expects to act on those relationships eventually, and possibly move out of the classroom.

The stigma against males working with young children is lessening. In addition, support groups are making the field a more comfortable place for males to enter and to remain.

Issues and Concerns

Early childhood education has experienced a number of growing pains during the past decade. Two major concerns are the shortage of qualified personnel to meet the demands for early childhood programs and the low wages and benefits paid to those working in the field. These two concerns are closely related.

Galinsky (1989) reported that programs throughout the country are having problems finding and retaining staff. She identified six factors contributing to the staffing crisis:

1. There is a shortage of people in the labor pool in the eighteen to twenty-four-year age range, a group that traditionally provides a large number of early childhood staff members.
2. Salaries in early childhood are lower than in many other fields.
3. Benefits, including sick leave, life insurance, health insurance, and retirement are either inadequate or unavailable to most early childhood workers.
4. There is a lack of status associated with the field.
5. The absence of a clearly defined career ladder is frustrating to many experienced teachers. They can work for years and have the same title and salary as a beginning teacher.
6. The working conditions are often poor.

According to Galinsky, the biggest obstacle to solving the staffing crisis is the fact that funding adequate pay for teachers will raise the cost of child care to a level that most parents cannot afford. Some parents are already spending between 10–25 percent of their gross income on child care. Poor people spend disproportionately higher percentages of their income on child care than wealthier people (Hofferth, 1989). Consideration is being given to a variety of federal and state initiatives such as tax credits and direct financial support as ways to help fund child care and, in turn, to improve the salaries of those working with young children.

The goal of the teacher-education reform movement is to improve the preparation of teachers, who will then be better equipped to help children learn. Salaries, benefits, working conditions, and other job-related factors will have to be improved in order to attract these better educated teachers to the early childhood classroom.

SUMMARY

There never has been a better time to enter the field of early childhood education. The field is growing. Jobs with children within the field and in related fields are plentiful. Society is beginning to recognize the importance of caring for and educating young children. However, this growth has raised a number of issues that have affected the field. We will have to come to grips with concerns for credentialing, certification, status, and professionalism in order for the field to focus on providing quality experiences for children. The fact that these issues have been raised is an indication of the vitality of the field. We have recognized many of the problems facing the field and we are moving to correct them.

In her book *The Early Childhood Educator at Work*, Millie Almy (1975) reflected on the fact that the early childhood educator is a double specialist in a number of ways. Early childhood educators teach and evaluate learning, work with children and adults, and think concretely and formally. Almy's description of the role identifies the complexity of being a practitioner in early childhood education. There are always at least two things to do at one time in order to meet the needs of the children.

REFERENCES

ALMY, M. (1975). *The early childhood educator at work.* New York: McGraw-Hill.

ALMY, M. C., AND A. SNYDER, (1947). The staff and its preparation. In *Early Childhood Education*, 46th Yearbook of the National Society for the Study of Education. Part II. Chicago: University of Chicago Press.

CAMPBELL, D. M., AND I. B. REED (1976). *Traveling toward competence: The California State College Child Development Associate project.* ERIC Document Reproduction Service No. ED 138359.

CARNEGIE FORUM ON EDUCATION AND THE ECONOMY (1986). *A nation prepared: Teachers for the 21st century.* New York: Author.

CATALDO, C. (1983). *Infant and toddler programs.* Reading, PA: Addison-Wesley.

CHILD DEVELOPMENT ASSOCIATE CONSORTIUM (1977). *Competency Standards.* Washington, DC: Child Development Associate Consortium.

CHILD DEVELOPMENT ASSOCIATE NATIONAL CREDENTIALING PROGRAM (1989). CDA professional preparation program geared for implementation. *Competence, 3*(3), 1–4.

COMBS, A. W. (1982). *A personal approach to teaching: Beliefs that make a difference.* Boston: Allyn & Bacon.

COMMONWEALTH OF VIRGINIA (1988). *Proposed child care center standards.* Richmond, VA: Commonwealth of Virginia Child Day-Care Council.

COUNCIL FOR EARLY CHILDHOOD PROFESSIONAL RECOGNITION (1989). *National directory of early childhood training programs.* Washington, DC: Author.

DAVIS, M. D. (1982). The Preparation of administrators, teachers, and caregivers. In M. Dickerson, M. Davis, and G. Rose (Eds.), *Young Children: Issues for the 80's*. Little Rock, AR: Southern Association on Children Under Six.

DAVIS, M. D., AND N. L. ALEXANDER (1982). Quality teaching and professional role responsibilities: Concerns for early childhood education. *Reading Improvement, 19*(3), 232–235.

GALINSKY, E. (1989). From our president: The staffing crisis. *Young Children, 44*(2), 2–4.

HOFFERTH, S. (1989). Public policy report: What is the demand for and supply of child care in the United States? *Young Children, 44*(2), 28–33.

HOLMES GROUP, INC. (1986). *Tomorrow's teachers: A report of the Holmes Group*. East Lansing, MI: Author.

HOSTETLER, L. (1984). The nanny trap: Child care work today. *Young Children, 39*(2), 76–79.

HOSTETLER, L., AND E. KLUGMAN (1982) Early childhood job titles: One step toward professional status. *Young Children, 37*(6),13–33.

HYMES, J. L., JR. (1982). Young children: Past accomplishments—future priorities. In M. Dickerson, M. Davis, and G. Rose (Eds.), *Young children: Issues for the 80's*. Little Rock, AR: Southern Association on Children Under Six.

KATZ, L. G. (1977). *Ethical considerations for working with young children*. ERIC Document Reproduction Service No. ED 144681.

LEEPER, S. H. (1968). *Nursery school and the kindergarten*. Washington, DC: National Education Association.

NATIONAL ASSOCIATION FOR THE EDUCATION OF YOUNG CHILDREN (1984). Research report: Results of the NAEYC survey of child care salaries and working conditions. *Young Children, 40*(1), 9–14.

———. (1984). *NAEYC position statement on nomenclature, salaries, benefits and the status of the early childhood profession*. Washington, DC: National Association for the Education of Young Children.

———. (1989). Code of Ethical Conduct and Statement of Commitment. *Young Children, 45*(1), 24–29.

PETERS, D. (1988). The child development associate credential and the educationally disenfranchised. In B. Spodek, O. Saracho, and D. Peters (Eds.), *Professionalism and the early childhood practitioner*, pp. 93–104. New York: Teachers College Press.

POWELL, D. R., AND L. DUNN (1990). Non-baccalaureate teacher education in early childhood education. In B. Spodek and O. N. Saracho (Eds.) *Yearbook in early childhood education, Vol. 1: Early childhood teacher preparation*. New York: Teachers College Press.

SEAVER, J. W., C. A. CARTWRIGHT, C. B. WARD, AND C. A. HEASLEY (1979). *Careers with young children: Making your decision*. Washington, DC: National Association for the Education of Young Children.

SEIFERT, K. (1983). *The achievement of care: Men who teach young children*. ERIC Document Reproduction Service No. ED 231542.

———. (1988). Men in early childhood education. In B. Spodek, O.N. Saracho, and D. L. Peters (Eds.), *Professionalism and the early childhood practitioner*, pp. 105–116. New York: Teachers College Press.

SPODEK, B., M. D. DAVIS, AND O. N. SARACHO (1983). Early childhood teacher education and certification. *Journal of Teacher Education, 34*(5), 50–52.

SPODEK, B., AND O. N. SARACHO (1982). The preparation and certification of early childhood personnel. In B. Spodek (Ed.), *Handbook of research in early childhood education*, pp. 399–425. New York: Free Press.

SPODEK, B., O. N. SARACHO, AND D. L. PETERS (1988). Professionalism, semiprofessionalism, and craftsmanship. In B. Spodek, O. N. Saracho, and D. L. Peters (Eds.) *Professionalism and the early childhood practitioner*, pp. 3–9. New York: Teachers College Press.

WEBER, L. (1982). Education: Issues for the 80's. In M. Dickerson, M. Davis, and G. Rose (Eds.), *Young children: Issues for the 80's*. Little Rock, AR: Southern Association on Children Under Six.

SUGGESTED ACTIVITIES

1. Interview a center director about problems with hiring and retaining staff. How would you characterize the problems? Are they related to money, background, training, or other factors?

2. Find out the early childhood teacher certification requirements for your state. How do they compare with the requirements to be a director of a child care center?

3. Write to the American Montessori Association or the Child Development Associate Consortium for information on their credentials. Compare their requirements with the requirements of the program in which you are currently enrolled.

4. Interview both a male and a female teacher of young children using the same set of questions. How are their answers similar? How are they different?

5. For one week keep a record of all the child-related references you see or hear on TV or radio, in magazines and newspapers, and from people. How many different careers are featured in your references? Choose one of the careers that particularly interests you and collect information about it.

6. Read three articles related to ethical behavior in early childhood education. How do the ideas in the articles help you to decide on appropriate teaching practices?

5

The Child in the Early Childhood Program

OBJECTIVES

After completing this chapter on the child in the early childhood program, the student will be able to:

1. Describe six developmental theories and their contributions to early childhood education.
2. Relate developmental theories to the nature and nurture of children's development.
3. Identify the general characteristics of children three through five years of age.
4. Describe physical development, cognitive development, language development, emotional development, social development, and the development of values.
5. Discuss influences on language development.
6. Describe individual and group differences in children's development.

Throughout this century the field of early childhood education has been influenced by the concepts and theories of the field of child development. Many of the most prominent theories about children's psychological development and behavior continue to influence the field today. These are presented in this chapter, along with information about their originators.

DEVELOPMENTAL THEORIES AND THEORISTS

Up to about one hundred years ago there was no field of child development or child psychology. What we knew about how children grew and learned came from the introspection of adults who wrote down what they remembered of their own childhood, or from the journals and diaries of parents who recorded their impressions of their own children. These sources provided an interesting basis for understanding young children, but the information was often of questionable validity. Before the beginning of the twentieth century the pioneering work of G. Stanley Hall led to the establishment of the child study movement, out of which grew the scientific field of child development.

G. Stanley Hall (1844–1924): The Child Study Movement

G. Stanley Hall contributed several original theories to the field of child development. One of the most significant was his evolutionary development or recapitulation theory. This theory reflected the theory of evolution, which suggests that humans evolved from lower animals. Hall speculated that children's behavior was a reflection of primitive aspects of those species from which humans evolved. Since these primitive aspects were no longer adaptive or necessary, they needed to be eliminated. Hall believed that children could lose these primitive behavior patterns through play. Children's water play, for example, can be traced to the play of fish, and their climbing and swinging can be associated with the play of anthropoids. These activities allow children to role-play some facets of their evolutionary past so they can work through their primitive needs and move on to more appropriate forms of behavior.

Hall sent questionnaires to teachers asking them to identify children's interests and activities. These questionnaires provided him with a great deal of information from many sources in a simple, quick, and inexpensive way. He conducted more than 100 questionnaire studies on a variety of topics (Kessen, 1965). According to today's research standards, these questionnaires would be considered a crude and inadequate research technique. However, his work stimulated many of the current interests of today's child developmentalists.

Hall's most enduring contribution was his focus on child study. His work stimulated psychologists to study children as a way to understanding the development of adult behavior. He believed that the study of children provides insight into adult behavior and that those who work in child-oriented institutions need to know more about children and their development. Hall believed that the educational system should be adapted to children's patterns of development.

G. Stanley Hall. (Archives of the History Museum of American Psychology, University of Akron, Ohio.)

Hall's work changed child study research. It led the field to use more sources of information than adult memory or parents' records. Researchers began to base their studies on information gathered on large numbers of children to understand general patterns of development.

Some of Hall's other contributions included bringing Sigmund Freud to the United States and assisting in the introduction of Freudian psychoanalysis to American psychologists. Hall, along with John Dewey, was influential in moving early childhood programs toward more progressive, developmentally appropriate forms.

Arnold Gesell (1880–1961): Developmental Ages and Stages

Arnold Gesell developed detailed descriptions of the changes in children throughout the period of childhood. These descriptions were integrated to provide norms or characteristic pictures of development for infants and children through ten years of age. He organized these norms into a series of stages.

For over forty years Gesell studied the development of children's motor behavior, language, visual capacities, adaptive functions, and personal and social relations. By 1950 he had studied more than 3,000 behavioral elements, which he described in detail at thirty-four stages or levels of maturity from birth to ten years of age (Gesell, 1952). For example, Gesell described 18-month-old children as able to scribble if they are given a paper and crayon. At two years of age they can draw vertical marks. Six months later they are able to include horizontal strokes to their drawing.

In addition to integrating and forming information about the develop-

Arnold Gesell. (Gesell Institute.)

ment of children, Gesell proposed a theoretical model of development. He believed that children's development depends on maturation. He strongly maintained that infants' minds evolve through the growth process. He felt that childhood represents a unitary action structure of behavior evolving in a consistent sequence. Behavioral tests could be used to assess children's development and thus determine their maturity and the status of their nervous system (Gesell, 1952). This maturational view of development supported a noninterventionist approach to early childhood education. Teachers are able to support development, but they are not able to influence it in a significant way.

Sigmund Freud (1856–1939): Personality Development

Sigmund Freud originated the psychoanalytic theory of personality development. His purpose was to understand the adult personality as it developed from childhood, beginning in the earliest periods of life through maturity. Although Freud's major interest was the adult personality, his psychoanalytic theory identified the importance of early childhood experiences in the development of that personality.

Freud felt that it was essential to know the child in order to understand the emerging adult. He believed that individuals develop through a series of conflicts derived from within their own nature. He thought that the roots of mature emotional life are developed in the early years.

Freud's theoretical explanation of behavior emphasizes the interaction of physical development and maturation with the early life experiences. Behavior is affected by biological drives, instincts, and unconscious motives interacting

Sigmund Freud. (Austrian National Tourist Office.)

with early family experiences. He believed that almost every experience is stored in the mind. While we are not consciously aware of these memories, they influence our behavior.

Freud believed that a person's essential psychological nature depends on biologically based desire rather than reason. The emphasis in psychoanalysis was primarily on individuals' passions or emotions, and secondarily on their rational abilities or intellect. The person was born with basic animal instincts functioning at the unconscious level of thought. Such instincts, or irrational needs, demand instant rewards. An individual's development relies in part on the transformation of these desires into socially acceptable, rational behavior (Langer, 1969).

Freud identified three elements of the human personality: the *id*, *superego*, and *ego*. The *id* is an inborn factor that includes the basic instinctive drive to seek pleasure. The *superego* develops through society's influence, as an individual's conscience strives to differentiate right from wrong. In seeking pleasure, the *id* and the *superego* (which does not permit pleasure) conflict. The *ego*, the rational or reasoning factor, functions to resolve this conflict. It develops socially acceptable ways to meet the pleasures of the *id*. For example, when a child gets angry with another child, he or she may feel the urge to hit out but has been taught that hitting others is not permitted. The child strives to decrease the conflict and handles the anger in a socially acceptable manner. The child may verbalize the anger or reduce the pent-up emotional energy by punching a bag or pounding clay.

Freud's psychoanalytic theory suggested a somewhat more active role for early childhood educators. Teachers still were not expected to intervene in the child's development to any great extent. They were, however, expected to provide a warm and nurturant environment. At the same time they could offer activities

TABLE 5-1   Freud's Psychosexual Stages

AGE	STAGE	CHARACTERISTICS
0–1 year	oral	Mouth and upper digestive tract is the center of sensual stimulation and pleasure.
1–3 years	anal	Anus and lower digestive tract is focal; pleasure in withholding or eliminating feces.
3–6 years	phallic	Pleasure focused in genital area, creation of Oedipal or Electra attachment, identification with parents.
6–12 years	latency	Focus on industriousness, suppression of sexual interest.
12 years and beyond	genital period	More mature sexual interests develop.

that would allow children to rid themselves of feelings they could not express at home. Teachers were also expected to help children find socially acceptable ways of expressing their emotional needs.

Erik Erikson (1902–   ): Psychosocial Development

Erik Erikson, like Freud, felt that a healthy adult is one who satisfies personal needs and desires while learning to meet the demands of society. In his early adulthood Erikson studied teaching and received a Montessori teaching certificate. He also studied psychotherapy with Anna Freud. He incorporated these two interests by applying psychoanalytic theory to educational issues. Later he conducted research in the area of children's play and child-rearing practices. He also became a long-term student of the growth and development of the ego.

Erik Erikson. (Jon Erikson.)

Erikson transformed Freud's psychosexual-stage theory of development to one of psychosocial stages, theorizing that people develop throughout their lives as they interact with their social environment, and that all individuals go through eight unique stages during the course of their lives. Each stage features a specific crisis. Individuals who are unable to resolve that crisis may move on to the next stage, but they are not capable of resolving the crisis of the new stage until the earlier ones are resolved. The crisis in each stage is related to the ego strengths that begin to form at birth and accumulate throughout development (Erikson, 1963). The epigenetic principle that development is predetermined by genetic principles is another important aspect of Erikson's theory. Erikson, like Freud and Piaget, felt that growth develops along a discontinuous or age/stage route (Erikson, 1968).

Whereas Freud focused on the importance of sexual or biological pleasure in development, Erikson emphasized the social, historical, and cultural influences on development. Like Sigmund and Anna Freud, Erikson was interested in the development of the ego. Although he was aware that the individuals' instinctual drives and interest in various parts of the body evolved in a prescribed sequence, he focused on children's interactions with their surroundings. He perceived the ego, not the id, as the main driving behavioral force.

In developing his theories, Erikson studied healthy personalities instead of analyzing neurotic people, as Freud did (Maier, 1978). He disagreed with Freud's concept of infantile sexuality, believing that society provided the major influences in developing children's behavior. He also believed that the develop-

TABLE 5-2 Erikson's Stages of Psychosocial Development

AGE	STAGE	CHARACTERISTICS
0–1½ years	trust vs. mistrust	Reliance on caregiver, predictability leads to trust in environment; or lack of care leads to basic mistrust.
1½–3 years	autonomy vs. shame and doubt	Environment encourages independence, pride, and sense of self-worth; or doubt and lack of self-esteem result from over-control.
3–6 years	initiative vs. guilt	Ability to learn and to enjoy mastery; or fear of failure and of punishment leads to guilt.
6 years–puberty	industry vs. inferiority	Valuing work, skill, and competence; or feelings of inadequacy and inferiority.
Adolescence	indentity vs. role confusion	Development of individuality; or confusion related to self.
Young adulthood	intimacy vs. isolation	Commitment to personal relations; or withdrawal from others and self-absorption.
Middle age	generativity vs. stagnation	Care of next generation, widening interests; or self-indulgence.
Old age	ego identity vs. despair	Gaining the meaning of one's existence; or disappointment with life and fear of death.

mental course can be reversed to the point that the later events can modify elements of children's personality that were developed during earlier periods. Freud, like Erikson, believed that the basic personality system is established by five years of age. For both Freud and Erikson, stages are linked to ages in the sense that the ego leads the transition to a new stage regardless of experience and reorganization at the previous stages.

Erikson's and Freud's developmental stages differ in two major ways. While Freud saw development as essentially complete by the end of adolescence, Erikson assumed that development was continuous throughout an individual's life. Therefore, his stages continue through early adulthood, adulthood, and maturity as well as childhood and adolescence. In addition, Erikson based his stages on a series of social, instead of sexual conflicts, which all individuals must successfully master before achieving maturity (Erikson, 1982). These conflicts could differ according to the culture and historical reference point.

Erikson's work suggests an even more active role for early childhood education. Teachers can help children cope with the essential crisis of their developmental stage. They can also help children develop competencies that will strengthen each individual's ego.

B. F. Skinner (1904–1990): Operant Conditioning

In the 1950s B. F. Skinner advanced the behaviorist school of thought in learning and development. He focused on exploring the nature of reinforcement and reinforcing stimuli in relation to learning. Skinner developed problem boxes to experiment with animals. The Skinner box dispensed a reward (food pellet)

B. F. Skinner. (Courtesy of B. F. Skinner.)

to an animal if it correctly manipulated a lever or button. Trial and error were linked to rewards for correct behavior. The animals learned to operate the mechanisms in the box as a result of being rewarded.

Skinner's theory of learning has been referred to as *operant conditioning* or *instrumental learning*. According to Skinner, consequences (either negative or positive) that follow a behavior control that behavior. Operant conditioning concentrates primarily on positive reinforcement because of the negative effects punishment can have. A correct response must provide a reward to encourage that behavior to occur again in a similar circumstance. Such instrumentally conditioned responses are referred to as *operants* because they operate on the environment. The nature of the consequences can be critical, because they determine the future behavior of the organism.

The role of early childhood education on an individual's development is considered to be a major one from a behaviorist point of view. The child's development can never be considered as separate from the events in the child's development. The early childhood teacher can design an environment that will elicit appropriate, desirable behaviors from the child. The teacher can also increase the chances of these behaviors appearing and being sustained by purposely reinforcing only those behaviors. Children increase their range of behaviors as they go through development, but there are no specific stages related to specific kinds of behavior.

Jean Piaget (1896–1980): Intellectual Development

Cognitive-developmental theory has been most completely elaborated on and described by Jean Piaget. He did not study children's emotions or their personality development, although he considered them important. Rather, his interest in examining thought processes and their developmental changes led Piaget to study changes in how children process information as they mature. Piaget believed that children's thinking differed in profound and significant ways from adult thinking and that children's thought processes were modified as they grew. He described their thought processes at different levels and demonstrated that they were active and self-motivated in the creation of their own knowledge. For Piaget, children's thinking abilities followed a consistent developmental pattern beginning early in their life and continuing until maturity.

Most of young children's play behavior reflects the child's important work of *equilibration*, that is, by assimilating new information and accommodating existing intellectual structures, the child develops a balance of understanding while investigating people and their environment (Piaget, 1962). Mental activity and parallel physical activity are essential as children construct their systems of knowledge in more and more mature ways and become effective, competent, thinking adults.

Piaget identified four major stages of cognitive development: (1) the sensorimotor stage (birth to two years), (2) the preoperational stage (two to seven years), (3) the concrete operational stage (seven to eleven years), and (4) the for-

Jean Piaget. (Wayne Behling/The Ypsilanti Press.)

mal operational stage (from eleven or twelve through adulthood). Children progress through these stages in a regular sequence but at their own rate of development, which is influenced by their experiences and their own maturing abilities.

While Piaget believed that children regulate their own thinking, his theory suggests an active role for early childhood education. The teacher should not tell children what they should know, either directly or indirectly through audiovisual techniques. Instead, the teacher should design developmentally appropriate activities which allow children to act upon concrete materials and develop conceptual skills. Teachers also can ask questions to develop a degree of cognitive conflict, posing issues that force children to think in more mature ways.

TABLE 5-3   Piaget's Stages of Intellectual Development

AGE	STAGE	CHARACTERISTICS
Birth–1½ or 2 years	sensorimotor	Children develop schemas based on sensory input and bodily motion.
2–7 years	preoperational	children develop language and other symbolic representations. Intuitive thought is not systematic or sustained.
7–11 years	concrete operational	Children deal with logical processes, can deal with only one form of classification at a time; logical thought requires actual physical objects or events.
11 years and beyond	formal operational	Children reason logically; formulate and test hypotheses; think abstractly.

This approach represents a major shift in theories about what schools can do for young children.

NATURE AND NURTURE IN CHILDREN'S DEVELOPMENT

The concepts that have been set forth by these developmental theorists vary from one another in considerable ways. One way relates to the areas of development each theory addresses. Some theories deal with all areas of development, while others address only a narrow range of development—for example, intellectual development or socioemotional development.

Another way they differ is the way in which they consider the individual's genetic makeup (nature) or the experiences of growing up (nurture) as being critical to each child's development. Some theorists suggest that an individual's development is primarily determined by nature; while a poor environment might limit any individual's ultimate development, it cannot be considered the prime cause of development. Other theories suggest that human development is more plastic and that ultimately it is the child's experiences that determine what the individual finally becomes. Most child development specialists avoid either of these two extremes, believing in the importance of both these influences and feeling that the environmental influences should never be ignored. Although the family serves as the major environmental influence for the young child, early childhood education is also important. Thus, the teacher of young children can have a significant impact on the life of each child in a class.

It should also be noted that developmental research has provided us with a picture of the normal development of children. While this picture represents the central tendencies of development, with half the children developing at a somewhat faster rate and the other half at a somewhat slower rate, it does represent the characteristics of most children at particular points in their lives. Teachers can plan for appropriate activities knowing about how most children mature, then making modifications for the individual differences that are found in a particular class. General characteristics of children age three to six that are considered important to teachers are presented in Table 5–4.

Any chart of developmental expectations should be used only as a general guide. Not all children will show the same characteristics at the same point in their development, though many do. This chart merely illustrates the order of development and provides you with a general sense of what to expect.

DEVELOPMENTAL AREAS

Physical Development

By the time the children reach the early childhood stage, obvious physical changes occur in relation to body proportions and physical skills. For example, a toddler's round, baby-like contours become more slender. Physical development affects the preschooler's muscular growth and general body build. This growth

TABLE 5-4 Characteristics of Early Childhood Development

THREE-YEAR-OLDS		
Socioemotional Behavior	*Perceptual-Motor Behaviors*	*Cognitive Behaviors*
Knows self as an individual	Climbs stairs unassisted	Likes to talk with adults
Plays by self and with others	Learns to hop	Talks to self in monolog
Learns to share toys	Jumps, walks, runs with music	Asks questions
Cannot share work space	Rolls ball with direction	Has 250–900 word vocabulary
Feels sympathetic	Throws underhand	Says full name
Rests for 10 minutes	Catches large ball	Tells action in picture
Waits and takes turns	Walks on tiptoe	Listens longer to stories
Enjoys dress-up clothes	Sits with feet crossed at ankles	Sings, laughs
Enjoys simple humor	Turns wide corner with tricycle	Says simple nursery rhymes
Enjoys praise	Stops or goes on slide	Speaks in 6-word sentences
Enjoys floor play	Walks a walking board holding	Repeats 3 numerals
Is proud of what he or she makes	adult hand	Counts to 5 in imitation
Helps with adult house activities	Buttons and unbuttons	Identifies own drawing
Separates from mother to go to	Enjoys easel paint	Works puzzles with as many as 7
preschool	Holds crayon with fingers	pieces
Invents people and objects	Copies a cross on paper	Builds tower of 5 graduated
	Cuts with scissors	blocks
	Toilets self during the day	Builds 3-block bridge
		Understands prepositions (on, under, inside)
		Can point to parts of body
		Can point to smaller of 2 squares
		Identifies big and little

FOUR-YEAR-OLDS		
Socioemotional Behaviors	*Perceptual-Motor Behaviors*	*Cognitive Behaviors*
Plays with small group	Walks alone up and down stairs,	Can identify and point to pictures
Likes birthday parties	one foot per stair	described
Talks about inviting or not inviting	Climbs ladder and trees	Matches and names 4 basic
someone	Runs on tiptoe	colors
Learns to express sympathy	Gallops to music	"Reads" pictures
Shows off in dress-up clothes	Hops on one foot	Counts and touches 4 or more objects
Likes to brag	Bounces large ball	jects
Likes to go on (field) trips	Cuts with scissors on line	Gives home address and age
Runs ahead but waits at corner	Eats with fork and spoon	Can tell what material objects are
Is interested in rules	Dresses self except tying shoe	made of
Plans ahead with adults	laces	Asks for explanations
Acts silly if tired	Builds building with blocks	Is interested in death
Answers telephone efficiently	Builds tower of 10 or more blocks	Makes up words and rhymes
Aware of sexual differences	Balances on walking board	Learns to distinguish between
Is courteous without verbal clues	Draws man with 2 or more parts	fact and fancy
	Adds 3 parts to incomplete man	Likes to finish activities
	Draws and paints recognizable	Can compare 3 pictures
	objects	Can tell likenesses and differences in 3 out of 6 pictures
	Folds and creases paper 3 times	ences in 3 out of 6 pictures
	Copies square	Carries out a series of 3 directions
		tions

(Continued)

TABLE 5-4 *(Continued)*

Socioemotional Behaviors	FIVE-YEAR-OLDS Perceptual-Motor Behaviors	Cognitive Behaviors
Pleased and conscious of new maturity	Is able to sit longer	Identifies pennies, nickels, dimes
Has more cooperative play	Explores neighborhood	Is interested in clock and time
Likes to play house and baby	Has more hand-eye control	Draws what he or she has in mind at the moment
Gets along well in small group	Prints first name	
Conforms to adult ideas	Prints numerals 1–5	Recognizes some numerals and letters
Asks adult help as needed	Can trace around a diamond	Tells what numeral follows another through 10
Likes to have rules	Draws a triangle	
Begins to show respect for group property and rights of others	Studies for reality in drawing and painting	Listens and takes turn in group discussions
Has poise and control	Is self-sufficient in personal care	Knows agent (producer) of 15 of 20 actions
Is proud of what he or she has and does	Does simple errands	
	Can roller skate	Works with several children to lay out simple "maps" with blocks, showing streets and buildings and their locations
Chooses own friends	Skips on alternate feet	
Begins to distinguish masculine and feminine roles	Can jump rope	
	Like to eat simple food	
Is irritable and cross only when tired and hungry	Runs, skips, and dances in response to music	Learns left from right
	Catches a ball 5″ in diameter	Speaks fluently and correctly except s/f/h
	Learns to use overhead ladder	
	Uses knife and fork	Loves stories and acts them out
	Washes and dries face and hands without getting clothes wet	Asks meaning of words
		Places 10 or more pieces to complete puzzle
	Draws person with major body parts and features	Can tell how a crayon and pencil are the same and how they are different

Missouri State Department of Elementary and Secondary Education, *Focus on Early Childhood Education; Resource Guide for the Education of Children Ages 3–6.*

allows the child to engage in numerous and diverse kinds of physical activities in preschool.

The preschooler's body is also transformed in other ways. When children enter preschool, most of them have all of their 20 baby teeth. Shortly after the beginning of the preschool years, they begin to lose their teeth. Permanent teeth do not appear until age six (Spock & Rothenberg, 1985). The children's muscle and skeletal systems continue to develop with age. The head and brain reach their adult size during this stage. Maturation increases the connectivity and transmission of nerve impulses, which are very important in more complex brain functions, including motor control (Helms & Turner, 1986; Malina, 1982; Schmidt, 1982).

In addition to physical developments characterizing the preschool years, certain factors also affect the overall course of development and the eventual expression of physical change. Physical development is a long-range process influenced by many elements. Some of the influences are related to an individual's internal characteristics, while other elements are related to the general environment, independent of the individual. Each of these sources plays an important role in the overall development of every child (Gardner, 1973). Sex, race, nutritional state, and general physical condition all affect children's physical growth, including their stature and body proportions. Although physical growth is genetically determined, environmental influences (such as nutrition, health, and exercise) significantly influence development.

Motor development proceeds in predictable patterns. Children (including infants) who are provided with adequate environmental stimulation and practice gradually acquire the capacity to control their bodily movements. Their brains process information from the environment and coordinate actions and interactions with the environment.

Physical development influences personality development in several ways. Physical appearance affects the way children act and how they think about themselves and others. Children's rates of maturity especially influence the personality development of handicapped children (Berger, 1986; McCandless & Trotter, 1977; Seifert & Hoffnung, 1987).

Children need time to develop, opportunities to explore, and freedom to experiment and test ideas and actions. Their personal drive to learn will motivate them, but they must be allowed to develop at their own rate. Teachers need to provide the space and materials, allow the time, and accept the children's idiosyncratic developmental rate.

Cognitive Development

Cognition refers to an individual's intellect or thinking. The development of thinking skills is based on changes in the child's mental structures. The ability of a child to coordinate various ways of thinking in order to solve problems is a good measure of intellectual growth.

Mature thinking and reasoning begin to develop with the discriminations and regular pattern of actions found in infancy and toddlerhood. Toward the end of their first year most infants are able to distinguish their mother from others in their environment, to understand simple relationships, to point to an object, and to develop fundamental attention and memory skills. As infants' memories are refined, they begin to consider themselves as unique individuals, separated from their environment. Children's limited memory capacities increase with age. Children begin to explore the world around them, developing a sense of object permanence. Toddlers also begin to use language as a vehicle for expression, substituting words for sounds or actions. Thus they develop mental processes that enable them to understand simple problem-solving situations.

Infants and toddlers can make rather fine sensory discriminations. Researchers have found that infants as early as their crawling stage show a high degree of sensory awareness. Perceptual development also takes place as the sense of hearing, taste, smell, and touch develop. Extraordinary developments during infancy and toddlerhood include progressively finer perceptions of shape and form, space, class, and time (Helms & Turner, 1981).

Infants' perceptions are soon transformed into *concepts*. A concept is an individual's mental construction of a class of things. Concepts change to a large extent from early childhood into late adolescence, when socially accepted meanings become stabilized (Klausmeier & Allen, 1978). Such changes are obvious even in the early years. Barry J. Wadsworth (1971) describes the changes in early childhood from preconceptual to intuitive thought.

Preconceptual thought characterizes children ages two to four and is especially important to those working with young children. Like Piaget's stage of sensorimotor development, preconceptual thought provides a basis for the appearance of later mature cognition.

During the stage of intuitive thought (four to seven years), children's thinking is marked by immediate perceptions of experiences rather than mental functions. The high degree of egocentrism tends to change with the cognitive change taking place at this time. The mental system that arises at each developmental stage does not have a lower form of egocentrism but conceals it in a higher form of the same thinking style. The form in this stage is an egocentrism of symbols represented by its objects.

Symbolic functioning produces mental images and develops the child's capacity to distinguish signifiers (words, images) from significates (the objects or situations to which signifiers refer). The meanings of words and other symbols accepted by social groups speaking the same language are also word concepts or mental constructs. Mental constructs are a critical element of a maturing individual's continuously modifying and amplifying cognitive structure. Individuals' own concepts guide them in interpreting and organizing incoming information, and in developing principles and other complex relationships among concepts. Maturing individuals acquire concepts based on their unique informal learning activities and their maturational patterns (Kagan, 1966).

Concepts are the underlying executors of intellectual work. The theoretical importance of cognitive concepts for symbolic mediators in psychological theory is similar to the fundamental role that genes play in biology or energy plays in physics. Concepts are perceived as the concentration of sensory experience and the crucial relationship between external inputs and overt behaviors.

Young children master their basic spoken language in the early years. Children who are 18-months-old know approximately twenty-five words and their developmental gains are remarkable. Figure 5–1 shows the children's progress in language development between the ages of three to six, when children acquire a vocabulary of more than 1,800 words. Preschoolers have a vocabulary increase of approximately 600 words each year, and have outstanding advances in knowledge of semantics and grammar (Corrigan, 1983; Helms & Turner, 1986).

Language Development

As children grow, their language production increases in quantity, range, and complexity. Studies of language development have focused on sequence and rate of development as well as on those factors influencing language acquisition from infancy throughout life. In a discussion of language development, three basic points need to be made:

FIGURE 5-1 Language Development in the Early Years

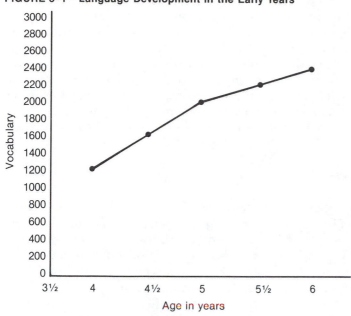

1. *There is a difference between language and speech.* Language is usually conceived as a complex system of grammatical and semantic properties, while speech consists of actual utterances. Although language and speech are closely related, they are not the same.
2. *Two areas of language growth are receptive (understanding) and expressive (producing) language.* Receptive language (such as listening or reading) refers to the children's capacity to understand and act on the language communications they process. Expressive language (speaking and writing) refers to the creation of language which is being communicated.
3. *Self-communication or inner speech must also be considered.* Children employ internal language when they daydream, plan ways to solve problems, provide directions, and coordinate their movements. This language component increasingly controls learning. (McCandless & Evans, 1973)

Children gradually make the transition from using sounds to communicate emotional expression, and from using movements and gestures to communicate personal purposes or desires, to communicating through appropriate elaborated language.

Preschool children use their developing speech skills to engage in entertaining conversations. They employ language in many ways, including questions, dialogues, songs, or chants. Most children also use language for experimentation, and for rhythm and cadence activities (Helms & Turner, 1986; Schwartz, 1981). The children's change in language relates to the development in their perception of the world around them. Two-year-olds have an intense interest in the names of things. Such interest continues to be strong for several years and helps children to quickly increase their vocabulary. In a sense, children construct their own world as they are able to name and/or describe their surroundings. Without this language ability, their surroundings would be a confusing set of vague and un-identified entities with no pattern. The elements in their surroundings come to have meaning when children know their names; experiences and situations become meaningful when children are able to use words to describe them. Using words to name objects or describe events helps children to construct an objective world they can share with others. Through language the listener can perceive the world as the speaker views it. Young children can use language with other forms of expression, such as role playing, expressive gestures, and art forms. Such expressions provide clues as to the children's perceptions of their world in relation to themselves and others.

Emotional Development

Emotional development is related to children's overall development. In-dividuals adapt to the existence of emotions—joy, anger, pain—through everyday experiences (i.e., as they feel, as they know they feel, and they know what they feel). Beyond this everyday knowledge, experts in emotional development have provided elaborate systems to categorize the various kinds of emotions. There has been a lack of agreement, however, on the definition of emotion and emotional development. Children employ unique but specific sets of behaviors, which are observed and from which emotional states are inferred. Fear, like other emotions, is a highly complex phenomenon requiring an understanding of the child's behavior, the circumstances in which the behavior takes place, and the attribution that the caregiver and society provide to that coherence of behaviors and circumstances (Lewis & Michaelson, 1983).

Children do not understand their emotions until middle childhood, when they actually acknowledge the experience of simultaneous positive and negative feelings (Whitesell & Harter, 1989). Harter and Budding (1987) describe the developmental changes in children's understanding simultaneous emotions, documenting a systematic, age-related progression in which children come to acknowledge increasingly complex multiple emotional experiences. This sequence culminates in the ability to describe simultaneous opposite-valence emotions directed toward a single target at about ten or eleven years of age.

Almost all theories of infant emotional development acknowledge that emotional expressions undergo transformation with age. Some research on the normative changes that occur in this development show that certain emotional expressions are present at birth (e.g. Demos, 1986; Izard, Hembree, & Huebner, 1987), although other research has found that these changes may not occur until later in children's development (Izard & Malatesta, 1987). Demos (1986) found that infants' emotional expressions are more guarded, subtle, and complex after their first year of life, while Cole (1985) showed that control of facial expressions occurs during the preschool years.

Each of the children's distinct facial expressions should be considered as a different internal experience. Although the meaning of an experience corresponding to a smile varies for infants and for adults, Malatesta, Culver, Tesman and Shepard (1989) contend that infants link their expression with the experience and social learning. Social learning processes are very important during the first two years. This is the time when young children blend emotions to disguise their feelings.

Beginning in the early years, children relate to others based on their interactions and the time spent with one another. Cooperation and reciprocity develop in relation to children's perceptions of friendship. Competition complicates the friendship relationship (Hartup, Laursen, Stewart, & Eastenson, 1988). Usually, friends rather than non-friends work to bring about more equitable outcomes in competitive exchanges (Berndt, 1985; Matsumoto, Haan, Yabrove, Theodorou, & Carney, 1986), although some research studies show that friendships support intense competition under some conditions.

During the early childhood period, children are socially vulnerable. They rely on others as they develop a contextual sense of self that is consistent across multiple settings such as in family, school, and peer groups (Reid, Landesman, Treder, & Jaccard, 1989). The development of attachment to their primary caregivers in infancy is important for children to establish strong relationships with others in their widening worlds (Bretherton & Waters, 1985; Cauce, 1986). The early establishment of a good social support network is critical in children's development because it promotes their emotional adjustment, life satisfaction, and mental and physical health (e.g., Cohen & Wills, 1985).

Individual differences in emotion can be considered by focusing on those emotional stages and experiences that are enduring. For example, an individual's mood is affected by differences in personality development and personality structure (Lewis & Michaelson, 1983).

Social Development

Social development usually refers to the child's developing ways of adapting to society's rules of behavior. With young children this means learning about cooperating and taking turns. Children first respond to other persons (usually their parents) using a recognizable, consistent, and predictable sign (such as a smile). Even crying is an early sign of socialization. These are social responses. Social development encompasses social controls as well as responsiveness. For example, children stop what they are doing when an adult says "No." Children follow such directions regardless of their desires.

The interchange of the total development is illustrated in the interplay of social and emotional behavior. It is important to understand the elements that create optimum socialization. Socialization is learned, it does not simply result from maturation. Social development requires maturity and the opportunity to learn individual responses. It is promoted in an early childhood classroom through the availability of interested, accepting, and communicative adults. A healthy social setting also facilitates the development of a positive self-concept, of social skills, and of readiness for formal learning. Play serves an important function in the social development of young children.

Development of Values

Attitudes and values are significant aspects of early childhood learning, which is partly nonintellectual. To some extent, values are learned the same way that general concepts are learned. A learner has expectations, experiences events, and seeks conformation for set expectations. Most prejudices, loyalties, and preferences are learned from others. The significant people in a child's life usually guide the children's testing of expectations, serving as models that children imitate. Since young children tend to view their teachers as models, we need to provide children with positive examples to follow. In learning the school's and community's values, young children imitate the models that are available. Teachers should encourage young children to adopt the desirable behavioral patterns that they and others present. Children need to learn to distinguish socially appropriate values while taking into consideration the feelings of others.

The subsystems of development described above continuously work together to affect behavior and development. They do not function independently but are integrated. In attempting to understand the children's behavior, one must take into account their development and the relationship of their whole system. For example, when a child is being administered an intelligence test, the results will be affected by that child's physical, language, emotional, and social state as well as by his or her intelligence.

REGULARITIES AND IRREGULARITIES IN YOUNG CHILDREN'S DEVELOPMENT

Teachers have a tendency to treat all children as average or slightly above average. Although this might be a reasonable approach most of the time, there are occasions when it is totally inappropriate. There are many children who differ from the average in profound and significant ways, and programs for them need to be specially designed to be responsive to those differences. Among the differences that are especially important in the development of early childhood education programs are cultural differences, language differences, social class differences, and differences that result in identifiable exceptionalities.

Cultural Differences

Culture has been defined as a set of attitudes and behaviors that have been learned and shared by a group of people. Each group of people live and function within a society that has specific cultural values and cultural techniques that are meaningful to the group.

American society has been characterized by cultural pluralism, with a number of groups having their own, somewhat isolated culture within the larger American culture. Cultural pluralism means that the values, attitudes, and behaviors that children acquire as they interact with persons closest to them may be different from those of other people they will meet throughout their lives. Our society requires that we help children learn to develop the flexibility they need to understand and accept cultural differences.

The contexts and cultures in which children are raised promote their cognitive development. Some research suggests that "domain-specific" sets of cognitive skills may develop as a function of different contexts and cultures (e.g., Feldman, 1980; Gardner, 1983). This would suggest that children in one culture might develop stronger social skills, while children in another culture might develop stronger intellectual skills. Descriptions of individual differences in cognitive ability show that culture and context do influence those who are exceptionally skilled, for example, in chess, in memory or in specific kinds of information or arithmetic-spatial skills (Greenfield & Lave, 1982; Scribner, 1984; Morris, Tweedy, & Gruneberg, 1985; Stigler, 1984). These studies on culture and cognition contribute to the understanding of domain specificity and contextual approaches to cognitive development.

Early childhood education programs socialize children by exposing them to the dominant values, customs, and habits of the culture. This exposure creates a cultural frame of reference that will become part of them and serve as a vital force in determining their behavior. Educators need to acquire a clear perspective on the role of culture in child development. Many of the children in our schools come from families that share a different culture. Teachers must be sensitive to the cultural roots of the children in their classes as well as those of others in our society. Teachers should keep in mind that there are some cultural values we all accept, but there are others that we must respect as being important to others, even though we may not accept them personally. Teachers need to use a variety of resources, including children, parents, and experts on culture, to help the children share the different cultures in the classroom. This approach communicates respect for cultural difference and shows that every culture is valued.

Language Differences

Just as children differ in their cultural roots, they may differ in their dominant language. Some children use words, grammar, and speech patterns that are different from the standard pattern. Within American society, children learn many different dialects and native languages. The grammar of children from rural New England, Appalachia, and parts of the South (for example, where Creole and black English are spoken) will be strikingly different from standard formal American English. Although children from these areas may not speak the established standard English, they may have achieved language competence in their own dialects.

There are also groups of people who have a first language other than English and who may incorporate rules of the first language into the standard English. These children may come from Native American tribes or immigrant families. They may be French- speaking, Chinese-speaking, or Spanish-speaking. Migrant children, regardless of their ethnic group, also speak differently since

Children differ from one another by age, sex, culture, language, and social class.

they move from place to place, becoming exposed to a variety of language patterns and meanings.

Teachers need to be careful that children are not demeaned or embarrassed because they do not speak standard English or because they speak a language other than English. Children need to feel proud of their own language and heritage. Teachers can provide opportunities in the classroom for children to share diverse languages and heritages and can provide meaningful learning experiences that enable children to learn to speak standard English.

Social Class Differences

Social class membership has been identified as one of the major causes for academic failure in schools. For several decades research has examined group differences in intellectual and academic tasks between low-income and middle-income children. Psychologists such as J. McVicker Hunt (1961) believed that these differences were not genetically determined and that changes in the environment could serve as a major stimulus to increase intellectual development. Since development is most heavily influenced in a child's early years, he suggested that preschool enrichment, preferably initiated at age two, be used as an effective "antidote" or compensation to enhance cognitive growth in low-income children.

A number of experimental early childhood education programs developed in the 1960s led to the creation of Head Start, an early childhood program for low-income children (see Chapter 3). Head Start has been characterized as a comprehensive child development program, providing health, nutrition, and social services along with education. Parent involvement is an important part of the program, extending children's learning beyond the classroom and ensuring that the program is responsive to the needs of the children, their parents, and their community.

Exceptional Children

Most schools now enroll some handicapped children in regular classes. These children deviate in one or more ways from other children; they may have behavior disorders, learning or developmental disabilities, mental retardation, visual or hearing impairment, communication disorders, and/or physical health impairments. Often these children are multiply handicapped, complicating diagnosis and remediation. Both the child's disability and strength must be taken into account when one designs or modifies an educational program. Each child's total developmental condition needs to be understood.

Handicapped children are usually assigned labels which may become stigmas. Such labeling can create low expectations of their learning, leading to a self-fulfilling prophecy. Once children are associated with a narrow educational path, it becomes difficult to change them to a different path (Spodek, Saracho, & Lee, 1984).

Teachers who work with exceptional children usually require special assistance. While severely or profoundly handicapped children should be educated in segregated settings, it is recommended that, whenever possible, exceptional children be "mainstreamed" or integrated in the regular class program so they can be educated in the least restrictive environment possible. The responsibility of identifying exceptional children and providing appropriate education in the classroom falls primarily on the classroom teacher with the help of special education teachers, psychologists, parents, and others who serve together as a team.

All children, regardless of whether they are handicapped or nonhandicapped, have special educational needs that require individualized educational programs. However, some groups of children have specific educational needs that require the modification of teaching techniques. *Mainstreaming Young Children* (Spodek, Saracho, & Lee, 1984) is a rich source of material for teachers who work with young handicapped children.

SUMMARY

Since the beginning of the child study movement, the field of child development has been closely related to early childhood education. Its theories have provided the foundations for early childhood curriculum practices. These theories have related to physical development, intellectual development, language development, and socioemotional development.

Child development research has also given us a clear picture of what children are like at various age levels. This knowledge has helped teachers establish expectations for how children will function and what they will accomplish at any particular age level. These norms, or expectations, are helpful, but they can also be harmful. Because a norm represents an average of everyone's characteristics, it cannot be used to characterize any single child. Each child at any age will be different from the average in important ways. Teachers must look at individual children and see how each one differs from the average before planning a program and establishing an expectation.

REFERENCES

BERGER, K. S. (1986). *The developing person through childhood and adolescence.* New York: Worth Publishers.

BERNDT, T. J. (1985). Prosocial behavior between friends in middle childhood and adolescence. *Journal of Early Adolescence, 5,* 307–318.

BRETHERTON, I., AND E. WATERS (1985). Growing points of attachment: Theory and research. *Monographs of the Society for Research in Child Development, 50*(1–2 Serial No. 209).

CAUCE, A. M. (1986). Social networks and social competence: Exploring the effects of early adolescent friendships. *American Journal of Community Psychology, 14,* 607–628.

COHEN, S., AND T. A. WILLS (1985). Stress, social support, and the buffering hypotheses. *Psychological Bulletin, 98,* 310–357.

COLE, P. M. (1985). Display rules and the socialization of affective displays. In G. Zivin (Ed.), *The development of expressive behaviors: Biology-environment interactions,* pp. 269–290. Orlando: Academic Press.

CORRIGAN, R. (1983). The development of representational skills. In *Levels and transactions in children's development.* New directions for child development, no. 21. San Francisco: Jossey-Bass.

DEMOS, V. (1986). Crying in early infancy: An illustration of the motivation function of affect. In T. B. Brazelton and M. Yogman (Eds.), *Affect and early infancy,* pp. 39–73. Norwood, NJ: Ablex.

ERIKSON, E. H. (1963). *Childhood and society.* New York: Norton.

———. (1968). *Identity: Youth and crisis.* New York: Norton.

———. (1982). *The life cycle completed: A review.* New York: Norton.

FELDMAN, D. (1980). *Beyond universals in cognitive development.* Norwood, NJ: Ablex.

FLAKE-HOBSON, C., B. E. ROBINSON, AND P. SKEEN (1983). *Child development and relationships.* Menlo Park, NJ: Addison-Wesley.

GARDNER, D. B. (1973). *Development in early childhood.* New York: Harper & Row.

GARDNER, H. (1983). *Frames of mind.* New York: Basic Books.

GESSEL, A. (1952). *Infant development: The embryology of early human behavior.* New York: Harper & Row.

GREENFIELD, P. M., AND J. LAVE (1982). Cognitive aspects of informal education. In D. A. Wagner and H. W. Stevenson (Eds.), *Cultural perspectives in child development,* pp. 181–207. San Francisco, CA: W. H. Freeman.

HALL, G. S. (1906). *Youth.* New York: Appleton-Century-Crofts.

HARTER S., AND B. J. BUDDING (1987). *Children's understanding of the simultaneity of two emotions: A developmental acquisition sequence.* Paper presented at the biennial meeting of the Society for Research in Child Development, Detroit.

HARTUP, W. W., B. LAURSEN, M. I. STEWART, AND A. EASTENSON (1988). Conflict and the friendship relations of young children. *Child Development, 59,* 1590–1600.

HELMS, D. B., AND J. S. TURNER (1986). *Exploring child behavior.* (3rd ed.) New York: CBS College Publishing.

HUNT, J. McV. (1961). *Intelligence and experience.* New York: Ronald Press.

ILG, F. L., L. B. BATES, AND S. M. BAKER (1981). *Child behavior: Specific advice on problems of child behavior.* New York: Barnes and Noble Books.

IZARD, C. E., E. A. HEMBREE, AND R. R. HUEBNER (1987). Infants' emotion expressions to acute pain: Developmental change and stability in individual difference. *Developmental Psychology, 23,* 105–113.

IZARD, C. E., AND C. Z. MALATESTA (1987). Perspectives on emotional development: 1. Differential emotions theory of early emotional development. In J. D. Osofsky (Ed.), *Handbook of infant development* (2nd ed.), pp. 494–554. New York: Wiley.

KAGAN, J. (1966). *A developmental approach to conceptual growth.* In H. J. Klausmeier and C. W. Harris (Eds.), *Analysis of concept learning,* pp. 97–116. New York: Academic Press.

KESSEN, W. (1965). *The Child.* New York: John Wiley & Sons.

KLAUSMEIER, H. J., AND P. S. ALLEN (1978). *Cognitive development of children and youth: A longitudinal study.* New York: Academic Press.

LANGER, J. (1969). *Theories of development.* New York: Holt, Rinehart & Winston.

LEWIS, M., AND L. MICHAELSON (1983). *Children's emotions and moods: Developmental theory and measurement.* New York: Plenum Press.

MAIER, H. W. (1978). *Three theories of child development* (3rd ed.). New York: Harper & Row.

MALATESTA, C. Z., C. CULVER, J. R. TESMAN, AND B. SHEPARD (1989). The development of emotion expression during the first two years of life. *Monographs for the Society for Research in Child Development, 54* (Serial No. 219), 1–2.

MALINA, R. M. (1982). Motor development in the early years. In S. G. Moore and C. R. Cooper (Eds.), *The young child: Reviews of research,* Vol. 3. Washington, DC: National Association for the Education of Young Children.

MATSUMOTO, D., N. HAAN, G. YABROVE, P. THEODOROU, AND C. C. CARNEY (1986). Preschoolers' moral actions and emotions in prisoner's dilemma. *Developmental Psychology, 22,* 663–670.

MCCANDLESS, B. R., AND E. D. EVANS (1973). *Children and youth: Psychosocial development.* Hinsdale, IL: The Dryden Press.

MCCANDLESS, B. R., AND R. J. TROTTER (1977). *Children: Behavior and development.* New York: Holt, Rinehart & Winston.

MORRIS, P. E., M. TWEEDY, AND M. M. GRUNEBERG (1985). Interest, knowledge, and the memorizing of soccer scores. *British Journal of Psychology, 76,* 415–425.

PIAGET, J. (1962). *Play, dreams, and imitation in children.* New York: Norton.

REID, M., S. LANDESMAN, R. TREDER, AND J. JACCARD (1989). "My family and friends": Six- to twelve-year-old children's perceptions of social support. *Child Development, 60,* 896–910.

SCHMIDT, W. H. O. (1973). *Child development: The human, cultural, and educational context.* New York: Harper & Row.

SCHMIDT, R. (1982). *Motor control and learning: A behavioral emphasis.* Champaign, IL: Human Kinetics.

SCHWARTZ, J. I. (1981). Children's experiments with language. *Young children, 36*(5), 16–26.

SCRIBNER, S. (1984). Studying working intelligence. In B. Rogoff and J. Lave (Eds.), *Everyday cognition,* pp. 9–40. Cambridge, MA: Harvard University Press.

SEIFERT, K. L., AND R. J. HOFFNUNG (1987). *Child and adolescent development.* Boston: Houghton Mifflin Company.

SPOCK, B. J., AND M. B. ROTHENBERG (1985). *Baby and Child Care.* New York: Pocket Books.

SPODEK, B., O. N. SARACHO, AND R. C. LEE (1984). *Mainstreaming young children.* Belmont, CA.: Wadsworth Publishing Company.

STIGLER, J. W. (1984). "Mental abacus": The effect of abacus training on Chinese children's mental calculation. *Cognitive Psychology, 16,* 145–176.

THOMPSON, G. G. (1952). *Child psychology: Growth trends in psychological adjustment.* New York: Houghton Mifflin.

WADSWORTH, B. J. (1971). *Piaget's theory of cognitive development: An introduction for students of psychology and education.* New York: McKay.

WAGNER, D., AND J. E. SPRATT (1987). Cognitive consequences of contrasting pedagogies: The effects of quranic preschooling in Morocco. *Child Development, 58,* 1207–1219.

WHITESELL, N. R., AND S. HARTER (1989). Children's reports of conflict between simultaneous opposite-valence emotions. *Child Development, 60,* 673–682.

SUGGESTED ACTIVITIES

1. Collect a set of photographs of a six-year-old child that had been taken at intervals since infancy. Compare the different photos. Describe the changes in weight, appearance, and body proportions.

2. Observe a pair of young children of different ages and record how they perform tasks such as holding a cup, painting a picture, and building with blocks.

3. Observe a three- to five-year-old child during the self-selected play period. Describe the social contacts the child has. Compare your observations with those of other students who observed children who are different in age, culture, social class, and/or who are handicapped.

4. Follow a child for a full school day in order to see him or her in a variety of environments and situations. Describe the consistencies as well as the differences in the behavior observed in these settings.

5. Interview parents of two infants of the same age. Ask them to describe their child's sleeping, eating, and toileting habits.

6. Interview parents of children of the same age but from different cultural backgrounds. Ask them to describe their children to you. Compare the descriptions. Are there differences in descriptions that you can relate to the cultures of the individual parents?

6

Planning and Organizing the Physical Environment

OBJECTIVES

After completing this chapter on planning and organizing the physical environment, the student should be able to:

1. Define activity centers and identify ways to use centers.
2. Describe safety guidelines for organizing a room, for designing an outdoor play area, and for choosing materials for young children.
3. Schedule daily, monthly and yearly activities for an early childhood class.
4. Develop a plan to arrange activity centers in a classroom.
5. Discuss the importance of the outdoor play area as a vehicle for fostering development.
6. Identify the relationship between classroom materials and physical, social, emotional, and intellectual development.
7. Identify the relationship between classroom arrangement and the development of independence.

Early childhood settings are not all the same. Some programs are in new build-ings that have been especially designed for educating young children. There are also programs in church Sunday school classrooms in which teachers need to put everything away on Friday afternoon and then set up again on Monday morning. There are even programs in places that were never originally conceived to serve young children: former stores, warehouses, and lofts, for example. Within these settings there may be fully furnished learning centers or centers containing only a bare minimum of resources, sometimes little more furniture than tables and chairs. Open-ended materials may be provided in the setting, such as manipula-tive and constructive materials, or the program might rely primarily on pencil and paper activities. Regardless of what resources are provided for a teacher at the beginning, all learning environments need to be enriching and the most ef-fective use possible must be made of resources.

In this chapter ideas are presented to help teachers plan and implement a physical environment that will be an inviting and stimulating place for chil-dren. The physical organization of the room is discussed, with attention given to activity centers, furniture, equipment, and materials. The outdoor play area is discussed as well. Ideas for scheduling the day are also included.

SETTING THE STAGE

Ideally, all early childhood classrooms should be provided with an adequate sup-ply of equipment and materials to serve the children assigned to the group. Real-istically, few teachers are given everything they would like to have in their class-room. Teachers need to supplement what is provided, as well as modify the setting in ways that will make it more useful. As teachers consider their physical setting and develop plans for their classrooms, they must ask, "How can I make this setting the best possible place for young children to live and to learn in?" The question should first be asked before the school year starts, but it should also be asked repeatedly during the year, for what works at one time may become stale and less useful as time goes by.

Teachers begin the year with limited knowledge of the children who will be with them. They set up their rooms, hoping the arrangement, materials, and equipment provided will continue to be suitable for most of the school year. However, arranging a room with only a limited sense of what you want to accom-plish and with only limited knowledge of the children who will live and work in the room may lead to error. An arrangement may be created that gets in the way of the program's goals rather than helping the children achieve them.

The classroom environment sends value messages to children. A sloppy room tells them that it is all right to leave things scattered when play is done. Rooms with carefully displayed children's work tells them that their efforts and products are valued. An organization that allows children to select their materials from easily accessible shelves is one that fosters independence. Teachers should approach room arrangement with an understanding of the messages they want to send.

Teachers begin their planning even before children enter school.

The first thing that must be considered in planning the classroom environment is the children involved. Although a teacher knows little about them, there may be sources of information. There may be records and reports written by the previous year's teacher. There may be an information form such as many preschools collect before a child is enrolled (see Figure 6–1). The children may have visited the class individually and a parent intake interview may have been held. All these are helpful in giving a teacher a sense of the class. These sources are limited, however. What a teacher thinks about the children and class at the beginning of the year will have to be modified as the teacher sees each child interacting with others and with the materials available. In addition, every group has a life of its own. A class represents more than a sum of its parts. The group is a growing organism that develops and changes just as each child develops and changes. Yet the knowledge gained from first impressions is important in getting teaching started at the beginning of the year.

The second question to ask is, "What do I want my children to accomplish?" If you expect children to accomplish a specific goal, you must develop a room arrangement that will support that goal. If you want to support socialization, you need to plan areas where children can work together. If you want children to be creative, then materials like blocks, wood and woodworking tools, and a range of arts and crafts material should be provided for them. The support of physical development requires space and equipment for both large-scale and small-scale activity. Most important, if you want children to develop independence you must design a room arrangement that allows them to explore the room and activities with minimal guidance. You must also recognize that many materials allow children to be working on two or more goals at one time. For example, children playing with Lego's may be sorting and classifying, which are intellectual tasks, while they are learning to share, a social task. Table 6–1 shows the relationship between specific developmental areas and materials and equipment provided in a classroom.

FIGURE 6-1   Child Enrollment Information

Name _____ Age _____

Address _____ Phone _____

Mother's name _____ Phone _____

Mother address _____

Mother's work place _____ Phone _____

Father's name _____ Phone _____

Father's address _____

Father's work place _____ Phone _____

Person responsible for child's transportation _____

_____ Phone _____

Name of doctor _____ Phone _____

Physical conditions that may affect the child's participation _____

_____

Required medications _____

_____

Special dietary needs _____

Sibling's name _____ Age _____

_____

_____

_____

In case of emergency who should be contacted?

Name _____ Phone _____

In the space below please list any other information you wish us to know:

_____

_____

_____

TABLE 6-1   The Relationship Between Developmental Areas and Early Childhood
Materials and Equipment

AREAS OF DEVELOPMENT	*MATERIALS AND EQUIPMENT*
Physical Development	Climbers, wheel toys, blocks, tires, balls, button frames, shoes for lacing, beads for stringing, pattern cards, balance beams, ladders, scissors, woodworking tools, sand tools, puzzles and any other equipment or materials that allow a child to develop large- or small-muscle coordination.
Social Development	Prop boxes, including materials related to the child's experience, such as post office, fire department, or grocery; housekeeping materials, blocks, dress-up clothes, activities or experiences that allow for two or more children to work together.
Intellectual Development	Animals, plants, manipulative materials, sand, water, wood, blocks, pan balance, magnifying glass, matching games, block props (stop sign, toy trucks, etc.), books, records, cassette players, leaves, stones, twigs, flowers, pictures, puzzles, cooking activities, other materials that allow a child to reflect on, act on, and learn from.
Creative Development	Varied kinds of paints, varied sizes, shapes, and textures of paper, markers, clay, "junk," beans, rice, macaroni, paste, wire, cloth, yarn, weaving frames, straight edges, scissors, crayons, brushes, materials for making prints, blocks, dress-up clothes, straws, wood, and any other materials children can use to represent their world.
Language Development	Books, records, materials for language experience charts, stories, finger plays, puppets, child-made books, dress-up clothes for make-believe, social situations, field trips, opportunities to interact with children and adults.
Emotional Development	Any materials that allow for success, that challenge but do not frustrate, that leave a child with a sense of accomplishment.

Another concern is for the number of children that will be in the group. Generally the minimum indoor space requirement for a preschool class is 35 square feet per child, although some authorities recommend 100 square feet. This includes space for equipment as well as room for children to move. No matter how large a room, however, there should be limits placed on the number of children in a group as well as the ratio of children to adults.

The National Day Care Study (Roup, Travers, Glantz, & Coelen, 1979) found that differences in program quality related to group size and staff/child ratio. They found the ratio of one adult to seven children to be the best for preschoolers ages three to five. They recommended that the size of the group be limited to twice the number of children recommended per adult. They also recommended group size and ratios for toddlers: an adult/child ratio of 1:4 for children under three years of age, with groups no larger than eight for children under two, and no larger than twelve for children between two and three.

Teachers often break the class into smaller groups for particular activities, such as cooking or block building. The size of these groups should be determined by the activity, the amount of supervision required, the space available for the activity, the amount of materials and equipment available, and the ability of the teacher to provide supervision.

Many teachers see planning as "busy work." In reality it is the most important part of the teacher's role. Planning is a professional responsibility that requires a teacher to make use of knowledge and experience in order to ensure the educational worth of children's activities. In planning, teachers make decisions that help determine the success of their program.

Sue Vartuli (1987) discussed three types of decisions teachers make on a regular basis: preactive decisions, interactive decisions, and reflective decisions. Preactive decisions occur during planning. They relate to individual differences, routines, content transitions, activities, experiences, centers, and interactions. These decisions are the basis for a teacher's plans. Interactive decisions occur while teachers are working with children. Examples include structuring (giving directions, coaching, stating expectations), monitoring (focusing, questioning, extending, enhancing), and pacing (using time wisely). These decisions modify the teacher's plans in the face of classroom realities. Reflective decisions are those made while reviewing the day's work. It is a time for teachers to revise old activities, to add new goals or to continue as planned. These decisions come from an evaluation of the teacher's plans, the way the plans have been implemented, and the consequences of the classroom activities. They should result in plans for the future.

Planning can take place for the day, week, month, holiday, season, or year. Figure 6–2 shows four different ways to divide the year by topics. The topics are familiar to children and, as such, have high interest. Each instructional unit contains objectives, experiences, concepts, and activities and may require special

FIGURE 6–2 Ways to Organize the Year into Units

Planning by:

Months	Seasons	Holidays	Themes
September	Fall		School and Me
October		Halloween	Self and Family
November		Election Day	Foods we eat
		Thanksgiving	
December	Winter	Winter Holidays	Helping Others
January		Martin Luther King Day	Animals
February		Valentines's Day	Communication
		President's Day	
March	Spring		Dinosaurs
April		Spring Holidays	Growing Things
May			Birds
June	Summer		Machines
July		Independence Day	Space
August			Transportation

materials or equipment. Teachers should keep in mind these special needs as they plan and arrange the room accordingly.

ORGANIZING FOR INSTRUCTION

Teachers plan for a variety of activities to take place each day. Large-group, small-group and individual activities all have different spatial requirements. Regardless of the type of activity, teachers should approach room organization with a goal of facilitating independence and eliminating potential problems. Evertson, Emmer, Clements, Sandford and Worsham (1989) suggest the following four key elements of classroom arrangement:

1. Keep high traffic areas all free of congestion.
2. Be sure that children can easily be seen by the teacher.
3. Keep frequently used teaching materials and children's supplies readily accessible.
4. Be certain that students can easily see presentations and displays. (pp 4–5)

The classroom should be designed to support a flexible educational program. Floors can be carpeted or covered with resilient tiles. Walls should be pleasantly but unobtrusively colored and there should be enough display space, including bulletin boards and a display shelf or table. A small chalkboard mounted on the walls may be useful. Window shades or blinds that both reduce glare and darken the room completely are helpful for resting as well as for controlling light. A drinking fountain and a sink for various activities and for cleaning should be readily available. Bathrooms should be immediately adjacent or close to the classroom.

The teacher needs to be aware of what elements can be arranged to accommodate the children and the program and what elements cannot be changed and must be adjusted to. Doors, windows, lighting fixtures, electrical outlets, plumbing fixtures, radiators, and heat registers are the kinds of elements that are built into a room and can seldom be changed. They can be modified, though. While windows cannot be shifted to another wall, they can be covered. Similarly, permanent shelves can become part of an activity center or display, and extension cords can be used to allow better placement of equipment as long as they are placed carefully and safely. In this way the best use can be made of a room's physical structure.

As teachers plan their room, they must consider the amount of usable floor space that is available and how it can best be allocated to meet the program's needs. How much space is needed for the movement of traffic, for large-group activities, for large-muscle activity, and for any special projects a teacher might have in mind needs to be considered. The room should be arranged so that a teacher can see students in all areas of the room and so that the teacher can be seen. The placement of blackboards, bulletin boards, film screens, and windows must be considered.

Bulletin boards provide opportunities to teach through displays.

The location of electrical outlets may determine where the record player, aquarium, or other equipment that needs electricity is placed. Electrical cords must be kept along the wall and off the floor. Extension cords should not be used unless absolutely necessary, and then only when they can be placed safely along the baseboards and fastened to the floor with tape. Loose wires left on the floor are sure to be tripped over. Teachers must always be sure to check that the physical arrangement of the room is safe in other ways as well. Furniture and equipment should have no sharp edges. Worn and unsafe equipment should be repaired or removed from the class. Traffic patterns should be designed to avoid unnecessary conflict. Climbing equipment should be installed over soft surfaces. When handicapped children are in a class, additional modifications may need to be made to make the learning activities as fully accessible as possible, and to provide a safe environment. Furniture might have to be rearranged or crutch tips placed on the legs of tables so they will not slip. In addition, teachers and children should establish and enforce safety rules for functioning in the classroom.

The aesthetic climate of the classroom should also be considered. Colors should be soft, not distracting. Attractive pictures and fabrics, fresh flowers, and pleasing displays all add to the children's learning experience. The teacher should regularly monitor the room temperature, noise level, and lighting. All of these can affect the way children behave and how well they learn.

Storage should be carefully planned. A classroom should have enough storage and locker facilities for children's coats, boots, extra clothing, and personal belongings, as well as for the teacher's needs. Providing a locker or cubby for each child's use is desirable. Teachers also need their own storage that is separate from the children's. Teachers' shelves should be isolated from the activ-

A classroom should have lockers for the children's clothing and personal belongings.

ity areas and be clearly identified. In addition, considerable and varied storage space should be provided for materials and equipment. Large wheel toys, paper, art supplies, and materials for different learning units all need different kinds of storage facilities. The room should be arranged so that children know where materials go, and the children should help with cleanup. Having the children responsible for putting things away is a way of helping to develop autonomy. The children should know what is expected of them and expectations should be related to what they are able to do.

It is important to keep the room neat and pleasing. Messy shelves, broken equipment, and careless displays all give the same message to children: that sloppiness is acceptable and that their activities are not valued. The materials in the classroom are tools for children's learning and should be treated with respect.

The classroom should be an attractive, inviting place for children to learn.

The room should be ready when the children walk in each day. The teacher should be at the door to greet them and invite them to participate in a carefully arranged, well-organized room. The physical setting should extend a personal invitation to learn.

Activity Centers

Early childhood classrooms are best organized into activity centers, each center supporting some portion of the program. Though the centers can be modified to serve the changing needs of the program, made larger or smaller, or even merged with other centers, most should be available as separate areas throughout the activity period. Activity centers allow rooms to become child centered rather than teacher centered. They help programs become more individualized and allow children to participate more actively and be more independent of the teacher (Blake, 1977). Figure 6–3 provides a floor plan for an early childhood classroom and demonstrates how activity centers might be arranged.

Early childhood programs generally include arts-and-crafts activity centers, dramatic-play centers, block-building centers, manipulative-materials centers, library centers, music centers, and display centers. Temporary centers can also be organized around specific themes, such as an environmental studies center or a transportation center. Materials and activities related to the theme would be organized and the center would remain for as long as the theme holds the children's interest.

Centers should include materials related to their purposes. All supplies and equipment should be readily accessible to the children. Table 6–2 provides examples of equipment to be included in various activity centers. The physical boundaries of a center should be clearly defined. Children should also know the acceptable limits for use of materials. Centers should be designed to be easily supervised, and their contents should support independent activity. Place the art center and water play center near the source of water, to avoid the need to carry buckets of water across the room. Centers should be arranged so that children have room to move around without disturbing the activities of others. Teachers should be sure that children have easy access to materials without climbing on chairs or tables. In addition, doors, water fountains, and restrooms should not be blocked. A child who has to use the bathroom is not going to wait until the easel is moved away from the door. A well-thought-out traffic pattern can eliminate many behavior problems, because children will not interfere with each other as they move from one activity to another.

Ample supplies should be available for the number of children who are going to participate in each activity. Nothing is more frustrating to a child than to run out of material when the child has been waiting all morning to participate. Materials that children can use should be separated from those that they are not supposed to use. Books, resources, and materials that are not for children's use should be stored out of sight and out of reach in the teacher's storage space.

A quiet area should be available for children who need time away from the group. This may be a rocker, a large pillow in the corner of the room, a cardboard box with the side cut out, or a loft. Quiet activities should be grouped

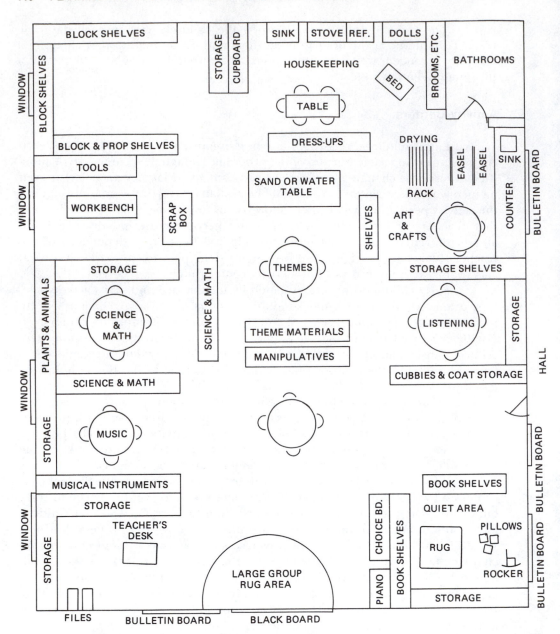

FIGURE 6-3 Floor Plan of an Early Childhood Classroom

TABLE 6-2 Provisions for Activity Centers

CENTER	EQUIPMENT
Arts and Crafts	Easels, tables and chairs, a drying rack for pictures, a place to store children's products, and a place for material storage.
Woodworking	A sturdy workbench, an adequate number and variety of tools, a scrap box for wood, and a tool board.
Housekeeping	A play sink, refrigerator, cupboards, stove, bed, table, and chairs; storage for cups, saucers, and utensils as well as a place to hang dress-up clothes, dolls of both sexes that represent various cultural groups.
Music	A board for hanging rhythm instruments, a record player, a listening center, and storage for records; a cassette player, cassettes, and piano are excellent additions to the music area.
Blocks	Storage for unit and hollow blocks, adequate floor space for building, and adequate storage for props.
Water/Sand	A table that can be used for water or sand, a plastic sheet to cover the floor, and a place to store the water/sand play props.
Reading/Language	A rocker, pillows, rug; and storage and display for books.
Science/Math	A pan balance, manipulatives, puzzles, Legos, attribute blocks, aquarium, plants, tables, chairs, display space and storage.

away from those that are noisier and more active. Reading or listening areas, for example, should not be next to the blocks or woodworking areas.

There should be enough space for the activities. For example, block building or other constructive activities can require considerable floor space. Good building space can be as important to block building as an adequate supply of blocks.

Each center should be analyzed to determine how many children can comfortably be involved at one time. The number of children allowed to use a center might need to be limited. The children should know what the limit is. Teachers should also establish rules so that each child has access to all of the centers in the classroom each week.

All activities, materials, or centers in a classroom do not have to be out at the same time. Too many things in a room may make it difficult for children to make choices. It is also helpful to rotate centers or materials throughout the year. If children begin to lose interest in a center, the materials can be put away for a few months. Bringing it back will make it seem as if the activities and materials are new. It will rekindle interest and will often turn the center into a desirable learning setting once more. Materials in centers should also be changed periodically to reflect the children's interests, seasons, holidays, and units. The new items will stimulate interest and enable children to extend their learning.

Furniture and Equipment

Furniture for an early childhood classroom should be movable, durable, and scaled to the children's size. Tables and chairs should be of varying heights since children in any age group vary in size. Tables of different shapes can be used for both art work and eating. Trapezoidal tables are nice to have in a class since they can be grouped and arranged to create many different shapes. Stackable chairs and tables can be stored in a corner of the room when not in use.

If young children stay in school for a full day, they will need cots for rest. Lightweight cots that stack for easy storage can be purchased. It is not necessary to have cots for children in a half-day program. Various cabinets, shelf units, and racks should also be provided for storing supplies, equipment, and books. If supplies are kept on open shelves, the children can help themselves to materials they need. In addition to providing storage, cabinets and shelves can be arranged to screen different centers from one another. Other furniture and equipment, such as housekeeping furniture or a water/sand table, will be needed in the activity centers.

When you are selecting equipment for the classroom, the following criteria should be used:

Safety. This is the first and most important consideration in selecting materials. The Public Action Coalition on Toys (1983) suggests that the following questions be asked about the children's toys and equipment:

> Are there any sharp edges or points, exposed nails, sharp wires or straight pins?
> Is is large enough so that it can't be swallowed?
> Does it have detachable or (poorly glued) small parts that can be removed and lodge in the windpipe, ears, or nose?
> Is it made of unbreakable material?
> Is it labeled "nontoxic," since infants put everything into the mouth?
> Does it have parts that can pinch fingers or toes or catch hair?
> Are the cords for crib toys shorter than 12 inches to avoid strangulation?
> Is the projectile toy (rocket, dart, model airplane) capable of inflicting dangerous eye injuries?
> Does the toy require electricity?
> Will the toy be safe when used in its surroundings?
> Are there any hidden hazards?
> Is the toy easily cleaned? (pp. 6–8)

Cost. All programs have limited supply budgets. Thus, the cost of an item often determines whether it will be purchased. While money spent for an object is critical to many programs, price should not be considered alone. Often more expensive items will last longer and cost less in the long run. Teachers should select materials and equipment that will be interesting to children and help further their educational goals.

Appropriateness for the Children. Materials should be matched to the interests, ages, and learning abilities of a particular group of children. Teachers need to look at individual children and judge what types of materials will be interesting and developmentally appropriate for them.

Quality and Durability. Equipment that is considered adequate for home use is often inappropriate for school. It may not be durable enough for heavy use or it may require too much supervision. The design and construction of each piece of equipment should be considered in relation to its use by a group of children.

Flexibility of Use.   Equipment should be selected that can be used in a variety of ways and situations. Dramatic play equipment that has few details can often be used most flexibly. A child's imagination can turn a simple box into a boat or an airplane. Of course, equipment designed for specific purposes should not be overlooked.

A number of guides are available for the selection of equipment for early childhood education. Useful lists include:

ASSOCIATION FOR CHILDHOOD EDUCATION INTERNATIONAL (1976). *Selecting educational equipment for school and home.* Washington, DC: The Association for Childhood Education International.

FEENEY, S., AND M. MARGARICK (1984). Choosing good toys for young children. *Young Children, 40*(1), 21–25.

PROJECT HEADSTART (N.D.). *Equipment and supplies: Guidelines for administrators and teachers in child development centers.* Washington, DC: Office of Economic Opportunity.

Free and Inexpensive Materials

Early childhood teachers will save *anything,* and anything that they save can be used as some part of a learning activity. Few teachers have enough money to purchase all the materials they feel they need. Most collect materials from various sources—parents, shopkeepers, and just about anyone else who has something usable to contribute. While no complete list of things that can be obtained for free can be compiled, here are some ideas:

- Parents can save buttons, string, cloth, milk cartons, yarn, old shirts, old toys, bottle caps, dress-up clothes, and magazines. Often a note sent home with the children will bring more than you will need.
- Shopkeepers can provide meat trays, props for dramatic play, cardboard boxes, old coupons, window advertisements, posters, wood scraps, carpet scraps, and wallpaper samples. You or your parent group need to ask for these things. Be sure that what is collected is *safe* and *useful.*

Other sources for materials include the Red Cross, post office, fire station, National Dairy Council, agricultural agencies, senior citizen centers, other teachers (who may be willing to trade materials), and local, state, and federal agencies.

Although there is no limit to the materials you can collect, don't collect more than you can comfortably store. Messing up a classroom with a lot of free "stuff" that you can't store can be counterproductive.

DESIGNING OUTDOOR PLAY AREAS

Local climate and weather conditions, as much as anything else, will determine what kinds of activities can be offered to children outdoors and in turn, will influence how the outdoor play area should be designed. Additional considerations include the problem of vandalism, and other uses that might be made of the area when school is not in session. The outdoor area should be considered an extension of the classroom, providing opportunity for exciting learning experiences.

Joe Frost and Barry Klein (1979) recommend that children's playgrounds be carefully planned, even before schools are planned, in order to preserve the natural terrain. Permanent facilities such as fences, storage sheds, waterlines, water fountains, hard-surfaced areas, and shade structures should be installed at the beginning. The range and arrangement of equipment in the playground should take into account such factors as: (1) the need for complex multifunction structures; (2) the availability of varied kinds of equipment to allow many different forms of play; and (3) the arrangement of equipment to allow play to take place across different structures. Zones can be created for different kinds of play and should be arranged to allow for movement across zones. Space should also be provided in the outdoor area for creative arts and activities using natural materials. In addition, safety, maintenance, and supervision must be considered when one is planning the outdoor space and its use.

Mildred Dickerson (1977), in describing the process of developing an outdoor learning center, refers to a number of concerns that need to be addressed. She suggests that the complete site be planned initially, even if it is going to be built in stages. The planners must consider regulations, insurance requirements, budget and resource limitations, and the labor needed to build and main-

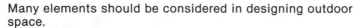

Many elements should be considered in designing outdoor space.

tain a site. She also suggests basic criteria to be considered in developing an outdoor learning center, including:

1. Children who will be using the area—their age, size, and abilities.
2. Space and location—closeness to toilets and to the classroom; whether it can be adequately supervised; the elimination of "blind spots" where children can hide.
3. Security—a fence is essential. It should be at least four feet high with no toe holes for climbing. It should have a single gate to allow children to come and go, and a double gate for maintenance.
4. Surfaces—the area should have good drainage and variations in terrain. There should be hard surface areas for some activities, as well as grassy areas, sand areas, and earth areas. A paved path for wheel toys is helpful.
5. Sun and shade—there should be a balance of both.
6. Storage—handy storage areas will keep things from having to be moved long distances.
7. It should support a variety of play opportunities.
8. It should allow for different equipment arrangements—to facilitate equipment use, and to accomplish the goals of the center.
9. Water—a convenient source of water for drinking as well as for water play should be provided.

Joe Frost and Sue Wortham (1988) suggest that playgrounds should allow for the outdoor exploration of indoor curriculum areas. When the weather is mild, music, art, science, social science, and math activities can all take place on the playground. The change in setting provides children with new perspectives and challenges them to approach familiar materials in new ways.

Selecting Outdoor Materials and Equipment

Outdoor equipment should provide for more than the exercise of large muscles. It should promote creativity and imagination, allowing children to act out ideas and themes in dramatic play.

The equipment provided in an outdoor play area is as important to the child's learning as the equipment provided indoors. Dramatic play props, wheel toys, balls, water play and sand play equipment, construction materials, and gardening materials are all necessary to the outdoor experience. A well-planned, well-organized, and well-equipped outdoor learning environment is an important part of the young child's program.

Besides program concerns, teachers should be concerned about potential safety hazards that may exist in outdoor equipment. Peter Werner (1983) reported that, according to the Consumer Product Safety Commission's 1975 study, playground equipment such as that in a school's outdoor area ranked sixth on the list of 100 most hazardous consumer products. Since that time, however, steps have been taken to improve the quality of equipment.

Frost and Wortham (1988) offer the following suggestions for maintaining a safe outdoor play area:

- A fence (minimum 4 feet high) protects children from potentially hazardous areas (e.g., street, water).
- Eight to 12 inches of noncompacted sand, pea gravel, shredded wood, or equivalent material is in place under and around all climbing and moving equipment.
- Resilient surface is properly maintained (e.g., in place, noncompacted, free of debris).
- The equipment is sized to the age group served, with climbing heights limited to the reaching height of children standing erect.
- There are no openings that can entrap a child's head (approximately 4 to 8 inches).
- Swing seats are constructed of lightweight material with no protruding elements.
- Moving parts are free of defects (no pinch, shearing, or crush points; bearings are not excessively worn).
- Equipment is free of sharp edges, protruding elements, broken parts, and toxic substances.
- Fixed equipment is structurally sound—no bending, warping, breaking or sinking.
- Large equipment is secured in the ground, and concrete footings are recessed in the ground.
- All safety equipment (e.g., guard rails, padded areas, protective covers) is in good repair.
- The area is free of electrical hazards (e.g., unfenced air conditioners and switch-boxes).
- The area is free of debris (e.g., sanitary hazards, broken glass, and rocks). (J.L. Frost and S.C. Wortham. "The Evolution of American Playgrounds." *Young Children, 43*(5), p. 24. Copyright © 1988 by the National Association for the Education of Young Children, Washington, D.C. Reprinted with permission.)

SCHEDULING ACTIVITIES

Scheduling is the teachers' arrangement of time for children's activities. Scheduling provides the structure for the best use of teachers' and children's time. The schedule should provide adequate time for a full range of activities that reflect the program's goals. Half-day, full-day, and extended-day programs require different schedules, but all schedules should be based on an understanding of young children: their patterns of movement, how fast or slow they respond, how much excitement or rest they need. In addition, when activities take place in a regular order each day over a long period of time, a sense of security develops based on a knowledge of what can be expected.

Schedules that are established should be followed. Children like the sense of order this provides. While young children may not be able to tell time, they do know when their day has been rearranged. There are special occasions, such as field trips, visitors, and holiday celebrations, when schedules should be modified.

In developing a schedule for a group of young children, a number of factors need to be considered. A time for the entire group to get together at the beginning of the day is helpful. It allows the teacher to inform the children of what will be happening that day as well as to get a sense of the children. It also helps to establish a feeling of groupness. A similar period at the end of the day can be used to summarize what happened and to set the stage for the next day.

There needs to be adequate time built into the schedule for self-care activities, such as dressing and undressing (on entering school, before and after outdoor play, and before going home), eating (breakfast, if needed, snacks, and lunch), and resting. Times for toileting should be provided, though the children should not be placed on a rigid schedule. High-energy activities should be scheduled as well as quieter activities to give children the opportunity periodically to rest, relax, and calm down and to make sure that children don't get lethargic.

When planning schedules, you need to consider the calendar as well as the clock. Time should be allotted during the year for special activities or themes. Most programs include units based on holidays, seasons, animals, or other interests that should have a place in the schedule.

Time must also be allocated for transition from one activity to another. Well planned transitions can save valuable time, while poor ones lead to chaos. Teachers must plan for adequate cleanup time and make sure that they warn children when the end of an activity is coming. Using a bell or timer is a good way to help them anticipate cleanup.

A number of factors contribute to difficulties around transition time: boredom, the insistence on conformity, the absence of a future orientation in some children, the absence of clearly defined tasks, and a possible fear of failure (Hirsch, n.d.). Planning for transition can ease potential difficulties. Sometimes specific children have problems during transitions, and a teacher can provide special support for them. Making a game of cleanup can help to make it less overwhelming. Giving children specific directions and setting expectations so that they are able to do what's expected of them also help. Having available some short games, stories, poems, and finger plays can help fill periods of waiting for some children while others are completing their task. Most important, the teach-

A warm greeting at arrival can start the day off well for a child.

er's sense of calm and order will help the children overcome whatever problems arise.

Extra time should be allowed for moving the children from one room to another. If children go to a special place for lunch, a teacher has to plan for time to clean up, to move children to the lunch room, eat, clean up, return to the classroom, use the toilet, and prepare for the next activity.

Although activities should follow the same order each day, teachers should not worry about varying the duration of activities from day to day. Some days children may have a very productive outdoor period, and providing additional time is a reasonable thing to do. On other days disinterest or fussiness may lead to cutting a period short. The teacher must be sensitive to children and be flexible enough to change to meet their needs.

The following schedule is suggested for a morning half-day nursery school and kindergarten:

8:15–8:45 A.M. *Teacher planning and preparation.*

8:45–9:00 A.M. *Arrival.* The children may enter the classroom at various intervals during a prescribed arrival time. Spaced entry allows the teacher to greet each child individually and allows the children an opportunity to make a gradual transition from home to school. During the arrival period they browse through books or work with manipulative materials. They might also be able to view displays the teacher has placed on the bulletin board or science table.

9:00–9:20 A.M. *Group time.* The teacher sits with the entire group to plan the day and take care of necessary routines such as attendance. Group time also allows for discussions on a variety of topics. A sharing or show-and-tell period might be appropriate if the children do not take the initiative in discussions. Once skills in group discussions are developed, the formal show-and-tell could be dispensed with.

9:20–10:10 A.M. *Activity period.* During this period the children are given a choice of activities and may change activities at any time during the period. Many of the children may work individually or in small groups. The teacher may work with a single child or a small group or may supervise the entire room. Included in the activities offered are an arts-and-crafts activity, dramatic play, and other activities planned by the teacher. Some children may work with manipulative materials. Others might work at a sand table or a water basin or might be involved in a planned science experience. All the activity is under the guidance of the teacher.

10:10–10:30 A.M. *Cleanup, snack, and rest.* After an activity period children need to clean their room and put away the materials they have been using. Time should be allowed for young children to go to the bathroom and wash up. Milk or fruit juice, crackers, raw vegetables, or fruit may be provided as a snack. This period can provide productive learning opportunities. Informal discussion can be stimulated, new food can be tasted, responsibilities and skills can be learned, and children can become aware of the characteristics and functions of the things used. A quiet period, such as listening to a story or record, might be substituted for a formal rest period.

10:30–11:00 A.M. *Music and story time.* A period of time is usually set aside for activities involving the entire class. Group singing or rhythmic activities allow the children to explore music as well as the use of their own body for creative expression. Teachers can read from picture books or tell stories.

11:00–11:20 A.M. *Outdoor activity time.* Children can be encouraged to climb, run, jump, and use wheel toys and large pieces of equipment. Sand and water play can also be included. The amount of time spent outdoors will probably vary with the climate.

11:20–11:40 A.M. *Preparation for dismissal and dismissal.* The children need time to get ready and collect their things before departing for home. If parents are expected to pick their children up, this time provides an excellent opportunity for mini-conferences and informal chats about the children.

11:40–12:00. *Teacher cleanup period.* At the end of the morning, teachers need time to reorder themselves and their rooms and take care of records before preparing for the next group.

In a program lasting fewer hours, periods can be compressed somewhat. In an extended or all-day program, other periods might have to be added. There might be an extended informal activity period at the beginning of the day to accommodate children who must be dropped off earlier. Breakfast might be served then, if needed. In addition, time for lunch, rest, snack, and individual activities might be added in the afternoon for an all-day program.

A day care program might use the schedule presented here for the morning. However, the day might start earlier for most children, who may arrive at 8:00 A.M. or as early as 6:00 A.M. Along with serving food, where appropriate, teachers might plan for informal activities for the early part of the morning, or they might shift the times of the various activities if most children arrive early. The rest of the day might look as follows:

11:30–12:00. *Lunch.*

12:00–1:30 P.M. *Rest on cots* (many children will nap). The teacher should arrange quiet activities for those who do not. Looking at books or playing with soft toys might help to relax the children. Sometimes playing quiet records on the phonograph helps.

1:30–2:30 P.M. *Outdoor time,* similar to that in the morning. This is an opportunity to set up activities such as painting or dramatic play outdoors.

2:30–3:00 P.M. *Cleanup and snack.*

3:00–3:30 P.M. *Music and/or story time.*

3:30–4:40 P.M. *Activity time.* More emphasis will be given to tables activities and other less physically demanding activities than in the morning.

4:30–5:00 P.M. (or later) *Informal activities* until the children are picked up.

The afternoon in an all-day kindergarten might be as follows:

11:30–12:00. *Lunch.*

A full-day program must provide for children's lunch and nap, as well as additional play activities.

12:00–12:45 P.M. *Quiet time.* Activities that do not require high levels of activity might be offered here. Table activities, including those related to preacademics, might be offered. Some children may still need naps.

12:45–1:45 P.M. *Project time.* Children might work on long-term projects that have been developed over time. Mural paintings, cardboard box constructions related to a social studies unit, or plantings related to a science unit are examples.

1:45–2:30 P.M. *Outdoor activity time.*

2:30–3:00 P.M. *Cleanup, story time, preparation for dismissal.*

3:00 P.M. *Dismissal.*

Each day will vary from this schedule, of course, as teachers modify their programs to meet the specific needs of their class or to carry on special projects. The schedule should be characterized by both regularity and flexibility.

SUMMARY

The physical environment includes the early childhood classroom, everything in it, and the outdoor area. These represent the context for children's learning. A room that is poorly equipped will present children with relatively few options for educational experiences. One that is well equipped with developmentally appropriate materials can be a stimulating and engaging learning site. The difference between the two is in the planning, organizing, and provisioning that is done by the teacher. Teachers need to consider the physical environment in which they work and arrange that environment to serve the goals established for their programs.

REFERENCES

BLAKE, H. E. (1977). *Creating a learning-centered classroom*. New York: Hart.

CONSUMER PRODUCTS SAFETY COMMISSION (1981). *A handbook for public playground safety*. Washington, DC: Consumer Products Safety Commission.

DICKERSON, M. G. (1977). *Developing the outdoor learning center*. Little Rock, AR: Southern Association for Children Under Six.

EVERTSON, C. M., E. T. EMMER, B. S, CLEMENTS, J. P. SANDFORD, AND M. E. WORSHAM (1989). *Classroom management for elementary teachers*, (2nd ed). Englewood Cliffs, NJ: Prentice Hall.

FROST, J. L., AND B. L. KLEIN (1979). *Children's play and playgrounds*. Boston: Allyn & Bacon.

FROST, J. L., AND S. C. WORTHAM (1988). The evolution of American playgrounds. *Young Children, 43*(5), 19–28.

HIRSCH, E. S. (n.d.). *Transition periods: Stumbling blocks of education*. New York: Early Childhood Education Council of New York City.

PUBLIC ACTION COALITION ON TOYS (1983). Guidelines for choosing toys. *Day Care and Early Education, 11*(1), 6–8.

ROUP, R., J. TRAVERS, F. GLANTZ, AND C. COELEN (1979). *Children at the Center: Final report of the National Day Care Study*, Vol. 1. Cambridge, MA: Abt Associates.

VARTULI, S. (1987). Ideas: Teacher decisions that maximize learning and minimize disruptions in an early childhood classroom. *Dimensions, 15*(4), 28–31.

WERNER, P. (1983). Children's needs and safety standards. *Dimensions, 11*(2), 11–14.

SUGGESTED ACTIVITIES

1. Observe in a classroom for four-year-olds. Make a list of the tasks that they do for themselves. Make a second list of those tasks that are done for them by adults. Try to make some generalizations about the two lists.

2. Design a dramatic play center for young children. Include a floor plan, list of materials, number of children and rules for participation.

3. Interview a teacher of young children about the importance of planning. Be sure to discuss the use of instructional units as a vehicle for organizing the year. Develop a beginning list of possible unit topics and related materials for your own class.

4. Critique the room arrangement that appears in Chapter 6. How would you modify the room for a half-day preschool program? An extended day child care program? A full-day kindergarten program?

5. Interview a parent about his/her expectations for child care. Which of the expectations can be met through a well-thought-out room arrangement?

7

Planning and Organizing the Social Environment

After completing this chapter on planning and organizing the social environment, the student will be able to:

1. Design an appropriate physical setting to support children's interactions with other children and significant adults.
2. Identify several ways of organizing young children.
3. Plan different types of grouping patterns to facilitate individual and group activities.
4. Describe and compare a number of models to improve young children's classroom behavior.
5. Develop a system of classroom management to help children develop self-control and responsibility.
6. Explain the strategies to teach young children positive social interactions.
7. Discuss appropriate ways of working with adults in the classroom, including paraprofessionals, volunteers, and resource people.

Once teachers establish the educational goals for their class, they often focus on creating the proper physical setting. The next step is to plan and organize a social environment that will also support the achievement of these goals. Such a social environment should be more than a management system to achieve program goals. While all teachers are justifiably concerned with managing the social context of their class, good teachers are also aware of the social dimensions of a setting. These dimensions help a teacher achieve important educational goals, especially those relating to the social development of young children. Children can be helped to become sensitive to the needs and feelings of other children, as well as to their own. They can also learn to control their impulses and behaviors and to become cooperative members of a social group. The relationships teachers develop with children as well as any other adults in the classroom will be reflected in the behavior manifest in that classroom.

ORGANIZING CHILDREN

When young children enter school for the first time, they give up the natural rhythm of their daily activities. They must now attend school at a specific time, sit in an assigned place for a determined period of time, take care of bodily functions at a prescribed time, and eat and play together at specified times. Children are expected to do all these things and others at the same time as their peers. They must adapt their behaviors to what the school considers appropriate and conform to group norms, regardless of how they function at home.

Teaching children in groups instead of one at a time requires the teacher to become aware of the need for individuals to adapt to the group. Yet, within this expectation, teachers must be sensitive to individual differences within the group. In achieving the complex task of organizing children, teachers use various types of organization, grouping children and adults in a workable classroom management system. Children must also be helped to learn the positive social interaction skills they will need.

Grouping

Children in any classroom are different from one another. However, since some will have similar interests and needs and will not differ in profound ways, teachers can often individualize through grouping. In addition, some children may work better in a group situation than alone; they can learn from each other's reactions and model one another's behavior. Some children may also feel less pressured in a group setting.

Four or five young children working together often constitutes a manageable group. Younger children like to sit close to the teacher. They feel that the nearness allows them to get a verbal or physical response easily, which may not be possible when they are lost in a large group. If the teacher has some help (such as an aide, mother helper, college student, or volunteer), the class should be divided into smaller groups for many learning tasks to make it more manageable.

As children learn to work in groups, group size can be increased. Even if the teacher keeps the entire class together, an assistant can help, joining in and participating with the group, and promoting the children's interests. Three-, four-, and five-year-old children are sometimes all brought together to introduce a unit, tell a story, or talk about an object or event.

Young children may be grouped for story time provided the teacher (1) plans for a smooth transition that allows the children to anticipate what will happen, (2) prepares the setting so that children can listen quietly, (3) has the story and any materials ready in advance, and (4) plans follow-up activities.

Group time should be used to develop receptive and expressive language, encourage thinking processes, and provide positive social experiences for young children. Group experiences should integrate logical and language activities by means of a variety of experiences such as poems, stories, action plays, songs, rhythms, creative movement, and discussion. Not all of these will be used on any one day. Long-range planning guarantees that children have a variety of experiences over time, whereas short-range planning ensures flexibility in teaching.

A word of caution: When teachers develop well-organized instructional plans and prepare all the resources necessary, they often feel the need to stick to them under any circumstances. There should be enough flexibility in planning to take into account any unanticipated events and to make use of opportunities that arise, even if it means dropping a set of planned activities. A frog that jumps into the room on a rainy day during story or sharing time, for example, will instantly distract the children. Rather than fight the distraction, teachers can change the topic and permit the children to become actively involved in the unexpected event. The teacher might seek out storybooks about frogs or use frogs as a theme for a movement activity. The teacher can achieve the same goal and, at the same time, build on an exciting occurrence, especially if the children have been physically confined for a long period of time.

Although formal instruction is seldom found in early childhood classes, children are grouped for a variety of activities. Many kinds of grouping patterns can be used to individualize instruction, including open grouping, paired grouping (Wilson & Ribovich, 1973), and multi-age grouping (Spodek, 1985). Learning centers, discussed in the previous chapter, can facilitate individual and group activities.

Open Grouping.   In open grouping children choose a group based on their interests. Children might, for example, choose to join a group in which a story is being read, or they may go to the block center to build with others. This type of grouping requires that activities be known to the children ahead of time to allow them to anticipate activities, plan their selection, and choose to participate in one of several group activities.

Paired Grouping.   In paired grouping, a child works for a while with one other child, the two helping each other learn. It assumes that all children can teach and be taught and that all children have strengths and needs that will com-

Children often group themselves according to their interests.

plement each other. A child's strengths can be demonstrated and internalized by his or her teaching another child, while at the same time each child's needs are met by receiving help from another.

Multi-age Grouping.   Multi-age grouping, which is also called *family grouping*, develops an enriched community of young children and provides an opportunity to mix the ages within a group (such as having three- to five-year-olds in the same class). This group of children of different ages functions much as a family does, with children helping, protecting, guiding, and teaching each other. There is also less concern about age level expectations in such groups so that pressure on individuals may be reduced.

Children vary in styles, interests, and needs. Classroom strategies that gear activities and expectations to the average child should be avoided. They create pressures and place restrictions on activities. These strategies punish children for their unique qualities. Individual differences need to be valued and enhanced in the classroom. Grouping practices that work well accommodate the class to differences among children.

One-to-One Interactions

Teachers usually see themselves as working with groups of children, either large whole-class groups or smaller groups. Yet much teaching takes place in the interactions they have with individual children. Some of these one-to-one interactions are short, informal and may even occur spontaneously. Other interactions are planned and deliberate. Working with a single child allows the teacher to focus only on that one child. A personal relationship can be built and the teacher can learn a great deal about the child that would not be evident in the group setting.

Using Children to Extend Teaching

In any classroom, the children themselves should assume some responsibility for classroom tasks. Children can restore toys and materials to their proper places when they are finished using them. They can serve snacks, clean up spills from tables and floors, and maintain a clean, neat, and orderly environment. They can monitor their own behavior and make sure that others do not break the classroom rules. Teachers can use this assistance to provide themselves with more time to teach and interact with the children. This is a good way for children to learn to assume responsibilities.

CLASSROOM MANAGEMENT

Classroom management focuses on maintaining order in the classroom. Many teachers make proper management their primary teaching goal, although different teachers may achieve that goal in different ways. Some teachers punish, lecture, guide, or persuade children to behave appropriately, with all the classroom controls coming from them. Other teachers help children develop self-control and responsibility. Some teachers strive for absolute quiet and limited movement. Other teachers value the movement and noise that come from purposeful activity. Generally teachers want children to behave as they are expected, to not defy the teacher, to be on task, to assume responsibility for classroom materials, and to have good interpersonal skills.

Setting Limits

It is always necessary to place limits on children's behavior. Such limits help to socialize children, and help them discriminate between acceptable and unacceptable behavior. In addition, since young children often lack appropriate experience and judgment, limits can protect children's health and safety.

Marian Marion (1989) states that good limits help children achieve self-control and develop positive interaction skills. They also protect children's health and safety. When developmentally appropriate, they are meaningful to children, and never degrade them. Teachers can help children comply with limits by orienting them properly to the situation, providing clear and helpful suggestions, giving reasons for the limits, using appropriate verbal and nonverbal cues, timing and pacing suggestions, supporting compliance, and using firm but gentle techniques to enforce the limits. Setting limits on children's activities is the basis for establishing positive discipline in the classroom.

Discipline is an important part of any classroom management system. Discipline is not the same as punishment. It represents an appropriate way of organizing and managing the classroom for children and adults. Simple rules for appropriate behavior should be established, and these rules should be taught through a variety of experiences. The teaching of appropriate behaviors should be planned and worked at just as language arts and other curriculum areas are planned and worked at.

Teachers need to develop a workable management system to meet the range of individual differences in the classroom. A classroom management system should help young children develop self-control in appropriate ways. Children should become more independent, learn to help themselves, and learn to cope with their environment. At the same time, children should be helped to manage their own impulses and drives.

For young children, learning to be independent includes acquiring self-caring skills such as dressing, toileting, feeding, and other essential tasks with the least amount of help. It also includes learning to keep busy, to develop positive relationships with other children, and to make independent decisions to the extent possible. Children should be helped not to be destructive, intrusive, exhibitionist, overly proud, overly assertive, or inappropriately competitive. Developing constructive patterns of self-care and work requires children to direct their impulses. In addition, children need to understand clearly the difference between acceptable and unacceptable behavior. Teachers are responsible for making sure that areas of appropriate, acceptable behavior are spelled out for the children and that children develop self-control.

Some educators and psychologists believe that children's behavior can be improved through specific approaches to discipline. C. M. Charles (1989) describes several models for the classroom environment that promote optimal learning. These include the behavior modification model, the Kounin model, and the Dreikurs model.

Behavior Modification

Psychologists consider behavior modification, or applied behavior analysis theory, to be a systematic way of changing children's behavior. Teachers study the behavior problem, then systematically apply reinforcement and punishment, which moves children toward the desired behaviors. Once children acquire the desired behavior, the teacher can eliminate the strategy.

In planning a behavior modification strategy, teachers need to (1) analyze the behaviors to be changed and (2) develop a specific plan to change those behaviors (Charles, 1989). The analysis should include a specific determination of what behaviors should be changed, as well as what they should be in the future. The conditions in the classroom that encourage inappropriate behavior should also be noted. These might include such factors as boredom, distractions, or difficult transitions between activities. It is also helpful to see what there is in the situation to be changed that provides reinforcement to the child's behavior.

Once the behavioral change or target behavior is identified, the teacher can decide on a system of consequences, or reinforcers and punishments, to be used. The teacher can then establish a schedule for reinforcing acceptable behaviors, possibly using praise, tokens, candy, play, or time to participate in a valued activity. Those conditions that encouraged the inappropriate behavior should also be modified. Transitions could be improved, or more interesting and appropriate activities could be planned, for example.

If the target behavior is to be sustained without continual attention from the teacher, the child must learn to reinforce him/herself by finding increased satisfaction in the target behavior. Once a child engages in block building, for example, the activity becomes a reinforcer. Children who develop a sense of accomplishment also reinforce themselves.

Kounin's Model of Classroom Management

The teacher's capacity to manage groups becomes the focus of Kounin's (1970) classroom management model. Teachers need simultaneously to cope with the whole class, subgroups, pairs of students, and individuals. In managing the classroom, Kounin's model avoids punishment and harsh teacher responses. He suggests that teachers should:

1. Be aware of what is going on everywhere in the classroom at all times and let the students know this.
2. Cope simultaneously with more than one problem.
3. Correct the appropriate target behavior immediately to avoid the increase of the misbehavior.
4. Learn to employ the *ripple effect* efficiently.
5. Use and keep a smooth and consistent momentum.
6. Sustain group focus by alerting and accountability.
7. Offer nonsatiating teaching strategies by using progress, challenge, and variety.

Kounin has identified the *ripple effect* in working with children. What a teacher does to one child, for instance a remark made to suppress behavior, modifies the behavior of all the children who witness the act. Kounin studied kindergartens to determine how teachers deal with misbehaviors, and he found three attributes of *desists*, or ways of stopping misbehavior, used by teachers:

1. *Clarity.* The desist provided information that identified the deviate behavior along with the acceptable behavior and provided the reasons for the desist.
2. *Firmness.* This attitude projects "I mean it" and continues until the misbehavior disappears.
3. *Roughness.* The desist is composed of anger, threats, physical handling, and punishment.

According to Kounin, the degree of clarity of the desist increased conformity of behavior in the children who witnessed the scene. Firmness in the desist increased conformity only in those children who misbehaved. Roughness failed to improve any behavior and made children upset, anxious, confused, and restless. These observations suggest that it is important to be clear and firm in handling problems; they also suggest that roughness should be avoided.

Kounin uses the concept of *withitness* to describe the teacher behavior that communicates that they know what is going on everywhere in the classroom at all times. This sense of what is going on often allows teachers to anticipate and avoid problems by intervening before situations get out of hand.

Timing affects the withitness strategy. Teachers who display withitness correct misbehaviors as soon as they occur. They take action before a misbehavior spreads. Kounin found that withitness induces more work involvement and less misbehavior, particularly in teacher-directed lessons. Correcting the child at once is more important to classroom management than the firmness or clarity of a desist.

Overdwelling refers to teachers' spending time providing directions and explanations that are not necessary. There are some teachers who overdwell on students' behavior, lecturing beyond what is required to eliminate the misbehavior and communicating that they are displeased. They may even lecture long and hard about misbehaviors that have not occurred. Students have a tendency to tune out this type of nagging, letting their mind wander while teachers talk on.

In effective classroom management, *variation* in teaching plays a crucial role in keeping children from becoming bored. Teachers need to change the dynamics of instruction and avoid repetition. Repetition reduces student involvement in and enjoyment of an activity. Teachers must vary the content of classroom activities to achieve better classroom management and more effective instruction.

Dreikurs' Model of Discipline

Rudolph Dreikurs developed a model of discipline based upon psychodynamic principles. It is concerned more with the causes of misbehavior than with the actual behaviors themselves. Dreikurs (1968) suggests that children misbehave for one of four reasons: (1) they wish to gain attention, (2) they wish to display power, (3) they wish to gain revenge, or (4) they wish to display a problem to gain them special attention. Rather than punish children for their transgressions, Dreikurs suggests that teachers and parents use what he calls *logical consequences*. These consequences express the reality of the social order, are directly related to the misbehavior, communicate no moral judgment to the child, and are related only to the immediate problem. That is, the child is still valued, but the behavior is not (Dreikurs & Grey, 1968).

In applying logical consequences, it is important that the teacher become aware of the child's reasons for the misbehavior. Rather than allow the child to achieve a desired goal through misbehavior, it must be demonstrated to the child that the behavior is both inappropriate for the situation and ineffective in achieving that result. The logical consequence should be inconsistent with the child's desired goal and the child should be informed of the reason the particular consequence was selected. For example, if a child plays around with his or her clothing instead of getting ready for outdoor play in order to have the teacher do the dressing, a logical consequence might be that the child remains indoors. A logical consequence for messing up the paint at an easel might be having the child clean up while others are engaged in different activities. While logical consequences can work in many situations, they should be avoided where dangerous physical conditions might be created.

Redirection

Teachers of young children often deal with a misbehavior by moving the child from the problem activity and redirecting that child to another activity. If a child is in conflict with another child over blocks needed for a building, the teacher might suggest that the child might enjoy woodworking, firmly guiding the child to the workbench. To be effective, the teacher must know which activities a child finds appealing and be able to offer attractive alternatives.

While redirection works for the short term and is used successfully and often by teachers, it does not help children learn to deal with and resolve conflict. There may be times when a teacher would find it more appropriate to help children negotiate a conflict, developing verbal skills at communicating and social skills at working together. These skills would allow children to be more socially independent in the classroom.

Guiding Children's Behavior

A major goal of education is to help children become self-directed and self-disciplined. Children become independent of authority by thinking and analyzing situations in order to make appropriate decisions. Teachers can guide children, influencing their behavior through social interactions and warm personal relationships. Teachers also help develop appropriate behaviors by arranging the physical environment and providing specific equipment and materials that guide children indirectly.

A well-planned environment helps maintain orderly traffic patterns while allowing for a variety of simultaneous activities. Providing children with

Teachers need to accept children's feelings and behaviors.

sufficient materials (such as paper, scissors, and paste) so that they do not have to wait turns or compete for scarce resources will also lead to fewer arguments. Teachers can also remove equipment that stimulates competition and elicits conflict.

Teachers can guide children's behaviors directly through speaking, demonstrating, helping, leading, approving, disapproving, restraining, and punishing. Dealing with children positively is usually most effective; negative strategies should be used only in extreme situations. Punishment stifles learning, develops negative attitudes toward school and teachers, and provides no directions that children can use for behavior change.

Teachers also may guide young children through physical actions, helping, demonstrating, leading, restraining, or removing the children. Physical guidance can be effective with young children when it is accompanied by verbal guidance.

When teachers speak to children, they should be sure they have the children's attention. They should also be careful to use language that children can understand. Teachers may squat or sit at the children's eye level, looking at them directly, then use simple words, appropriate facial expressions, and gestures to extend communication. When possible, teachers should speak to one child at a time or to small groups, rather than to the whole class. They should give clear and simple directions, telling children exactly what to do. Using the word "don't" in a command may confuse young children. For instance, the statement "Walk" tells children what to do, while the statement, "Don't run!" does not include information about what is acceptable. Teachers should also explain why some behaviors are unacceptable, building on children's reasoning. Teachers can help children learn to follow directions by making them simple and providing enough time to complete tasks. Before moving to another activity, teachers should caution children that it will soon be time to change activities. The children will be able to anticipate change and can finish their project and get ready for the next activity.

All teachers serve as models of appropriate behavior. Children will do what their teachers do. Consistency, patience, and firmness are essential in working with children. The rules children are expected to follow need to be communicated clearly and enforced consistently. They should be specific, concrete, simple, and inclusive. They should be explained and discussed regularly. Teachers should avoid unrealistic expectations of children, which can create frustrations and other problems.

Managing Problem Behavior

Even when teachers have taken all precautions to manage the children's behavior, situations do get out of hand. Teachers can stop and request the children's help. They can be honest, sometimes saying: "We have a problem to solve. This is not working. The problem is that . . ." Children can suggest solutions to the problem, establish and enforce realistic rules, and assist in organizing the situation.

TABLE 7-1   Guidelines for Managing Behavior

1. BEHAVIORS EXPECTED OF CHILDREN SHOULD BE KNOWN TO THEM. Children should be told what is expected of them. Children's improper behavior may be a result of ignorance. Instructions will have to be repeated many times in many contexts before they are understood.

2. CHILDREN NEED TO BE TOLD WHY RULES ARE IN EFFECT. Even if they cannot fully *understand* them, children need to be given the reasons for rules. Most rules for school behavior are reasonable. Children can begin to see the purpose of lining up at a slide or limiting the amount of time one child can ride on a bicycle. They can understand why they should behave differently in a crowded lunch room than in their own room and why rules are promulgated for behaving certain ways in class, others in the hall, and still others on a school bus.

3. CHILDREN SHOULD HAVE OPPORTUNITIES TO OBSERVE AND PRACTICE PROPER BEHAVIOR. Children need demonstrations; they learn through modeling. They must also have opportunities to *practice* proper behavior, with feedback from the teacher.

4. THE BEHAVIOR EXPECTED OF CHILDREN OUGHT TO BE POSSIBLE FOR THEM. Children are not miniature adults and should not be expected to behave like adults. Teachers should develop goals of reasonable childlike behavior.

5. CHILDREN CANNOT ALWAYS BE EXPECTED TO BEHAVE PROPERLY AT ALL TIMES. Nobody is perfect, including adults. We do not expect adults always to be on their best behavior. The same is true for children. They should not be expected to conform to standards of model behavior at all times any more than adults should.

6. TEACHERS SHOULD BEHAVE WITH CONSISTENCY. The teacher's behavior communicates a message to the children about what is acceptable and appropriate and what is not. If teachers vacillate or accept certain kinds of behaviors one time and reject or punish the same behavior another time, they confuse children and blur their goals. Though teachers cannot always behave consistently, this is a goal for which they should aim.

B. Spodek, *Teaching in the Early Years,* 3rd ed. (Englewood Cliffs, NJ: Prentice-Hall, 1985), p. 241.

One of the most important strategies teachers can use to deal with behavior problems is to provide children with a good educational program. Teachers need to carefully examine the children's entire day, including their daily routines like scheduling, toileting, cleanup, dressing, and snack. Every component of the program contributes to each child's behavior and to the dynamics of the group. Problems may easily emerge during transitions as children move from one activity to the next.

Scheduling should provide a balance between active and quiet activities. Children may get restless if teachers schedule a long sequence of activities in which children have to be inactive. They will become restless and will seek their own relief by fidgeting, moving, and possibly disturbing others. Having several consecutive active periods, such as free play, creative movement, and outdoor play, can also cause problems. Children may become too tired to be attentive.

Inappropriate tasks can also produce management problems. Having all the children line up to go to the bathroom at the same time, for example, should be avoided. Young children do not have the self-control to wait. Children who cannot perform these tasks can be individually guided or held by the hand. Children should be permitted to drink water or go to the bathroom at times that suit their needs. A few children at a time can wash up while the rest of the class is busy working.

Keeping young children in a straight line when they move about a building or through the streets demands a great deal of the teacher's energy and can cause frustration. Children can be guided to walk on sidewalks instead of lawns and they can learn to walk the halls without running or bumping into someone. Lines are not needed to achieve these purposes, although there are times when teachers use lines to maintain safety.

Activities in which children assume responsibility and develop autonomy should be planned to help children develop self-control. Learning opportunities that are appropriate for individual children need to be provided to help them use learning resources, both in and out of school, to become a responsible group member, working with others without having their wishes submerged but considering the feelings of others.

Teaching Positive Social Interactions

Children often have had no contacts with adults except for those in their home, until they enter preschool. These children need help in adjusting to a new situation and responding to new adult authority figures, including the classroom teacher and other staff members. They need to learn to function effectively in society. The socialization process requires children to interact with others in appropriate ways. Young children need to become sensitive and considerate of others' feelings. They need to develop social competence and learn to work and play with other children.

Children need to learn to deal independently with social problems.

The younger child or older children with little experience in playing with others may not be ready to cooperate and engage in play with other children. Children who spend many hours watching television and little time playing with others often lack social skills. Their play requires the teacher's support.

Teachers need to accept a child's patterns of play as it exists, gradually inviting children into small-group activities without forcing any child to function in a way he or she is incapable of. When children join the group for a music or story time activity, a child who refuses to participate should be excused and provided with an acceptable substitute. Children's cooperative play behaviors require the children to consider others, to cooperate with others, to conform, and to become assertive without being aggressive. Some children prefer to play alongside a friend, other children prefer to play together, while still others prefer to play alone with materials, investigating their properties and creating themes.

Supporting Children's Prosocial Behavior

Most children in preschool and kindergarten classes are skilled in initiating social interactions with other children. Their circle of friends is relatively small and may not be as stable as is the case with older children. In order to continue to develop friendships, these children need to learn that others do not necessarily share their point of view and to be able to be aware of the perspectives of others. While they don't easily make sacrifices for the sake of others or help others who suffer fear, deprivation, or anxiety, they should be making progress in that direction (Moore, 1986). Young children can be helped to become more sensitive to the needs of others and more capable of providing for those needs. They can be taught to show kindness and consideration, as well as to help, others.

Young-ok Kim and Joseph Stevens (1987) have reviewed the research on the development of prosocial behavior in young children and on strategies that teachers can use to nurture prosocial behavior. Children can be taught to be more considerate and less aggressive. They can consider other people's points of view and display more empathy. They can also learn to reason more systematically about social problems. The authors suggest that young children can be tutored in role play to consider alternative actions in social situations and to anticipate the consequences of each action. Teachers can modify their use of time, space, and materials to promote social learning. They can encourage children to work and play together, providing children with opportunities to negotiate social interactions with each other. They can also model acts of kindness, consideration, and generosity. In thinking through their program, teachers should plan classroom activities that nurture children's prosocial abilities and characteristics, allowing their positive feelings to become more manifest in their behavior.

Play Intervention

Teachers can prolong and extend children's interaction to enrich their social experience, intervening when necessary, but otherwise staying out of play activities. They must be careful to avoid becoming the center of attention or the source of most of the play ideas, thus discouraging the children's play initiatives. On the other hand, teachers can go to the other extreme and fail to promote children's play, allowing situations that lack richness to fall apart too soon. Intervening appropriately in children's play is important in developing children's social skills.

Children's play does not always take a positive turn. Sometimes play bogs down, becoming overly repetitive and not seeming to go anywhere. Sometimes play can lead to conflict among children. It can even lead to destructive behavior. When such things occur, teachers must intervene in order to make the children's play more educationally productive.

Ann Spidell (1985) studied a number of preschools and analyzed how teachers intervened in children's play. She identified a number of strategies that teachers used. One form of intervention was labeled *instruction*. In this intervention teachers told children a fact or concept they felt would move the play along. Teachers also used *praise* to intervene in children's play, showing approval to a child whose behavior they wanted to support or to have other children model. Teachers also used *maintenance* strategies, dealing with issues relating to crowded space, not enough materials or equipment, disputes about rules, or similar housekeeping details.

Among the other strategies that teachers used were *conversation*, engaging children in a dialogue about their interests or activities; *demonstration*, showing children how to do something or how to carry on an activity; and *redirection*, suggesting alternative activities. *Participation* was also used as a play intervention, with teachers joining into play for brief periods of time.

Not all of these interventions were used to the same extent by all teachers. Each teacher seemed to use some interventions more often than others. Nor were all the strategies equally effective in moving the children's play along. In most cases, teachers used a combination of intervention strategies in helping play remain dynamic and productive.

Teachers may enter into children's play for a short time in order to stimulate it or extend it.

One of the most powerful strategies teachers use for play intervention is never observed in the classroom. It is not seen because it occurs before the children begin their play. This strategy consists of setting the stage for play before the children arrive in school. The teacher intervenes best in children's play by organizing a play center, providing enough space and materials, and establishing proper ways of behaving in the classroom. As the stage is set, the teacher makes suggestions for play activities and provides resources that allow the activities to unfold. Feeding information about the play theme to children by reading books to them, holding discussions, inviting resource persons, or taking a field trip allows children to extend their play and elaborate on what the teacher has originally provided.

Teachers need to keep in mind that play intervention may only require a suggestion or a supportive comment. Teachers can also add accessories to encourage children to participate in a play activity.

Children who prefer to play by themselves should not be forced to engage in cooperative play. Teachers can foster cooperative actions by asking these children to help clean up after snack time or put away library books or housekeeping equipment. These kinds of activities can also be supported by the children who have been playing in these areas. Cleanup activities also provide the teacher with an opportunity to model appropriate behavior for children and encourage them to engage in cooperative activities. The children will soon initiate cooperative play behavior upon the teacher's suggestion or on their own initiative.

ORGANIZING ADULTS

Staffing patterns vary among early childhood centers. The number of persons who are employed in any early childhood center depends on the size of the center, the kind of agency sponsoring the program, and the level of funding provided. The type of staff employed, their relationship, and the program's administrative system depend on the setting.

Adults play a number of different roles in these programs. Directors and supervisors perform administrative duties, though they may also be responsible for some teaching. Head teachers, teacher-directors, and classroom teachers are primarily responsible for planning and implementing the classroom program. Teacher aides and assistants, along with volunteers and community resource people, may do some teaching and engage in other supportive activities under the guidance of a classroom teacher. Every staff member who is in contact with the children has some influence on them. The cook, custodian, and bus driver, for example, have no responsibility for instruction but still influence the children's education in significant ways. They can facilitate program development or retard activities. Although teachers are not responsible for the children's experiences with these school personnel, they must be aware of their experiences and use them to support positive learning opportunities.

Adults working in the classroom must know the school's philosophy, its routines, teaching strategies, classroom management, and appropriate ways to guide children. Teachers need to define clearly each volunteer's specific roles. Adults may be expected to perform duties in school in ways that differ from those they have performed before. Teachers also need to tell others the reasons for the procedures used and provide practice sessions.

A good management system is essential when a number of people (such as specialists, parent volunteers, college students, or teacher aides) participate in the educational process. The teachers must work cooperatively with the adults and communicate to them all decisions that have been made. Teachers should possess the academic and practical knowledge required to plan creatively, schedule appropriate activities for young children, and develop a good management system, including working with paraprofessionals, volunteers, and community resources. The teachers are responsible for ensuring that each child succeeds in some learning experience each day.

Working with Paraprofessionals

Paraprofessionals, such as teacher aides and assistants, generally share classroom responsibilities with the teacher and provide important assistance. Those who work in the classroom can help with routine jobs to support children's learning experiences and can be used to individualize interactions. Aides and assistants can also help teachers with exceptional children who may need special attention. However, it is the teachers who are responsible and who assess the children's individual needs and plan their educational activities.

The teacher aide or assistant can extend the teacher's influence, managing the classroom environment, working with a small group of children, and monitoring the children's behavior and activities. The teacher assistant's supportive role is crucial in the effective functioning of the classroom and may reduce disruptions. The aide or assistant should be included in the planning of the daily and weekly schedules. Open lines of communication must be maintained so all can work effectively as a team. Planning sessions are important for maintaining communication and providing an opportunity to discuss any problems that have emerged.

Working with Volunteers

Some early childhood programs, including parent cooperatives, do not employ adults to assist the teacher in the classroom. Parents may participate in the classroom but the teacher is the one responsible for supervising. Teachers might use volunteers such as parents, community persons, and students to help in the classroom.

Volunteers can be valuable resource persons in a center. Teachers can invite them to the classroom on a regular basis to join with the regular teaching staff, as in cooperative schools, or they can bring them in for short visits. Teachers must coordinate all of the experiences children have with volunteers in school to maximize their use. This means that the teacher must plan and organize for the use of volunteers, orient them to the school, and even train them.

Retired adults can often be used as volunteers in the classroom.

In training and organizing these volunteers, teachers can meet with them to explain their responsibilities and show how to carry them out. Volunteers can also be asked for their reactions to daily and weekly plans. At the beginning, teachers should explain the basic ground rules for functioning in the classroom and should try to make the volunteers feel at ease. Sharing a list of possible tasks, such as reading a story to the children, cooking with them, discussing a picture, or providing additional adult supervision on a field trip, can give them a sense of the duties they might perform. The volunteers should be able to select from these activities so they can feel comfortable in working with the groups. Some volunteers may have to be given very specific directions in order to function adequately. Teachers should sense what is necessary and respond to each volunteer as needed.

Teachers need to make the volunteers feel truly welcome and comfortable and show them that their assistance is appreciated. Volunteers deserve to be thanked for their help and encouraged to return. They can become a continuing source of help in the class.

Working with Community Resources

Though most of the early childhood program is offered inside the classroom, teachers also can make use of resources outside. Taking young children into the community on field trips can provide a great deal of interest, enjoyment, and information, but these field trips must be properly planned. The children should know the purpose and focus of the trip and be able to anticipate what will happen. Although there is much incidental learning on a field trip, its planning cannot be left to chance.

Reading stories to a child is a worthwhile task for a volunteer.

Field trips need not be elaborate excursions. Simple trips can be meaningful to young children: A walk to the corner to watch the traffic lights and cars, or a visit to a local bakery to see bread baked, can provide an enriching experience. Even though some children may have the same experience outside of school, the teacher's planning and preparation can help them focus differently and learn new concepts within a familiar situation.

In addition to taking field trips, teachers can invite resource persons to visit their classroom. Persons in the community who have specific skills or knowledge can help extend the children's knowledge and motivate their interest. Community resource persons can include firefighters, mail carriers, garbage collectors, police officers, highway patrol officers, retired persons, musicians, baton twirlers, dancers, clowns, football players, artists, hobbyists, storytellers, nurses, mothers and babies, custodians, weavers, anthropologists, and anyone else who has some first-hand knowledge that would be of interest to the children.

Before the resource person visits the classroom, the teacher should be sure that both the children and the resource person know the purpose of the visit, what will take place, and the basic ground rules for participation. Children can serve as hosts to the visitor in their classroom.

SUMMARY

Teachers must create a social environment in their classes to help children function well with both adults and other children. Teachers can group children in a variety of ways for different activities and support children in helping one another. There are a variety of classroom management techniques that can be used to maintain order. Good techniques help children manage their own needs and develop autonomy. Through careful teacher interventions children can be helped to develop positive social interactions and can have their play activities extended.

Paraprofessionals, parents, community volunteers, and student teachers can provide assistance to the teacher in the classroom, but teachers must be prepared to spend the time to maximize their effectiveness. Teachers need to plan for each person's involvement, introducing them to the philosophy of the program and the roles of adults in the classroom. Teachers also need to orient volunteers to specific activities in the classroom: reading to young children, supervising outdoor play, assisting at meals, or teaching a concept are all helpful. Having the extra pair of "helping hands" in the classroom, though, will require a teacher to shift some attention from the children to the other adults.

REFERENCES

CHARLES, C. M. (1989). *Building classroom discipline: From models to practice.* (3rd ed.) New York: Longman, Inc.

DREIKURS, R. (1968). *Psychology in the schools* (2nd ed.). New York: Harper & Row.

DREIKURS, R., AND L. GREY (1968). *Logical consequences: A handbook of discipline.* New York: Meredith Press.

KIM, YOUNG-OK, AND J. H. STEVENS, JR. (1987). The socialization of prosocial behavior in children. *Childhood Education, 63,* 200–207.

KOUNIN, J. S. (1970). *Discipline and group management in classrooms.* New York: Holt, Rinehart & Winston.

MARION, M. (1989). *Guidance of young children* (2nd ed). Columbus, OH: Merrill.

MASDEN, C. H., JR., AND C. K. MASDEN (1974). *Teaching/discipline: A positive approach to educational development* (2nd ed.). Boston: Allyn & Bacon.

MOORE, S. (1986). Socialization in the kindergarten classroom. In B. Spodek (Ed.), *Today's Kindergarten: Exploring the knowledge base, expanding the curriculum,* pp. 110–136. New York: Teachers College Press.

SPIDELL, R. A. (1985). *Preschool teachers' interventions in children's play.* Unpublished Doctoral dissertation, University of Illinois at Urbana–Champaign.

SPODEK, B. (1985). *Teaching in the early years.* (3rd ed.). Englewood Cliffs, NJ: Prentice-Hall.

WILSON, R. M., AND J. K. RIBOVICH. Ability grouping? Stop and reconsider. *Reading World, 13,* 84–91.

SUGGESTED ACTIVITIES

1. Visit an early childhood center. Record instances where the teacher attempts to modify a specific child's behavior. Describe the teacher's strategy and the child's changed behavior after intervention.

2. Describe the personal and professional qualities that a teacher needs in order to successfully organize adults for classroom instruction.

3. Interview a teacher of a group of toddlers about problems of teaching them to share. Interview a kindergarten teacher on the same topic. Compare their responses.

4. Interview a preschool teacher to find out how the children in the classroom are managed. Prepare a short report about the teacher's major procedures or principles.

5. Observe a session in an early childhood classroom and note the following:

   a. Number of children working in groups.

   b. Ratio of boys and girls in each group.

   c. Ratio of children and adults in each group.

   Ask the teacher what factors were considered in grouping these children.

6. Interview a nursery teacher, a day-care teacher, and a kindergarten teacher to find out how and why they developed their daily schedules.

8

Working with Parents

OBJECTIVES

After completing this chapter on working with parents, the student should be able to:

1. Define blended family, nuclear family, extended family, single-parent family, and foster parent family.
2. Explain the purposes of different kinds of parent programming, including parent involvement, parent education, and parent advisory groups.
3. Describe ways to involve parents who cannot come to the center, those who can come to the center but who do not want to work with children, and those who want to work directly with children.
4. Describe how to plan and conduct a parent conference.
5. Discuss some of the ways that a parent involvement program can be modified to meet the needs of all parents.
6. Develop formal and informal ways of communicating with parents.
7. Explain why parent education is a necessary part of any early childhood program.
8. Describe strategies that can be used for parent–teacher problem solving.

While the child is the first priority in early childhood education, parents are the second priority. Parents and teachers are partners in helping children to learn. Parents are their children's first teachers, and they continue to have the primary responsibility for their children's development even after the beginning of school. While teachers have an important role in guiding a child, an early education program that does not respect the importance of the parent cannot be successful. A review of the Urban Education Project (Norwood, 1984) noted that one common quality of the most successful schools in the country was the active involvement of parents and citizens in planning curriculum and instruction.

This chapter focuses on working with parents: parents as learners, parents as volunteers, parents as decision makers, and parents as members of the teacher–parent team, providing the best possible support for the young child's optimal growth and development.

The importance of parents being involved in early childhood education can be seen by the results of a number of studies that have been completed over the past twenty years. These results have led to the requirement of parent involvement in Head Start programs.

Rebecca S. Heinz (1979) suggests that three things occur when schools and parents cooperate: (1) parents' and children's self-concept increases, (2) children's motivation accelerates, and (3) children's achievement advances. Heinz also reported that the mothers in Ira Gordon's Florida Parent Education Program who perceived improvement in their children's growth experienced growth in their own self-esteem as women. At the completion of the program, many of the parents moved to better homes, found better jobs, and returned to school. Heinz also suggests that parent involvement in the preschool years is crucial to the formation of achievement motivation in children.

Ira Gordon, Pat Olmstead, Roberta Rubin and Joan True (1979) reported that the Follow-Through Parent Education Program Model had an impact on two areas: (1) changes in the home–school partnership and in parental teaching behavior, and (2) changes in the school, community, and career development of parents, paraprofessionals, and professionals. These Follow-Through parents exhibited more desirable teaching behaviors with their children than did non-Follow-Through parents. They functioned as decision makers, adult learners, and audiences.

This chapter describes various kinds of families. It also discusses different ways of working with parents in school, including forms of parent involvement, the use of parent advisory groups, and different kinds of parent education. In addition, it examines both formal and informal ways of communicating with parents.

FAMILIES

At one time teachers who worked with parents could assume that all families consisted of a mother, father, and a few children. Today, there are many different kinds of families. While someone takes the parenting role(s) in each, each type of family has its own particular needs and expectations from early childhood programs. Family types include but are not limited to the following:

Nuclear families consist of mother, father, and children.
Extended families include more distant relatives (possibly grandparents) living with the nuclear family.
Single-parent families have just the mother *or* the father, but not both, living with children.
Foster parent families consist of parents who care for children other than their own for temporary periods of time.
Blended families are formed when two single parents, each with children, marry and form a new family group.

It has been shown that single-father families, while much less common than single-mother families, can be successful family structures. Beverly Briggs and Connor Walters (1985) reported that research indicates single fathers who choose custody and who had previous experience with household tasks and child care were satisfied with both their children's adjustment and development. However, some fathers did decrease overtime and work-related travel as well as forego promotions if the position would involve more time away from their children.

Single parents, whether fathers or mothers, may experience task overload. This is caused by the frustration of not being able to complete everything that must be done at home and at work. Such an overload can lead to a feeling of failure (Weiss, 1979). As single parents learn to delegate some tasks to children and to eliminate others, their workload becomes more manageable.

Blended families (or stepfamilies) present the teacher with a special situation. Patsy Skeen, Bryan Robinson, and Carol Flake-Hobson (1984) report that there are approximately 25 million stepparents in this country and that most blended families are formed by divorce and remarriage. Since most adults have not had prior experience in living with a stepfamily, it is difficult for them to acquire stepparenting skills. Teachers may have children who are members of a blended family and are experiencing difficulty in learning their place. They may also have to communicate with parents who are at a loss as to how to best respond to children in the new family situation.

Yet, when you consider the number of changes that can occur in a nuclear family—moving to a new home, the birth of a baby, mother or father going back to work, or family illness—it is apparent that teachers need to be aware of changes in the families of all the children. Foster families are also continually changing. Since foster children come into a new family for only a short period of time, the family unit is always evolving. This constant shifting affects not only the new children, but the children who are permanent members of the family.

In fact, no single type of family can guarantee that children will not need special assistance from a teacher at some time. Skeen, Robinson, and Flake-Hobson (1984) offer the following suggestions for working with children from blended families; most of them are appropriate for children from all types of families:

1. Observe carefully, looking for clues that can help you understand what a child is feeling.
2. Make a plan on how to help the child. Talk with parents and counselor, observe the child, and read related literature before forming a plan.
3. Provide opportunities for the child to work through feelings via dramatic play, art, or media.
4. Help the child to understand the new family.
5. Maintain a stable classroom environment.
6. Work with the parents, and be supportive of their efforts to help the child.
7. As needed, refer families to competent counselors who specialize in family matters.

While each family type has different needs, an understanding teacher can be an asset to all families.

WORKING WITH PARENTS

Parents and teachers both want the best for children. Even though they may not always agree on methods; the health, welfare, and education of the child are always of primary concern for all parties. Parents and teachers, however, may have different views on discipline, the appropriate relationship between adults and children, differences between boys and girls, and cultural or religious differences (Kortz, 1984).

Doreen Croft (1979) suggests that there are a number of things that parents have in common:

1. Parents look to the school staff to maintain the health and well-being of their children.
2. Their training and ideas about raising children might be quite different from those of the teachers.
3. They probably have some feelings of guilt about leaving their children in someone else's care.
4. Parents expect teachers to have the expertise to help them raise their children.
5. Their ideas about teachers are colored by their own past experiences in schools.
6. The advice of teachers is more likely to be respected if parents are convinced that the teacher truly cares about the children in their class.
7. They worry about their children.

Working with parents in early childhood education includes both parent involvement and parent education. *Parent involvement* refers to parents participating in their children's education as classroom volunteers as well as serving on advisory committees or policy boards. *Parent education* refers to providing parents with the skills and knowledge necessary to be more successful parents. The two components complement each other, though they have different purposes and require different teaching approaches.

Parent Involvement

Parent involvement programs benefit parents in a number of ways. As parents participate in these programs, they have an opportunity to learn about the teacher's way of guiding children's growth and development. They also gain a sense of competence and a feeling of being needed by the program. In addition, they have an opportunity to develop relationships with other parents in the school (Feeney, Christensen, & Moravcik, 1983). In addition, they have an opportunity to develop relationships with other parents who may be experiencing similar problems in coping with the demands of family and career (Feeney, Christensen & Moravcik, 1983; Hall, 1989).

Involving parents in programs is often difficult. There are already considerable time pressures on the many dual-career families and single-parent families. Parent may find it seemingly impossible to add another activity to their schedule. Additionally, teachers are burdened with a variety of out-of-class responsibilities and they, too, may find it difficult to fit parent involvement activities into an already packed calendar (Hall, 1989). As the benefits are clear, however, all parties should recognize that sacrifices must be made in order to have a successful parent involvement program.

Planning for parent involvement takes time and thought. The level of involvement that the teacher will be able to handle should be considered. Shari Nedler and Oralee McAfee (1979) suggest that beginning teachers might start involving parents slowly, setting limited, short-range goals. They can plan to expand the levels of parent involvement as they grow into the teaching role. Rebecca Heinz (1979) suggests that teachers who involve parents in a classroom need to be able to listen to these parents in an active and accepting way and should be skilled in the art of confrontation without explosion.

Doreen Croft (1979) provides some guidelines for increasing the success of parent–teacher interactions in classrooms. Teachers should:

1. Recognize, understand, and accept the concerns and expectations each person brings to the classroom.
2. Carefully plan training sessions.
3. Provide clear rules.
4. Have goals that are agreed upon by parents and teachers.
5. Offer careful instructions about the options that are available to parents during the decision-making process.
6. Show genuine commitment, patience, perseverance, and a good sense of humor.
7. Develop an atmosphere of mutual cooperation and interdependence.
8. Provide time to talk.

When making arrangements for parent involvement, you need to be able to see things from a parent's point of view and consider the parent's needs. You may need to arrange for child care for other children in the family. You may also need to:

- Provide for alternate times for workshops in order to meet the varied schedules of parents.
- Plan for more than one type of involvement.
- Consider the needs of the single parent.
- Avoid creating father–son or mother–daughter activities that may limit some parents' and children's participation.

Parent involvement can range from doing things at home for school to assisting the teacher in the classroom. Parents who help in the classroom can either work directly with children or be involved in tasks that assist the teacher. All parents are different, with individual needs and interests. Providing a range of activities helps to ensure that parent participants will be doing something they enjoy and that is useful as well. It is helpful to communicate the kinds of tasks that parents can do so they can anticipate what they will be doing. Teachers should also look beyond using only parents as classroom volunteers and include other persons from the family and from the community.

Parents who can come to school but who are not comfortable working directly with children may:

- Record attendance.
- Assemble samples of children's work for booklets or displays.
- Arrange details for field trips.
- Help file pictures or collections of poems, songs, or finger plays.
- Gather information for some of the reports teachers must do, such as the number of children eating meals at school, or types and numbers of health services.
- Prepare materials for class activities such as art, games, and water play.
- Locate resources and materials in the community for the teachers and children to use at school.

Parents can make an important contribution by participating in classroom activities.

Not all parents can come to school during class time. There are other ways to involve parents. Parents who cannot come to school can:

- Launder or mend dress-up clothes from the dramatic play area.
- Collect scrap materials for craft projects.
- Paint or fix school toys that need repair.
- Serve as telephone tree coordinators to facilitate communication regarding meetings or other topics.
- Make instructional materials.
- Arrange field trips.
- Work on parent newsletter.

Parents who are interested in working with children in school could be asked to:

- Assist a small group of children (under the teacher's guidance) with a language game or a short math or science activity.
- Read (or tell) a story or poem.
- Help with art and music activities.
- Be available to talk with and listen to the children as they work.
- Supervise children's activities, such as cooking, caring for pets, or fingerpainting.
- Assist during transition periods by helping with cleanup or preparing for the next activity.
- Help a child with table activities such as counting, seriating, or classifying.
- Take one or two children on short trips in the neighborhood.
- Help with arrival and dismissal times.
- Be available in emergencies (for example, taking a child to the toilet in a hurry, or soothing a child who skins a knee).
- Let the teacher know if any child seems to need special attention.

Teachers who invite parents into the classroom have an obligation to help them learn more about children. One way to do this is to provide opportunities for parents to observe in the classroom before they begin working with children. K. Eileen Allen and Betty Hart (1984) suggest providing parents with a clipboard with a simple observation form as a way to focus observations. Teachers would then arrange time for parents to discuss their observations. Teachers must always respond to parent questions about children, program, or participants' work. Talking with volunteers not only broadens their knowledge about children but also indicates that you value their work.

An orientation meeting can also be provided before parents begin participating with children. During the meeting parents can learn about the program, they can be provided with a schedule of activities, they can go over rules for behavior and the sanctions that are used in class, and they can learn their specific responsibilities (Spodek, 1985). It is far easier to orient parents to the program before they begin to work with children than it is to do so while they are working. It is also important to allow time for parents to talk together informally so that they can become acquainted with one another.

Parent Advisory Groups

Another level of involvement includes parents on advisory or policy committees. At this level parents have input into the educational decision-making process. Advisory committees give advice to teachers, supervisors, and administrators regarding the educational program.

Parent *policy councils* allow parents to make decisions about programs, in contrast to parent *advisory groups*, which provide advice. These councils are generally found in parent cooperative nursery schools and in federally funded preprimary programs such as Head Start (Nedler & McAfee, 1979). The parents in a parent cooperative own the school and so they must be involved in making decisions. Many federal programs, including Head Start, have regulations which require that parents be involved in program decisions.

Center accreditation standards of the National Academy of Early Childhood Programs require parents to be informed about the program and to be welcome as observers and resource people (NAEYC, 1984). Table 8-1 presents the criteria for staff-parent interactions.

Regardless of the level of involvement, when parents participate, both parents and children benefit. Parents and teachers come closer together as teachers learn more about the children's families and parents come to value the school more highly.

Parent Education

Parent education programs are not limited to teaching parents to teach their children. Rather, they range broadly from programs that help parents develop positive self-concepts to programs designed for unwed teen-age mothers. No one

---

TABLE 8-1   Criteria for High-Quality Early Childhood Programs

STAFF-PARENT INTERACTION

GOAL: Parents are well informed about and welcome as observers and contributors to the program.

RATIONALE: Young children are integrally connected to their families. Programs cannot adequately meet the needs of children unless they also recognize the importance of the child's family and develop strategies to work effectively with families. All communication between centers and families should be based on the concept that parents are and should be the principal influence in children's lives.

C-1. Information about the program is given to new and prospective families, including written descriptions of the program's philosophy and operating procedures.

All programs need a written statement of philosophy and goals that is readily available to parents and staff members. Written statements of philosophy and policy do not ensure good communication but they provide a basis for good communication and understanding between parents and staff. Such information enables parents to make an informed decision about the best

(Continued)

TABLE 8-1   (*Continued*)

STAFF-PARENT INTERACTION

possible arrangements for their child. Programs with significant numbers of non-English speaking families need to provide materials in the parents' native language.

C–2. A process has been developed for orienting children and parents to the center which may include a pre-enrollment visit, parent orientation meeting, or gradual introduction of children to the center.

The transition from home to center can be a difficult one and must be planned. There are numerous methods of orientation for both children and parents. The criterion does not require that one particular method be implemented but it does require that an orientation for both children and parents be provided.

C–3. Staff and parents communicate regarding home and center childrearing practices in order to minimize potential conflicts and confusion for children.

Parents have the responsibility for selecting the best possible arrangements for their children. It is very important that parents are informed of the center's philosophy so that they can make an educational choice for their children. It is also important that parents and staff discuss their views on childrearing to minimize potential conflicts and confusion for children. Staff do not capitulate to parent's demands, but they should demonstrate respect for parents as the principal influence in the child's life.

C–4. Parents are welcome visitors in the center at all times (for example, to observe, eat lunch with a child, or volunteer to help in the classroom). Parents and other family members are encouraged to be involved in the program in various ways, taking into consideration working parents and those with little spare time. The center's policy should openly encourage parent involvement. Parents should be free to visit the center unannounced at any time.

C–5. A verbal and/or written system is established for sharing day-to-day happenings that may affect children. Changes in a child's physical or emotional state are regularly reported.

Since verbal systems are not always workable in programs where several staff members interact with children during the day, written systems are often necessary. Such communication systems allow for reporting important information about children to parents and encourage parents to communicate about their children to staff.

C–6. Conferences are held at least once a year and at other times, as needed, to discuss children's progress, accomplishments, and difficulties at home and at the center.

Conferences do not take the place of daily communication but allow opportunities for in-depth discussion of children's development; and for parents to ask questions, express concerns, or make suggestions about the program. Conferences should be scheduled at least annually, but may be called as requested by either parents or staff.

C–7. Parents are informed about the center's program through regular newsletters, bulletin boards, frequent notes, telephone calls, and other similar measures.

Individual programs may be as creative as possible in communication efforts as long as such efforts are seen by parents as effective.

Parent education meetings can put parents in touch with specialists
in the field.

parent education program can meet the needs of all parents. Each teacher or school
should develop programs that reflect the specific needs and interests of their parents.

Alice Honig (1979), referring to a "Parents Bill of Rights," suggests that
parents have the right to:

1. Knowledge about child development.
2. Observation skills for more effective parenting.
3. Alternative strategies for problem solving and discipline.
4. Knowledge about how to use a home for learning experiences with children.
5. Language tools and story reading skills.
6. Awareness of being the most important early teachers of their own children.

These parent rights also suggest some guidelines for parent education
programs. Parents' right to acquire both skill and knowledge means parents need
to have opportunities to learn about children and how to work with children.
Parent education programs should provide information about the child's physical development, social development, emotional development, and cognitive development. They should also help parents develop the skills necessary to work
with their own children. Parent educators should show parents what to do, give
them an opportunity to practice what they should do, and provide feedback on
how well they are performing (Spodek, Saracho, & Lee, 1984). Guided practice is
more likely to bring about change in a parent's behavior than is a lecture.

One form of parent education has been to involve parents in the classroom as volunteers and then to discuss the parents' observations with them. This
gives the parents an opportunity to learn more about children while working

with them. This strategy was used in Head Start as a way to reach the program's objectives. It allows low-income parents to gain skill and confidence while encouraging them to become involved in the classrooms (Travis & Perrault, 1980).

A second way of providing parents with a knowledge base is through the use of family-based programs. These programs, which are set in the child's home, provide professional support to teach the parents how to be effective educators. Alice Honig (1979) refers to family-based programs that can increase the level of consciousness of parents, help them obtain information they need to be effective parents, and make them aware of their importance in their children's lives. Again, in a family-based program parents have the opportunity to refine their skills by doing.

Another form of parent education that has been particularly successful is parent group meetings. Group meetings give parents an opportunity to gain knowledge and to obtain a sense of fellowship that comes from being with others who have similar concerns or needs. Groups can focus on either children's or parents' needs. Some groups have helped parents to gain self-esteem; others have focused on training parents for new job skills.

Jane Hall (1989) reported on a North Carolina center that switched from having two large meetings a year for all parents to a family group approach. Parents were divided into small groups based on the number of children and staff in a classroom. A toddler class that had twelve children and two teachers would have two parent groups, with one staff member being assigned to each group as a facilitator. Each group was autonomous and would arrange their own meeting times and agendas.

The family groups did a variety of things, including generating learning activities for home and center, having its members serve as resource persons in the classroom, and viewing and discussing videotapes of children. The informality of the small group arrangement led to parents feeling comfortable sharing ideas and concerns. The success of the groups was attributed to the parents being involved in activities that they considered to be important.

Group meetings allow parents to develop a sense of fellowship.

An informal way of providing for parent education is to develop a place for parents in the center. If space is available, an area can be set aside with comfortable chairs, a teapot, a bulletin board for announcements, and bookshelves containing books and periodicals on children, families and other interesting topics. When permanent space is not available, a double set of shelves on wheels can become a portable parent center (Kortz, 1984).

The large number of children born to teen-agers in this country has necessitated the development of parent education programs designed for young adults. In 1986, there were 878,500 live births to unmarried women in the United States. Thirty-two percent of these babies were born to mothers who were fifteen to nineteen years of age, and 9 percent were born to mothers who were younger than fifteen (U.S. Bureau of the Census, 1989). Programs for young mothers should focus on nutrition and health care as well as on parenting and child development knowledge. They also have to encourage and help the mother to complete high school.

COMMUNICATING WITH PARENTS

Parents have a right to know about their children's progress. Teachers have a corresponding obligation to respond to parents' requests for information. However, the communication process should not be just one way, from the teacher to the parent. Effective communication requires that both the teacher and the parent send and receive information about the child.

There are at least three good reasons for administrators and teachers to develop good communication links with parents. First, educators must understand the needs and expectations of children and parents if they are going to develop appropriate programs. Second, parents need accurate information if they are going to make sound judgments about how the school is doing. Third, close communication helps to establish public support for the schools (Cattermole & Robinson, 1985).

Communication techniques range from informal to formal, from those that take little time to those that take a great deal of time. They are all important and they all increase parents' and teachers' insight into the nature of the child and his or her learning.

Parents are not as concerned about global generalization as they are about the specific things their own child is doing. Generally, they want to know about:

1. Their child's activities in school.
2. How their child responds to other children.
3. How other children respond to their child.
4. How their child gets along on the playground.
5. What their child likes and dislikes about school.
6. Whether or not the teacher is truly concerned about their child. (Heinz, 1979)

Informal Communication Techniques

Informal techniques are those simple procedures that convey information about what happened during the day or about special situations that have arisen. One informal technique is to greet parents and speak to them briefly when they drop off children in the morning or pick them up in the afternoon. Teachers can find out if Joey had a bad morning or if something happened at home that may affect his behavior. The afternoon provides an opportunity to tell the parents about an interesting event that happened in school or a special milestone that Debbie accomplished that day. These brief encounters can provide important pieces of information. Because these encounters are public, the topics should be ones that are not confidential and that can be discussed in front of the child (Allen & Hart, 1984).

Because some parents may not get any further than the front door, a clothesline hung by the door with a clothespin labeled for each family provides an easy way for parents to access materials such as announcements and newsletters. This technique also provides an easy way of checking to see which families received the messages (Kortz, 1984).

Another type of informal communication is the personal note. By taking the time to write to parents about an important event, you indicate to them that you care about them and their child. Sending notes home with children of this age has an inherent danger: Children may lose the notes before they arrive home. It is a good idea to pin such notes to the children's clothing or tape them to their lunch boxes as they leave for home.

Telephoning parents is another way to communicate with parents. Sometimes calls can be made during the school day, but often they need to be made in the evening. If the topic is such that the child should not be involved, it might be wise to prearrange a time to call or to call after a child is asleep.

Formal Communication Techniques

Formal techniques include all endeavors that have a set agenda and specific theme. Parent conferences, home visits, parent meetings, and newsletters all provide formal ways to communicate information to parents.

Parent Conferences. For many teachers, parent conferences are the least favored way of communicating with parents. It takes time to confer with each parent and even more time to plan for each conference. In addition, teachers may feel threatened by having to report a child's progress to parents in a face-to-face situation.

There are some guidelines for conferences that, if followed, can help make the conference a positive, productive meeting. The first guideline is to use everyday speech that can be understood by parents. Educational terms may not be understood and may intimidate some parents. In addition, if you are meeting with parents who are not fluent in English, it might be helpful to arrange for an interpreter.

Keep in mind that the parent is coming to you for a conference and needs to be made as comfortable as possible in an unfamiliar environment in which you work daily. Be prepared for the conference. Have notes and files on each child as well as children's work samples ready before the parent arrives. Rely on your professional training and ethical standards. Be gentle with parents in commenting on children. Parents identify closely with their children and criticism often implies criticism of the parents as well. Negative comments should be stated in a positive way and qualified, if necessary. Concrete examples are more useful than generalizations in helping parents understand their children. Most important, a complete picture of the child, presenting strengths along with weaknesses, should be offered. Do's and don'ts for parent conferences are presented in Table 8–2.

Parents and teachers are not always going to agree on a single solution to a problem. Parents may feel possessive about their child. Teachers and caregivers may also become attached to children and develop possessive feelings. Many times both sides feel that the other doesn't fully understand the nature of the problem and therefore cannot arrive at a reasonable solution (Galinsky, 1988).

Ellen Galinsky (1988) suggests a six-step approach to teacher–parent problem solving (Table 8–3) that provides for equal input from all parties in resolving conflicts.

TABLE 8-2   Do's and Don'ts for Parent–Teacher Conferences

''DO'S''
Prior to each conference, decide its main purpose.
Have a folder for each child containing dated samples of his/her work, and any anecdotal records you have kept on the child.
Have a positive attitude regarding the conference.
Check that the classroom appears neat and organized.
Begin a conference by reviewing positive aspects of the child's work and/or behavior.
Listen carefully.
Focus on parent and what the parent says.
Be aware of non-verbal as well as verbal cues.
Use language that the parent can understand (avoid jargon).
Personalize your communication with each parent.
Recognize and accept the parent's feelings and attitudes.

''DON'TS''
Don't put the parent on the defensive.
Don't talk about other children or compare this child with other children.
Don't talk about other teachers to the parents, unless the remarks are of a complimentary nature.
Don't belittle the administration or make derogatory remarks about the school.
Don't argue with the parent.
Don't interrupt the parent to make your own point.
Don't go too far with a parent who is not ready and able to understand your purpose.
Don't ask parents personal questions which might be embarrassing.
Don't repeat any confidential information which the parent may volunteer.

TABLE 8-3   Six Steps to Teacher–Parent Problem Solving

1. Describe the situation as a problem out front. Avoid accusations or the implication that the source of the problem resides in the personality of the parent or the child.
2. Generate multiple solutions. Parents and professionals should both do this, and no one's suggestions should be ignored, put down, or denounced.
3. Discuss the pros and cons of each suggestion.
4. Come to a consensus about which solutions to try.
5. Discuss how you will implement these solutions.
6. Agree to meet again to evaluate how these solutions are working so that you can change your approach, if necessary.

Derived from: E. Galinsky, ''Parents and Teacher-caregivers: Sources of Tension, Sources of Support,'' *Young Children, 43*(3), 4–11.

Home Visits.   Home visits follow many of the guidelines for a parent conference. You should arrive at the home on time and you should not overstay your welcome. Forty-five minutes to one hour is a reasonable length of time for a home visit. Limit the discussion to prearranged topics and *listen* to what the parent says. Listening is an important part of any successful communication. It needs to be practiced regularly. In addition, observe the home carefully so that you have a good sense of the setting in which the child is growing up.

TABLE 8-4   Guidelines for Parent Meetings

BEFORE THE MEETING

1. Involve parents in planning the meeting.
2. Establish a convenient time for the meeting.
3. Find a comfortable, convenient place to meet.
4. Announce the topic and format of the meeting well in advance; inform parents of what they should bring.
5. Send out notices of the meeting with return slips.
6. Follow up on parents who do not return slips.
7. Arrange for transportation and baby-sitters if necessary.
8. Check with parents about refreshments.

DURING THE MEETING

9. Start and end the meeting on time.
10. Establish ground rules early (e.g., smoking, breaks, confidentiality).
11. Be flexible in following the agenda.
12. Vary program activities (e.g., discussion, role playing, lecture, film, games).
13. Provide opportunities for everyone to be involved in the discussion.
14. Allow some time for informal interaction at the end of the meeting.

AFTER THE MEETING

15. Make a brief record of what happened.
16. Plan for follow-up activities.

From: B. Spodek, O. N. Saracho, and R. C. Lee. From *Mainstreaming Young Children,* p. 169 © 1984, Wadsworth, Inc. Reprinted by permission of the publisher.

Parent Meetings.   Teachers are often called upon to plan or direct parent meetings. These meetings might be used to orient parents to the schools, providing information about the school's philosophy, school policies, or school rules and procedures. Such a meeting is helpful at the beginning of the school year. Other meetings might be called to tell parents about the program, to show them their children's work, or to answer questions about what the children are doing. Parent meetings are a good vehicle for parent education as well. Experts might be asked to talk about a particular topic, or a film or videotape might be shown, or a discussion might be held.

Teachers need to be aware of the purposes of the meeting and see that the activities are related to that purpose. Resources need to be collected before the meeting and the physical setting arranged to be as comfortable and as helpful as possible. Meetings should be scheduled so that most parents can attend, or the schedule could be varied so that all parents have a chance to attend some meetings. Sometimes it is necessary to provide some form of baby-sitting for parents who don't have a place to leave their children.

In addition to the formal meeting, it is helpful to schedule an informal time when parents can get to know one another and where teachers can chat with them briefly. It is also important that the meeting not take too long. Table 8–4 presents guidelines for parent meetings.

Newsletters.   A periodic newsletter is a good way to inform parents of current school events and to provide them with ideas for working with their own children. Thelma Harms and Deborah Cryer (1978) offer the following purposes for a newsletter:

1. To keep parents informed about current classroom activities.
2. To give parents some insight into the educational purposes underlying instructional activities.
3. To enhance children's and parent's abilities to communicate with each other.
4. To reinforce and extend school learning into the home and family, especially in the area of language development.

TABLE 8-5   Ideas for a Parent Newsletter

1. Describe special events that are happening or will happen in your center.
2. Bring parents up to date about ongoing activities (e.g., how the garden is growing or how the baby guinea pig is doing).
3. Provide parents with activities that they can do at home with their children. Describe very specific activities so parents know exactly what to do.
4. Provide parents with a "talk-about" section discussing children's school activities that can be extended at home. The children enjoy discussing their "work" with parents; a "talk-about" section stimulates communication.
5. Highlight one staff person in each newsletter. Detail his or her background, training, special interests, and experience.
6. Describe special projects that individual children have completed. Be sure to feature each child at some time during the year.
7. Request materials or assistance that you might need.
8. List community services and activities of interest to parents.
9. Provide short descriptions of articles or books that parents may find helpful.

To be most effective, newsletters should be sent home on a regular basis and they should be short enough to be read by busy parents (Hanley, 1980). A two- to three-page newsletter might work well. Table 8–5 offers some suggestions for what to include in a newsletter.

WORKING SUCCESSFULLY WITH PARENTS

Working with parents is an important element in educating young children. In order to do this successfully, teachers must understand and value the beliefs and cultural backgrounds of each family. They must be willing to accept the parents as the final authority in matters relating to their own child, except in cases of abuse and neglect. Teachers must be willing to modify their own program to meet the expectations of parents, while educating parents in relation to what they see as important. Forcing parents to adhere to the value orientation of the teacher often leads to mistrust of teachers' motives and an impression that the teacher feels superior and is insensitive.

Teachers must understand that no two families are alike; each will treat their children differently. There is no single set of behaviors and experiences that leads to optimal child development. Nor is there one body of knowledge that would enable a person to be an effective parent. Any approach to working with parents must take into account the individual differences that occur in any family group. Joseph H. Stevens, Jr. (1980) feels that parent programs should be considered developmental and should be designed to be appropriate for all parents. This is important, since parents function at their own levels of development. Teachers must be able to identify the needs and interests of the parents and plan programs flexibly to include their changing interests and concerns.

Teachers need to be aware of the forces that are affecting family life today. Included in these are:

- Economic forces — the need for two salaries in many families.
- Technological forces — new household utensils and tools changing the nature of housekeeping.
- Political forces — provision of special services for families; concern for child abuse and neglect.
- Social forces — many smaller families, nonnuclear families, high mobility.
- Psychological forces — changing identity of women. (Swick, 1984)

In working with parents, teachers must keep two ideas in mind. The first is that the role of the teacher is not to do something to parents but rather to provide an opportunity for parents to influence as well as to be influenced (Spodek, 1985). Second, the parent–teacher relationship need not be confrontational in nature. Too often inexperienced parents and teachers tend to think the worst of each other. Receiving a note from the teacher requesting a conference frightens many parents. They automatically assume the child is having a problem.

Conversely, many teachers who receive a note or call from a parent requesting a meeting assume that they will be accused of having done something wrong to the child. The more parents and teachers know about each other and the more they work together, the more comfortable and trusting the relationship will become.

SUMMARY

Working with parents is critical to working well with children. In planning a parent program, teachers need to be sensitive to the kinds of families represented in their classroom. Different families will have different needs as well as different ways of responding to the school.

In working with families, teachers need to determine what levels of parent involvement are appropriate for the school and community. Parents might participate in the classroom, serve on various committees, or serve the program in other ways. Teachers must also determine what kind of parent education program is most reasonable.

Teachers must also develop both formal and informal ways of communicating with families. Parent conferences are most useful in communicating with individual parents, but meetings, home visits, newsletters, and informal chats are also helpful. A teacher's insight into the needs of children and families, and the range of options the teacher has available, will determine the success of any parent program.

REFERENCES

ALLEN, K. E., AND B. HART (1984). *The early years: Arrangement for learning*. Englewood Cliffs, NJ: Prentice-Hall.

BRIGGS, B. A. AND C. M. WALTERS (1985). Single-father families: Implications for early childhood educators. *Young Children, 40*(3), 23–27.

CATTERMOLE, J. AND N. ROBINSON (1985). Effective home school communication—from the parents' perspective. *Kappan, 67*(1), 48–50.

CROFT, D. J. (1979). *Parents and teachers: A resource book for home, school and community relations*. Belmont, CA: Wadsworth.

FEENEY, S., D. CHRISTENSEN, AND E. MORAVCIK (1983). *Who am I in the lives of children: An introduction to teaching young children* (2nd ed.). Columbus, OH: Merrill.

GALINSKY, E. (1988). Parents and teacher-caregivers: Sources of tension, sources of support. *Young Children, 43*(3), 4–11.

GORDON, I. J., P. P. OLMSTEAD, R. I. RUBIN, AND J. H. TRUE (1979). How has Follow Through promoted parent involvement: *Young Children, 34*(5), 49–53.

HALL, J. S. (1989). Family groups: A link between parents and preschool. *Dimensions, 17*(4), 4–7.

HANLEY, P. E. (1980). Working parents: Ideas for classroom participation. *Dimensions, 8*(2), 45–47.

HARMS, T. O., AND D. CRYER (1978). Parent newsletter: A new format. *Young Children, 33*(5), 28–32.

HEINZ, R. S. (1979). *Practical methods of parent involvement*. ERIC Document Reproduction Service No. ED 188776.

HONIG, A. S. (1979). *Parent involvement in early childhood education* (2nd ed.) Washington, DC: National Association for the Education of Young Children.

KORTZ, N. (1984). So what are the issues? A survey of teachers, directors, parents. *Beginnings*, Fall, 35–37.

MORGAN, E. L. (1989). Talking with parents when concerns come up. *Young Children, 44*(2), 52–56.

NATIONAL ASSOCIATION FOR THE EDUCATION OF YOUNG CHILDREN (1984). *Accreditation Criteria & Procedures of the National Academy of Early Childhood Programs.* Washington, DC: The Association.

NEDLER, S. E., AND O. D. MCAFEE (1979). *Working with parents: Guidelines for early childhood and elementary teachers.* Belmont, CA: Wadsworth.

RANZONI, P. S. (1984). Places for parents: Providing for mothers and fathers in child care settings. *Beginnings*, Fall, 6–9.

SKEEN, P., B. E. ROBINSON, AND C. FLAKE-HOBSON (1984). Blended families: Overcoming the Cinderella myth. *Young Children, 39*(2), 64–74.

SPODEK, B. (1985). *Teaching in the early years* (3rd ed.) Englewood Cliffs, NJ: Prentice-Hall.

SPODEK, B., O. N. SARACHO, AND R. C. LEE (1984). *Mainstreaming young children.* Belmont, CA: Wadsworth.

STEVENS, J. H., JR. (1980). Our romance with parenting. *Dimensions, 8*(2), 78–81.

SWICK, K. J. (1983). Parent education: Focus on parent needs and responsibilities. *Dimensions, 11*(3), 9–12.

———. (1984). *Inviting parents into the young child's world.* Champaign, IL: Stipes Publishing Co.

TRAVIS, N. E., AND J. PERRAULT (1980). *Day care as a resource to families.* ERIC Document Reproduction Service No. ED 190198.

U. S. BUREAU OF THE CENSUS. (1989). *Statistical abstract of the United States: 1989.* Washington, DC: U. S. Government Printing Office.

WEISS, R. S. (1979). Going it alone: The family life and social situation of the single parent family. New York: Basic Books.

SUGGESTED ACTIVITIES

1. Collect parent newsletters from a number of centers. Compare them as to layout, content, and clarity. Discuss the characteristics that seem to make the most attractive newsletter.

2. Attend a parent orientation session at a child care center. List the topics covered that relate to parent involvement and to parent education. List some of the things that made the meeting effective. Describe how it could have been improved.

3. Interview the director of a Head Start program and the director of a privately owned child care center about their parent education programs. Present your findings by listing the characteristics of one program in column A and the second in column B. Then compare the two columns.

4. Ask a number of parents what schools could do to make parent conferences more beneficial. Then ask a number of teachers the same question. Compare and contrast the responses.

5. Interview a single father about his child care concerns and then interview a single mother using the same set of questions. Discuss their responses in terms of similarities and differences.

9

Evaluation in Early Childhood Programs

OBJECTIVES

After completing this chapter on evaluation in early childhood programs, the student will be able to:

1. Identify and describe the different ways to gather information for evaluating children.
2. Judge the validity of standardized tests for young children.
3. Describe different ways of observing young children that can be used in an early childhood classroom.
4. Design an evaluation plan that reflects important elements of an early childhood program.
5. List the characteristics of a classroom environment that supports educational activities.
6. Describe screening procedures for identifying exceptional children.
7. Record and interpret the results of an evaluation.
8. Identify several ways of reporting to parents about their child's progress.

Evaluation is helpful in making classroom decisions as well as in developing educational policies. Many agencies and organizations use it to improve their performance. It is equally useful to teachers as an aid in improving the education of the children in their classes.

At one time educational evaluation was considered the same as testing. Test scores were used to assess individual children in school, and their performance on a test was used to evaluate the school program. Children's test scores, however, provide only a limited amount of information about a child's performance. Achievement tests do not provide information about children's interests or about how they learn. They are only one narrow method of evaluating learning and have limited use for early childhood classrooms. In addition, we need to know much more than just the children's levels of achievement to evaluate a program.

This chapter describes ways of gathering and analyzing information about children, including different kinds of tests and observations. It discusses the evaluation of classrooms and programs. Forms of screening handicapped children and recording and communicating the results of evaluation are also presented.

WAYS OF GATHERING INFORMATION

An evaluation that provides insight on an entire program (e.g., its rationale, development, operations, achievements, and problems) requires different ways of gathering information. Such an evaluation assesses the school context, the children's learning environment, the teaching method used, and the program's outcomes. It should use a combination of methods, including different types of observations along with standardized and informal tests. Each of these will be discussed separately.

Observations

An observation is a way of gathering information about a situation by looking at and listening to what is happening, then recording it accurately. The observer receives impressions and records ongoing events, just as a camera might. Teachers can use observation to understand what is happening to children in a classroom. A number of observation methods have been developed over the years for these purposes. Olivia Saracho (1983b) describes the different kinds of observation strategies that can be used in an early childhood class, including anecdotal records, rating scales, semantic differential scales, and checklists.

Anecdotal Records. An anecdotal record is a brief account of a situation. By means of words, it draws a picture and provides a factual description of an incident, behavior, or event. Several guidelines should be followed in recording anecdotes:

1. *Descriptions should be specific.* Specific descriptions of what actually happened and the children's reactions, actions, and comments need to be carefully recorded. Care should be taken not to use words that are easily misinterpreted (such as "yelled" or "screamed"). In recording factual descriptions of events, observers much select words or phrases to be used consistently throughout the description. (For example, every time someone talks, the word "said" is recorded.)

2. *The collection of anecdotes should be purposeful.* Although anecdotal records identify unanticipated behaviors, observations should describe specific situations and focus on a selected behavior.

3. *Recordings should be systematic.* A system must be designed to record descriptions of events in order to identify patterns in young children's behavior. For example, a child may be observed during outside play so the teacher can record his or her progress in motor development.

4. *Background information should be provided.* The date, time, child's name, and setting in which the event occurred should be recorded.

Figure 9–1 presents an example of an anecdotal record.

FIGURE 9–1   Anecdotal record.

Child _Ralph Samson_	Age _5 yrs. 1 mo._ Sex _male_
Date _November 21, 1987_ Time _9:15 – 9:30_ (a.m.) p.m.	Setting _Story Hour_
Observer _Janie Smith_	Observation No. _6_

Record exactly what you observe under observations and record any interpretations under interpretations.

Observations	Interpretations
The teacher read the book <u>Snails, Where Are You?</u> Ralph said, "In the book." The teacher said, "Look, very carefully and raise your hand." Ralph did not raise his hand and said, "At the beach." The other children said, "On the cat's tail!" The teacher finished the story, put the book away and told the children to go back to their chairs. Ralph sat on the carpet and would not move until the teacher talked to him and both went together to his chair.	Ralph seems to like to participate in group discussions. He likes to answer questions even if they are not correct. He seems to have trouble following directions and paying attention. He will follow directions, but he requires the attention and assistance of the teacher.

Rating Scales. Rating scales are used for making an estimate of a child's specific behavior or trait. To develop a rating scale, you first identify traits that need to be evaluated. Statements, units, or categories relating to the trait are written as statements on the scale. A teacher or observer can mark along a continuum the extent to which they agree or disagree with a description of that trait or behavior as represented in a child.

Placing equally distanced units, points, numbers, or descriptive statements along a continuum can help an evaluator make the judgment. An odd set of intervals (for example, three or five) are often used in order to provide a neutral midpoint. On a five-point scale, the highest score will be a five while the lowest score will be a one, or vice versa (see Figure 9–2).

Teachers can design a rating scale with as many items as they feel are necessary and appropriate. Each statement needs to be clearly defined and represented by a set of rating units. The teacher observes the behaviors and places a mark on an appropriate point on each rating scale line. Rating scales can easily be used to develop a profile of each child's strengths and needs.

Semantic Differential Scales. A semantic differential scale is similar in many ways to a rating scale. The person using it makes an estimate of a behavior or trait, but makes the estimate by judging where on a scale between two opposite adjectives the individual fits. For example, some pairs of opposite adjectives that could be used to describe a person are "happy–sad," "strong–weak," "reflective–impulsive," "interesting–boring," and "active–passive." Each set would allow the teacher to make a judgment on that particular characteristic.

Each adjective pair is placed at opposite ends of a line. As many as seven equally separate points between the adjectives can then be marked along that line. The observer checks that point on the line that most closely describes the characteristic being assessed in relation to these adjectives. The closer to the end

FIGURE 9-2

STRUCTURED OBSERVATION TECHNIQUES

Examples of rating scales

1. The child engages in cooperative play.

1	2	3	4	5
never	seldom	sometimes	often	always

2. The child likes to look at pictures.

1	2	3
disagree	unsure	agree

FIGURE 9-3

Examples of semantic differential scales

active	—	—	—	—	—	—	—	passive
happy	—	—	—	—	—	—	—	unhappy
misbehaves	—	—	—	—	—	—	—	behaves

of the continuum the mark is made the more strongly the observer considers that particular adjective as describing the behavior or trait (see Figure 9–3).

Checklists. A checklist is a list of items, behaviors, or traits; the teacher is to determine whether these traits exist in a child or not. Behaviors or traits that are essential in learning are used for a checklist to assess young children in a school setting. The observer checks off the presence of the items by placing a check mark or marking a "yes" or "no" next to each item. This is an easy method of assessing behaviors or traits (see Figure 9–4).

Anecdotal Records. Anecdotal records should describe extensively the actions, reactions, statements, and personal cues (such as postures, gestures, and facial expressions) observed. The record of the behavior should be as complete as possible, including people, things, and the physical environment. Teachers who feel overwhelmed by classroom events, and do not have the time to observe and record them, can videotape classroom situations. An older student from another class or a volunteer could be used to run the video camera. The teacher can use planning time to view the videotape and record the events using the observation procedures suggested above.

FIGURE 9-4

Examples of checklists

Check off the presence of each behavior.

_____ 1. Child can categorize objects.

_____ 2. Child looks at books.

Circle a "yes" to indicate the presence of each behavior and circle a "no" to indicate the absence of each behavior.

yes   no   1. Child manipulates objects.

yes   no   2. Child plays in dramatic play area.

Olivia Saracho (1983b) also suggests the following procedures for record keeping:

1. Observations must record pertinent information (e.g., date, time of day, time interval, and place of observation), as well as other information which might have a bearing on the situation—such as weather, unpleasant surroundings and incidental events.
2. The observer must place herself/himself in a location which does not interfere with the classroom activities but allows one to see everything that is relevant.
3. A shorthand system should be developed record the actions in the classroom quickly and clearly. For instance, a circle with an X on the side records a child's location on a round table.

Example:

Before selecting the type of recording technique to be used, it is important to be clear about the purpose for the recording. The technique chosen should be determined by what use is to be made of the record, as well as by which technique will provide the clearest picture of the situation. A class log or diary, for example, can be used to record events of the day. Charts and checklists, on the other hand, can serve as reminders of the extent to which activities and materials were used throughout the day. Table 9–1 summarizes the observation techniques.

Summary. Each observation method above represents a way to systematically assess children's behaviors or traits. They each provide a different kind of information that is helpful in identifying the strengths and needs of a program or an individual child. A more detailed description of observational techniques can be found in the following books:

ALMY, MILLIE, AND CELIA GENISHI (1979). *Ways of studying children* (2nd ed.). New York: Teachers College Press.
BEATTY, JANICE J. (1986). *Observing development of the young child.* Columbus, OH: Merrill.
BENTZEN, WARREN R. (1985). *Seeing young children: A guide to observing and recording behavior.* Albany, NY: Delmar.
BOEHM, ANN E., AND RICHARD A. WEINBERG (1987). *The classroom observer: Developing observation skills in early childhood settings* (2nd ed.). New York: Teachers College Press.
CARTWRIGHT, CAROL A., AND G. PHILIP CARTWRIGHT (1984). *Developing observation skills.* New York: McGraw-Hill.
COHEN, DOROTHY, AND VIRGINIA STERN (1983). *Observing and recording the behavior of young children* (3rd ed.). New York: Teachers College Press.

After all the information is gathered, a report can be written. This can be used as a basis for planning programs or for parent conferences. To facilitate writing the report, sketch rough notes after observing an event. Return to the observation form later and read it to remember any forgotten details. The report can consist of three sections: (1) background comments (e.g., pre-observation impressions, sketches, and comments) that can add to the reader's perceptions of the situation; (2) a detailed description of the report; and (3) a summary.

TABLE 9-1   Selecting the Appropriate Observation Techniques

METHOD	DESCRIPTION
Anecdotal Record	Recording in a narrative form specific behaviors or incidents that illustrate the situation.
Rating Scale	Recording the child's degree of measurement (e.g., development, performance, interest, scaled behaviors).
Semantic Differential	Rate the child on a continuum between differential descriptions of opposites on specific characteristics.
Checklist	Recording the existence or absence of materials, behaviors, etc. It serves as an inventory of materials or expected behaviors to achieve the teacher's educational goals.

Standardized Tests

Standardized tests include a fixed set of items that are carefully developed to evaluate a specifically defined area of achievement. Precise instructions are used in administering and scoring the tests. In addition, standard criteria are established at a national level for such tests, based on the average scores of large numbers of individuals who are similar to those who will be taking the test. These standard criteria or norms allow teachers to compare an individual's test score with those of a representative group who have taken the same test. Thus, they are able to make judgments about that child's performance in relation to all other children's performance. Standardized tests provide a national frame of reference in judging an individual's achievement. The content and procedures that are established for such a test are also standardized. Since an identical test is administered in the same way to all individuals everywhere, comparisons are considered to be valid.

There are several types of standardized tests, including (1) *norm-referenced,* (2) *criterion-referenced,* and (3) *domain-referenced* tests. *Norm-referenced* tests compare the performance of an individual against a group average or norm. These tests are used in a wide range of educational and developmental areas. Such tests allow an objective assessment of achievement or developmental characteristics.

Criterion-referenced tests are specifically constructed to evaluate a person's performance level in relation to some standard. Most teacher-made tests that are used in classrooms are criterion-referenced. The criterion may be knowing how to spell all the words on a list or being able to compare one configuration of blocks with another. There is no group average or norm to which a child's score can be compared.

Domain-referenced tests represent a special case of criterion-referenced testing, which emphasizes the respondent's performance concerning a well-defined level or body of knowledge. Domain-referenced testing is used to describe the content and skills sampled by the test and clearly specify the nature of the tested performance to provide a foundation to evaluate a specified competency (Baker, 1988).

William Goodwin and Laura Goodwin (1982) describe the types of instruments that are available for use in measuring young children. Each standardized test assesses certain elements of school content and academic skills, has different objectives, and uses different testing materials. Even tests with similar titles may be very different from one another. Because of these differences, standardized tests need to be carefully selected by the teacher in relation to the purpose for which the information will be used (Anastasi, 1988; Gronlund, 1981).

The standardized tests that are used in early childhood education usually assess the children's readiness for learning tasks. They measure basic concepts and skills that are important in order for children to achieve what will be expected of them. For example, the *Boehm Test of Basic Concepts* (Psychological Corp., New York, NY) indicates the children's knowledge of verbal concepts (e.g., biggest, nearest, several) that are essential to understand oral communication and gain from school experiences. Children listen to test items read aloud and then mark an X on pictures that indicate the proper response. Similar tests include the *Cooperative Preschool Inventory* (Addison-Wesley Testing Service, Reading, MA), *Stanford Early School Achievement Test* (Psychological Corp., New York, NY), and *Tests of Basic Experience* (CTB/McGraw-Hill, New York, NY), which measure basic concepts and other kinds of preschool learning (for example, knowledge of the child's environment). Although these other tests have a broader scope than the *Boehm Test*, their purpose is essentially the same: to evaluate the children's knowledge of important concepts and skills as well as to identify learning deficiencies.

Reading readiness tests are widely used in preschool, kindergarten, and first grade to determine the children's ability to benefit from reading instruction and to be a basis for grouping for such instruction. Examples of reading readiness tests include the *Metropolitan Readiness Tests* (Psychological Corp., New York, NY) and M*urphy-Durrell Reading Readiness Analysis* (Psychological Corp., New York,

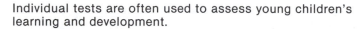

Individual tests are often used to assess young children's learning and development.

NY). These tests attempt to identify whether children have the knowledge and skills needed for beginning reading instruction, but test scores are only one indication of children's readiness to read. They do not provide information about children's mental ability, physical development, experiential background, social and emotional adjustment, or the desire to read. All of these elements are also important for beginning readers (Anastasi, 1988; Gronlund, 1981).

There are some advantages to using standardized tests. The tests are relatively available, so teachers do not have to spend time constructing their own instruments. In addition, test scores can be compared with those of a standard population or a different school. Unfortunately, there are disadvantages as well. Young children often do not respond well to standardized tests. Also, these tests are not available to measure all valued educational outcomes. When programs are evaluated by such tests alone, there is a danger that the tests will determine the curriculum. Other possible dangers in using standardized tests include relying on tests that have no established validity or reliability, and using tests for purposes for which they were not designed (Meisels, 1987). For the best possible assessment, a variety of different kinds of information should be gathered using different kinds of instruments.

For a proper assessment, other kinds of information need to be gathered.

Informal Tests

Another way of gathering information is through informal testing. Informal test scores cannot be compared nationally. The tests are based on what the children are actually being taught in a particular class, and the information can be used directly by a teacher in planning and modifying the instructional program. (See Figure 9-5). Once a teacher determines the purpose for testing children, items related to what they are learning can be developed or selected. For example, informal placement tests can help determine the children's readiness for planned instruction. Informal formative tests given during teaching can be used to gather information about how well children are learning from the activities presented; the results will help to improve and guide the selection of future activities. Informal prescriptive tests can be used to identify what instruction needs to be provided and to plan activities designed to teach to the goals. These tests can also help improve children's performance and identify any learning problems. Informal summative tests are given at the end of a unit of instruction in order to evaluate the degree to which children have achieved the expected learning outcomes (Gronlund, 1981).

Since informal tests are related to the specific goals of a particular class, teachers can use them to determine if they are succeeding in helping the children achieve the educational goals. In developing these tests, teachers must carefully select items that are developmentally appropriate, since no norms are available to provide guidance. Irrelevancies that might influence the children's responses must be eliminated.

FIGURE 9–5 The Following Are Examples of Items That Can Be Included in an Informal Reading Test for Five- or Six-Year-Old Children.

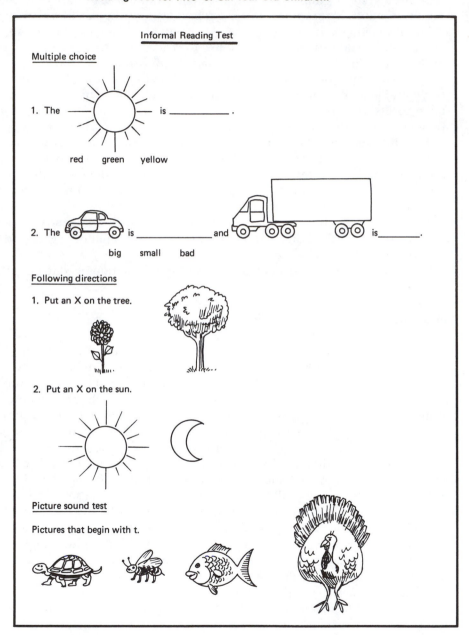

PROGRAM EVALUATION

There is no single early childhood program that meets all the needs of all children or their parents. However, all programs must meet the general needs of the children they serve for good education and care, providing opportunities for children to develop physically, socially, intellectually, and emotionally, and helping them to overcome or cope as well as possible with any handicaps they may have.

Each early childhood program uses its own specific ways to achieve its particular goals. These goals need to be evaluated along with the educational program that is designed to achieve them.

Using test scores to assess the worth of a program is an inappropriate evaluation task. Instead, all components of a program must be considered. Olivia Saracho (1983a) suggests that a wide range of information sources, including observations, dialogue, anecdotes, interviews, slides, photographs, samples of children's works, students' logs, audio tapes, videotapes, films, group discussion sessions, and conferences, can be used to look at the worth, effectiveness, practicality, and other attributes of the program. This type of evaluation appraises all of the elements in the program.

In evaluating the worth of a program, it is important to consider the way it creates its effects and the way it defines the parameters that influence its effectiveness, and to obtain insights into the students' educational learning (Saracho, 1987).

Bernard Spodek (1975) has suggested that each program be evaluated on the basis of its *worth, practicality,* and *effectiveness.* The program's worth depends on its underlying values. These may be made explicit, or they may have to be extracted by one's identifying the program's priorities. Information on the program's practicality can be gathered by examining the way a program works and identifying the resources it uses. An assessment of student outcomes can provide one type of information on the program's effectiveness.

A careful evaluation plan can guide teachers in understanding the important elements of an early childhood educational program and how these elements operate within their specific context. It should include an analysis of all components of the program. One way to get at such an understanding is through *responsive evaluation* (Stake, 1976), which focuses on actual program experiences rather than on what the program intends to do. Responsive evaluation looks at "what people do naturally." Information about the program is gathered through observations, interviews, and reactions. The perceptions and values of individuals are observed; records are examined. The report of such an evaluation may be presented formally or informally, orally or in writing, and in a variety of forms. It might consist of brief narratives, portrayals, product displays, or graphs, depending on the needs of the audience. (Saracho, 1983a).

An early childhood program evaluation may also focus on the success of different types of curriculum, such as one based on applied behavior analysis. Some teachers have difficulty evaluating their early childhood curriculum, lacking the background or competence to do it by themselves. They can work with an evaluator who has the particular expertise necessary. Since teachers are the ones who implement the program and thus have the practical knowledge of their classroom and their children, their judgments provide important and practical information that should be included in any evaluative process (Saracho, 1983a; Spodek, 1985).

Huber Walsh (1980) believes that all teachers can formulate effective strategies for assessing children's learning if (1) the learning objectives are stated clearly and accurately, and (2) the teachers have a rudimentary knowledge of evaluation techniques.

Teachers who work with children under six years of age should limit the use of pencil-and-paper testing. Instead, they should use more informal evaluation techniques such as observations, structured interviews, and analysis of children's products. These techniques can be used to evaluate the total early childhood program or just a specific area such as language arts, mathematics, or dramatic play.

In evaluating a literacy program for a group of three-year-old children, teachers can check to see if the children are attentive while listening to stories, if they can describe things in pictures, and if they can remember the sequence of events. Teachers can also note if the children ask to see the pictures relating to a story or repeatedly ask for a particular book or one on a particular topic. Olivia Saracho (1984) suggests that the way young children feel about reading may be as important as their reading skills in getting ready to learn to read. She developed a checklist teachers can use to determine how children feel about reading.

The evaluation of young children's learning experiences should include both *feedforward* and *feedback* dimensions. Feedforward is a preliminary assessment, an evaluation of the children's knowledge about the topic, setting, and objectives before a topic is introduced. Feedback is a final evaluation, referring to the children's responses after a learning activity. It provides information on how well the children have learned and what else they need to learn about a specific topic. These processes are similar to what is called *formative evaluation* and *summative evaluation*.

Formative evaluation consists of frequent judgments that are made while an activity is taking place, whereas summative evaluation refers to the overall worth of an activity and is usually made at the completion of the activity to be evaluated. These judgments are designed to improve the ongoing activity (Scriven, 1967).

EVALUATING CLASSROOM SETTINGS

The classroom environment is composed of objects and people organized into some relationship with one another. This environment is deliberately designed to support activities that the teacher values and that are expected to lead to learning outcomes. If teachers know about the characteristics of a classroom environment, they can act on this information and change the environment to improve a program's effectiveness.

Children react to all aspects of a classroom environment—the physical environment, the interpersonal environment, the activities, and the time schedule. The physical environment communicates many messages, including those about the kind of child–teacher and child–child relationships that are valued in the classroom. For example, when chairs are placed in a circle, they communicate the expectation of child–child learning interactions. The interpersonal environment should be warm and accepting. The environment should also include challenging and complex activities. In addition, long periods of unbroken time should be provided to enable children to become deeply involved in the activities.

Each setting must be individually assessed in relation to the unique combination of children, facilities, and staff. Thelma Harms (1979) has developed an evaluation checklist that consists of questions organized into four categories: physical environment, interpersonal environment, activities to stimulate development, and schedule. Rating the environment in relation to these questions allows teachers to become more aware of the setting. The following are examples of each:

The Physical Environment

1. Can quiet and noisy activities go on without disturbing one another? Is there an appropriate place for each?
2. Is a variety of materials available on open shelves for the children to use when they are interested? Are materials on shelves well spaced for clarity?

The Interpersonal Environment

1. Is there a feeling of mutual respect between adults and children; children and children?
2. Do children feel safe with one another?

Activities to Stimulate Development

1. Are there many opportunities for dramatic play indoors and outdoors: large housekeeping corner, small dollhouse, work-related props, dress-up clothes for boys as well as girls?
2. Is there a variety of basic visual art media: painting, drawing, clay, salt-flour dough, wood-glue sculpture, fingerpaint, collage?

Schedule

1. Is the time sequence of the school day clear to both teachers and children?
2. Has the schedule been designed to suit the physical plant and particular group of children in the school?

Harms' checklist has proven helpful to many teachers. Other, more direct systems of observing the environment can also help determine an early childhood program's quality and its effects on children. Ilse Mattick and Frances J. Perkins (1973) provide a set of observation guidelines containing three major categories: (1) physical setting, including spatial structure (use of space), materials, and temporal structure (timing); (2) interactional setting (relationships), including teacher–child, child–child, staff, and teacher–parent interactions; and (3) program, including curriculum content, teaching strategies, and socioemotional climate. The following are examples of items from their guidelines:

Physical Setting. The guidelines take into consideration ways in which the physical environment provides for each child's developmental progress in physical, social, cognitive, and affective areas.

Spatial Structure (use of space)

Are facilities and adequate, both inside and outdoors, in terms of numbers and ages of the children and the number of hours they spend at the center?

Materials

What specific materials are there in activity areas that indicate intended use of the area?

Temporal Structure (timing)

Is the sequence of different segments of the day's program clear and comprehensible to the observer (without having to ask)?

Interactional Setting. The guidelines take into consideration relationships regarding a variety of learning that can occur only in an environment of trust, pleasurable involvement, and support for autonomy.

Teacher–Child

Note the teacher's facial expression as he or she talks and reads to children or engages them in learning projects. (Animated, impassive, "bored to tears," angry?)

Child–Child

What kinds of overtures do the children make to each other? How are these responded to? Can give-and-take encounters be observed frequently? Is there conversation between children?

Staff

Do individual staff members give evidence of being responsible for particular children?

Teacher–Parent

How many parents are involved in the instructional or caretaking aspects of the program?

Program. The guidelines take into consideration ways in which the program helps children to increase their understanding of self, other people, and the world around them and to be able to act upon this understanding.

Curriculum Content

Describe (a) a water play sequence, (b) a cooking project, (c) a discussion guided by the teacher, and (d) a music period. (What learning is going on? Which educational goals are being met?)

Teaching Strategies

Does the teacher guide different children toward different activities for specific reasons (e.g., hammering for a restless child, table games for a timid, inhibited child on a certain day)?

Socioemotional Climate

How are good working and learning conditions ensured? (e.g., Do children have minimal interference with the activities, get the supplies they need in order to follow through on a project, etc.?)

Teachers must be concerned with the quality of the physical setting in early childhood education because of its effects on their interactions with young children. Both the degree of creativity and the opportunity for discovery provided in the classroom environment are directly related to the number and types of elements in it. For example, research has shown that young children's preferences for toys and the kinds of social interaction they display depend on the kinds of materials provided to the children and on the opportunities available to carry out activities without disruptions or distractions. Elizabeth Phyfe-Perkins (1980) offers the following criteria for judging educational toys:

1. *Holding power, attention span, and social value of materials.* Children interact with a variety of materials in different ways. They prefer to use some materials more often and to be involved with some activities for longer periods of time. These social interactions among children differ with the materials.

2. *The variety and complexity of materials related to an overall index of space quality.* Each play material differs in its play potential. Play equipment can be analyzed, according to Elizabeth Prescott (1978), by level of complexity, the variety, and the quantity for each child. Simple materials can be used only one way and do not have subparts. Complex units (such as a play house with furniture or a water table with equipment) have subparts or require the juxtaposition of the different kinds of material, permitting children to improvise and manipulate. Super complex units require three or more types of materials (such as water and measuring equipment added to the sandbox, boxes and boards for use with the jungle gym). A more complex unit provides children with more choices as they play. Complexity sustains attention and promotes dramatic play and social interaction. According to Elizabeth Prescott (1978), complexity, variety, and amount to do for each

child, influence such young children's behaviors as attention span, group participation, dramatic play, nondisruptive free choice of activities, and goal-directed
behaviors.

3. *The amount, type, and display of materials as they influence children's behavior.*
Deciding which behaviors must be fostered depends on educational philosophy
and values. The type of materials provided for young children is important to
increase their attention, to facilitate their social interaction, and to elicit their
cognitive play modes. Raw materials (clay, sand, blocks) are popular; sand and
clay encourage solitary and parallel play as well as functional cognitive levels of
play. A number of different materials can provide a purposeful activity, and a
sufficient number of play spaces must be available for each child in order to
promote the flow of children from one activity to another during play. An appropriate amount of materials encourages positive behavior in children who are
required to follow a rigid schedule of activities.

To evaluate an early childhood program, a teacher needs to access the
classroom environment from the children's point of view. Children respond to
the total setting: the way people treat them, the materials that are available on
the shelf, the space available in the play areas. Everything in the classroom, including the spatial arrangement and the materials available, communicates to
children what is valued. The teacher's way of speaking, as well as the teacher's
gestures and even the pace of walking, are part of the overall setting. The children's interactions with adults and other children are also important elements
of the preschool setting. Since the preschool setting provides strong messages to
young children, it must be evaluated and modified as necessary to provide a high-
quality learning environment.

SCREENING EXCEPTIONAL CHILDREN

Sometimes teachers identify particular problems in a child beyond those usually
found in a regular class of children. If the teacher's assessment suggests a serious
handicap, the teacher should request the assistance of a specialist to make additional assessments. For example, a speech-and-communication disorders specialist could be called in to assess communication skills, examining the child's ability
both to articulate sounds and to use normal communication procedures. The
teacher and the specialist can then discuss specific problems and, together with
a team including parents and others, can develop an individual educational plan
for the child. Specialists may suggest activities for the teacher to use in class. They
may also provide special activities for the child outside of class.

The teachers' observations can help to develop a problem list to serve as
a focus of the assessment. This list may contain a series of questions, and the
responses from the specialist would help them make plans for working with the
child. For example, if a teacher's classroom observation indicates that a child's
leg movements seem impaired, the teacher may want to ask the physical therapist
the following questions:

A variety of screening devices are used to identify handicaps in children.

1. What is the extent of the child's impairments?
2. How will the child's leg movements affect his or her other skills (such as walking)?
3. What type of skills will the child be able to perform?
4. What types of activities should be planned for this child?
5. Who should be involved in working with this child?
6. What precautions need to be taken to safeguard the child?

Once information is gathered, a program needs to be developed by a team, including, in the above instance, the teacher and the physical therapist. The therapist might work with the child regularly for a period of time. The teacher could supplement this treatment with additional activities within the regular class. Educational activities might be combined with leg exercises, for example, through movement exploration, games, and creative dramatics. The progress of the treatment would be continually assessed.

Teachers need to assess the instructional program they are offering to be sure they are meeting the needs of both their handicapped and nonhandicapped children. Evaluation can help teachers judge the effects of any modifications they make in the instructional program and can help to improve educational services for all children, including exceptional students.

RECORDING AND COMMUNICATING THE RESULTS OF THE EVALUATION

Information collected about each child in class should be regularly and systematically recorded. Carefully maintained records help teachers plan the child's instructional program and assist in individualizing instruction by identifying further learning possibilities, assessing individual growth, determining the child's personal characteristics, and planning for materials and resources needed to enrich the instructional program.

Teachers need to keep their students' records up to date, including those that document diagnostic-prescriptive processes, checklists related to particular performance areas, and work plans developed for the child, which might contain goals, objectives, materials, procedures, and evaluations. For the exceptional child, the resource team should check and discuss these records at regular intervals.

It is the teacher's responsibility to evaluate carefully the instructional program designed for every child. The most expert consultant can make a mistake about a remediating procedure. The teacher's assessment can also monitor the effects of a special procedure or an entire program designed to eliminate or reduce a child's problem. The teacher should consider the information that is on file and organize it to present to others in a comprehensive report about the child.

Reporting to Parents

Reporting on the evaluation of children is an important element in an early childhood program. The five methods that are most often used are informal reports, individual conferences, report letters, check sheets, and report cards (Decker & Decker, 1988). Report cards are seldom used in early childhood classes. The first two of these elements are also described in the discussion of parent programs in Chapter 8.

Informal Reports. Informal reports are usually provided in early childhood programs. They include casual conversations with parents in which the staff member discusses something about the child, such as the child's learning to skip, language development, vocabulary building, or self-care skills such as buttoning a sweater.

Individual Conferences. Individual conferences are usually scheduled with the children's parents, providing face-to-face contact. Teachers need to plan intensively for a successful conference. A letter should be sent explaining the purpose of the conference and inviting parents to make appointments during specified times. A schedule of appointments should be made and each appointment confirmed. A place for the conference should be identified and a waiting area provided for parents who arrive early. A baby-sitter may be needed for parents with younger children.

A guide sheet is helpful in planning a conference on children's progress. It can include an outline of what will be covered at the conference. While teachers should focus on the most important items, they should also present a picture of the whole child. Teachers must examine records on the child, and carefully transfer to the guide sheet all of the information that needs to be shared with the parents. A copy of the guide sheet can be given to parents.

Supplementary material should also be made available during a conference. Samples of children's work can be collected that represent all or most developmental areas, and these can be shown to parents to offer a fuller picture of their children's progress. The last step of the conference is to summarize it. After the conference the teacher should write a report of the conference to keep in the child's file.

Report Letters.   Writing individual letters can be burdensome. Therefore, report letters are usually designed as a form that can be used for each child. Several headings may be used, such as psychomotor learning, personal-social adjustment, cognitive development, language growth, work habits, problem solving, aesthetics, and self-reliance. Whatever headings are used, teachers should be sure that all parents understand their meaning. Teachers can record brief comments about a child's progress under each heading. In using report letters, teachers are able to concentrate on a child's specific strengths and needs without recording letter grades or satisfactory/unsatisfactory ratings. Individual report letters take a lot of time to complete, and teachers need to be careful not to stereotype their comments after writing the first few letters.

Check Sheets.   Check sheets contain checklists of expected achievements. Teachers check off the child's development of a particular skill or concept. While check sheets can be one of the methods of reporting, they should not be the only means of reporting. They are generally most helpful when shown to parents during an individual conference or when enclosed in a report card or letter.

SUMMARY

Evaluation helps teachers make judgments about the programs they are offering and about their children's learning and development. A number of different techniques can help teachers gather and record information about children and about their classroom. Once this information is recorded, it can be compared over time to assess the children's progress and the program's appropriateness. The results of evaluations can be communicated to parents and to others.

Although the pressures on children to achieve are not as strong at the preschool level as at the elementary school level, it is essential that parents work with teachers to evaluate their children's progress. Teachers must consider the progress of each child as they keep in mind that there are differences in parents from group to group. Reports should be presented based on the needs and interests of the parents and the extent of their participation in preschool activities. For a group of parents not familiar with the evaluation process, the report may include a brief, encouraging note at the end of the year to increase parental pride, parental appreciation of the child, and parental participation in preschool group activities.

REFERENCES

ANASTASI, A. (1988). *Psychological testing* (6th ed.). New York: Macmillan Publishing Company.

BAKER, E. L. (1988). Domain-referenced tests. In J. P. Keeves (Ed.), *Educational research, methodology, and measurement: An international handbook,* pp. 370–372. New York: Pergamon Press.

BERK, R. A. (1988). Criterion-referenced tests. In J. P. Keeves (Ed.), *Educational research, methodology, and measurement: An international handbook,* pp. 365–370. New York: Pergamon Press.

DECKER, C. A., AND J. R. DECKER (1988). *Planning and administering early childhood programs* (4th ed.). Columbus, OH: Merrill.

GOODWIN, W. AND L. D. GOODWIN (1982). Measuring young children. In B. Spodek (Ed.), *Handbook of research in early childhood education,* pp. 523–563. New York: Free Press.

GRONLUND, N. E. (1981). *Measurement and evaluation of teaching.* New York: Macmillan.

HARMS, T. (1979). Evaluating settings for learning. In D. W. Hewes (Ed.), *Administration: Making programs work for children and families,* p. 187–190. Washington, DC: National Association for the Education of Young Children.

HARTER, S., AND B. J. BUDDING, (1987). *Children's understanding of the simultaneity of two emotions: A developmental acquisition sequence.* Paper presented at the biennial meeting of the Society for Research in Child Development, Detroit.

HARTUP, W. W., B. LAURSEN, M. I. STEWART, AND A. EASTENSON (1988). Conflict and the friendship relations of young children. *Child Development, 59,* 1590–1600.

HELMS, D. B., AND J. S. TURNER (1981). *Exploring child behavior.* New York: CBS College Publishing.

HUNT, J. McV. (1961). *Intelligence and experience.* New York: Ronald Press.

ILG, F. L., L. B. BATES, AND S. M. BAKER (1981). *Child behavior: Specific advice on problems of child behavior.* New York: Barnes and Noble Books.

IZARD, C. E., E. A. HEMBREE, AND R. R. HUEBNER (1987). Infants' emotion expressions to acute pain: Developmental change and stability in individual difference. *Developmental Psychology, 23,* 105–113.

IZARD, C. E., AND C. Z. MALATESTA (1987). Perspectives on emotional development: 1. Differential emotions theory of early emotional development. In J. D. Osofsky (Ed.), *Handbook of infant development* (2nd ed.), pp. 494–554. New York: Wiley.

KAGAN, J. (1966). *A developmental approach to conceptual growth.* In H. J. Klausmeier and C. W. Harris (Eds.), *Analysis of concept learning,* pp. 97–116. New York: Academic Press.

KESSEN, W. (1965). *The Child.* New York: John Wiley & Sons.

KLAUSMEIER, H. J., AND P. S. ALLEN (1978). *Cognitive development of children and youth: A longitudinal study.* New York: Academic Press.

LANGER, J. (1969). *Theories of development.* New York: Holt, Rinehart & Winston.

LEWIS M., AND L. MICHAELSON (1983). *Children's emotions and moods: Developmental theory and measurement.* New York: Plenum Press.

MAIER, H. W. (1978). *Three theories of child development* (3rd ed.). New York: Harper & Row.

MALATESTA, C. Z., C. CULVER, J. R. TESMAN, AND B. SHEPARD (1989). The development of emotion expression during the first two years of life. *Monographs for the Society for Research in Child Development, 54*(Serial No. 219), pp. 1–2.

MALINA, R. M. (1982). Motor development in the early years, In S. G. Moore and C. R. Cooper (Eds.), *The young child: Reviews of research,* Vol. 3. Washington, DC: National Association for the Education of Young Children.

MATSUMOTO, D., N. HAAN, G. YABROVE, P. THEODOROU, AND C. C. CARNEY (1986). Preschoolers' moral actions and emotions in prisoner's dilemma. *Developmental Psychology,* *22,* 663–670.

MATTICK, I., AND F. J. PERKINS (1973). *Guidelines for observation and assessment: An approach to evaluating the learning environment of a day care center.* Washington, DC: The Day Care and Child Development Council of America.

McCANDLESS, B. R., AND E. D. EVANS (1973). *Children and youth: Psychosocial development.* Hinsdale, IL: The Dryden Press.

McCANDLESS, B. R., AND R. J. TROTTER (1977). *Children: Behavior and development.* New York: Holt, Rinehart & Winston.

MEISELS, S. J. (1987). Uses and Abuses of developmental screening and school readiness testing. *Young Children, 42*(2), 7–8.

PHYFE-PERKINS, E. (1980). Children's behavior in preschool settings—A review of research concerning the influence of the physical environment. In L. G. Katz (Ed.), *Current topics in early childhood education,* Vol. 3, pp. 91–125. Norwood, NJ: Ablex.

PRESCOTT, E. (1978). Is day care as good as home? *Young Children, 33*(2) 13–19.

SARACHO, O. N. (1983a). New dimensions in evaluating the worth of a program. *Education, 103*(1), 74–78.

———. (1983b). Using observation techniques to plan inservice education. *Child Care Information Exchange,* 14–16.

———. (1984). Using observation to assess young children's reading attitudes. *Reading Horizons, 25*(1), 68–71.

———. (1987). An instructional evaluation study in early childhood education. *Studies in Educational Evaluation, 13,* 163–174.

———. (1988). A study of the roles of early teachers. *Early Child Development and Care, 38,* 43–56.

SCRIVEN, M. (1967). The methodology of evaluation. In R. Stake (Ed.), *AERA Monograph Series on Curriculum Evaluation,* No. 1, pp. 37–83. Chicago: Rand McNally.

SPODEK, B. (1975). *Evaluating teacher education.* Paper presented at the annual Conference of the National Association for the Education of Young Children, Dallas.

———. (1985). *Teaching in the early years* (3rd ed.). Englewood Cliffs, NJ: Prentice-Hall.

STAKE, R. E. (1976). *Evaluating educational programmes: the need and the response: A collection of resource materials.* Paris: Organisation for Economic Cooperation and Development.

WALSH, H. M. (1980). *Introducing the young child to the social world.* New York: Macmillan.

SUGGESTED ACTIVITIES

1. Observe and compare two play areas for young children. List the characteristics you would evaluate.

2. Observe a preschool or kindergarten class and identify specific examples of appropriate and inappropriate uses of evaluation methods. Describe the evaluative situation and the role of the early childhood teacher in each situation.

3. Interview a school principal. Ask him to describe how standardized tests are used in the school's kindergarten. Suggest alternative assessment procedures that could be used.

4. Interview a school psychologist concerning the value and the confidentiality of records. Discuss professional ethics and the dangers involved when a child's file is used inappropriately.

5. Develop a checklist to assess the physical environment of a classroom.

6. Develop and use an informal test on reading or language for a group of young children.

7. Observe an all-day preschool program and write an anecdotal record of one child in the early morning and another of the same child in the late afternoon. Compare the child's behavior at both times.

8. Construct a semantic differential scale to assess the extent to which you have achieved the objectives of this chapter.

10

Play in Early Childhood Education

OBJECTIVES

After completing this chapter on play in early childhood education, the student will be able to:

1. Define play.
2. Distinguish between classical and dynamic theories of play.
3. List several criteria to identify play.
4. Describe the classical theories of play.
5. Compare stages in play development.
6. Describe and compare ways to support outdoor play.
7. Describe and compare ways to support indoor play.
8. Develop outdoor play activities.
9. Develop indoor play activities.

From the time when special programs were first developed for young children, there has been a belief that play is the way that these children learn. Not all early childhood programs include play as a learning activity, however. While traditional Montessori programs provide environments to support a wide range of manipulative activities, Montessori activities are considered work rather than play. In addition, fantasy activities, dramatic play, and activities that nurture creative expression are not a part of traditional Montessori programs. There are also programs for young children consisting of direct instruction that do not view play as a form of learning. These programs focus primarily on academic achievement and exclude play activities except as a form of relaxation from the work the children do. Even when the activities are in the form of games, they may not meet the criteria for play that we present in this chapter. Barring these exceptions, however, most early childhood programs contain a significant amount of play activities. Teachers consider these to be an important part of the education of young children.

This chapter discusses definitions and theories of play. It also describes ways of developing play activities and supporting indoor and outdoor play.

DEFINING PLAY

Play as a phenomenon has intrigued educators, psychologists, philosophers, and others for many decades. They have tried to define it, explain it, understand it, and see it in relation to other activities in which humans engage. Play has been a particularly difficult concept to understand because it appears in so many different forms. In addition, play is not only an activity of young children but of adults and nonhuman animals. In this chapter we deal with play only in relation to the activities of young children.

We see play so regularly in our lives that we have no problem identifying it, although there are times when we are not sure when someone is serious or "merely playing." It is not an easy matter, however, to spell out exactly what makes an activity play and what makes it nonplay, that is, work or serious activity.

Often we define play in terms of what it is not. Helen B. Schwartzman (1978), for example, states:

> Play is not work; play is not real; play is not serious; play is not productive; and so forth. . . . [Yet] work can be playful while sometimes play can be experienced as work; and likewise, players create worlds that are often more real, serious and productive than so-called real life. (pp. 4–5)

You will note that even a serious scholar can sometimes have trouble in formally separating work from play.

One possible explanation for this confusion is the fact that play and work are not concepts that can be identified in an all-or-none manner. Often activities will be "more work" or "more play." Eva Neumann (1971) has identified criteria that can help us in judging the nature of an activity as more work or more play. Neumann's criteria for play include *inner control, inner reality,* and *intrinsic motiva-*

tion. To the extent that children control their own activities rather than being subjected to the control of outsiders, the activity may be considered play. To the extent that the child allows fantasy to operate rather than being limited by the outer reality of the situation, the activity may be play. And to the extent that the child is motivated to engage in the activity for its own sake rather than for some external reward, the activity may be play.

In a similar vein, Kenneth Rubin, Greta Fein, and Brian Vandenberg (1983), after reviewing definitions of play, suggest that most definitions identify play by the state of mind of those who are playing. A person's motives for being involved in an activity provide a clue to whether they are playing or not. We need to consider also the individual's concern for goals, concern with the material involved in the activity, and concern for rules and for other elements. They suggest, then, that play can be identified by the following criteria:

1. Play is personally motivated by the satisfaction embedded in the activity and not governed either by basic needs and drives or by social demands.
2. Players are concerned with activities more than with goals. Goals are self-imposed and the behavior of the players is spontaneous.
3. Play occurs with familiar objects, or following the exploration of unfamiliar objects. Children supply their own meanings to play activities and control the activity themselves.
4. Play activities can be nonliteral.
5. Play is free from rules imposed from the outside, and the rules that do exist can be modified by the players.
6. Play requires the active engagement of the players.

Understanding Play

There have been a number of theories developed to explain play. J. Barnard Gilmore (1971) identified some of these theories, including the following classical theories of play:

1. The *relaxation theory* suggests that play serves to restore the energy we use up during work. Thus, after a period of sustained work we need a period of play in which we can relax. During that time we generate and store enough energy so that we may resume work once more.
2. The *surplus energy theory* suggests that, as organisms, we generate energy continually. Most of that energy is used up by working. When we have energy left over beyond what we need for work, we rid ourselves of it by playing.
3. The *recapitulation theory* suggests that individuals go through stages in their personal development that are similar to the stages we have gone through in the development of the human race. Play is an instinctive way of getting rid of primitive skills and drives that have been carried over through the epochs of civilization through heredity. By allowing a person to move through these primitive stages, play allows the child to become prepared for the activities of modern life.

4. The *preexercise theory* suggests that play is an instinctive way of preparing children for the activities of adult life. Young children's play activities parallel the activities they will engage in as adults. In this way, play allows the child to practice skills that will be important in adult life.

The first two of these theories seem to have a ring of truth to them. We ourselves often become tired at the end of a week of work. The weekend gives us a chance to relax and store up enough energy to allow us to face the serious tasks of a Monday morning. Similarly, if we watch a class of children after a long spell of bad weather, we seem to feel their pent-up energy. The energy that was not used in vigorous outdoor activities seems to build up. We will probably find the teacher looking for ways to help the children rid themselves of their excess energy.

Early theories of child development were built upon the recapitulation theory. It was attractive to think of the young child maintaining continuity with the entire human race. Play provided the link between the young child, the new generation, and the oldest generations of mankind. Children's play did seem primitive when compared with how adults functioned.

Play also seems to have a preexercise function. If you walk through a toy store, or the toy department of a larger store, you see toys that are simplified miniature replicas of what adults use in their lives. There are rows and rows of dolls and miniature homemaking equipment. There are mechanics' tool sets, doctor kits, toy typewriters, and many other playthings that reflect adult reality. These toys allow the children to engage in activities that parallel those of adults. In many ways the world of child's play does seem to serve as preparation for the world of adult work.

Despite the fact that there is a certain attraction to each of these theories, none of them is adequate in helping to explain children's play. Other theories have evolved within the last several decades to help us understand what happens in children's play and what occurs as the result of this play. These include the following:

The *psychodynamic theory* of play has its roots in the psychoanalysis of Sigmund Freud. According to Freud, play allows children to express and get rid of fears and anxieties by bringing them to a level of consciousness and having them expressed in play. Children use the fantasy of play to deal with those parts of reality that they cannot deal with directly. Problem situations are scaled down in play. At the smaller, simpler play level children may be able to handle problems that cannot be handled on a larger scale, or situations can be changed in play so that they can be mastered. Because of the way play is used by children to express conflicts and problems, psychoanalysts are able to use play as a form of therapy. The language of play serves the same function that verbal language serves for adults in psychoanalysis.

Constructivist theory is rooted in the work of Jean Piaget. Piaget viewed the development of knowledge in children as being created by two complementary processes. One process, called *assimilation,* allows the individual to take in information that is gained as a result of experiences. As that information is fit into the individual's already developed sense of understanding, it is considered to be assimilated or absorbed. Sometimes new information cannot be fit into an existing framework of understanding; it may be in conflict with what a person seems to know or it may contradict past understandings. As a result, people are required to change their way of viewing and understanding the world: They must become involved in *accommodation,* changing their sense of what they know in relation to the new information. They create a new balance or *equilibrium.* Play is a way of taking in information from the outside world and working that information through so that it fits with a person's already developed scheme of understanding.

Other theories also exist that help explain various aspects of children's play. According to Vygotsky (1967), play is helpful in the development of language and thought. Mental structures are formed through the use of signs and tools, and play helps in this formation. Play also frees the child from the constraints of the real world that surrounds the child. In this way play gives children greater control over a situation than they would have in reality. Children play with meanings as well as with objects as a result of being freed from reality. They are thus allowed to engage in higher-order thought processes through play.

Jerome Singer (1973) views imaginative play as children's efforts to use their physical and mental abilities in an effort to organize their experiences. Play, according to Singer, is used by children to explore the world, to develop competence in dealing with the world, and to develop creativity.

Michael Ellis (1973) seeks to understand play as a form of information processing. He suggests that human beings normally are mentally active. They continually work at making sense out of the information they gather. If the individual has too much or too little information to process, there is an uncomfortable feeling, and a proper balance needs to be created. Thus, we stop paying attention to some things in our environment that seem overwhelming. We also daydream when we get bored, that is, when too little information is coming our way. The young child uses play as a way of creating that balance. The child can create information internally through fantasy play.

Robert White's theory of competence motivation has also been used to explain some things about children's play. Children require no rewards for playing; they play for play's sake. White (1959) suggests that children gain personal satisfaction from feeling competent. Being able to do something well or having an impact on the surrounding world carries its own rewards. Play serves as a way that children can act on their own in an effective manner. Thus, play activities are themselves rewarding.

While no one of these theories alone explains all about children's play, when taken together they can be used to help us understand that play serves many functions. Play is an activity that children engage in naturally; they do not need to be prodded to play. Play is useful to children in helping them understand and express the world, both at a thinking level and at a feeling level. Play gives children a sense of mastery or control over some aspects of their world. Play involves the use of symbols, actions, or objects that stand for something other than themselves. Because play is not tied to reality, it allows flights of fancy in children that are as important in the development of their understandings as in the development of their creativity.

Gender Differences in Play

For years, those who have studied the play of young children have observed that the play of girls is different in many ways from that of boys. Some suggest that these differences are a function of the nature of being male or being female and are genetically determined. Others say the differences are the results of being treated differently from the moment of birth. For example, a baby girl will be given a doll as a present while a young boy will be given a ball. It is quite possible that both explanations have some truth to them. More and more developmental psychologists are finding gender differences in children's functioning even from birth. At the same time, we are learning that the way that we treat boys and girls and the expectations we have for them shapes their behavior so that they become more alike or different.

In reviewing the research on gender difference, James E. Johnson, James F. Christie and Thomas D. Yawkey (1987) note that boys engage more in rough-and-tumble play and often appear more active than girls. Boys are also more likely to engage in adventuresome play involving superheroes and supervillians. Girls are more likely to engage in constructive and other table play, show interest in a greater variety of toys and play materials, prefer to play in smaller groups, and tend to have imaginary friends more than boys do. Boys and girls also tend to choose playmates of the same gender.

It is important to remember that such gender differences in the play of children as have been noted are differences in central tendencies. They do not apply to individual boys and girls, who may differ in their behavior from the generalizations noted. Teachers may support the segregation of children by gender in their class, and the play differences that might be evident, by inviting children to play with materials or in themes that reflect gender stereotypes. Such actions will undoubtedly highlight such differences and lead to sex-segregated play. A better alternative is for teachers to design a program that is anti-gender bias, as it should be anti-racial and cultural bias. They should create physical and social play environments that invite all children to select from a wide range of play activities and play themes, encouraging children to participate in activities that are not gender stereotyped. Thus, play activities, like all other educational activities in the preschool and kindergarten, will reflect the values of the teacher and the community in which the school is set.

Stages in Play Development

Another complicating factor in studying the play behavior of children is that it changes as children grow. Changes in the social and intellectual dimensions of play have been noted by a number of child development specialists. As early as 1932 Mildred Parten identified the changes in the social play of children as they move through the early childhood period. She observed children at the age of three as either *unoccupied* (not playing), as *solitary* players (playing alone), or as *onlooker* (looking on at the play of other children). By age four children were involved in *parallel* play (playing side-by-side with other children), and by age five they were observed in *associative* or *cooperative* play (play in which they engage other children).

Parten saw parallel play as a bridge between solitary play and cooperative play or group play. There have been a number of more recent studies that suggest that children often move directly from solitary play to social play, with parallel play serving as a bridge to allow children to adjust to social situations in play. Other studies suggest that solitary play may not be entirely age related and that both older and younger children engage in solitary play, although it is used in a more constructive or educational manner by older children (Johnson & Ershler, 1982).

Jean Piaget (1962) outlined early stages in play development as *practice* play, *symbolic* play, and *games* with rules that correspond to *sensorimotor, preoperational,* and *concrete* operations stages of intellectual development. The sensorimotor stage of play builds on the infant's and toddler's existing patterns of social behavior. Symbolic play is best represented in the dramatic play we see in preschool children. Children in kindergarten and beyond shift from overwhelming involvement in dramatic play and spend more and more time playing games.

Sara Smilansky (1968) adapted Piaget's play stages for studying preschoolers. She defined *functional* play as the routine or stereotyped use of play materials or as simple motoric activity. *Constructive* play was defined as sequential and purposive play that resulted in a finished product. *Dramatic* play was seen as thematic role play that involved transforming situations or objects.

Teachers can combine the work of Parten with that of Smilansky to get a better sense of the level at which children are playing in their classes. Kenneth Rubin, Terence Maioni, and Margaret Horning (1976) have done this in researching the impact of interventions on the play behavior of children. Teachers can observe their children's play, noting the level at which they play in various activity centers. They can then intervene by modifying the setting, by adding new materials, by raising questions of the children who are playing, or by stepping in momentarily to move play in a particular direction and then stepping out again. Knowing the criteria for play, the teacher can be sensitive that the activity remains play even when there are adult interventions. It should not be distorted to the point that the children become so reality oriented or sensitive to authority that the activity loses its playfulness.

Using Play to Achieve Educational Goals

Educators often make a distinction between play activities and learning activities. Play, as noted earlier, is seen as an activity that is done for its own sake, while learning activities are goal oriented. All play, however, is not free, unstructured play, and all learning activities are not necessarily work. Bernard Spodek (1985) differentiates between *educational play* and *noneducational play*. The difference between these two forms of play is not in the degree of enjoyment the child receives, but in the purposes established for the play. Educational play has the child's learning as its prime purpose.

Doris Bergen (1988) developed a schema of play and learning. She conceives of a continuum from free play to work, with guided play, directed play, and work disguised as play as forms of classroom activity that fall between the two extremes. Free play and guided play support discovery learning and guided discovery learning, while directed play supports reception learning. The two forms of work identified in this schema support rote learning and drill. Bergen sees a limited role in early childhood education for directed play and work disguised as play.

When free play and guided play activities are used in early childhood settings, they enable children to become active learners—active in using the information they have gained from a variety of sources to create knowledge structures that are personally meaningful to them. In this active form, the educational functions of play relate to the areas of cognitive, creative, social, and physical development. In cognitive play, children create objects and roles, often using the objects symbolically. In dramatic play, for example, as children process a wide range of information and consider their playmates' points of view, they develop more mature levels of logical thinking.

Playing also allows children to suspend reality and use their creative imagination. While children's dramatic play typically starts with the recreation of familiar situations, play is usually more inventive than imitative. As the children play, they experiment with words, manipulating their use, meaning, and grammar. Play with language helps children use language more flexibly and in a more expressive fashion. It also helps children become aware of the rules for conversations.

Through play, young children learn to get along with one another. They discover that other children have points of view that are different from their own. They learn to revise their views of the world and negotiate differences. They also learn to share and cooperate. Play also helps to extend children's physical skills. Through play, children learn to manipulate a variety of toys and use their bodies in novel situations, becoming skillful as they engage in play activities. Thus, all the areas of development can be nurtured by appropriate play activities (Spodek & Saracho, 1988).

DEVELOPING PLAY ACTIVITIES

Reviewing the theories and definitions of play has helped to pinpoint the fact that play is an important activity for young children. Play serves as a way for children to express ideas and feelings as well as to explore understandings about the world. Play also helps to build social relations among children. Thus, it is valuable in supporting the well-rounded development of young children. The important point for the teacher is to be aware of children's play and especially the kinds of play we want to support. By nurturing selected play activities, we can increase the educational power of children's play in school.

Almost all preschool and kindergarten programs devote a considerable portion of the school day to play. The teacher needs to plan for this play, providing the necessary supporting environment, making sure that enough materials and equipment are available, feeding into the positive social relations that develop among children at play, and helping the children to extend their play.

Play takes place both indoors in the classroom and out-of-doors in the play yard. Most outdoor play differs in important ways from indoor play, and therefore different supports and controls need to be provided.

Outdoor Play

Outdoor play is usually noisier and more vigorous than indoor play. There is more space out-of-doors, so it is a better place for children to run, jump, and use wheel toys like tricycles and wagons. Also, because there are no walls or ceilings, loud noises are less disturbing. There may be grassy, dirt, or sandy surfaces outdoors which make falling less dangerous for children than the wood or concrete floor indoors.

Even though all this is true, outdoor areas should not be limited to large-muscle activities. Many of the activities of the classroom, including music, art, storytelling, and dramatic play can take place outdoors as well. Of course, some of these activities will be limited by climate and weather.

Most schools, including preschools, are in session from about the beginning of September until some time in June, although summer sessions are often held. In some regions of the country this period includes severe winter weather. Not only may it be too cold to do many of the things we do indoors, but the clothing children wear outdoors in winter limits their mobility and the activities in which they can engage. At other times of the year extreme heat or rain may also limit the outdoor activities that can take place reasonably and comfortably.

There are almost always times, however, when useful play activities can take place outdoors. The play should be designed to support a range of activities. There should be areas for vigorous activity, where climbing equipment can be placed and a proper ground surface arranged to support safety. There needs to be some paved surfaces for wheel toys. There should be a sandpit or dirt area for digging. Many large-muscle activities can be extended to include elements of dramatic play if teachers provide props and suggestions for play themes.

There should also be areas that support quieter activities. Arts and crafts or less vigorous dramatic play can take place outdoors. Construction with large hollow blocks is also a basic outdoor activity. Much of the year water play can be provided as well. These ideas may suggest the need for a zoned outdoor play area, with different places developed for different activities, much like activity centers in the classroom. A further discussion of the physical setup of outdoor play areas is presented in Chapter 6.

It is important to note that outdoor play time is not a recess for children. We do not send young children outside so that they can rid themselves of excess energy. Rather, this is a setting for valuable play activities. If value is to be gained, then teachers must do more than monitoring for safe, nonaggressive behavior. True, teachers must be on guard to see that children are not hurt or that children do not fight, but they need also to observe the children's outdoor play so that they can extend it just as they do indoors.

Indoor Play

Indoor play is usually a little quieter and more constrained than outdoor play. The room should be arranged so that different kinds of play can occur in different areas at the same time without interfering with one another. To this end, the classroom is arranged into activity centers. Each center has space allocated and materials available for one type of activity or play, such as dramatic play, block building, or manipulative and fine motor play. In addition, if gross motor play is provided indoors, there is usually a room set aside with a lot of space, some large pieces of equipment, and some gym mats.

Each activity center is designed to serve a particular purpose. The materials and equipment are readily accessible to the children, and the boundaries of the center are carefully delineated, although children should be able to carry their play beyond those boundaries when necessary.

Some ways we guide play apply to all activity centers; others apply only to specific centers. After we present here some general strategies for guiding play, we will look at each type of play separately.

Initiating Play Activities

Sometimes it is enough simply to make play materials available to children to start a play activity. If the materials are attractive, if they offer reasonable play opportunities, and if there is some novelty to the materials and the setting, that may be enough. It is helpful, however, to have a short meeting with the children to present a new piece of equipment or a new toy. You can talk about the uses that can be made of the materials and the limitations on its use. If the new equipment seems to be particularly attractive, it may be helpful to develop another, equally attractive activity, to limit conflict or arguments over taking turns.

Often you can stimulate new interest in a play activity by bringing a degree of novelty to it. Rearranging the block area, setting up some signs in the dramatic play area, or introducing a few new materials will make something that has become "old hat" an attractive new activity once again.

In starting a new play activity, it often helps to stimulate the children's imagination. A walk through the neighborhood, reading a book related to a particular play topic, or showing a film or filmstrip each serve to get children's play started.

Moving Children's Play Along

Every preschool teacher is presented with a dilemma in guiding play. On the one hand, we want children's play to be as productive as possible; we need to involve ourselves in it to some extent to achieve this goal. On the other hand, we want children to be independent in their activities. We do not want to structure the play for the children. If we impose ourselves too much, the activity is limited and stops being play. Teachers need to check on the consequences of what they say and do regularly. If a teacher goes too far, it is easy to pull back without causing too much distress, if that teacher is sensitive to what is happening in the play.

Ann Spidell (1985) studied preschool teachers to identify how they function to guide, modify, and extend children's play. She identified a number of teacher strategies that she characterized as *play interventions,* or methods of guiding play. If children do not seem to be playing effectively, it is helpful for the teacher to observe what is happening and then decide what is the most effective way to intervene. Sometimes it is helpful to tell children what they might do, or talk to them about how they are playing and to suggest some new possibilities. If the play seems particularly productive, a teacher might praise a child as a way of encouraging the continuation of this play. Teachers might also join in the play briefly to demonstrate some alternative ways of functioning in the play situation.

Teachers can also guide children's play by adding or taking away material from the play situation. At the beginning of supermarket play, for example, there are a number of things that can be provided: A doll carriage or other wheeled toy can be a supermarket cart, boxes and empty food containers can represent the store's merchandise, and tables can serve as shelves. Signs can be written, indicating what kinds of food are on what table, and even the price can be noted. The teacher might ask the children what they need, or might suggest materials, or might simply put some things out so the children themselves can choose what to use. As the play progresses, a toy cash register and some play money might be added.

Sometimes the teacher will guide play by suggesting roles that children can play. "Who is doing the shopping?" or "Who is the supermarket clerk?" may be enough to suggest new roles and move play along. A teacher might also join the play for a while. The teacher could become a shopper for a period of time, purchasing, asking about the price of things, and asking who should be paid as a way of suggesting roles.

If the children seem blocked in their play, the teacher might take them on a field trip or bring in a book to provide more information. For example, the teacher could take just a few children or the whole class on a trip to the supermarket. A few purchases might be made to show the children the entire shopping process. They will pay more attention in this situation than when they visit the store with their parents. The children also could observe the way the store is arranged, how food is stored, and so on. If plans are made in advance, you might be able to take the children to the storage area, the butchering area, the bakery, or other places not normally seen in the supermarket.

Teachers may also need to use strategies to change children's play if it is becoming destructive or nonproductive. One strategy often used is redirection, suggesting alternative play activities and even guiding a child into another play area. Such an intervention strategy is extreme, since it distorts the play intentions of children, and should be used judiciously.

Teachers must be careful not to disrupt the flow of activities when intervening in play. They must also be careful not to provide too much for the children—too much material, too much information, or too much structure. If there is too much, children either ignore what the teacher introduces or may lose interest in the activity. Teachers can intervene in other play areas, through the way we have suggested they intervene in dramatic play.

SUPPORTING OUTDOOR PLAY

Much of the outdoor play of young children consists of large-motor activity: climbing, running, jumping, swinging, and crawling. Other outdoor activities involve wheel toys, building structures, playing with sand and water, engaging in dramatic play, and playing games. Each of these will be discussed separately.

Large-Motor Activity

Relatively little intervention is required when children engage in large-motor activities. Equipment needs to be provided that is both challenging and safe, and that avoids creating frustration. Whatever equipment is available must be carefully checked to ensure that it is in good condition. It should also be matched to the developmental level of the children. For very young children a set of low steps provides plenty of challenge for climbing. You will see little children going up and down such steps repeatedly. When children are older and more capable, wooden or metal ladders can be introduced, along with ramps, rope ladders, platforms above ground level, cargo nets, and climbing ropes. Often these pieces of equipment are integrated into large play structures that provide a range of options so that children can establish their own challenges. Some children's centers are even fortunate enough to have trees in their play yards that are suitable for children to climb.

The ground surface under any climbing equipment should allow children to fall or jump without being injured. Sometimes dirt or grassy surfaces are adequate. At other times sand, tanbark, corn cobs, or other appropriate materials

Large structures allow a range of outdoor play activities.

A large see-saw extends both physical and social play.

need to be provided. If the play area is subjected to heavy traffic, the grass will not survive.

In addition to climbing apparatus, there ought to be things for children to crawl under, jump over or down from, swing on, and slide on. Although separate pieces of equipment can serve these purposes, larger pieces of stationary equipment are sometimes placed permanently in the play area for children's use. These can be augmented with other props to extend the children's play. Barrels and large cardboard cartons are fun for children to crawl through. Smooth boards can be used to provide added slides, and hanging pieces of cloth can provide privacy.

Wheel Toys

Some space which is paved with concrete, asphalt, or a similar material should be provided so that children can use wheel toys. These can include tricycles, wagons, Irish Mails, Big Wheels, miniature trucks, or similar vehicles. Children will use wheel toys in a variety of ways. They will ride on them alone or with others; they will carry things or pull things with them. Traffic patterns and rules need to be established. Since there are often more children than wheel toys and these toys may be quite popular, the teacher may want to work with the children to develop rules for taking turns.

Building Structures

Not many years ago, the *Adventure Playground* movement that had been popular in Europe caught the imagination of American educators and recreation workers. Adventure playgrounds provide children with the opportunity to create their own play structures. Children are given tools and raw materials and, with help and supervision from adults, they create their own play equipment. Supervisors check that the structures are safe before children use them. The beauty of the structures rested in the fact that they were built by children for their own use rather than for their visual beauty.

Few children of kindergarten age or younger are capable of constructing their own adventure playgrounds. However, young children are capable of combining pieces of equipment to create their own play structures when the proper equipment is available. In many large city playgrounds and school yards the play equipment is solid and permanent, anchored into place to be safe and vandal-resistant and to require little maintenance. Too often these structures leave little flexibility to children. However, smaller pieces of equipment can be given to young children outdoors to allow them to create their own play structures. Sawhorses, ladders, cleated boards, large hollow blocks, large wooden packing crates, and other such pieces of equipment can be combined and recombined to provide a variety of play structures. Often these can be used in combination with more permanent structures in the play yard. The fact that children can continually modify and elaborate the structures they build means that these structures are continually being renewed, providing novelty and a sense of adventure and challenge that permanent structures cannot offer. Since they are created by the children themselves, such structures are even more attractive.

For children to build adequate play structures, there must be enough equipment to allow them to extend from what is provided. There also needs to be some storage facilities available outdoors so that when the play is over, the structures can be taken down and the pieces stored. This way new ones can be created at a later time.

Sand and Water

Sand and water can be used both indoors and outdoors. When used indoors, they are usually in a large basin or tub set on a table, or in a special lined sand or water table. When they are used outdoors, more freedom can be allowed and, since there is more space, more sand or water can be provided.

Outdoors a large sandbox or sand pit can be used. It can be recessed or placed low to the ground so that children can kneel over the edge or even be allowed to play inside it. It is important that a sandbox be designed to drain easily and that it can be covered and kept clean.

Children can play with sand with no tools, just feeling, molding, and modeling damp sand. Nevertheless, tools are useful for children to use. Pails and shovels, large wooden spoons, strainers, funnels, plastic jars, and empty cans all make excellent tools to use with sand. Toy trucks or construction vehicles might also be provided. If the weather is good, a water hose, a sprinkling can, or a plastic bottle filled with water will allow the children to dampen or wet the sand.

Indoors or out, water play can be provided with water made available in galvanized or plastic tubs. There should also be various containers to pour the water into. Hoses, funnels, plastic boats, and other objects that float or can be filled with water can be used to extend the child's play.

A sand pit will allow children to use many props in their sand play.

As in other areas, rules need to be established for children who use sand and water. Wetting other children or throwing sand may need to be clearly indicated as taboo. Proper protection, such as plastic aprons, may be needed to protect children's clothing, or shoes and socks may need to be removed when children step into a sandbox. Also, children can help with cleanup here, as in all areas.

Dramatic Play

Although most of the dramatic play of children takes place indoors, children will engage in such play in the yard if we allow them to, and if we provide supports. Many of the elements of dramatic play, discussed later in this chapter

Sometimes the ground itself serves children's play well.

in relation to indoor play, also apply to outdoor dramatic play. Climbing apparatus can be turned into homes, castles, airplanes, or any number of other settings that will allow the children to extend their activities through their imagination. Interventions here will be much like those indoors. The teacher needs to observe the children's play, keeping it going by making sure there are enough props, feeding ideas when necessary, and maybe even moving into the play for short periods of time.

Games

Teachers can help to develop outdoor games with children. Games differ from other forms of play in that there are rules that provide structure. Many children's games are too elaborate for the preschooler. It is difficult for young children to follow the rules or even remember the intent of the game. Many simple games, however, can be played with the teacher providing the leadership. Simple sing-along games like "Ring Around the Rosie," "Paw Paw Patch," and "Loobie Loo" can be played by preschoolers. Other games might also be played as children develop skills in game playing and an understanding of how games work. Ruth F. Bogdanoff and Elaine T. Dolch (1979) provide a set of developmental guidelines that can help in selecting games that match the developmental level of any particular group (see Table 10–1).

TABLE 10–1 Developmental Guidelines For Choosing Games

LEVEL	CHILD'S THOUGHT DEVELOPMENT	GAME REQUIREMENTS	SUGGESTED GAMES
I	Preoperational	Pattern or sequence game Two-step sequence	Ring Around the Rosie Roll the Ball (small group)
	Very limited verbal understanding	No verbal instruction necessary to teach game	Hokey Pokey (modified) Humpty Dumpty and other nursery rhymes
	Strong egocentrism	Continuous participation by all No waiting necessary Two to four children	This is the way the _____ walks (tune of Mulberry Bush)
	Little group awareness, child involved primarily with adults	Game depends on adult action No role alternation required	
II	Preoperational	Basic pattern game Not more than three steps in sequence	Punchinello (circle style) Did You Ever See a Lassie?
	Verbal understanding not dependable	No verbal instruction required	Hide the clock
	Egocentrism still strong	Continuous participation Five to eight children	Little Sally Walker Paw Paw Patch
	Awareness of other children's presence but most interest in adult's expectation of child's behavior	Role alternation with help of the leader only	Variation of Mulberry Bush (with child's choice of action)

TABLE 10-1 (*Continued*)

LEVEL	CHILD'S THOUGHT DEVELOPMENT	GAME REQUIREMENTS	SUGGESTED GAMES
III	*Preoperational*	Basic pattern game	Looby Loo
		Four to five steps in sequence	Doggie Doggie, Where's Your Bone?
		Limited choice of action within framework of game	Musical Chairs (modified)
			Are You My Kitten?
	Coordination of language with action nearly complete	Some verbal instruction supported by demonstration	Duck, Duck, Goose (modified)
	Egocentrism less strong in game situation	Wait short periods for turn with group action interspersed	
	Good awareness of all players but limited understanding of their roles in game	Six to ten players	Mulberry Bush
		One-to-one interaction possible	
	Primary interest in own role	Role alternation between players may now be part of game	
IV	*Late preoperational*		
	More objective understanding of rule in action of game	Players required to make some choices of action	A Tisket-a-Tasket
			Squirrel in the Trees
			Charlie over the Water
	Good verbal understanding	May use verbal clues as well as action	Find My Child
	Egocentrism diminishing	Turn taking can be part of game	London Bridge
			Knock, Knock
	Enjoy coordination with group	Understand and enjoy role alternation and some role reversal	
	Will subject own interests to group effort	Eight to twelve children	
V	*Concrete operational*		
	Reversible thought and lessened egocentrism	Decisions of strategy determine outcome of game	Word games (G-H-O-S-T)
			Tag (modified)
	Understand rules as objective framework for action		Hide and Seek
			Kick the Can
	New interest in competition within coordinated effort	Competition may be used	Competitive races and relays
		Team action may substitute for personal involvement	Follow the Leader
			Darts
	Use language easily for thought	Verbal element can be definitive part of game	Horseshoes
			Pease Porridge Hot
			Simon Says

R.F. Bogdanoff, and E.T. Dolch, "Old Games for Young Children: A Link to Our Heritage." In L. Adams and B. Garlick (Eds.), *Ideas that Work with Children*, vol 2. (Washington, DC: National Association for the Education of Young Children, 1979), pp. 169–177.

There is usually more room outdoors to allow a large number of children to play a game together. In addition, there is usually plenty of space for other activities, so that all children do not have to be required to participate.

SUPPORTING INDOOR PLAY

Indoor play is usually organized into activity centers. The most important centers for play are the Block Center, the Housekeeping Center, and the Table Activities Center. Other centers are also provided for other activities.

Block Building

Wooden blocks provide an excellent material for children's construction. There are two types of wooden blocks that preschool children use: large hollow blocks and the smaller solid wooden unit blocks. Cardboard blocks are also available and are less expensive to purchase, but they are much less durable and, because of their lightness, they are not as productive in children's use.

Hollow blocks are usually based on a unit of about one foot square by one-half foot deep. The blocks also come in half units and double units as well as triangular ramps and boards. Some sets of hollow blocks are made of hardwood with two open sides to allow children to slip their hands inside to carry them easily. Other sets are made of plywood, closed on all sides, though often with hand-holes on two sides. Because of their size and their sturdiness, children can build structures that are relatively stable and strong enough to climb on or crawl into. Children build them to their own specifications to serve their own

Even the simplest buildings allow for social as well as physical learning.

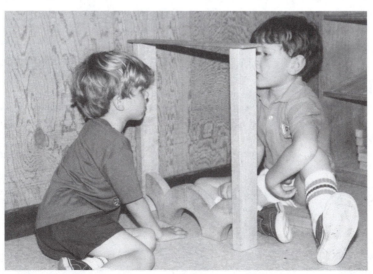

purposes. While providing a good medium for construction, hollow blocks also serve as props for dramatic play, substituting for many structured play props. Blocks can represent buildings, vehicles, or funiture. When the children are through with a particular prop, it can be taken apart and reassembled in a different way to represent another prop.

Unit blocks are much smaller than hollow blocks. The structures created with them are used by children in a very different way. Unit blocks are solid pieces of wood, the best ones made of hardwood. They are based on a unit with multiples and variations of that unit. The basic unit is a brick-shaped block measuring $5\frac{1}{2} \times 2\frac{3}{4} \times 1\frac{3}{8}$ inches. Double units and quadruple units are two and four times the length of the unit, and a half unit is one-half its length. Ramps, triangles, pillars, boards, switches, and curved units are all made in proportion to the unit. Figure 10–1 provides examples of unit blocks typically found in a classroom set.

The advantage of basing the dimensions of all the blocks on a unit is that the structures that are built with the blocks, even large, elaborate ones, will be in proportion and will be stable and sturdy. If the blocks are made of hardwood, they are less likely to wear significantly with use; the proportions will remain constant throughout the life of the blocks, and these blocks, if used properly, will last a long time.

Unit block structures are constructed on the floor. They are too small for children to use dramatic play, but in time they will be used fancifully. At first, children will be content to build simple structures and take them down. As children mature, they will use blocks to represent objects and structures in the outside world. Once children use blocks representationally, their play with unit blocks is much like playing with a dollhouse: they will manipulate objects to represent dramatizations rather than perform in them themselves.

Many years ago Harriet Johnson (1933) identified stages in young children's block building. In the first stage children may simply walk around carrying blocks in their hands. In the second stage children will take blocks and pile one upon the other. Children go from this stage to building towers. They will also lay blocks side by side in rows.

In later stages children will start bridging space with their blocks, separating blocks on the floor and then putting one block over two spaced blocks. After this, children will start to build enclosures of various kinds. In later stages children reproduce elements in their structures over and over again as they make patterns; they also begin to build balanced structures through their patterning. In the final stages children use blocks to represent large objects in the real world. School buildings, city streets, airports, and other real things will be represented and children will use them to play through the processes they observe in the world.

In the early stages of block building, small sets of blocks with limited amounts of space are adequate for children. As children move through the stages of block building, their more elaborate structures need more blocks, as well as more space. These more elaborate block structures take a long time to complete. It helps if block buildings can be left up for more than one day. Children can

FIGURE 10-1   Types of Unit Blocks

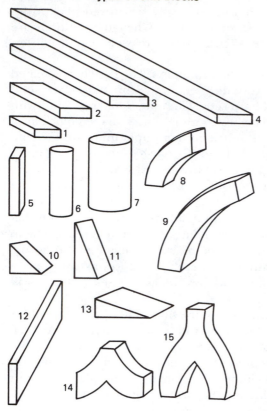

1. Half unit
2. Unit
3. Double unit
4. Quadruple unit
5. Pillar
6. Small cylinder
7. Large cylinder
8. Circular curve
9. Elliptical curve
10. Small triangle
11. Large triangle
12. Floor board
13. Ramp
14. Right-angle switch
15. Y switch

Blocks may come in other sizes and shapes as well.

From Elisabeth S. Hirsch (Ed.), *The Block Book* (Washington, DC: National Association for the Education of Young Children, 1984), pp. 202–203.

As children develop, their block structures become more complex and more representational.

build and rebuild them and the structures will be used in many different ways as well.

Blocks are expensive. They also take up a lot of classroom space. Nevertheless the learning that can result from block building makes the investment worthwhile. Not every block builder will become a great architect, as did Frank Lloyd Wright, but block building does teach a great many things. Physical coordination and eye–hand coordination are just the beginning. Through blocks children learn math concepts as they balance their buildings and find that equivalent lengths of blocks cover the same space. They learn informal measurement of length, area, and volume and begin to understand topological geometry. Also blocks are representational. They can be used to help in developing social studies understandings. They also help develop abstract thinking, for they allow children to use relatively abstract objects to represent reality in an arbitrary way, developing the rules of representation themselves. (See Elizabeth Hirsch, *The Block Book* [1984] for an excellent discussion of learning through blocks.)

The teacher needs to establish a sense of order in the block area. Blocks should be stored on shelves clearly marked so that children can replace them in the same spot from which they took them. There need to be limits on how children use blocks—leaving space around the shelves so others can move by, respecting the buildings of other children, using blocks safely, not throwing them or hitting with them, and not using them inappropriately. There might also be limits on how high children should build with blocks.

When working with very young children, teachers might show them how to stack or make rows. They might also build alongside the children, making bridged structures. However, teachers should not tell children how to build or what to build. Block structures should always be the children's. Suggestions can

Blocks can be combined with other toys to extend children's play.

show alternatives without imposing them on children. As children mature, teachers should provide props to extend their block play. A pulley system can allow airplanes to land and take off at an airport. A battery, buzzer, and door button can extend children's play in their personally created dollhouse. A field trip to see how things are built and organized in the world outside the school can stimulate more block building.

Dramatic Play

Dramatic play is probably the most studied, though not necessarily the most understood, form of young children's play. In dramatic play children pretend at being persons other than who they really are and use objects to represent things other than what they really are. Dramatic play incorporates a great deal of fantasy. When it is rooted more in reality, when children act out the roles and relationships they see in the social world that surrounds them, it is often called sociodramatic play.

In dramatic play children develop their own evolving play situations, setting the stage and creating their own dialogue. Even when the play is based upon an observed or experienced situation, dramatic play is an important avenue young children use to express and explore their own personal feelings as well as their understandings of the world they have experienced. In playing with others, children are able to work through their feelings and test their understandings against those of others. Thus, this form of play helps children develop an understanding of their world as well as an ability to cope with their environment.

Most preschool classes have dramatic play centers. Often these represent the home life situation of children. It may be called the "doll corner" or the "housekeeping corner." Miniature tables, chairs, stoves, sinks, refrigerators, and beds are provided along with dolls, toy pots and pans, small brooms, and other things that allow children to act out the roles they see at home. They can be a

Dress-up clothes and a housekeeping corner are a part of most dramatic play centers.

parent and cook, clean, and feed the doll/baby. Or they may be the baby and have another child nurture them. The way children play out these roles, relations, and feelings reflects how they understand them in their own life.

Teachers can extend children's play beyond the confines of the home. A range of community settings can serve as the basis for children's sociodramatic play. The supermarket, post office, auto repair shop, barber, or hairdresser, to name just a few settings in the neighborhood, can provide stimulation for interesting play in children.

Judith Bender (1971) suggests creating a set of "prop boxes" as a way of organizing material for dramatic play. The teacher can collect and store material related to each play theme in a box. The following suggestions might prove helpful in creating some prop boxes:

Grocery store or supermarket. Empty food boxes or cans, a cash register, play money, signs, supermarket advertisements, a white apron. (These can be augmented by shelves, tables, and other equipment that can be found in the classroom.)

Barber/hairdresser. Mirror, combs, brushes, hair rollers, hair clips, shampoo containers, empty hairspray cans, a cloth to cover the child's clothes, a toy razor, a shaving brush.

Post office. Used stamps, envelopes, postcards, a rubber stamp and stamp pad, play money, empty milk containers to serve as letter boxes, paper, pencils.

Doctor's office or hospital. A stethoscope, gauze bandages, a toy hypodermic syringe, a white coat or shirt.

Restaurant. Dishes, silverware, napkins, menus, order pads, pencils, sponges, fake food, cooking utensils, a cash register, a telephone.

Construction work. Tools such as hammers, saws, screwdrivers, wrenches and pliers, a tool box, a hard hat, painter's and carpenter's hats, overalls, a tape measure.

Airport. Airline boarding passes, ticket envelopes, maps, small suitcases, a pilot's cap, serving trays, plastic cups, a steering wheel, oil cans.

Auto repair shop. Screwdrivers, wrenches and other tools, an air pump, empty oil cans, clean used automobile parts, toy cars and trucks.

Telephone store. Toy telephones, wire, plastic tape, pliers, screwdrivers and other tools, telephone directories.

Teachers can think of other sets of props to organize into prop boxes as they watch and listen to children to find out what interests them. In each case, some attempt toward authenticity of materials is helpful. Safety, however, is the most important consideration when you are selecting material.

One of the prime responsibilities of the teacher is to set the stage, providing equipment and materials that will invite children to play. In addition, teachers need to observe play to augment the material as needed. The teacher may also provide information that will feed into the play and suggest play ideas. On occasion, the teacher may also join in the play. With all the possible interventions, however, it is important that the teacher does not distort the situation. Play should always remain in the children's control.

Table Activities

Most early childhood classes will have a portion of the room set aside for table activities. Along with tables there will be open shelves to store a variety of small materials for children's play. Each set of materials can be kept in its own container, possibly a plastic see-through box, basket, or tray. The children can take a set of materials from its shelf to the table. When they are through, they can gather the materials back into their container to replace on the shelf.

Many of these materials are designed to promote small-muscle development and improve eye–hand coordination. Many of them can also be used to help develop perceptual and conceptual skills. The materials in such a center might contain the following, depending on the developmental level of the children and the resources of the school:

Stacking and nesting toys. Even the youngest preschoolers can use toys that contain smaller and larger parts. These can be ordered by size and stacked one upon the other, placed on a dowel, or nested one into the other. Cups, dolls, and rings are among the more common materials used in these toys. Children learn to distinguish one part from another by size and put them together in the proper manner.

Puzzles. A wide range of wooden puzzles are available for young children. Some of the simplest are formboards, in which spaces are cut out in different forms (such as triangles, squares, rectangles, or trapezoids) and children must put the correct form into the matching space.

A wide range of puzzles should be provided.

More complex are picture puzzles. These puzzles will vary from a simple one with a single part made up of the pictured object, to complicated puzzles in which the shapes of the pieces have no relationship to the shapes of the objects pictured. There may be as many as two or three different levels of difficulty available in a class. Not too many puzzles are needed at one time, though, since young children enjoy completing the same puzzles over and over again.

Fastening frames. A very useful manipulative device is a fastening frame. This usually has two pieces of cloth stretched over and attached to a wooden frame. Attached to these are one of the many fastening devices that we use in clothing: zipper, hooks and eyes, buttonholes, snaps, or eyelets and shoelaces. The children enjoy fastening and unfastening these devices. Practicing with these frames not only improves motor skills but also helps children learn self-care skills, for the skills learned can be transferred to the fastenings on children's clothing.

Locking devices. There are a number of commercial sets of locking boards available. Sometimes parts of the boards can move to resemble the opening and closing of doors and windows. Often teachers find they can make the same apparatus themselves with materials from a local hardware store. Hinges can be used to fasten the moving parts, and hooks and eyes, sliding door bolts, hasps, cupboard catches, window locks, and even locks that use keys can be mounted for children's use.

Construction sets. There are many excellent sets of materials that children can use to build on a table surface. Table blocks, which are smaller versions of the unit blocks, are the simplest of these. In addition, there are plastic interlocking blocks, such as *Lego,* as well as *Lincoln Logs, Tinkertoys,* and many others. These are designed commercially and each is given its own brand name. Often these can be combined with small figures of people or animals, with doll furniture, and with small toy vehicles to allow children to add to their constructions as they play out their own dramatizations in miniature.

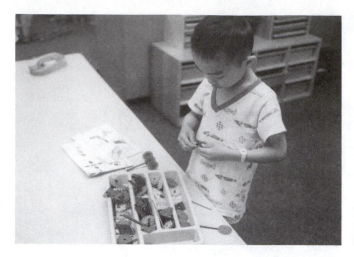

Sets of construction materials allow children to create many structures.

Games. A number of simple games can also be included in the materials in this center. Some games, like *dominoes,* might be played independently by children. Others, like *Lotto,* might require the attention of an adult working with a group of children. Somewhat more elaborate games such as *Candy Land* or *Chutes and Ladders* might also be included for more mature children.

Academically oriented material. A number of sets of material can be included in this area to provide academic readiness for children. Templates, along with paper and pencil, allow children to trace shapes; this activity prepares them for writing letters. Number cubes or puzzles designed to teach number meanings can also be included, along with wooden or plastic letters that can be combined to make simple words. These materials allow children to explore the meanings of numbers and the uses of letters independently. They let children discover meanings on their own and become more comfortable with academic concepts.

Other manipulative materials. A glance through any early educational catalog will provide illustrations of material far beyond those discussed here. Many of them are worth having in a classroom. Montessori material, for example, has proven useful over the years with young children. These and other materials can also be used in inventive ways. As with other areas of the room, however, there are limits to the way materials should be used. It is helpful to introduce new materials to the children, showing them how they should be used. The routines of caring for and cleaning up the area must also be shown to each group.

PLAY AND THE EARLY CHILDHOOD CURRICULUM

A separate chapter in this book has been devoted to the topic of play in early childhood education. Because of the way books are written and printed, play has been treated as a topic separate from the other curriculum areas. This should not give the false impression that play is a separate curriculum area from language, science, social studies, mathematics, or the arts. As a matter of fact, all of these areas should be interrelated in a well-integrated program of early childhood education and play activities can well be used to achieve educational goals in these important curriculum areas.

Play and Social and Personal Learning.   Dramatic play especially serves an important function in generating personal and social learnings. Dramatic play is particularly useful in helping children to understand their social world. Children generally begin their dramatic play by acting out roles and relationships in social settings as they perceive them and comprehend them. This form of play helps children to take what they see of the social world surrounding them—the world of family, school, and community—and act out what they see as a way of understanding that world. Teachers who observe children in dramatic play can gain a good sense of the child's understanding of that social world. As children play with others, they share their understanding and test it against the understanding of other children. Psychologists have used play as a form of psychological therapy since children can act out events and understandings that they cannot articulate in words. While teachers cannot and should not act as therapists in the classroom, they can help children deal with misunderstandings by guiding play and by introducing new information to children when the play indicates that there is either a lack of information or misinformation.

Just as children symbolize their understanding of the social world in their dramatic play, they can symbolize their understanding of the physical world in their block structures and the structures they create in the sand area. As children mature and go beyond the creation of abstract forms, they can construct buildings, neighborhoods, roads, airports, and a variety of other geographic elements. Teachers can help by making available a variety of play props, such as toy people and vehicles, strips of plastic for road surfaces, road signs, battery operated street lights, and a host of other things that they find or that they create to stimulate the children's representations. Talking to children about what they are building, making suggestions, and providing additional information through pictures or field trips will also help to extend the children's understanding of their geographical world.

Play and Science Learning.   Play can help children learn about scientific phenomena in a variety of ways. In manipulative play children learn about the physical attributes of objects. But play should teach young children more about science than that. Hawkins (1965) has suggested that play is an important stage in science learning for all persons, young or old. Only after an individual has had the opportunity to play, or "mess about" with a phenomenon, is he or she able to make productive use of more directed learning opportunities in understanding science.

Play and Mathematics Learning.   A great many manipulative materials have been designed to help children gain mathematical understanding. There are many materials that are commercially available to help children to learn number concepts, count, match numbers to objects, and discriminate shapes and sizes.

Teachers can also develop their own manipulative materials and games to serve the same purpose.

Other play settings can provide opportunities to help children develop mathematical concepts. Dramatic play, for example, offers many such opportunities. In playing store, children can weigh merchandise. In playing restaurant, they will have the opportunity to match the number of plates, napkins and utensils to customers. In many play situations that require the use of money they can learn to differentiate denominations, and count the money that must change hands. Teachers need to seek such opportunities in children's play and make good use of them.

Play and Language Learning. A number of early childhood educators have identified a positive relationship between children's play prior to the primary grades and their ability to learn to read (e.g., Gentile & Hoot 1983; Pellegrini, 1980; Wolfgang & Sanders, 1981). Dramatic play, like language, is symbolic activity. Children use objects and people to stand for things other than themselves in play just as they use sounds to stand for objects or ideas and later use written symbols to stand for sounds. The symbolic learning children achieve in play enhances their ability to function in the area of language and literacy. As children mature, their play contains a larger amount of discursive language and children learn to play with language as they play with objects. In time stories tend to supplant the dramatic play of children.

Play and the Creative Arts. Play and the arts are both ways that young children express ideas and feelings. They are also both media for creativity. Little research has been done on the relationship between play and the arts, mainly because few educators are as interested in children's achievement in the arts as they are in children's achievement in academics. There does seem to be a self-evident relationship between children's play and the arts—the creative use of color, shape, form, sound, and movement related to the creative use of objects and people. Children play with various media in achieving forms of creating expression. This would suggest that it is helpful for teachers to allow the children's activity to flow easily between the various play areas and the different art areas.

SUMMARY

In this chapter we have discussed the nature of play. We have identified both classical and current theories of play. We have also discussed the importance of play for the development of the young child. We have focused on how play can be used in an early childhood class and have identified the role of the teachers in supporting and extending children's play. Finally we have presented the various play areas of the early childhood class, both indoors and outdoors, discussing the significant aspects of each.

Play is a critical element of any early childhood program. It is the responsibility of the teacher to see that the children's play serves an educational func-tion. Equally important, it is the teacher's responsibility to see that the activity remains play. Young children in school must be allowed to maintain their sponta-neity and creativity as they use the materials we provide for them.

REFERENCES

BECHER, R. M. AND C. H. WOLFGANG (1977). An exploration of the relationship between symbolic representation in dramatic play and art and the cognitive and reading readiness levels of kindergarten children. *Psychology in the Schools, 14,* 377–381.

BENDER, J. (1971). Have you ever thought of a prop box? *Young Children, 26*(3), 164–169.

BERGEN, D. (1988). Using a schema for play and learning. In D. Bergen (Ed.), *Play as a medium for learning and development,* pp. 169–180. Portsmouth, NH: Heinemann.

BOGDANOFF, R. F., AND E. T. DOLCH (1979). Old games for young children: A link to our heritage. In L. Adams and B. Garlick (Eds.), *Ideas that work with young children,* Vol. 2, pp. 169–177. Washington, DC: National Association for the Education of Young Children.

ELLIS, M. J. (1973). *Why people play.* Englewood Cliffs, NJ: Prentice-Hall.

GENTILE, L. M. AND J. L. HOOT (1983). Kindergarten play: The foundation of reading. *Reading Teacher, 36,* 436–439.

GILMORE, J. B. (1971). Play: A special behavior. In C. Herron and B. Sutton-Smith (Eds.), *Child's play.* New York: John Wiley.

HAWKINS, D. (1965). Messing about in science. *Science and Children, 2*(5), 5–9.

HIRSCH, E. S. (Ed.) (1984). *The block book* (rev. ed.). Washington, DC: National Association for the Education of Young Children.

JOHNSON, H. (1933). *The art of blockbuilding.* New York: Bank Street College (reissued, 1966).

JOHNSON, J. E., J. F. CHRISTIE, AND T. D. YAWKEY (1987). *Play and early childhood development.* Glenview, IL: Scott, Foresman and Co.

JOHNSON, J. E., AND J. J. ERSHLER (1982). Curricular effects on the play of preschoolers. In D. J. Pepler and C. H. Rubin (Eds.), *The play of children: Current theory and research,* pp. 130–143. Basil, Switzerland: S. Karger.

NEUMANN, E. A. (1971). *The elements of play.* New York: MSS Modular Publications.

PARTEN, M. B. (1932). Social participation among preschool children. *Journal of Abnormal and Social Psychology, 27,* 243–269.

PELLEGRINI, A. D. (1980). The relationship between kindergartners' play and achievement in prereading, language, and writing. *Psychology in the Schools, 17,* 530–535.

PIAGET, J. (1962). *Play, dreams and imitation in childhood.* New York: Norton.

RUBIN, K. H., G. G. FEIN, AND B. VANDENBERG (1983). Play. In M. E. Heathering (Ed.), *Carmicheal's manual of child psychology: Social development.* New York: John Wiley.

RUBIN, K. H., T. L. MAIONI, AND M. HORNUNG (1976). Free play behaviors in middle and lower class preschoolers: Parten and Piaget revisited. *Child Development, 47,* 414–419.

SCHWARTZMAN, H. B. (1978). *Transformations: The anthropology of play.* New York: Plenum.

SINGER, J. L. (1973). *The child's world of make-believe.* New York: Academic Press.

SMILANSKY, S. (1968). *The effects of sociodramatic play on disadvantaged preschool children.* New York: John Wiley.

SPIDELL, R. A. (1985). *Preschool teachers' interventions in children's play.* Unpublished doctoral dissertation, University of Illinois at Urbana-Champaign.

SPODEK, B. (1985). *Teaching in the early years* (3rd ed.). Englewood Cliffs, NJ: Prentice-Hall.

SPODEK, B. AND O. N. SARACHO (1988). The challenge of educational play. In D. Bergen (Ed.), *Play as a medium for learning and development,* pp. 9–22. Portsmouth, NH: Heinemann.

VYGOTSKY, L. S. (1967). Play and its role in the mental development of the child. *Soviet Psychology, 12,* 62–76.

WHITE, R. F. (1959). Motivation reconsidered: The concept of competence. *Psychological Review, 66,* 297–333.

WOLFGANG, C. H. AND T. S. SANDERS (1981). Defending young children's play as the ladder to literacy. *Theory into Practice, 20,* 116–120.

SUGGESTED ACTIVITIES

1. Observe an early childhood program for young children. Identify the different stages of play development observed. Describe each in concrete terms.

2. Record the shapes of blocks and accessories that young children use in an actual play situation. Describe what the teacher did to support block play.

3. Interview a parent. Ask what his or her child had learned from play.

4. Develop a directory of sources of early childhood play material and equipment.

5. Survey the local community schools for the different types of outdoor play equipment and play surfaces used in their outdoor areas.

6. Follow a preschool or kindergarten teacher during an activity period. Note the different ways she guides the children's play. Tally the times she uses each intervention strategy.

7. Observe and record a play situation in a preschool. Analyze your notes to identify children's activities related to different curriculum areas.

11

Creative Activities

After completing this chapter on creative activities, the student will be able to:

1. Define creativity.
2. Describe the developmental characteristics of creativity in children ages three to five.
3. Develop activities that support creativity.
4. Prepare a variety of two- and three-dimensional art activities.
5. Design craft activities for young children.
6. Discuss the purpose of music activities for young children.
7. Prepare a variety of early childhood music experiences.
8. Develop a movement program for young children.
9. Design movement activities for children's physical development.

Young children freely express their feelings and thoughts through many different materials. Often the way young children express themselves is more important than what they express. These expressions help them achieve self-satisfaction and acquire self-confidence, helping them develop positive self-concepts. It is more important that young children have personal forms of self-expression than polished products which display well but which might be based upon an imitation (e.g., drawing the same scene as everybody else in class or memorizing a specific poem). Such products are educationally irrelevant and have no relationship to the child who is producing them. A basic goal of education should be to deveolp in children the capacity to create, using their own abilities, without having to follow a specific pattern or a particular set of directions and without having to depend on external rewards for satisfaction.

In developing these forms of self-expression, children need to be provided with opportunities to use open-ended materials, such as wood, clay, or paints. As they explore these materials, their creative work must be respected and their talent be encouraged. This chapter discusses issues related to self-expression and creativity. It also presents ideas for offering developmentally appropriate opportunities for children to express themselves in two-dimensional and three-dimensional art work as well as in music and movement.

SELF-EXPRESSION

Young children express themselves in many ways. They use words to communicate ideas and feelings. They also use pictures, sounds, movement, and a variety of other media. Teachers can stimulate self-expression by challenging children to use their imagination. For instance, children can listen to music with their eyes closed. The teacher can ask them to imagine moods or images and to draw or paint what they have imagined. Or teachers can play background music, then invite the children's brushes to dance as they paint. Children's imaginations can also be stimulated by questions such as: "Can you make this ball of clay look like something you eat?" "What parts of your hand can you use to create something from the forest?" "What materials do you need to create a puppet who could be anyone?" or "How many different ways can you draw a castle?" (Lasky & Mukerji, 1980).

In order to stimulate self-expression, teachers can tell stories, present well-illustrated picture books, show films, filmstrips, and other media, and share songs and games about specific topics related to the children's lives. They can ask children to think of how things would look through the eyes of someone else, such as a bird in the sky or a fish under water. Children can be organized to work in groups with one child beginning a project drawing on a large piece of paper, then every other child being asked to continue the work, in turn, until it is finished. It is often helpful for teachers to collect project ideas, writing them on index cards and storing them in a file box which can be shared with children. Often the children themselves will be the source of these ideas. For those children who cannot read, directions can be provided through pictures.

A climate of self-expression should characterize all early childhood programs. Self-expression is healthy for young children and should be fostered and nurtured. Doing so requires providing more than a supportive climate for children. To develop such a program, it is helpful for you to know something about the development of creativity.

Creativity

In the past several decades educators have realized that creativity is as natural to the average person as it is to the genius (Torrance, 1962). Ligon (1957) has identified age-related developmental characteristics for children's imagination. He also suggested methods to promote young children's imagination. These developmental characteristics for birth to six years of age include the following:

Birth To Age Two. Children begin to develop their imagination during the first year of life. As they develop speech, they begin to ask questions about the names of things and try to reproduce the sounds and rhythms they hear. They are very curious and examine everything they touch, taste, and see.

During this period, creative growth can be stimulatd with simple materials, large blocks, dolls, and the like. Teachers can encourage verbal play and should accept the names that children use for their creations. Once the children begin to use words with meaning, songs can be sung about objects rather than the child's being asked to "say dog," or "say daddy."

Ages Two To Four. These children learn about the world through their own direct experiences as well as through verbal and imaginative play. They have short attention spans and shift activities at random. They begin to become independent of others as they do things for themselves. They continue to be curious about their evnironment as they explore the world in their own unique way and ask questions.

Children of this age can be provided with toys that can be used to represent a variety of things. They can be made aware of the wonders of nature in budding flowers, growing seedlings, baby kittens, and the varied colored leaves of fall. These children need freedom to explore, but they also need to be prepared for new experiences so that they can respond to strangeness.

Ages Four To Six. During this third period children begin to develop planning skills. They anticipate play and work and they enjoy planning and working through their plans. They learn different roles through pretend play and experiment with many of these roles.

Many refer to these early childhood years as the age of creativity. An observation of an early childhood school shows a world graced with young children's imagination and inventiveness. Children build with blocks, paint, shape objects out of clay, or work with other materials. Others will sing melodic fragments or familiar tunes or move their bodies to the rhythm of music they hear. Children of this age will play with language as they play with toys.

Teachers need to encourage creative growth by integrating creative activities into the educational program. Activities that support creativity include experiences in art, music and movement.

ART EXPERIENCES

Young children express themselves through art in ways that require no words. They enjoy printing, constructing, modeling, painting, stitching, and weaving. They act selectively, interpreting and expressing their experiences as they think and feel about them. In this process, art serves a dynamic and integrative function.

Just as children go through stages in cognitive development, so they go through stages of artistic development. Victor Lowenfeld and W. Lambert Brittain (1987) describe such stages. The stages that are of concern to early childhood teachers are the scribbling stage (ages two to four) and the preschematic stage (ages four to seven).

Children at the *scribbling* stage have a kinesthetic experience through drawing, feeling their drawings through the movement of their arms and hands. They make longitudinal, then circular, motions. As they mature, their actions become more coordinated. Children experiment with material, first making drawings, then comparing what they have drawn to what they see in the real world to give the drawing a name.

In the *preschematic* stage, children discover the relationship between drawing, thinking, and reality. They start out knowing what they wish to represent, even though their picture may change in the process. They are beginning to create representational drawings and they are developing form concepts.

These stages suggest the kinds of activities that are most appropriate for children at various ages. Teachers need to be aware of children's level of art performance and provide activities to move them to somewhat more mature levels. The following are the kinds of material that children can use in two-dimensional and three-dimensional art projects in an early childhood class.

Two-Dimensional Art

Two-dimensional art is art that is created with materials on a flat surface. Among the materials young children can use are paints, chalk, crayons, finger-paints, and collages.

Tempera Paint. Tempera paint is an opaque water color. This type of paint allows children to work quickly. Tempera paint is easy to control and details can be painted over because the material dries very quickly. Any type of paper, including cardboard, can be used with tempera paints.

Although tempera paints can be purchased premixed, dry tempera or powdered paint is often used in schools since it is less expensive. It can be mixed

Young children need only a small range of colors for painting at an easel.

with water to be used with brushes or fingers. Children can paint in solid areas, outline areas of color, or combine interesting mixtures. Dry paint can also be sprinkled on a moistened paper. Children can also dip a wet brush into the dry powder and then brush the paint on an absorbent paper surface.

Young children should probably be offered only a small range of colors so they will have no problems in selecting the colors and there will be little distraction. Small amounts should be given at first, since young children will mix colors until they are unusable. Primary colors (red, yellow, and blue) should be introduced first; other colors can be made by mixing these.

As they mature and children's paintings become more representational, the color range should be widened.

Colored Chalk. Young children enjoy drawing on wet pieces of paper with various colored chalks. Colors should be limited at first. As children mature and acquire more experience with chalk, they learn to blend colors and explore the use of chalk in combination with other media. For example, they may brush over the chalked areas with paint. Chalk pictures can be sprayed with a fixative or hair spray to keep the pictures from rubbing off.

Ask the children to moisten a newspaper or newsprint with a wet sponge. They can then draw anything they like with colored chalk, charcoal, or dry tempera powder, then hang them in the room to dry. It is helpful to have a designated place with a clothesline and clothespins to hang drawings to dry in the art area. If the drawing is painted over with liquid starch, the chalk designs will not rub off or the teacher can spray it with fixative when the drawing is dry.

The fixative can be applied with a spray gun or old perfume atomizer if it does not come in a spray container. The paper must be laid flat for spraying or it can be pinned to a backing of newspapers or the back of a large carton to protect walls while spraying. The teachers can make a fixative by mixing 1 teaspoon of paste in ½ cup of water.

Crayons. Wax crayons are available for drawing in almost every early childhood class. They are easy for children to use, require little teacher preparation, and need less cleanup than most art materials. Large half-round or hexagonal crayons are easy for young children to grasp and control. Their shape also keeps them from rolling away. A large variety of crayon colors are available, although young children need only a few basic colors. Crayons work best on the rough texture of manila paper, but almost any paper can be used for crayoning.

As children develop greater control over their drawings, teachers might wish to provide marking pens as well. These pens allow children to make pictures

Crayons provide a single medium that young children can control.

with deep vivid color and firm edges. The feel of the marking pen is also different from that of a crayon or a paint brush and offers an interesting alternative to children. Care needs to be taken that the markers selected for young children contain washable and not permanent color.

Experiences:

TEXTURE DRAWINGS. The classroom has surfaces with a variety of textures. Children can take crayons and make crayon rubbings by placing paper over these surfaces. These rubbings can be compared and discussed by the children. On a nice day, children can go outside and rub different surfaces (e.g., tree trunks, rocks).

WAXED DRAWINGS. The teacher can have children save discarded crayons in a box or coffee can for later use. When there are sufficient crayons, children can shave them with a cheese grinder, spray them over a piece of waxed paper, fold the waxed paper, place it between several sheets of newspaper and press it with a warm iron to melt the crayons. The melted shavings provide a drawing with pretty colors and designs.

Caution: An adult should supervise this activity. Children need to know that they always use a hot pad when handling hot cans or pots.

Fingerpaint. Fingerpaints permit the children to work with color and form more freely than do paint brushes. Glazed paper can be moistened either by dipping it into water or sponging the water on the paper. A tablespoon of fingerpaint can be placed on a dampened paper or spread evenly over the surface. Children can use their fingers, the sides of the hands, their elbows, combs, sticks, or pieces of cardboard to draw an image or design. At the beginning children use one color at a time; as they gain experience and maturity with this kind of painting, colors can be used together. Finger paintings can be dried on a flat surface covered with newsprint. The paintings may have to be pressed flat to avoid curling.

Children do not always need to fingerpaint on paper. Fingerpainting can be done on any smooth washable surface. A print can be made from the surface by pressing a sheet of paper to it if the child wishes to preserve the painting.

You can make fingerpaint by combining tempera paint or powder paint with liquid starch or wheat paste and mixing until smooth. Making fingerpaint in the classroom is fun, but commercially prepared fingerpaint will usually produce a better result.

Collage. A collage is a composition in which a variety of materials are selected and organized to produce interesting patterns, textures, and colors. Colored paper, cloth, feathers, straws, and almost any kind of material that can be pasted on paper can be used in a collage. Materials and textures can be overlaid to add depth. Since the materials are largely flat and are pasted or fastened against a flat background, a collage is still considered two-dimensional art. With collage, young children's primary concern is with form and color.

Experience:

TISSUE PAPER COLLAGE. Children can tear different colored pieces of tissue paper and put them in a box. The teacher can dilute white school glue with water in a bowl. Children can brush the diluted glue on the cardboard and place the tissue paper pieces of cardboard to create an artistic form. The children can then brush a second and third coat of diluted glue and add more tissue paper. The children's art work should be left to dry overnight. The children's artistic products can last longer by applying varnish or shellac to it.

Colored Sand. Children can paint with ordinary brown or white sand or sawdust that has been colored with tempera paint or food coloring. They draw designs with white glue, which they can squeeze out of a nozzle-topped plastic bottle. Colored sand is then sprinkled over the paper. The sand sets as the glue dries, and the excess sand can be shaken off. This process can be repeated on the same paper with another color of sand.

Murals. Most art projects are independent activities, but children can also be organized into groups to make murals. These can use a variety of materials and a variety of surfaces. Since mural painting uses a larger surface than either painting or drawing, more space will be needed for the project. Children can each be given their own section to work on or they can work on the whole mural together. Children should be helped to plan and work together as a group on a mural.

Experience:

COLLAGE MURAL. Children may make a mural of their neighborhood, school, community, or a place they have visited on a field trip. The children can use tempera paint, construction paper, crayons, magic markers and other available art media. Odds and ends of material with different textures can be used (e.g., yarn, string, corrugated paper, wood, foil, pipe cleaners, buttons, twigs, leaves, soap flakes). The teacher can cut off one side of a refrigerator box or other large corrogated cardboard box and cover it with butcher paper. Children can be creative in representing ponds, puddles, apartment houses and other features.

Other Materials. Children can use other materials to extend the basic use of two-dimensional art materials. Texture can be provided with the addition of materials such as sawdust, sand, flour, salt, liquid soap, and other items with different textures. Each child can take a piece of paper, one color of paint, and a brush and can experiment with mixing these materials in the paint or sprinkling it over the painted paper.

Providing tools other than brushes also adds variety to painting. Rollers, whisk brooms, straws, marbles, dispenser bottles (the squeezable kind), tinfoil pie plates, and cardboard box halves all work well with paint. Children can choose to paint with one or more of these tools.

Children can also dip a piece of string into paint and then drag it or drop it on the paper. They can place the string on a paper and fold the paper

Marking pens allow children to produce vividly colored drawings.

over, pressing down with one hand while pulling the string with the other. The paper is then opened and allowed to dry. Young children can drip some paint onto a paper and then blow through a straw over the paint to make patterns. If they blow from different points around the paper, the design can be varied.

The teacher can have the children paint with marbles to develop eye–hand coordination while creating pleasing designs. Take a muffin pan, put a different color of paint in each muffin holder, and drop a marble into each. Children can place a sheet of paper at the bottom of a shallow, open-top box. They can then take one of the paint-covered marbles from the muffin pan, drop it in the box, and move the box to allow the marble to roll over the paper. Then a marble of a different color can be substituted and the process repeated.

Three-Dimensional Art

Materials that are three-dimensional provide children with the opportunity to produce width, breadth, and depth. Three-dimensional media include blocks, wood, clay, and sand.

Blocks.   All early childhood classrooms should have a good set of wooden unit blocks. Unit blocks were discussed in the previous chapter as a play material. They can also be regarded as an art material, since block constructions resemble sculpture. It is helpful to provide accessories that extend the block structures. These can include the following:

Toys are useful accessories. Small cars, rubber or wooden people and animals, pulleys, airplanes, and trucks can all be used.

Colored cubes can be added to blocks, as can parquetry blocks or large dominoes. Assortments of odd-shaped small blocks or sewing thread spools can be put into boxes for use in decorating buildings.

Pebbles, small stones, and little sticks can serve as cargo for trains, boats, and trucks.

Lumber scraps, especially flat pieces for constructing roofs and wide bridges, will enhance block constructions.

Small, familiar signs such as "one way," "school crossing," or "bus stop" can be added to children's construction. Tongue depressors or popsicle sticks stuck in clay or play dough can be used to anchor these signs.

Thin pieces of rubber tubing tacked to a cylinder block can become a simple gas pump.

Excelsior makes good hay for farm animals.

Trees can be drawn on paper, cut out, stapled to a tongue depressor or popsicle stick, and stuck into a piece of clay or play dough to stand.

Pulleys, with ropes and containers, make wonderful elevators.

Dry cell batteries with bell wire and flashlight bulbs are popular accessories.

Magazine pictures of bridges, roads, constructions, or city scenes can be mounted on cardboard and displayed on the walls of the block area.

Children's books can be provided for the class to develop ideas for block construction. For example, if a theme is "city scenes," the books might include the following:

ZION, G., (1957) *Dear Garbage Man.* New York: Harper & Row.
GOODSPEED, J. (1956) *Let's Go Watch a Building Going Up.* New York: G. P. Putnam's Sons.
SCHNEIDER, H., AND N. SCHNEIDER (1954) *Let's Look Under the City.* New York: W. R. Scott and Co.
TRESSELT, A. (1957) *Wake Up City.* New York: Lothrop, Lee and Shepard Company.
ZOLOTOW, C. (1944) *The Park Book.* New York: Harper & Brothers.

Volunteer can be used to supplement the teacher when working on art projects.

Woodworking. Woodworking provides children with visual, motor, and problem-solving experiences. Constructing small objects with scrap wood, tools, glue, nails, and a variety of woodworking accessories helps children learn about tools and develop skills in using them.

A workbench, with a thick wooden top and with wood vises attached, should be provided for the woodwork area. Children learn to work with many types of tools including a hammer, saw, screwdriver, plane, vise, drill, clamp, and rasp. The tools should be of good quality. Hammer heads should be forged, not cast, and all tools should be in good repair, with saws and drills kept sharp to avoid frustration and to maintain safety. Proper care and safety are important considerations in the use of woodworking tools. Tools might be stored on a peg board or on shelves that are marked so that each tool gets placed in its proper position. Having children wear eye protectors while woodworking is a wise precaution.

Wood can easily be combined in different ways with other materials to develop satisfying results and interesting art forms. Since most of the wood used will be scrap material, it is important that teachers select only soft woods that can be worked by the children. Woodworking is especially useful for children who have experience primarily with store-bought toys. Many excellent suggestions regarding woodworking can be found in the NAEYC publication, *Woodworking for Young Children* (Skeen, Garner & Cartwright, 1984).

Experiences:

WOOD EXPERIENCES. Before introducing young children to carpentry with real tools, they can build with small bits of wood blocks to become familiar with and use shapes in different combinations, planning their work, and changing their building as they see new possibilities. Building and inventing with various shapes of wood blocks helps children to become aware of the many possibilities in ordinary shapes. Scraps of wood can be found in lumber yards, building supply stores, and carpenters' or cabinetmakers' shops. Wood to be used with children should be soft; it should also be clear (no knots or blemishes) and smooth (no splinters or jagged edges). A wide choice of materials can motivate children to create a boat (large block of wood at the bottom and a small one at the top), an airplane (two narrow strips glued at right angles with small pieces used to represent other parts, e.g., tail, motor). When children feel their project is completed, white glue can be introduced to hold it together. Working with glue will also help children combine wood with all other materials. Later, when they also know how to use other tools to shape and fasten wood, this skill will be useful.

Clay. Clay is a plastic art material which allows young children to mold three-dimensional objects. It provides children with an opportunity to create and recreate different shapes and sizes. At first, young children are not particularly concerned with making something with clay. They prefer to manipulate it, sense its feelings, experience its pliability, smell its earth odor, and notice its reaction to patting, pulling, twisting, squeezing, rolling, and shaping.

Experiences:

Children who have not had experience with clay or have trouble experimenting with clay need to hold the clay and describe how it feels.

Example: The teacher can ask such questions as: Is it cold? Can you squeeze it? How high can you make it? Can you push your finger through it? Can you make it smooth? Can you make it lumpy (Lowenfeld & Brittain, 1987)?

Such questions help children become aware of their own senses and help them identify with their work. The children's first successful experiences with clay will encourage other means of expression using clay. If the above questions do not stimulate children to use clay, the teacher may need to provide them with specific directions.

Example: The teacher can ask the children to:

1. Take a lump of clay and pat it into a ball with their hands.
2. Hold the clay in one hand.
3. Pinch the clay out, bend it, and pull it into as many different directions as they can.
4. Squeeze the clay into a fat sausage.
5. Roll the clay into a long coil.
6. Roll thin and fat coils out of clay.
7. Blend the coil of clay to find out how many shapes they can make out of the clay.
8. Bang the clay back into a ball.
9. Pat the ball of clay into a pancake.
10. Tear off parts of their pancake into different shapes.
11. Make their shape stand up.
12. Create an animal out of clay.

After they are allowed to spend time manipulating the clay, they can squeeze it into a fat sausage, roll it out into a long coil, or shape it in a variety of ways. They can compare the length and thickness of the coils they make. They can then see how many things they can make with their coils.

When children have some experience manipulating clay, they can begin making simple pots and bowls. Have them make balls and then use their thumb to make holes in them. By squeezing the hole toward the outside, they can shape a bowl. If they hold the ball of clay in one hand, they can pinch out a pot with the thumb and fingers of their other hand. They can pull up the pots to make them tall, or pull out the pots to make them wide. When they have finished shaping the pots, they can press them gently on the table to make flat bottoms (See Figure 11–1).

Clay, like blocks, can be used with accessories. These include paints (to color dry clay objects), rolling pins, tongue depressors, plastic knives and forks for cutting and designing, buttons and yarn, acorns or other vegetables for making prints, and waxed paper or aluminum foil for molding clay objects.

There are several variations of clay which can provide different textures, different feeling, and smell. These include:

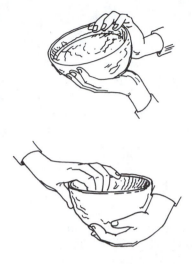

FIGURE 11-1   Making Pottery

Plasticine, an oil-based nonhardening clay. It is stiffer and harder for children to manipulate. It does not dry out, however, and can be used over and over again.

Sawdust and wheat paste mixtures provide a rough texture, but children find they offer a pleasing feeling. This medium cannot be molded too thickly because it will not dry properly. Objects made with this type of clay can be dried more quickly by being placed in a slow oven to evaporate the water.

Papier-mâché is made by tearing newspaper or newsprint into small pieces and adding warm water. Once the paper is completely wet, any excess water is squeezed out and wheat paste is added to make the material into a malleable clay. Once papier-mâché is molded and dried, it will not break. Objects that are molded too thickly may mildew, however. To avoid this, a hole can be made in the bottom of the molded object to allow circulation of air and to hasten drying. While it is drying, the object can be turned from side to side until it becomes hard. Projects using papier-mâché should be simple for young children and should not take so long that children lose interest.

Play dough can be made by mixing two cups of flour with one cup of salt and then adding enough water to make it into a "clay." The children can mold it, or can roll it and cut out forms. Food coloring or tempera paint can also be added. Adding a bit of vegetable oil or glycerine to the recipe will keep the dough from drying too quickly.

Cornstarch clay is made by cooking cornstarch and water until the starch is dissolved. The starch is cooled until it thickens, and then tempera paint can be added for color. When ready, the children can mold it.

Sand.   A sand table kept in class allows for excellent modeling activities. The sand should be sprinkled with water each morning to allow it to become moist enough for the children to mold. Sandboxes can also be used in other ways. Instead of sand in the sandbox, wood shavings, small pebbles, or rice can be substituted. Although these do not lend themselves to modeling, they are fun to have for activities such as measuring and pouring.

Cornstarch clay offers a medium for modeling.

Craft Activities

Craft projects have the same characteristics as three-dimensional art projects, though they tend to be more practical. Craft projects can serve different purposes. For example, children can create Christmas ornaments to decorate the tree, or they can create Mother's Day gifts. Although some craft projects require teacher direction, an emphasis should be placed on the children's personal creativity.

People: Spoons and Clothespins. Help the children to select objects such as corks or short sticks, and add bits of scrap materials to make small people. Only

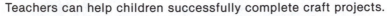

Teachers can help children successfully complete craft projects.

FIGURE 11-2   People: Spoons and Clothespins

a small amount of scrap material is needed to convert a spoon or clothespin into a little doll. These can be stuck into a wad of play dough or clay so they can stand up straight. Bits of fabric and yarn can be glued on for clothing and hair, and a crayon, felt tip pen, or small pieces of fabric can be used to make the eyes and mouth for the face (see Figure 11-2).

Walnut Shell Boats.   Let children place small balls of clay into unbroken walnut shell halves. A sail the size of a postage stamp can be drawn and cut out of a piece of cloth or soft material, then mounted on a toothpick or dowel and pushed into the clay (see Figure 11-3).

Walnut Shell Boats

Cupcake Bells   FIGURE 11-3

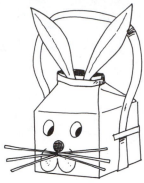

Nut and Candy Dish for Thanksgiving

Easter Basket

FIGURE 11–4

Cupcake Bells. Have the children join three or more cupcake papers with different lengths of strings. The strings can be inserted through the middle of the cups with a tapestry needle. The bells are adjusted so that they fall at different levels (see Figure 11–3). Cupcake papers of assorted colors will be more colorful. Jingle bells can be attached for clappers.

Easter Basket. Have the children open the top of a half-pint milk or cream container. The container can be cleaned, then painted inside and out with quick-drying paint. The children cut two long ears and a round circle for a nose from construction paper and staple or glue these on the container. Children can add other features, like whiskers made from pipe cleaners or thick strips of paper. A handle made of fancy string can be attached to make this Easter Bunny into a basket (see Figure 11–4).

Thanksgiving Nut and Candy Dish. Have the children twist two pipe cleaners together and shape them to make a head and long neck. Insert these in the base of an aluminum foil mini-cup, separate them at one end, overlap these ends so that the head remains steady. Shape another aluminum foil mini-cup into a lady's fan to form the turkey's tail and glue or tape it to the outside of the aluminum foil mini-cup, opposite the side where the head and neck were inserted. Adjust it for balance. This can be used as a candy/nut dish, or a table setting (see Figure 11–4).

MUSIC ACTIVITIES

Music is as important a part of young children's experience as it is to adults. Music shows the essence of the human spirit and brings joy to the quality of living. A good music program should be integrated in an early childhood curriculum. Sally Moomaw (1987, p. 7) suggests the following music goals for young children:

- Children should have many opportunities to explore music through their voices, through their body movements, and through making sounds with instruments.
- They should have opportunities to express emotions through music.
- They should gain increased understanding of what makes different kinds of sounds.
- They should have opportunities to expand listening skills.
- They should develop awareness of body image and self-identity.
- They should develop enjoyment of music.
- They should explore their own creativity in music.
- They should have experiences that reflect their developmental needs.
- They should have opportunities for group participation.

Young children become engrossed in music activities. Their eyes sparkle, their body moves, their mind discovers rhythmic language as their mood and feelings surface. Young children enjoy music, singing spontaneously when they work and play, clapping their hands and moving their bodies to the different sounds they hear, and creating their own sounds.

Teachers can provide young children with a wide variety of musical experiences while allowing them to be unique and creative. Music experiences in early childhood education should allow for both individual experimentation and group participation. Just as teachers can have a good art education program without being artists themselves, they can also plan and implement good music experiences with young children even though they are not musicians. Early childhood music experiences should include rhythmic activity, singing, and playing musical instruments.

Rhythmic Activities

Even infants love to experiment with rhythms, playing such rhythmic games as pat-a-cake. Young children sense rhythms and easily match movement with music. Rhythmic activities offer children ways to explore the pulse, relative duration, and flow of sound. They keep time with music when they hear recordings, sing songs, act out nursery rhymes, or chant songs or poems. Exploratory and imitative experiences provide young children with a range of rhythmic movements, both musical and nonmusical.

Children create informal and spontaneous rhythms which teachers can extend by adding a chant, encouraging hand clapping, or playing an instrument. Teachers should not be concerned if the movements do not synchronize with the beat. Repetition helps children to control their rhythmic responses. Young children learn to synchronize movement with the beat as they experience music with instruments, action songs and games, visual devices (e.g., clocks and metronomes), and recordings with predominant rhythmic character.

Children who have better motor coordination can test out rhythmic patterns through clapping and chanting word rhythms of poetry and songs. They can improvise, share ideas, and verbalize their rhythmic knowledge through basic musical terms such as fast–slow, long–short, and even–uneven (MacDonald,

1979). They can further develop their knowledge of low, medium, and high notes by demonstrating these concepts through movement: squatting down for low notes, kneeling or touching their waists for middle notes, or standing on tiptoe and reaching high in the air for high notes. They can also find other ways of illustrating the differences in musical pitch.

Teachers can encourage rhythmic experiences by playing music on a piano, guitar, or record player and having the children walk, run, spin, or slide. Playing different rhythms on an instrument such as a drum or tambourine also helps. Slow beats can be played for walking, fast beats for running, and other beats can call young children to skip, roll over, slide, jump, or stretch. If children move around a circle in the same direction during movement activities, they can avoid colliding as they move. Young children should be given the opportunity to select the music for their movements or asked how the music they hear makes them feel.

Scarves extend children's movement. They can hold scarves above their head and run with them, pretending that they are airplanes, flying, landing, and taking off again. Or they can roll the scarf into their hands, pretending that they are balls, then throw the scarves up high. As the scarves begin to float downward, children can retrieve them and move with them. A scarf can also be a cape. Or if two children hold a scarf up in the air, they can lower it and raise it, pretending they are ocean waves. As children listen to different kinds of music, they can move their arms and the scarf.

Young children are particularly interested in repetitive songs, chants, action plays, nursery rhymes, and any form of expressions that link rhythm to words and sounds. Repetitive songs provide interesting musical experiences and usually encourage movement participation. *Here We Go Round the Mulberry Bush, London Bridge, Old McDonald, Are You Sleeping,* and the *Farmer in the Dell* are popular with young children. Nursery rhymes are also repetitive and add rhythm and bounce to the children's chanting experiences.

Example:

Mary Had a Little Lamb

Mary had a little lamb
Little lamb, little lamb
Mary had a little lamb
His fleece was white as snow

And everywhere that Mary went
Mary went, Mary went
And everywhere that Mary went
The lamb was sure to go.

Teddy Bear

Teddy Bear, Teddy Bear,
Turn around
Teddy Bear, Teddy Bear,
Touch the ground.

The rhymes encourage the use of children's action and become more enjoyable if you insert the child's name wherever possible. For example, Jane had a little lamb or Michael, Michael turn around.

The People on the Bus

The people on the bus go up and down, up and down, up and down.
The people on the bus go up and down, all through the town.
The wheels on the bus go round and round, round and round, round and round,
The wheels on the bus go round and round, all through the town
The horn on the bus goes toot, toot, toot, toot, toot, toot, toot, toot, toot
The horn on the bus goes toot, toot, toot, all through the town.
The money in the box goes ding, ding, ding, ding, ding, ding, ding, ding, ding.
The money in the box goes ding, ding, ding, all through the town.
The wipers on the bus go swish, swish, swish, swish, swish, swish, swish, swish, swish,
The wipers on the bus go swish, swish, swish, all through the town.
The driver on the bus says, "Move on back, move on back, move on back."
The driver on the bus says, "Move on back," all through the town.

Singing with Young Children

As children listen to and learn songs, their listening skills are developed and they gain an emotional release, just as adults do. The use of their own voices provides young children with the concrete experience which is essential to their understanding of what makes a vocal sound. Young children, while singing, test their ideas of soft and loud, high and low, fast and slow.

Young children's first musical experience is often group singing. MacDonald (1979) believes that young children can integrate movement, speech, and

The autoharp serves as an excellent accompaniment for group singing.

singing to develop chants in accord with their melodic configurations, repetitive character, and rhythmic movement. Teachers can employ these chants to describe daily events and as an aid in making transitions from one activity to another as well as to teach the value of singing.

It is not unusual for young children to create spontaneous songs about what they are doing. Young children sing when they work and play, often singing bits and pieces of works that they create to match their rhythmic movements. They may chant, "I'm baking an apple pie," or "See me swing up and down." Teachers can sing the chants and songs children create. They can ask the children to repeat the songs, and the melody and words can be recorded. The children will enjoy seeing their songs written down or hearing them played back on the piano or guitar or replayed on a tape recorder.

Young children usually prefer songs with a good melody, easy words, and actions. Children who do not know the song well will repeat whatever they know over and over again. Their singing may be off pitch or loud and it may have more gusto than skill. Any enthusiastic and repetitive music experience can be an enriching one.

Singing demands that words and vocal pitch be combined. Teachers should present songs that are developmentally appropriate for young children, starting with songs that have a limited melodic range, then gradually introduce songs with greater tonal variety. When young children are ready, teachers can teach them concepts about melody through singing. Appropriate teaching strategies include physical motions according to the direction of a song's melody, and visual cues composed of dashes or musical notes (which do not have to be presented on the musical staff) showing high–low, same, and up–down tones. Visual/tactile music experiences can include song bells, piano keyboard, or step bells. The children's knowledge of pitch can be used as they sing familiar songs and demonstrate the melodic flow.

The variety of cultures and backgrounds of children in our society require that a variety of musical experiences be included. Some appropriate songs can be found in a music textbook. The children themselves are often the best sources in selecting the songs.

There are also a variety of songbooks that teachers can use as resources. Bernard Spodek (1985) suggests the following songbooks to use with young children:

DIETZ, B. W., AND T. C. PARKS (1964). *Folk Songs of China, Japan, and Korea*. New York: John Day.

FOWKE, E. (1969). *Sally Go Round the Sun*. NY: Doubleday.

GLAZER, T. (1973). *Eye Winker Tom Tinker Chin Chopper: Fifty Musical Fingerplays*. Garden City, NY: Doubleday.

JENKINS, E. (1969). *The Ella Jenkins Song Book for Children*. New York: Oak Publications.

LANDECK, B. (1950). *Songs to Grow On*. New York: William Morrow.

———. (1954). *More Songs to Grow On*. New York: William Morrow.

LANGSTAFF, N., AND J. LANGSTAFF (1970). *Jim Along, Josie*. New York: Harcourt Brace Jovanovich.

SEEGER, R. C. (1948). *American Folk Songs for Children*. Garden City, NY: Doubleday.

———. (1950). *Animal Folk Songs for Children*. Garden City, NY: Doubleday.

SENDAK, M. (1975). *Maurice Sendak's Really Rosie: Starring the Nutshell Kids.* New York: Harper & Row.
WINN, M. (1966). *The Fireside Book of Children's Songs.* New York: Simon & Schuster.
———. (1970). *What Shall We Do and Allee Galloo!* New York: Harper & Row.

Good songs can have several characteristics, including:

1. They are short or divided into several verses and a chorus.
2. They contain verbal or melodic repetition.
3. They suggest physical activity or instrumental accompaniment.
4. They relate to the familiar.
5. They stimulate the mind and imagination.
6. They may relate to other areas of the program being covered. (Joan, Haines, & Gerber, 1984)

In selecting songs for young children, the teacher should look for songs:

1. That appeal to children through their clear rhythm, pleasing and simple melody, their limited, singable range, and the interest of their content.
2. That are known and liked by the teacher.
3. Whose meaning is reflected in the style of the music. (Joan, Haines, & Gerber, 1984)

Teachers need to view themselves as participants to be able to relax and concentrate on the musical activity rather than themselves (Jalongo & Collins, 1985). Thus, teachers should not be performers but should sing *with* the children.

Many popular artists have recorded children's songs on a wide range of topics (e.g., patriotism, animals, community workers). Young children enjoy records from these artists (such as Ella Jenkins, Tom Glazer, Steve Millang). Records of songs young children enjoy can be obtained from the following companies:

Bowmar Records
622 Rodler Road
Glendale, CA 91201

Folkways Records
701 Second Avenue
New York, NY 10036

Children's Records of America
159 W. 53rd Street
New York NY 10019

Silver Burdett Co.
250 James Street
Morristown, NJ 07960

Columbia Children's Record Library
CBS, Inc.
15 W. 52nd Street
New York, NY 10019

New songs should be introduced in a simple and easy way. Teachers should introduce the songs themselves. The children may not respond the first or second time the songs are presented. It takes a while for young children to understand and remember the words, and it takes even longer to get a clear idea of the melody. Listening capacity and vocal control are acquired more slowly by some children than others, although most children will acquire these skills to some degree if they are exposed to music and no one pressures them. Teachers need to encourage young children to sing, even if they are not singing the right tune. Drill on either words or music should be avoided with preschool children. Teachers should sing a song straight through, helping the children understand its meaning and allowing young children to catch what they can, even if it is only the last note.

Using Musical Instruments

Musical instruments should be provided in early childhood classes for children to play both independently and in a group. While some of these musical instruments can be made by teachers or children, commercial instruments should also be available since most homemade instruments do not have fine tone quality. Drums, tambourines, gourds and maracas, metal triangles, a variety of bells (for example, jingle bells, dainty table bells, cowbells), a xylophone, and cymbals should be included.

Children need to explore the instruments. They can use them with songs, chants, and records, exploring melodic directions (such as up, down, same), tempo (such as fast, slow, getting faster, getting slower), and rhythmic patterns, and producing original tunes and rhythm sounds.

Young children should experiment with both pitched and unpitched instruments. Each type of instrument makes a different sound, and by playing even an unpitched instrument differently (e.g., hard or soft, fast or slow), they can produce a different sound. They also learn that the size of an instrument affects

For the youngest children it is best to experiment with unpitched musical instruments.

the sound it makes: large drums make a lower tone than little drums, and the long bars on the xylophone make a lower tone than the short bars.

Experiences with instruments develop young children's understandings of sounds and music. Instruments can also help children express their feelings and promote their creativity. In addition, they improve children's eye–hand coordination and fine motor skills.

Sally Moomaw (1987) identifies three different types of instruments to be used with young children: rhythm instruments, melody instruments, and accompanying instruments (See Table 11–1).

Rhythm instruments are those that are struck or scraped to create nonpitched sounds. Rhythm instruments for young children are those usually found in the percussion section of an orchestra. They include tone blocks or wood blocks, rhythm sticks, claves, guiros, triangles, and cymbals.

Melody instruments are those that make sounds with certain pitches to create tunes or melodies. These include xylophones, melody bells, and zithers.

Accompanying instruments produce tones or chords, such as do the piano, autoharp, and guitar. Teachers usually play these instruments. While the piano is an excellent accompanying instrument, it requires considerable training for someone to accompany songs.

There are many homemade instruments that can be made by the teacher. Children can make some instruments as well. Kathryn Bayless and Marjorie Ramsey (1982) have provided suggestions for making several instruments, such as coconut shell clappers, rhythm blocks, and hand shakers (see Figure 11–5).

For *coconut shell clappers,* take a coconut that has the ends rounded to fit in the children's hands. Tap a hole in it and let it dry for several months so that the substance inside shrinks away from the sides. Place the coconut in a vise and saw through the middle, then lift out the substance inside the coconut with a

TABLE 11-1   Types of Instruments and Examples of Each

RHYTHM INSTRUMENTS	MELODY INSTRUMENTS	ACCOMPANYING INSTRUMENTS
tone blocks or wood blocks	xylophones	autoharps
rhythm sticks	melody bells	guitars
claves	zithers	drums
triangles	glockenspiels	pianos
cymbals		
finger cymbals		
maracas		
castanets		
tambourines		
drums		
jingle bells		
jingle sticks		
cowbells		
sand blocks		

Rhythm Blocks

Coconut Shell Clappers

Hand Shaker

FIGURE 11-5   Homemade Instruments

knife. Children can take the shells and clap them together to make a hollow sound similar to horses' hooves.

To make *rhythm blocks,* match two scraps of wood, 1 inch or less thick, which are similar in shape, size, thickness, and length. Sand the blocks until they are smooth. A design can be painted on them. Attach drawer handles or empty thread spools to be used as holders. Different sets of rhythm blocks of different sizes, shapes, thickness, and length will make different sounds when struck together.

To make a *hand shaker,* carve a handle at one end of a wooden board approximately 1 inch wide, 8 inches long, and ¼ inch thick. It should now look like a paddle. Straighten out four soft-drink bottle caps and punch a hole in the middle of each. Place a ½-inch washer between two of these and nail them to the wood on the opposite end of the handle. Nail another set of bottle caps and washer further back.

A *drum* can be made out of a coffee can with a plastic cover. A more authentic drum can be made by removing both sides of the can and stretching rubber or animal hide across the openings at each end. A *gong* can be made by suspending a 50-gallon steel drum from ropes. A garden hose *flute* can be made out of a foot-long piece of garden hose corked at one end, with holes bored down one side. A *washtub bass* can be created out of a galvanized washtub, a broom handle, and a 5-foot piece of heavy string or cord. The tub is placed upside down on the floor. One end of a cord is attached to a screw eye in the end of the broom handle and the other to an eye-bolt set in the center of the tub. The other end of the broom handle is notched and placed on the tub's edge. The cord is tightened and loosened by rocking back with the broom handle. The cord can be plucked like a bass fiddle.

Instruments allow young children to experiment with sounds, join in a rhythm band, observe older children playing instruments, create original tunes, and play spontaneously. Teachers must be careful that they do not pressure young children to participate or to produce rigid patterned musical activities.

Teachers of young children should encourage their students to explore and discover musical instruments.

MOVEMENT EDUCATION

Adults enjoy moving in certain ways as well as watching the movement of others. For example, they delight in seeing a person score a point at tennis, make a basket, or win a track race. Precision and grace are qualities that can be found in activities such as dancing, skating, diving, and gymnastics. Movement education teaches young children physical skills related to moving. Children should learn and acquire the necessary understanding and self-confidence at their own rate. Carol Copple, Irving Sigel, and Ruth Saunders (1979) note three factors relating to the children's early movement development: children respond to music, emotion, or mood. They use these factors to provide an understanding of the representational possibilities of movement. Movement education also emphasizes an appreciation of individual differences, task persistence, self-motivation, self-esteem, and enjoyment.

A movement education program should reflect differences in children's development. Characteristics of children's physical development and their program needs and implications are noted in Table 11–2.

TABLE 11–2 Characteristics, Interests, and Needs Important in Program Planning

PRESCHOOL (NURSERY SCHOOL)	
Characteristics	*Program Needs and Implications*
Cognitive Domain	
Is unable to sit still for more than a brief period.	Utilize movement experiences for learning activities.
Constantly explores environment.	Allow for creative effort, exploratory opportunity.
Shows little differentiation of fantasy from reality.	Offer activities that include elements of reality and fantasy so that they can learn to identify both.
Uses numbers without understanding concept of quantity.	Play active games that require simple counting.
Can make a choice between two alternatives.	Provide opportunities for children to make appropriate decisions.
Is capable of following directions if not more than two ideas are given.	Keep directions simple and straightforward, with one or two points of emphasis.
Begins to use words to express feelings.	Emphasize dramatic play.
Affective domain	
Has fear of heights, of falling.	Provide successful experiences in climbing and jumping off boxes (moderate height).
Can have strong fear of failure.	Allow to progress at own rate, but encourage experimentation.
Likes rhythmic activities.	Gross motor activities to rhythm. Simple rhythms. Marching. Action songs.

(Continued)

TABLE 11-2 *(Continued)*

PRESCHOOL (NURSERY SCHOOL)

Characteristics	Program Needs and Implications
Is self-conscious	Avoid sarcasm, ridicule, laughing at children. Seek emotional satisfaction.
May be shy.	Bring out through participation and acceptance. Encourage to "show."
Has great desire to imitate.	Offer opportunities to imitate animals, machines, professional personnel, and parental figures.
Needs constant encouragement.	Place emphasis on effort rather than reward for quality performance only.
Likes to play individually or in small groups of two or three.	Allow time for individual play and aid children in learning to play with others.
Shows great imagination.	Offer play opportunities where imagination is valued. New ways of playing games or creating make-believe characters that move are excellent.

Psychomotor Domain

Is awkward; shows inefficient movement.	Keep activity within the maturity level.
Binocular vision is slowly developing.	Provide hand-eye, object-handling experiences.
May walk well, but have difficulty with other loco-motor skills.	Provide wide variety of motor challenges. Stress hopping, skipping, galloping, etc.
Climbing skills need development.	Offer experiences of climbing over low, inclined planks, packing boxes, on jungle gyms, stairs.
Balance skills are developing.	Offer activities involving simple balancing.
Begins to develop throwing patterns.	Allow for hand-eye experiences with appropriate balls, beanbags, etc.
Is learning to use the hands.	Offer experiences of handling and guiding objects such as scooters, little cars, building blocks, etc.
May have trouble with eye control.	Provide low-level hand–eye experiences.
Toilet routines may need control.	Get children to accept this responsibility.
Physical growth slows down comparatively.	As physical growth slows, the child's readiness to learn motor skills increases.
	Allow many opportunities for the child to practice gross and fine motor skills.
Starts to develop agility in movement.	Offer hurdles to jump and mini-obstacle courses as challenges. Offer practice in starting, stopping, dodging, and changing direction.
	Offer game activities that require few rules and offer activity for all children.
Catching skills begin to mature.	Practice catching skills with objects that move slowly (balloons, beachballs) and will not cause fear.
Many motor learning patterns become ingrained.	Show children the proper way to perform various skills.

KINDERGARTEN AND FIRST GRADE

Characteristics	Program Needs and Implications
Cognitive Domain	
Has short attention span.	Change activity often. Offer short explanations.
Is interested in what his body can do. Is curious.	Offer movement experiences. Give attention to basic movement.
Wants to know. Asks "why" often about movements.	Explain reasons for various activities and movements.

TABLE 11-2 *(Continued)*

KINDERGARTEN AND FIRST GRADE

Characteristics	Program Needs and Implications
Expresses individual views and ideas.	Allow children time to do their own thing. Expect problems when children are lined up and asked to perform the same task.
Begins to understand the idea of teamwork.	Allow some opportunity for situations that require group cooperation. Discuss the importance of such.
Sense of humor is expanding.	Insert some humor into the teaching process.
Is highly creative	Allow opportunity for students to try new and different ways of performing activities. Sharing ideas with friends will encourage them to create.
Affective Domain	
Shows no sex differences regarding interests.	Offer same activities for both boys and girls.
Is sensitive and individualistic. The ''I'' concept is very important. Accepts defeat poorly.	Encourage taking turns; sharing with others; and winning, losing, or being caught gracefully.
Likes small group activity.	Use entire class grouping sparingly. Break into small groups.
Is sensitive to feelings of adults. Likes to please teacher.	Offer needed praise and encouragement.
Can be reckless.	Stress sane approaches.
Enjoys rough-and-tumble activity.	Include rolling, dropping to the floor, etc., in both introductory and program activities. Stress simple stunts and tumbling.
Seeks personal attention.	Recognize children through both verbal and nonverbal means. See that all have a chance to be the center of attention.
Loves to climb and explore play environments.	Provide play materials, games, and apparatus for strengthening large muscles. Examples are climbing towers, wagons, tricycles, jump ropes, miniobstacle courses, and turning bars, to name only a few.
Psychomotor Domain	
Is noisy, constantly active, egocentric, exhibitionist. Is imitative and imaginative. Wants attention.	Offer vigorous games and stunts; games with individual roles—hunting, dramatic activities, story plays; few team games or relays.
Large muscles are more developed; game skills are not developed.	Stress basic movement and fundamental skills of throwing, catching, bouncing balls.
Is naturally rhythmical.	Provide music and rhythm with skills: creative rhythms, folk dances singing games.
May become suddenly tired, but soon recovers.	Use activities of brief duration. Provide short rest periods or include moderately vigorous activities.
Eye–hand coordination is developing.	Offer opportunity to handle objects such as balls, beanbags, hoops, etc.
Perceptual-motor areas are important.	Offer practice in balance, unilateral, bilateral, and cross-lateral movements.
Pelvic tilt can be pronounced.	Give attention to posture problems. Provide abdominal strengthening activities.

Robert P. Pangrazi & Victor P. Dauer, *Movement in Early Childhood and Primary Education* (Minneapolis: Burgess Publishing Co., 1981), pp. 13–15.

Creative Movement

Movement serves both a communicative and aesthetic function. Though the movement components are the same in both, communication is the major function in pantomime, while the aesthetic quality of the movement is more important in dance.

Movement education, based on an understanding of various movement elements developed by Rudolph Laban (1971), is a relatively new approach to learning. The parts of the body vary in their relationship to each other and to objects (near, far; on, around, under). The number and variation of actions (such as stepping, balancing, crawling) are infinite. Movement in space occurs in several directions, at different levels along pathways of certain kinds (such as straight, curved, zigzag), and in a wide range of movement from small to large. Speed and rhythm also affect movement. Their force fluctuates in a continuum from strong to weak and in quality from sudden to sustained, while the flow varies in its degree of freedom. Children experience, experiment, observe, discover, analyze, and formulate ideas as they acquire knowledge and form concepts. Ideas are classified and analyzed to associate information into meaningful concepts. Emphasis is placed on the children's intellectual development and the wide range of skill and maturity which is found among the individuals in any class.

Laban has proposed the use of movement exploration to make children aware of the diverse capacity in the movement of the body rather than dictating to children specific directions in movement. Open-ended problems with wide alternative solutions requiring no right or wrong answers are offered. Follow-up questions encouraging children to explore additional alternatives should also be provided. Laban urges that an understanding of the movement education structure and its process lay the foundation for physical education. He employs the media of games, gymnastics, and dance to promote the child's physical and emotional development through movement concepts such as body awareness, space, quality of movement, and relationships.

Movement Activities for Physical Development

Robert P. Pangrazi and Victor P. Dauer (1981) suggest that movement activities at the early childhood level should include (1) movement experiences and body mechanics, which are locomotor, nonlocomotor, and manipulative; (2) rhythmics; (3) apparatus; (4) stunts and tumbling; (5) simple games; and (6) sports' skills and activities. These activities can provide a balance in games, gymnastics, and dance, although less emphasis should be placed on games.

Games.   The main purpose of early childhood games is personal challenge; in games with older children, one challenges an opponent. Competition is an element of all games, but young children enjoy it only when they have mastered the required skills. The skills developed in the early years that are fundamental to games include visual perception (e.g., spatial body awareness, spatial relations, form constancy, figure/ground), auditory discrimination (e.g., sound localization, rhythm discrimination, figure/ground selection), tactile-touch, kinesthetics, sensory integration (e.g., balance, exploration, eye–hand coordination), strength, endurance, flexibility, and motor ability (e.g., balance, power, coordination, speed, agility, rhythm). The movements related to these skills include balancing, bouncing, catching, hopping, jumping, pushing, running, tagging, twisting, and many others (Eason and Smith, 1976). Games can provide opportunities for children to practice these skills. Teachers can offer children individual assistance as well.

Gymnastics. Gymnastics helps children control their bodies so they can move skillfully, safely, and aesthetically. Gymnastic activities should be related to children's developmental level. The activities should be individualized, with tasks provided to each child that are challenging but not frustrating.

Coordinating Movement Activities. Movement activities should include a balance of games, gymnastics, and dance. Themes can be used that touch on specific concepts and skills. The theme of flying, for example, can incorporate a series of activities to emphasize jumping and landing. They explore basic jumps, such as jumping from one foot to another, on one foot to the same foot, and so on. Using a theme ensures that relationships are clarified and similarities and differences are accentuated (Spodek, Saracho, & Lee, 1984).

The activities for a movement theme can evolve around an obstacle course, a structured arrangement that includes a series of obstacles to develop all the movement attributes. The children must crawl under them, jump over them, climb on them or walk around obstacles. Objects are spaced so that several children can work on them separately but simultaneously. In the obstacle course illustrated in Figure 11–6, a child may move in different ways between the tractor tires on the ground—jump on one foot, jump on two feet, or turn in the air while jumping; another child may balance in the balance walk; still another child may climb or run through the ladder. The obstacle course can be used individually or with a group. It allows children to use the equipment without waiting for or interfering with each other. Children enjoy going over, under, and through the objects.

Movement activities can be coordinated with other areas of the curriculum. In teaching children to follow directions, the teacher can offer instructions for children to perform as follows:

Clap walk, walk clap
Clap step, step clap
Give a little twist
Then clap, clap, clap.

Teachers and children can change the words and make up songs similar to this with different actions. This activity can be extended, with the instructions becoming more complicated. Young children can be given the following directions:

Clap, clap your hands
Pat your knees
Rub your arms
Touch your nose
Crawl around
Walk on your knees
Jump up and down
Jiggle all over
Turn around
Jump around
Jump up and down
Rub your legs
Wash your hair
Jump up and down (again)
Sit back down

The teacher can also teach counting, asking the children to join her or him in a small circle. They all sit down. Children are asked to count slowly to ten and to clap their hands as they say each number. When they reach number ten, they get up, jump high into the air, shout their name, and immediately come back to their beginning sitting position with the palms of their hands flat on the floor. This activity can be varied by shouting the name, saying it in a whisper, or saying different words.

Through movement activities children can develop increased skills and control of their muscles. Their bodies become a medium for creative expression as the children learn to use the various parts of their bodies competently. Self-concept becomes more positive as children feel they can do more with their own selves.

Movement activities should be individualized so that children can learn without being pressured. Children should work on their own capabilities at their own rate, disregarding any specified standards. A practical method for individualizing instruction is using activity centers, which can be set up in a gymnasium, a playground, an all-purpose room, or a regular classroom. Figure 11–7 provides an example of three activity centers for skills and activities. An activity sign at each center displays designated skills and tasks. Each child selects an area and takes a skill sheet; since children this age are usually unable to read, the sheets can have pictures instead of words. Students can move to other areas before mastering all levels of a particular skill.

Several learning alternatives should be provided for each skill to be taught, with the activities within each area varying in complexity. Children can work on the skill they need to develop, following the directions given on the sheet. For example, instructions on developing a skill may consist of a series of pictures illustrating how a specific skill may be mastered and the types of activities that develop these skills.

Activity centers make it easier for the teacher to work with the children on a one-to-one basis without taking time from the class or embarrassing them. Elsie C. Burton (1977) identified several steps to implement activity centers: (1)

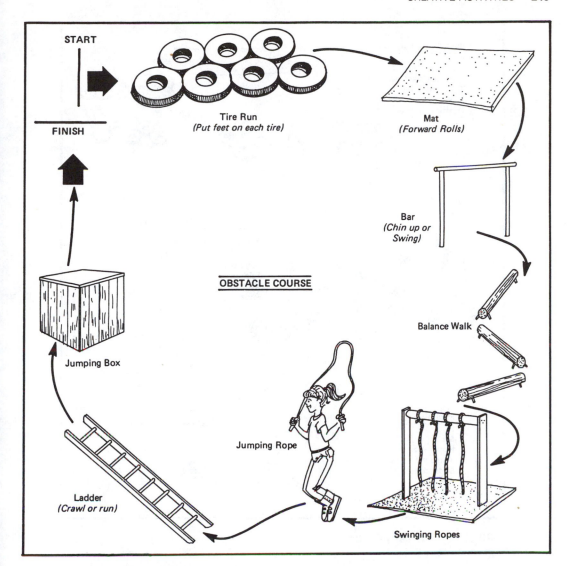

START

FINISH

Tire Run
(Put feet on each tire)

Mat
(Forward Rolls)

Bar
*(Chin up or
Swing)*

OBSTACLE COURSE

Balance Walk

Jumping Box

Jumping Rope

Ladder
(Crawl or run)

Swinging Ropes

FIGURE 11-6   Obstacle Course

the teacher presents to the children the different types of learning experiences that are available; (2) she or he provides the children with the opportunity to select the skill(s) they wish to pursue; (3) the teacher and the children discuss the process and the performance objectives for each child; (4) the teacher recommends instructions on how the task can be completed, where equipment and supplies are located, and the time limit; and (5) the teacher offers instructions and enrichment materials. Instructional materials and resources help children work toward their own goals independently, with a partner, or in a small group.

Activity centers must be varied to propose a wide range of options. However, activity centers depend on facilities, equipment, instructional materials,

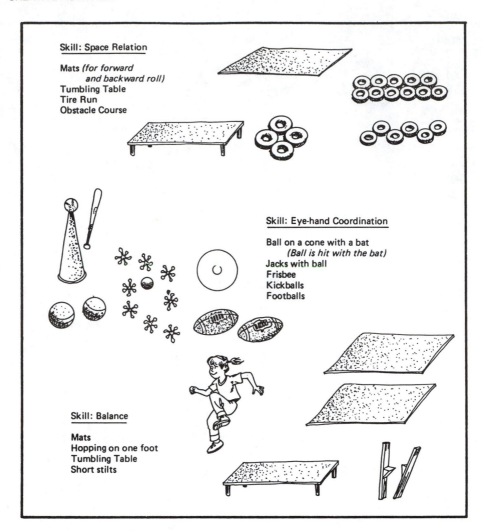

Skill: Space Relation

Mats *(for forward and backward roll)*
Tumbling Table
Tire Run
Obstacle Course

Skill: Eye-hand Coordination

Ball on a cone with a bat
(Ball is hit with the bat)
Jacks with ball
Frisbee
Kickballs
Footballs

Skill: Balance

Mats
Hopping on one foot
Tumbling Table
Short stilts

FIGURE 11-7   Activity Centers

and, most important, the teacher's philosophy concerning the students' responsibility and decision making.

SUMMARY

Young children can learn to express themselves through a variety of media. Art, music, and movement all offer opportunities for children to use their imaginations. As they develop skills in each area, the children can become more creative in their productions.

Young children express themselves in a variety of ways. Early childhood programs should support this expression using art, music, and movement as forms of expression. A balance of skill development and opportunity for creative expression should characterize these program activities.

REFERENCES

BAYLESS, K. M., AND M. E. RAMSEY (1982). *Music: A way of life for the young child* (2nd ed.). Saint Louis: C. V. Mosby.

BURTON, E. C. (1977). *The new physical education for elementary school children.* Boston: Houghton Mifflin.

COPPLE, C., I. SIGEL, AND R. SAUNDERS (1979). *Educating the young thinker.* New York: Van Nostrand.

EASON, R. L., AND T. L. SMITH (1976). A perceptual motor program model for learning-disabled children. *Physical Education Research Journal, 33* (1), 4.

JALONGO, M. R. AND M. COLLINS (1965). Singing with young children. *Young Children, 40*(2), 17.

JOAN, B., E. HAINES, AND L. GERBER (1984). *Leading young children to music.* Columbus, OH: Merrill.

LABAN, R. (1971). *The mastery of movement.* London: Macdonald and Evans.

LASKY, L., AND R. MUKERJI (1980). *Art: Basic for young children.* Washington, DC: National Association for the Education of Young Children.

LIGON, E. M. (1957). *The growth and development of Christian personality.* Schenectady, NY: The Union College Character Research Project.

LOWENFELD, V., AND W. L. BRITTAIN (1987). *Creative and mental growth* (8th ed.). New York: Macmillan.

MACDONALD, D. T. (1979). *Music in our lives: The early years.* Washington, DC: National Association for the Education of Young Children.

MOOMAW, S. (1987). *Discovering music in early childhood* (2nd ed.). Boston: Allyn & Bacon.

PANGRAZI, R. P., AND V. P. DAUER (1981). *Movement in early childhood and primary education.* Minneapolis: Burgess Publishing Co.

SKEEN, P., A. P. GARNER, AND S. CARTWRIGHT (1984). *Woodworking for young children.* Washington, DC: National Association for the Education of Young Children.

SPODEK, B. (1985). *Teaching in the early years* (3rd ed.). Englewood Cliffs, NJ: Prentice-Hall.

SPODEK, B., O. N. SARACHO, AND R. C. LEE (1984). *Mainstreaming young children.* Belmont, CA: Wadsworth Publishing Company.

TORRANCE, E. P. (1962). *Guiding creative talent.* Englewood Cliffs, NJ: Prentice-Hall.

SUGGESTED ACTIVITIES

1. Visit an early childhood school that uses commercially made musical instruments. After practicing on the available instruments, design and implement a musical activity with a group of four children.

2. Create a number of homemade instruments with some of your classmates. Use them to accompany a song.

3. Begin a file of songs that are appropriate for young children.

4. Collect drawings of different age groups and place them in sequence related to the children's ages. Compare the developmental differences reflected in the drawings.

5. Collect a box of scrap materials for use in art activities with young children.

6. Begin a file of art activities for young children.

7. Design and implement an art center for children to use during activity time. Include a wide variety of materials.

8. Observe a young child for at least half an hour during a movement activity. Record the different kinds of movements observed.

9. Go through current catalogs and make up a supply and equipment order for an art program for a particular class. In your order include quantity, quality, colors, and costs.

12

Language and Literacy

After completing this chapter on language and literacy, the student will be able to:

1. Identify the components of communication skill in an early childhood language arts program.
2. Describe the goals of a language arts program in early childhood education.
3. Organize expressive language experiences relating to children's literature, poetry, storytelling, puppetry, and creative dramatics.
4. Identify the goals for a literature program in early childhood education.
5. List the criteria for selecting young children's books.
5. Describe several ways to present poetry in the early childhood classroom.
7. Discuss the value of storytelling, puppetry, and creative dramatics.
8. Describe how to prepare to tell a story.
9. Describe the development of young children's written language.

Children differ in their language development. Some start to talk early, others start late; some are highly verbal, others are quiet. Some of these differences are developmental, others are children's reactions to their environments. Research shows that an individual's language development is related to sex, class, position in family, and ethnic group membership.

By the time children enter the preschool, they have learned a language at home. Once in school the children are ready for their language to be extended and enriched. Both teacher and other classmates make language demands to which they must adapt. This chapter presents aspects of the language art program, including children's literature, poetry, storytelling, puppetry, and creative dramatics. It also deals with the beginnings of reading and writing.

LANGUAGE ARTS PROGRAMS FOR YOUNG CHILDREN

Language is an important communication tool enabling individuals to develop new means of speaking with, for, and to others about any subject or event. At four or five, young children have mastered the basic grammar of their language and a great deal of vocabulary. They have learned the four rule systems of their language: pronouncing and combining sounds (phonology), constructing grammatical sentences (syntactics), conveying a wide range of meanings as they join words (semantics), and varying speech patterns based on the social interaction and context (pragmatics) (Honig, 1982).

Semantics refer to the meaning that language communicates through both content words and function words (Durkin, 1987). *Content words* carry meaning themselves, while *function words* have no easily definable isolated meanings, although they show relationships between other words in a sentence. Function words include prepositions, conjunctions and determiners (Pflaum, 1986).

There are two kinds of communication skills in an early childhood language arts program: *receptive* and *expressive* language skills. Listening and reading are used to *receive* communications, while speaking and writing are used to *express* communications. All four of these components—listening, reading, speaking, and writing—have equal importance in the language arts program. A high-quality language arts program for young children needs to provide many opportunities for children to hear, read, speak, and write the language in a flexible way, though reading and writing are usually not part of early childhood programs.

Goals of a Language Arts Program

A language arts program for young children needs to have multiple goals. Spodek, Saracho, and Lee (1984) suggest the following general goals:

1. *Developing basic oral language skills.* Learning to speak in sentences, express ideas in logical sequence, enunciate clearly, and pronounce words correctly.
2. *Developing listening skills.* Learning to attend, increase attention span, and understand what is said.

3. *Building a meaningful vocabulary.* Developing a vocabulary to use in a variety of contexts.

4. *Developing writing skills.* Learning to express thoughts in writing as in speech. (p. 204)

To achieve these goals, the early childhood language arts program needs to integrate the receptive activities of listening and reading and the expressive activities of speaking and writing. For young children, activities are used to develop *preliminary* learnings in the written communication skills, with actual reading and writing skills developed later. Thus, the focus is on oral language experiences. In time, young children will recognize the relationship between the spoken and the written language. They will learn to receive ideas and impressions as they read, just as they learned to listen; they will learn to express ideas, impressions, and feelings as they write, just as they learned to speak. At the preschool level we must offer a wide range of receptive and expressive language experiences with children's literature, poetry, storytelling, puppetry, and creative dramatics.

Children's Literature

Experiences in literature consist of two elements: the book and the reader. Maurice Sendak's (1963) *Where the Wild Things Are* is considered a great book for children. However, before children are capable of experiencing it as literature, they need to understand fantasy, to understand the complexity of the plot (story within a story), and to be able to respond to its emotional appeal through pictures and words. Children need to be able to consider the purpose of the book's words and pictures. They also need to understand how symbols create an aesthetic experience and guide the reader to understand the patterns, relationships, and feelings which are all part of the experience. The aesthetic experience in a book can be seen as a meaningful reconstruction of past experiences, an extension of experiences, or a development of a new experience (Cullinan, 1989; Huck, 1979)

Children's literature presents words and illustrations to help the reader/listener recognize an order of events, a unity of action, a balance of occurrences, or a new frame of reference for situations. Children can learn new things that they integrate with what is already known. Literature allows both an intellectual and an emotional response. The reader/listener learns to understand the characters, settings, and problems. He or she can enjoy beauty, wonder, and humor of the story or experience the despair of sorrow, injustice, and ugliness; can have vicarious experiences in other places, times, and lifestyles; can identify with others. The reader/listener can observe nature from a different perspective; can experience risks, mystery, and suffering; can enjoy a sense of achievement or a sense of belonging. Literature allows readers the opportunity to dream, to think, and to ask questions about themselves (Cullinan, 1989; Huck, 1979; Sutherland & Arbuthnot, 1986).

Literature experiences for young children should be enjoyable. At the same time they need to be planned in order to promote the children's appreciation of language and literature. Paul M. Williamson (1981) suggests five goals for a literature program in early childhood education:

1. *Many types of literature must be recognized, enjoyed, and valued.* Young children need to know literature well and to enjoy it to the point where they feel it "belongs" to them. Learning to value literature helps them learn to value the worth of learning to read.
2. *A strong sense of story must be developed.* Children need to learn the concept of a story. The younger children will probably be aware of it only when the same story is presented to them repeatedly, even if in a different way, and will remember the sequence of events.
3. *Literature must be actively and appropriately responded to in different ways.* Young children can learn to acquire meaning from literature. This process can be enriched through dramatization, art projects, field trips, cooking, performance, puppetry, and other expressive experiences.
4. *The magic and power of words must be recognized and appreciated.* Words have power, but individuals transmit the power over words. Young children need to be provided with many experiences using words, to develop their language and to help them understand how meaning is conveyed through artful use of language.
5. *Literature must provide identification with characters.* Young children can identify their own lives and experiences and relate them to those of characters in the literature. Many excellent books focus on issues that are important to young children.

The first step in a literature program is to help children enjoy books. Experiences can be provided both before and after reading a book to intensify the children's participation and perception. These literature experiences can be structured to develop understandings and appreciations while maintaining the sense of spontaneity, pleasure, and exuberance. Literature can be shared to enrich the lives of both children and teachers (Williamson, 1981).

Good literature experiences require a careful selection of books. Leland B. Jacobs (1955) developed a set of criteria for selecting young children's books:

1. The story should have a fresh, well-paced plot.
2. It must have unique individuality.
3. It should contain plausible, direct conversation.
4. It must have well-delineated characters.
5. It must have an authentic outcome. (p. 194)

In addition, books must possess a main plot, an arousing climax, and a predictable outcome. Young children also prefer books that have action, conflict, heroic characters, and tongue-teasing language. Illustrations should be synchronized with the text.

A number of categories of books can be used with young children. A small collection of books from the following categories can provide a balanced literature program (Coody, 1983; Cullinan, 1989; Morrow, 1989).

Teachers should carefully select books to read to children.

Mother Goose.   Mother Goose stories have a strong appeal for the young. Young children find their humanism, nonsense, high adventure, and rhythmic language fascinating. These old folk rhymes are among the best available literature. Several editions of Mother Goose as well as puzzles, art prints, pillows, figurines, filmstrips, and other materials can be provided in the early childhood classroom. Examples of Mother Goose books are:

> *Book of Nursery and Mother Goose Rhymes,* compiled and illustrated by Marguerite de Angeli, Garden City, New York: Doubleday and Company, Inc., 1952. This book has a good collection of art work with its soft, delicate black and white drawings interfused with mellow pastel paintings. It has 376 of the most popular rhymes.

> *The Real Mother Goose,* illustrated by Blanche Fisher Wright with an introduction by May Hill Arbuthnot, Chicago: Rand McNally and Company, 1944. This edition has been continuously popular with young children for more than 40 years. It includes an interesting description of the origins of Mother Goose.

Alphabet Books.   Children cherish ABC books as they learn the letters and sounds of the alphabet. Photographs, realistic paintings, or semi-abstract art are used to illustrate ABC books. In good alphabet books, meaningful objects are used to represent each letter of the alphabet, not more than two objects are used on each page to introduce each letter, and the letters are projected conspicuously. Examples of ABC books are:

The ABC Bunny by Wanda Gag, New York: Coward-McCann, Inc., 1933. Soft black and white drawings illustrate a small bunny's adventures. Each alphabet letter is printed in bright red.

Peter Piper's Alphabet, illustrated by Marcia Brown. New York: Charles Scribner's and Sons, 1959. The sounds of the alphabet are represented through famous old tongue-twisting nonsense rhymes. The pictures are loaded with fun and silliness.

Counting Books. Counting books present single mathematical concepts and their symbols, introducing the language of mathematics in an entertaining way. These books should be chosen much like ABC and other books. Two important criteria are good-quality art and each numeral being located on its own page. Shapes and forms presenting the number must be clearly and simply balanced and spaced on the page. Examples of counting books are:

My First Counting Book, written by Lilian Moore and illustrated by Garth Williams. New York: Simon and Schuster, 1956. A sturdy book with each number (one to ten) introduced using a similar plant or animal. A complete review is provided at the end of the book.

The Very Hungry Caterpillar, written by Eric Carle. Cleveland: Collins, William and World Publishing Company, Inc., 1972. This colorful book can be used to teach numbers, the days of the week, and the caterpillar's life cycle. A hungry caterpillar eats through an amazing group of foods throughout the book. The holes allow young children to follow the caterpillar's life cycle from egg to butterfly.

Concept Books. Concept books help young children learn specific concepts, such as size, shape, speed, and weight, which are introduced in graphic and artistic form. Examples of concept books are:

Big Ones, Little Ones by Tana Hoban. New York: William Morrow and Company, 1976. This book of black and white photographs depicts large and small zoo animals and domestic animals.

Symbols, written and illustrated by Rolf Myller. New York: Atheneum, 1978. This colorful and attractive book shows that a symbol represents something and that symbols communicate a concept. It also shows young children that symbols are everywhere and are an essential component in everyone's life.

Machines Personified. Machines and other inanimate objects are often personified and given human qualities in young children's books. The purpose of these stories is usually to inspire: The plot is constructed around some staggering, overwhelming problem which a machine or inanimate object must overcome. The ending is always successful and happy, providing the reader or listener with a feeling of satisfaction. Examples of books in which machines or inanimate objects are personified are:

The Little Engine That Could by Watty Piper. New York: Platt and Munk Publishers, 1955. A little engine attempts to achieve a difficult task while repeating the phrase, "I think I can, I think I can." This book tells young children they can overcome big obstacles.

Mike Mulligan and His Steam Shovel, written and illustrated by Virginia Lee Burton. Boston: Houghton Mifflin Company, 1939. Mary Anne, a steam shovel with personality, digs her way into a deep hole and cannot get out. The story ends in a humerous and satisfying way.

Animal Stories.   Young children like stories in which animals show human qualities. They work, play, laugh, cry, make silly mistakes, and perform kind and wise acts. These stories can be told, read aloud, and dramatized. Examples of books on animal stories are:

Curious George by Hans A. Rey. Boston: Houghton Mifflin Company, 1941. A curious little monkey explores and examines his environment. When his curiosity gets him into trouble, his friend in the yellow hat always helps him.

Millions of Cats by Wanda Gag. New York: Coward-McCann, Inc., 1928. Among millions of cats, only one was humble and modest. This cat is also the most beautiful and lovable. The modern folk tale is illustrated with black and white drawings.

Humerous and Nonsense Books.   Humerous books make children laugh. Children need to understand humor in a book in order to enjoy its wit. Examples of humerous and nonsense books are:

Horton Hatches the Egg by Dr. Seuss (Theodor Seuss Geisel). New York: Random House, 1940. This book has the type of humor that appeals to young children. Horton is an elephant up in a tree. Its ending is happy and surprising.

Sylvester and the Magic Pebble by William Steig. New York: Simon and Schuster, 1969. Sylvester Duncan, a young donkey, lives with his parents at Acorn Road in Oatsdale. Sylvester finds a magic pebble and finds himself in humorous and suspensful events. The book is illustrated in cartoon style that complements the witty text.

Picture Books.   In picture books the pictures are essential to the text. Young children often prefer to have pictures transmit the story so they do not have to read the text. Beginning readers can benefit from experiences with these books. Each year the artist with the most distinguished American picture book for children wins the Caldecott Award, presented by the Association for Library Services to Children of the American Library Association. Examples of picture books are:

Crow Boy, written and illustrated by Taro Yashima. New York: The Viking Press, 1955. Chibi, a young Japanese boy, really appreciates school. Every day for six years he leaves his home and goes to school at sunrise. At the end of the year, he is the only one in his class who is honored for perfect attendance. Chibi's classmates do not accept him until his schoolmaster finds out that Chibi can imitate crows.

Cinderella, illustrated by Marcia Brown. New York: Charles Scribner and Sons, 1954. This is a delightful folk tale with delicate illustrations about rags-to-riches.

Storybooks that are read to children can stimulate art projects.

Easy-to-Read Books. Easy-to-read books have a controlled number and range of words which are used often throughout the book. The print tends to be large. Pictures assist in telling the story and the text encompasses a large degree of conversation. Examples of easy-to-read books are:

Grasshopper on the Road, written and illustrated by Arnold Lobel. New York: Harper and Row Publishers, 1978. A grasshopper journeys on the road, where he interacts with some strange creatures who find it difficult to accept his philosophy.

Little Bear's Visit, written by Else Holmelund Miniarik and illustrated by Maurice Sendak. New York: Harper and Row Publishers, 1961. Little Bear visits Grandmother and Grandfather Bear in their little house in the woods.

Participation Books. Participation books provide children with sensory experiences of looking, feeling, patting, and smelling. In addition, they involve children in searching for visual cues, solving problems, and making decisions. These books require some manipulation; therefore, they may seem more like a toy or game than a book. They are fascinating and irresistible to children, especially toddlers, and they are a good way to introduce children to literature. Examples of participation books are:

Brian Wildsmith's Puzzles, written and illustrated by Brian Wildsmith. New York: Franklin Watts, Inc., 1970. A colorful illustrated book providing all of the answers to Brian Wildsmith's brain-teasing questions. Its good humor is integrated with beautiful art work to produce an outstanding participation picture book.

Zoo City, written and photographed by Stephen Lewis. New York: William Morrow and Company, Inc., 1976. This book is about machines, plumbing, cars, and other city fixtures which are similar to animals. It has beautiful black and white photographs with pictures of their real-life counterparts. The book has a split-page, puzzle format that allows children to match animals with look-alike objects.

Information Books.   Information books can enhance the young children's inquiring minds. They need to be carefully selected for the knowledge presented and the language used. The language must be understandable to young children without being condescending. Examples of information books are:

Kites, written and illustrated by Larry Kettlekamp. New York: William Morrow and Company, 1959. This book describes the basic types of kites and tells how to build and fly them. It provides information about kites in other lands and what their practical uses are.

Your Friend, the Tree, written by Florence M. White and illustrated by Alan E. Cober. New York: Alfred A. Knopf, Inc., 1969. This book provides information about the uses of trees. It urges children to be kind to trees. "When a tree is cut down, a new one should always be planted, because we cannot live without trees."

When young children are read to regularly, they begin to view reading as an important and integral component of their lives. Reading aloud to young children is part of reading readiness and is reading in the fullest sense of the word. The children examine the pictures in the book and follow the story lines as the adult unlocks the printed symbols for them.

To attract children to books, the teacher needs to provide a library area that offers a comfortable physical setting and materials that will help make liter-

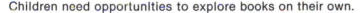

Children need opportunities to explore books on their own.

acy experiences enjoyable. The library area should be easily visible and inviting to anyone who enters the classroom. It should provide immediate access to a well-balanced literature program. Privacy and physical limits can be provided by using dividers on two or three sides. These can be bookshelves, a piano, file cabinets, or freestanding bulletin boards. The size of the library area depends on the number of children in the class and the space available. At least six children should be able to read together comfortably in the library area.

A throw rug and several pillows can project a cozy and soft atmosphere. The library area should include a small table with chairs for children to look at or create their own books, a rocking chair, and a tape recorder with headsets to listen to taped stories.

Children can enjoy manipulating figures of story characters from favorite books if a flannel board is available. Puppets can also help children to acting out of favorite stories. Mobiles made from book jackets can be used to attract children to particular books. Posters that are available from several sources can also encourage reading. For information on these posters, contact:

Children's Book Council
67 Irving Place
New York, NY 10003

American Library Association
50 East Huron Street
Chicago, IL 60611

Children enjoy cuddling with dolls and/or stuffed animals in the library area, especially if they relate to a favorite book. For example, a stuffed bear and a doll with blond hair can be placed next to the book *Goldilocks and the Three Bears,* a stuffed pig next to *The Three Little Pigs,* and a stuffed rabbit next to *Peter Rabbit.* Children will enjoy reading to these dolls and stuffed animals, or simply holding them as they look at books. Most young children can easily use Viewmasters with story wheels, which can supplement books.

The library area should also include materials that invite young children to create their own books, felt board stories, and roll movies. Many publishers and local magazine agencies will donate outdated periodicals to schools for the cost of mailing and shipping. Such materials can be used by children in their books or stories.

Children should help plan and design the library area. Along with the teacher, they can continuously evaluate the area, set up rules for its use, be responsible for keeping it neat and orderly and naming it (e.g., Book Nook, Look at a book). Figure 12–1 illustrates a library area.

Dealing with Stereotypes in Children's Literature

Unfortunately, among the books that are available to young children are many that portray stereotypes regarding race, sex, age, physical condition, and class. Women may be shown as being dependent on men or serving only in traditionally female roles. The elderly may be pictured as ugly, mean, and incapable.

FIGURE 12-1   Library Area

Lesley Mandel Morrow. *Literacy Development in the Early Years: Helping Children Read and Write* (Englewood Cliffs, NJ: Prentice Hall, 1989), p. 87

Members of ethnic groups may appear as having limited capacities. The handicapped may be pictured as incapable of doing anything. Some of the stereotypes relate to how society viewed these groups at the time the books were originally written. This is true of many fairy tales and children's classics. In some books stereotyped portrayals appear because the authors did not know enough about members of these groups to provide more distinct characters. Sometimes it is just easier to use stereotypes when picturing people (Chambers, 1983).

It is important for teachers to be aware of stereotypes in the books they use and to be able to identify the stereotypes. A decision might be made not to use a book because of the way it characterizes people in words and pictures. At other times a teacher might feel that a book is good overall and should be read even though it projects a stereotype. In this case the book might be used to start a discussion about similarities and differences among people and how a portrayal in a book is different from how people really are. A good source for teachers to use in choosing books is *Guidelines for Selecting Bias-Free Textbooks and Storybooks,* Council on Interracial Books for Children, 1980. This is available from the Council, 1841 Broadway, New York, NY 10023.

Poetry

Poetry communicates experience by attracting the reader's or listener's thoughts and feelings. Rich sensory reflections and intensive emotional reactions are strongly elicited as one becomes involved in the experience. Poetry requires the listener to respond intellectually, emotionally, and imaginatively. While children's poetry varies slightly from adults', poetry for everybody must be meaningful, must use poetic language, and must have content that is appropriate and fascinating to its audience.

Young children tend to be poetic in nature. They use their senses to enjoy and react to their experiences. Children are like poets who explore and attempt to arrange the elements of their experiences according to facts and emotional symbols. They even coordinate their body in a rhythmic way and are fascinated with the expressive qualities of the time, sight, and sound. They become aware of how persons coordinate their work and play as they adapt to their everyday life situations.

Young children enjoy the language they hear in school. They immediately recite those expressions that are most appealing to them and enjoy new and original ways to use language intellectually and emotionally. According to Betty Coody (1983), children enjoy poetry that has the following characteristics:

> *Rhythmic language.* Poetry for young children must constantly have words and phrases that sound melodious and harmonious. Lilting language sets poetry aside from other literature. An appropriate poem for young children must have rhythm and melody in its language.

> *Emotional appeal.* Poetry elicits emotional reactions from its listeners: sadness, delight, reflection, empathy, or anger. A poem can stimulate the young children's emotions. Teachers should mirror their feelings about the poem.

> *Familiar themes.* Poetry for young children should be related to children's life experiences. Young children tend to favor poems that tell a story or that are about animals, people, or places or that are fun, humorous, and nonsense.

> *Sensory appeal.* Poetry should provoke the children's senses of touch, taste, smell, sight, and sound.

Good poetry must be shared in the early childhood classroom so children develop a lifelong fondness for many types of poetry. Leland B. Jacobs (1972) suggests several ways to present poetry in the classroom:

- Read poetry to young children regularly enough that children begin to expect and ask for it.
- Read poetry relating to an immediate situation: the season, weather, holiday, or experiences in science, social studies, mathematics, or reading.
- Share poetry with young children, especially original poems that children have written themselves.
- Pantomime and dramatize poetry.
- Use a variety of media including paint, clay, wood, or wire to illustrate poems. Murals of favorite poems are successful with young children.
- Develop poetry anthologies by collecting favorite poems from newspapers, magazines, and books or those composed by the children.
- Schedule poetry reading based on themes related to children's interests and school events.

- Have poetry recordings available to listen to alone or with music.
- Record the children's own interpretations of poetry.

Appealing poetry should be carefully selected and presented to children. Sutherland and Arbuthnot (1986) provide the following suggestions on achieving this task:

1. Read poetry aloud often.
2. Provide a variety of poems in records, books, and tapes.
3. Select contemporary poetry as well as older material.
4. Avoid sing-song reading aloud.
5. Select poems with comprehensible subject matter.
6. Encourage children to write poetry.
7. Select poems with action or humor.
8. Try choral speaking.
9. Make several anthologies available to children.

Children who are in the process of learning to read should hear poems first and then see the poems on the printed page. Hearing poetry before reading it may give young children greater pleasure. Contemporary poets are more likely to be of interest to today's children than older poets, whose work may be better understood and more easily introduced in junior or senior high school. If the teachers knows of a local poet, he or she might be invited to work with the children. It is amazing what these poets can do with young children.

Among the fine anthologies of young children's poetry available are the following (Coody, 1983):

The Complete Nonsense Book by Edward Lear. New York: Dodd, Mead & Company, 1912. This anthology has Edward Lear's nonsense rhymes, his nonsensical drawings, his famous limericks, "The Owl and the Pussy Cat," and other nonsense songs and stories.

Hailstones and Halibut Bones, written by Mary O'Neill and illustrated by Leonard Weisgard. Garden City, NY: Doubleday and Company, 1961. This popular anthology is appropriate for all ages. It can be used as a springboard for other activities, such as art, creative writing, and dramatization. It describes colors in rhyming verse, naming familiar objects, feelings, and concepts.

Hey Bug! and Other Poems about Little Things, selected by Elizabeth M. Itse and illustrated by Susan Carlton Smith. New York: American Heritage, 1972. This anthology consists of poems about beetles, mice, snails, and other small creatures which are fascinating to young children. Its illustrations are scientifically accurate drawings.

Oxford Book of Poetry for Children, compiled by Edward Blishen and illustrated by Brian Wildsmith. New York: Franklin Watts, Inc., 1963. This anthology has a variety of poems to introduce young children to poetry and help them to make the transition from nursery rhymes to more serious verse. The illustrations establish the mood for the poems.

Poetry provides a different kind of language experience for young children. They experience the way an artist manipulates words and they hear words in a different arrangement than in conversation. Children usually experience poetry for the first time in school. Teachers should see that these first experiences are as glorious and pleasurable as possible.

Storytelling

The art of storytelling began long before there was written language to record the tales. In ancient times people would gather to share their problems, to discuss natural phenomena, to admire their heroes, to commemorate victories, and to grieve tragic losses. The storyteller was a musician, a newscaster, an actor, and a spinner of tales.

Storytelling provides young children with many values. Betty Coody (1983) suggests that through storytelling:

1. The child is introduced to some of the best literature.
2. The child is acquainted with many cultures from around the world.
3. The child is presented with many characters with whom he or she can identify.
4. A wholesome relationship between the child and the adult is developed.
5. The child is helped to understand life and to develop worthwhile goals.
6. The child is stimulated to want more literary experiences and to develop an interest in reading.
7. The child's vocabulary is enriched and expanded.
8. The child's listening and comprehension skills are improved.
9. The child's creative writing and other creative activities are stimulated.
10. The child is provided with valuable information and knowledge.

Children interpret stories they hear according to their experiences. When they listen to a story, they perceive the characters in relation to people they have known. A story must be read or told with unusual care, and the teacher should learn the story well before telling it.

The following suggestions may prove helpful to a teacher preparing a story to be told (Baker & Greene, 1977; Ward, 1957):

1. *Read the story over and over again.* Read the story several times until you learn it well and have a feeling for the story's rhythm and style. The story should become part of your experience.
2. *Learn the major incidents in sequence.* Learn the story by incidents. Doing this helps to organize the story so that you can remember it easily and tell it in an orderly way. For example, in "Chicken Little," the incidents might be:

When Chicken Little felt an acorn fall on his tail.
When Chicken Little met Henny Penny.
When Chicken Little and Henny Penny met Cocky Locky.
When Chicken Little, Henny Penny, and Cocky Locky met Ducky Lucky.

When Chicken Little, Henny Penny, Cocky Locky, and Ducky Lucky met Turkey Lurkey.

When Chicken Little, Henny Penny, Cocky Locky, Ducky Lucky, and Turkey Lurkey met Hooty Tooty, the owl, who went to help Chicken Little discover that an acorn had fallen on his tail and not the sky.

3. *Describe the characters in the story.* Use words to draw a picture of the characters, their clothes, their unique characteristics, their personalities, their ways of speaking, and their mannerisms. For example, in "The Little Rabbit Who Wanted Red Wings," Carolyn Sherwin Bailey describes the rabbit in the following way:

Once upon a time there was a Little White Rabbit with two beautiful pink ears, and two bright eyes and four soft little feet. Such a pretty little white rabbit, but he wasn't happy.

4. *Plan the presentation of the story.* Do not memorize the story. If you do, it can sound formal and forgetting something can leave you helpless in the middle of the story. Some dialogue may need to be memorized, especially in a story that is a well-known classic or with a conversation that is very clever or funny. For example, the dialogue may need to be memorized for better effect in the "Three Little Pigs."

WOLF:	Little pig, little pig, let me in.
LITTLE PIG:	Oh, not by the hair of my chinny chin chin.
WOLF:	Then I'll huff and I'll puff 'til I blow your house in.

Picturesque or humorous words, phrases, or sentences may also be memorized in telling the story.

5. *Tell the story.* Have a relaxed and intimate atmosphere in an informal setting. Sit the children facing you in a semicircle that is not too wide. Children should sit in several rows of not more than eight children each, with no child directly behind another. Children need to sit facing away from the sunlight or from any distractions that can divert their interest.

Before settling them down, ask the children to put everything they are carrying (such as books, marbles, purses, dolls) on a separate table or under their chairs. These can easily distract other listeners.

Use a a warm, friendly manner in telling the story. At the same time be direct, including all the children. Consider the children's point of view, their understanding, and their interest. Make the story simple enough for the children to understand but do not talk down to them. The setting, the presentation, the plot, and the characters must be clear to the children. Tell the story in such a way that the children see pictures vividly. Good action words are valuable in helping children picture the story.

Experience in telling stories will sharpen your storytelling skills. Remember, a story that is presented well will be remembered and dramatized by the children.

Some books that have good stories for telling are the following:

Merry Tales for Children by Carolyn Sherwin Bailey. New York: Platt and Munk Publishers, 1943. This contains a series of humorous short stories about home, stories about animals, folk tales, and holiday stories that can be read and told to young children.

Stories for Little Children by Pearl S. Buck. New York: The John Day Company, Inc., 1940. Short stories based on the lives of five young children who strive to understand such phenomena as daylight, darkness, and the seasons of the year.

Tales from Grimm by Wanda Gag. Eau Claire, WI: E. M. Hale and Company, 1936. (Translated from German.) Her interpretations of Grimm in both text and the small black and white sketches are delightful.

Professional Materials for Storytelling

Storytellers have provided a valuable legacy of materials and techniques. Ruth Sawyer, in *The Way of the Storyteller,* discusses the history of folklore, the preparation of tales for telling stories, and some of her favorite stories such as the "fairy gold." Recordings of Ruth Sawyer reading Christmas stories from her book *Joy to the World* and storytelling by Frances Clarke Sayers using some of Carl Sandburg's *Rootabaga Stories* and Hans Christian Andersen's stories are available from Weston Woods. Marie L. Shedlock's *The Art of the Storyteller* is an excellent resource for beginning storytellers (Cullinan, 1989).

Cullinan (1989) suggests the following collections of stories for use with young children:

Storytelling: Art and Technique by Augusta Baker and Ellin Greene, 2nd ed. New York: R. R. Bowker, 1987.
Handbook of Storytellers by Caroline Feller Bauer. Chicago: American Library Association, 1977.
Tell Me a Story by Eileen Colwell. New York: Penguin, 1962.

Puppetry

Puppetry is an old art form. Puppets provide children with a disguise as they become active in manipulating strings, paper bags, or their fists. This activity eases their self-consciousness and allows them to express their feeling more freely.

Puppets also make it easy for children to penetrate a magic world of fantasy. In this world children are able to solve all of their problems. They give evidence of their inner world through puppets (Jenkins, 1981; Petty, Petty & Salzer, 1989). The use of puppetry can accomplish the following:

- Develops children's creative thinking and imagination.
- Provides children with the opportunity to test life circumstances.
- Helps children become aware of their own behavior.
- Allows children to expose their anxieties and release their tensions.
- Develops communication skills.
- Promotes critical listening skills and critical thinking.
- Expands children's attention span.
- Assists children in acquiring knowledge.
- Offers children opportunities to work cooperatively and share ideas.
- Develops problem-solving skills.

Puppets help children explore the world of fantasy.

Young children can make many kinds of puppets including hand puppets, head puppets, and body puppets (see Figure 12–2) (Hennings, 1982). Following are some suggestions:

Hand Puppets

1. Felt tip pens, crayons, construction paper, yarn, or colored pictures clipped from magazines can add characteristics to puppets made out of hand-sized paper bags.
2. Buttons, yarn, scraps of material, twine, and glitter can add characteristics to puppets made out of socks, stockings, or white work gloves.
3. Faces can be drawn on the balls of each finger.
4. Styrofoam or ping-pong balls can be taped to the ends of fingers or to the ends of ice cream bar sticks, or the sticks can be inserted into them for support. The puppets can be elaborated with glitter, tinsel, buttons, and yarn.

Head Puppets

1. Crayon and felt tip pens can be used to add characteristics to paper plates; holes are cut for children to see through.
2. Eyes, nose, and mouth openings can be cut in a full-sized paper bag. Carpet fringe can be stapled across the top of the bag for curly hair, long lashes can be drawn around the eye openings, and a nose can be stapled above the nose opening.

Body Puppets

1. Large-sized cartons can be colorfully painted; one side is removed and a head hole is cut in the opposite side.
2. Children's bodies can be traced on heavy cardboard to make people-shaped and sized cut-outs. The children can cut on the line and color the body.

Figure 12-1

Hand Puppets

Head Puppets

FIGURE 12–2

Body Puppets

Sock Puppets

1. Select a cotton (or loosely woven knit) sock that is approximately the same size that you wear. Experiment with both solid colored and patterned socks.
2. Slip the sock over your hand, with the *heel* resting on your knuckles.
3. Holding all four fingers tightly curled together, spread your hand open very wide, with the fingers "curled" slightly over, forming an arc.
4. Use your free hand to invert and stuff the toes of the sock back toward the palm of the hand.
5. The inversion of the toe into the palm of the hand forms the "mouth" of the sock puppet. Experiment shaping the mouth until you achieve an effect that is pleasing to you. When you are satisfied with the shape and fit, secure it by hand sewing it in place.
6. You may add padding to the top or back of your hand to add a fuller shape to your puppet. Old rags, cotton, or a household sponge may be used for padding.

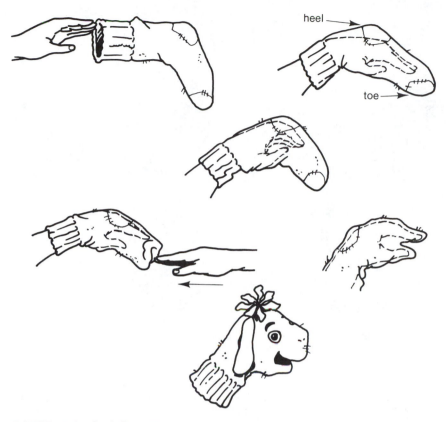

FIGURE 12–3   Sock Puppet

7. External features—eyes, ears, horns, nostrils, etc.—may be added. Buttons, iron-on-tape, yarn, and similar material may be used for that purpose. You may also add features by drawing them with a marking pen.

Paper Cup and Styrofoam Ball Puppets

A styrofoam cup or styrofoam ball can provide the basis for constructing a quick and easy puppet. Features and hair can be made from yarn scraps, pipe cleaners, old buttons, or construction paper. An old scarf or piece of fabric may be used to "dress" the puppet. Experiment creatively in constructing different puppets. If possible, provide materials and let the children make their own.

Directions

1. Glue or pin features and hair onto the styrofoam cup or ball.
2. Punch a hole in the bottom of the cup or ball large enough to insert your middle finger.
3. Cover the entire hand with a scarf or large piece of fabric.
4. Insert the scarf-covered middle finger into the hole in the ball or base of the cup.
5. Extend the thumb and little finger for puppet arms.

FIGURE 12–4   Paper Cup and Styrofoam Ball Puppets

Note: A quick and easy puppet stage may be constructed from an old cardboard box. A table turned on its side can also provide a place where a puppeteer may hide while giving a puppet play.

Shadow puppets can also be used for creative drama. Puppets are held behind a thin curtain with a strong beam of light shining from behind the puppets through the curtain. In a darkened room, the puppets look like silhouettes. A puppet can represent a person, an object, or any shape.

Children can make their own simple puppets to share a story. Provide materials such as ribbons, bows, twine, scraps of fabric, lengths of old yarn, paper bags, worn-out but clean socks, gloves, paper plates, buttons, and other odds and ends to allow children to make puppets with which to share their stories.

Puppets can be characters in a story, which can be read or told by one child while the other children manipulate the puppets according to the plot. Or children can manipulate and talk for their own puppets to share a personal story.

Creative Dramatics

Creative dramatics is informal drama. In creative dramatics a story may be dramatized. Ideas and feelings may be explored, developed, and expressed through dramatic enactment as the players create the dialogue.

According to McCaslin (1990), creative dramatics is valuable for young children because it:

- Develops the imagination.
- Develops independent thinking.
- Develops one's own ideas.
- Provides an opportunity for cooperation.
- Builds social awareness.
- Releases emotion.
- Develops speech habits.
- Provides experiences with good literature.
- Introduces the theater arts.
- Provides a form of recreation.

Dramatization helps children to interpret and understand literature. In creative dramatics there is no script, lines are not memorized, and few, if any, properties or costumes are required. Although the drama is unstructured, young children take their roles very seriously.

Selections from children's literature often serve as vehicles for dramatization. If used skillfully, creative dramatics can add to literary understanding and provide an opportunity to use language skills.

Creative drama can be introduced for the first time with simple activities, such as finger plays, single action poetry, action songs, and simple pantomimes. Later, when drama periods are longer, these simpler activities can be used for warm-up (Heining & Stillwell, 1981).

Children's language can be developed through creative dramatics. Creative dramatics also increases children's understanding and frees their responses to literature. It helps children to respond to experiences and to interpret the printed page in spoken word and gesture.

Finger Plays

Finger plays—little rhymes, songs, or chants—can be acted out as young children recite them. Some examples are "Eensy Weensy Spider" and "Hickory, Dickory Dock" (see Figures 12–5 and 12–6). There are many sources for finger

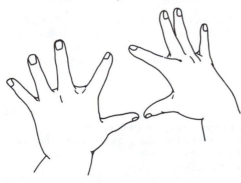

FIGURE 12-5   Eensy, Weensy Spider

Eensy, Weensy Spider

Eensy, weensy spider
  (Let opposite thumbs and index fingers climb up each other.)
Climbed up the waterspout.
Down came the rain
  (Let hands sweep down and open wide.)
And washed the spider out.
Out came the sun
  (Form circle over head with arms.)
And dried up all the rain.
So the eensy, weensy spider,
  (Let opposite thumbs and fingers climb up each other again.)
Climbed up the spout again.

LESSON PLAN FOR CREATIVE DRAMATICS

Story:

Goldilocks and the Three Bears

Goal:

To identify and describe the characters who help develop the story and the main character (Goldilocks).

Materials:

Book, pictures, flannel board characters, and puppets of Goldilocks and the Three Bears.

Arrangement:

Children sit on the carpet in a semicircle.

Prerequisites:

1. Children know the story.
2. Children can place the pictures in sequence.
3. Children can tell the story using flannel board pictures.
4. Children can tell the story using puppets.

Procedures:

After the children have achieved the prerequisites, the teacher explains the purpose of the activity. The teacher than guides the discussion by asking questions such as:

Who is the story about?
What is her name?
Can you describe Goldilocks?
Who else was in the story?
Can you describe Baby Bear?
Can you describe Mama Bear?
Can you describe Papa Bear?
If Baby Bear were bigger and fatter, how would the story be different?
What could Mama Bear and Papa Bear have done to change the story?

The number and types of questions asked depend on the children's interests and developmental level.

Follow-up Activities:

- Children can dramatize the story according to the book.
- Children can dramatize the story by changing the characters and discussing how the characters changed the story.
- Children can illustrate the characters.

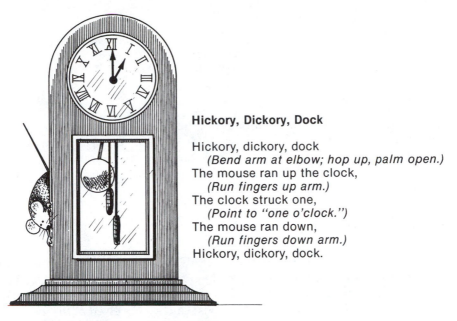

Hickory, Dickory, Dock

Hickory, dickory, dock
   (Bend arm at elbow; hop up, palm open.)
The mouse ran up the clock,
   (Run fingers up arm.)
The clock struck one,
   (Point to "one o'clock.")
The mouse ran down,
   (Run fingers down arm.)
Hickory, dickory, dock.

FIGURE 12-6   Hickory, Dickory, Dock

plays, such as *Let's Do Fingerplays* by Marion F. Grayson (1962). Teachers can also make them up from favorite nursery rhymes. A variety of anthologies of nursery rhymes are available that can be helpful.

Action Stories

Some stories have actions that children can perform. Someone tells the story and does the actions. Then the children imitate the actions. "Bear Hunt," in which children can use actions to describe the hunter going through grass, mud, hills, and so on, is an example of an action story.

Original stories can be made up, with actions being assigned to story characters or to frequently used words. Children act out each word, or specific words can be assigned to rows or groups. Original action stories based on the children's experiences or field trips can also be made up, with actions or words assigned in the same way. The children can also change posts.

Actions can be added to popular stories such as *The Hare and the Tortoise* (Galdone, 1962). Children can agree on a dialogue to act out the story such as the following:

Characters: hare, tortoise, fox
Setting: woods
Story:

HARE: Good morning, Mr. Tortoise. Ha! Ha! Ha! Ha!
TORTOISE: What's so funny?

HARE:	Ha! Ha! Ha! Ha!
TORTOISE:	What's so funny!!!
HARE:	Your little legs. Ha! Ha! How can you walk?
TORTOISE:	I can walk and even run faster than you.
HARE:	What?

The dialogue continues throughout the story. This story can be acted out by three children or three groups of children. With groups, when the Hare speaks, for example, the group of children who have selected that character will speak and act in unison on the agreed-upon dialogue.

TEACHING READING AND WRITING

Readiness is the stage when children are ready to learn something without intellectual or emotional stress, and when they can feel the satisfaction of having achieved that learning. Generally, reading readiness refers to the ability of a child to profit from reading instruction. Readiness can be conceived of for many learning stages of reading from beginning to mature reading in adulthood (Downing & Thackeray, 1978). Many use the term readiness to refer to the child's maturational state. If readiness depended only on maturation, then teachers could wait until each child matures. However, there is more than maturation involved in reading readiness, and a purely maturational approach to reading readiness is simply not effective. A reading readiness program must teach the prerequisite skills for reading.

Designing a Reading Readiness Program

A reading readiness program for young children must integrate expressive and receptive oral and written language. It must help children achieve fluency in speaking and listening abilities. An emphasis on oral language helps children develop an extensive speaking and listening vocabulary, an asset to developing a reading vocabulary. Listening to stories provides them with the opportunity to manipulate books and to become aware that information is found on the printed page, even in pictures. Children acquire simple skills like holding a book, opening it, turning its pages, and caring for it. These experiences also make children aware of the relationship between the written and oral language. As a result of this awareness, they establish the concept that the written word has the same power to communicate meaning as the spoken word. They also need to be provided with many opportunities to dictate personal stories to the teacher, and these stories can be read repeatedly. Both informal and formal language experiences guide children into making the transition to actual reading.

In addition, a reading readiness program must provide learning activities that help children acquire competencies in the specific skills required for reading. Hillerich (1977) recommends the following progression in developing reading readiness skills:

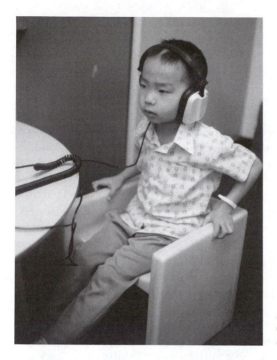

A listening station allows the child to control the number of times he or she hears a story read.

Auditory discrimination. Children need to hear the difference between phonemes in words, such as "book" or "look."

Listening comprehension. Young children need to expand their understanding of what they hear. Children must learn to understand conversational, informal oral language in order to comprehend written language.

Recalling sequence of events. Young children need to be able to remember events as they occur in order.

Language development. Children need to be capable of using the spoken language before beginning reading. Oral language can be developed through experiences that stimulate language.

Oral language development—basic vocabulary. Young children need to learn to understand and use a vocabulary of common words. An effective technique to develop vocabulary is through direct and personal experiences. If direct experiences are not feasible, good pictures or models can be provided.

Following spoken directions. Listening comprehension should be initiated by the teacher's giving simple one-step oral directions. Playing a game like Simon Says or Hokey Pokey provides practice in following oral directions.

Using oral context. Most four-year-olds intuitively know how to use oral context. They can easily provide a missing word to complete a sentence. Children can also develop their own incomplete sentences for the class to provide the missing words. This activity can be varied with riddles, which also help develop skills that employ oral context.

Emergent Literacy

The term "reading readiness" is heard less often in educational circles these days, replaced by the term "emergent literacy." Emergent literacy describes the early stages in children's development toward literacy; it precedes the conventional reading of print (Clay, 1979). Literacy development begins early in life and continues to develop continuously in the contexts of the home and community. Children at every age have some degree of literacy skills, which later develops into mature reading and writing (Teale, 1986). In emergent literacy, a child's scribble marks on a page, even when no letter is discernible, is considered writing. However, children who can differentiate between their scribbles and drawing know the difference between writing and pictures. Similarly, a child who is acting as if he or she is reading is demonstrating knowledge of literary behavior. Although such behavior cannot be called reading in the conventional sense, the activity is legitimate literacy behavior. For instance, when children narrate a familiar storybook at the same time they are looking at pictures and print, they reflect an understanding of the reading process (Morrow, 1989).

Literacy integrates all of the communication skills (reading, writing, listening, and speaking). Each skill compliments the others and they are learned concurrently. According to Morrow (1989), (1) reading is acquired through socially interactive and emulative behavior, (2) children acquire the ability to read as the result of life experiences, (3) children acquire reading skills when they see a purpose and a need for the process, and (4) being read to plays a role in the acquisition of reading.

Children acquire literacy through interacting with literate people. Literacy is the result of the children's involvement in reading activities mediated by persons who are literate themselves (Teale, 1982). The social interactions with the mediating person teach children the functions of reading and its conventions in society. Children also come to associate reading with enjoyment and satisfaction, thus developing children's desire to participate in literacy activities. Social relationships internalize high mental functions. Children prefer participating in reading activities that interact with more literate others.

Holdaway (1979) states that

> The way in which supportive adults are induced by affection and common sense to intervene on the development of their children proves upon close examination to employ the most sound principles of teaching. Rather than provide verbal instructions about how a skill should be carried out, the parent sets up an emulative model of the skill in operation and induces activity in the child which approximates towards use of the skill. The first attempts of the child are to do something that is like the skill he wishes to emulate. This activity is then "shaped" or refined by immediate rewards. . . . From this point of view, so called "natural" learning is in fact supported by higher quality teaching intervention than is normally the case in the school setting. (p. 22)

Holdaway believes that this form of "developmental" teaching is appropriate for school-based literacy instruction. His model of literacy instruction is based on observations of home environments where children have learned to read without direct instruction.

Children acquire reading as a result of life experiences. Many children read early; they acquire literacy skills before starting school and without formal instruction but surrounded by a literate environment. Even three-year-old children can read common words—such as Burger King, McDonald's, Exxon, and Sugar Pops—that they see around them (Goodman & Altwerger, 1981; Harste, Wood & Burke, 1984; Hiebert, 1986; Mason, 1980; Saracho, 1984, 1985a, 1985b). In a literate environment children discover the purpose, organization, and functions of print. Children's reading abilities need to be developed using their knowledge of and strengths in reading (Jewell & Zintz, 1986).

Children acquire reading when they see its purpose and feel the need. Young children gain their first information about reading and writing through their functional uses (Goodman, 1980; Heath, 1980; Mason, 1977; Mason & McCormick, 1981). Grocery lists, directions on toys, packages, household equipment, medicine containers, recipes, telephone messages, school-related notices, religious materials, menus, environmental print inside and outside the home, mail, magazines, newspapers, storybook readings, television channels, telephone numbers, conversation among family members, and letters are examples of functional literacy information that children encounter daily.

Children acquire reading by being read to. Reading to children promotes their literacy skills, their interest in books and in reading, and their sense of story structure. A well-structured story provides a *setting* (a beginning time, place, and introduction of characters), a *theme* (the main characters' problems or goals), *plot episodes* (a series of events where the main character tries to solve the problem or achieve a goal), and a *resolution* (the accomplishment of the goal or solving of the problem and an ending). Children who are aware of a story's structural elements can predict what will happen next in an unfamiliar story (Morrow, 1985). Written language in books differs from oral language. Children need to become familiar with the written language codes by experiencing them over and over again. As they hear stories read to them, they will gain a sense of this written language code. Similarly, children's comprehension skills are developed as they assimilate familiar vocabulary and syntactic structures in books they have heard. Children who have frequently listened to stories read tend to read earlier and easier than others (Clark, 1984; Durkin, 1966; Hiebert, 1981; Saracho, 1987). In addition, children who have listened to stories at school or at home usually perceive reading as enjoyment and information; thus developing a positive attitude toward reading (Saracho, 1987).

Reading the same story to children over and over again is an important technique (Morrow, 1986; Sulzby, 1985; Yaden, 1985). It helps children acquire an understanding of the functions of print, a sense of how print is used, and of what people are doing when they are reading (Smith, 1978). Reading stories to children also develops positive attitudes toward reading (Saracho, 1987). In addition, storybook experiences teach children how to handle a book: its front-to-back progression; the beginning, middle, and end of a story; and the concept of authorship (Clay, 1979; Torvey & Kerber, 1986). Listening to stories helps children become aware of the functions, form, and convention of print, as well as develop their metacognitive knowledge about reading tasks and interaction with teachers and parents (Mason, 1980). *Metacognition* refers to the individual's own awareness and understanding of the cognitive process.

Children acquire reading as they understand the reading process. Literacy is a form of representation: things can stand for something other than itself. Children acquire representation skills in infancy, representing things sensorily. As they mature, they develop pictorial and play representations. Words written on a page are a highly abstract form of representation. Reading is gaining meaning from these abstract symbols. The goal of reading instruction is to teach children to interpret the written code in order to gain meaning. Learning experiences that develop children's representation skills and lead to competent reading must be provided in early childhood classrooms (Saracho, 1985b). Most children who read fluently and understand what they read have good comprehension. This comprehension is helped through the use of multiple sources of information about the written message, such as word forms, syntactical structures, and the context of words. Readers who have problems gaining immediate comprehension from the printed word can use mediated comprehension, translating the written word into its oral form in order to gain meaning.

Schema Theory

Psychologists and educators have been concerned about how children come to comprehend meaning in what they read. Garner (1987) describes several views of reading comprehension such as a representative interactive model for text processing. Schema theory is one view which is most widely accepted today.

A schema, which is a repertoire of expectations, evolves as individuals have many experiences with objects and events. It is an abstract knowledge structure that is built into an individual's memory system and is used to interpret new information (McNeil, 1984). Incoming information is matched to the individuals' repertoire of expectations. The individual will try to place this new information into existing memory system "slots." Information which fails to conform to those sets of expectations may not be encoded or it may be distorted. The set of expectations guiding the encoding of information also guides the retrieval of information (Anderson, 1984).

An example of a schema that has been used is a *ship christening*. Individuals who have experienced or read about ship christenings develop a set of expectations regarding such events. A celebrity is expected to be mentioned in a description, a new ship is the major focus of the ceremony, a bottle of champagne is broken on the ship's bow, and so on. Inferences about the event can be made even if the description is incomplete.

Reading is a thinking and understanding act; learning to read is a constructive problem-solving process. Children are provided with information to learn and practice in a stepwise fashion so that they can interpret and relate the ideas in printed passages to their own knowledge and experience. It is essential that children monitor their understanding and actively engage in their own information processing. They must be helped to think about their own reading process and thinking techniques as they learn and remember information in print (Mason, 1986).

Children who lack experience with the reading process may have problems in comprehending written passages. If they have not been read to, for example, they may focus more on word calling rather than on the flow of meaning. Having been read to and told stories, as well as having a rich background of information helps beginning readers associate reading with language and thinking processes (Spodek, Saracho & Lee, 1984).

The Relationship Between Reading and Writing

Reading and writing are closely related processes. In writing meaning is constructed in texts, while in reading text is reconstructed by constructing anticipated meanings (Morrow, 1989). There is an obvious parallel between writing and reading that young children need to appreciate. Children test their ideas in writing and reading by: (1) inventing and decorating letters, symbols, and words; (2) mixing drawing and writing; (3) inventing messages in various forms and shapes; and (4) continuing to use invented writing after they have begun to master conventional ones.

As children experiment with writing they construct and refine their knowledge about written language that makes reading possible. As Marie Clay (1979) states:

> The child who engages in creative writing is manipulating the units of written language—letters, words, sentence types—and is likely to be gaining some awareness of how these can be combined to convey unspoken messages. The child is having to perform within the directional constraints that we use in writing English. The child is probably learning to generate sentences in a deliberate way, word by word. He makes up sentences which fit both his range of ideas and his written language skills. Fluent oral language may permit the young reader to depend almost entirely on meanings and the eye may overlook the need for discriminating details of letters and words. Creative writing demands that the child pay attention to the details of print. To put his message down in print, he is forced to construct words, letter by letter, so he becomes aware of letter features and letter sequences, particularly for the vocabulary which he uses again and again. (p. 2)

Children integrate their knowledge of reading and writing when they write. Morrow (1989) believes that early writing is acquired when:

1. Children's literacy experiences are integrated in familiar situations and real-life experiences such as family and community memberships.
2. Children's early writing process moves from playfully making marks on paper to communicating messages on paper to making texts as artifacts.
3. Children learn the purpose of written language before they learn the forms.
4. Children constantly invent and reinvent the forms of written language.
5. Children's writing is integrated in self-initiated and self-directed social situations and interactions.
6. Children's writing is motivated by story making.
7. Children observe and participate in literacy events with more skilled writers.
8. Children work independently on the functions and forms of writing that they have experienced through interactions with literate others.

According to Teale (1986), these exploratory activities make it possible for children to develop literacy as well as to develop knowledge about language, their "metalinguistic" knowledge. Their knowledge about language increases their ability to direct and control their attempts at writing. It is important that children practice what they learn about writing. Self-initiated practice plays a fundamental role in the development of the children's writing abilities (Morrow, 1989).

Children's writing evolves in stages. Saracho (1990) found the following levels in her writing study of 50 three-year-olds:

Level 1—Aimless Scribbling: In this level children attempt to write their name by moving the writing tool on the paper. Using their arms and hands, they make longitudinal and circular motions. Many times they draw a picture instead of writing their name.

Level 2—Horizontal Movement: The children's marks on paper soon go beyond aimless scribbling. The marks tend toward the horizontal and some systematic "up and down" squiggling. They make hasty scribbling in an up and down motion progressing across the page. The children attempt to imitate the adult's manner in rapid cursive writing.

Level 3—Separate Symbol Units: A horizontal movement with greater regularity in the vertical strokes still exists. However, the children tend to make discrete symbol units, some of which are scarcely recognizable as letters.

Level 4—Incorrect Written Letters: Letters are written incorrectly. Separate symbol units have become more easily discerned. The children seem to become more aware of separate letter units. The waviness in imitation of adult cursive writing is almost absent. Although most of the letter units are recognizable, occasionally an incorrect letter is made. There is more construction in space. The children have discovered separate letter units and have developed an interest in writing those letter symbols.

Level 5—Correct Spelling of First Name: A mixture of correct and incorrect letters appear in this level. Correct spelling of the first name is seen.

These levels are reflective of one study of young children's early writing attempts. They are provided as an example of how writing changes for children. The categories and stages should not be considered as representing a developmental order among all children.

Teaching about the Written Language

Writing experiences help young children to read. When children try to copy letters, they become aware of the distinctive shapes of letters and words. Many young children write by themselves, and some early writers become quite independent.

Young children's writing involves more than just print markings on a page. They know that writing communicates ideas. Several research studies (e.g., Clay, 1975; DeFord, 1980; Hildreth, 1936) show that children progress in a series of sequential stages as they gain writing skills.

Marie Clay describes how children explore the variation in their early writing efforts. She has identified principles that can guide teachers in understanding young children's writing efforts. Teachers can observe the children's written responses in order to identify each child's perception of written language. They can collect a large number of writing samples and the necessary information to develop an appropriate writing program for young children. Vu-

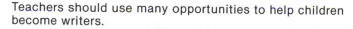

Teachers should use many opportunities to help children become writers.

kelich and Golden (1984) suggest that the following activities and opportunities be included:

- Daily opportunities to write.
- A writing center where children record on paper their thoughts and words.
- Writing materials such as pencils (both regular and primary size), pens, magic markers, and paper (with and without lines).
- Other materials that promote writing, such as a typewriter, magnetic letters, wooden letters, and blocks with letters.

For some children, writing is a forerunner of reading. They copy signs, labels, or letters. They are intrigued with using pencils, crayons, and paper. Many researchers provide evidence that young children are interested in learning to write in the early years. Marie Clay (1977) observed that three- to five-year-old children recognize that people write for a purpose, and they are therefore motivated to express their ideas in written form.

The "language experience approach" is a way for children to express their ideas through written language. Children dictate individual or group stories to a teacher or other adult. The teacher may set up a field trip or other exciting activity to motivate the children's thinking. A discussion follows in which children share their experience and the teacher clarifies concepts. The children then dictate a story which is written on a chart or chalkboard. Each child may contribute a sentence. The teacher uses the child's exact words and reads it back immediately, emphasizing left to right progression. The teacher then asks the children

After a field trip, the children dictate a letter of thanks to the teacher, which they can all sign before mailing.

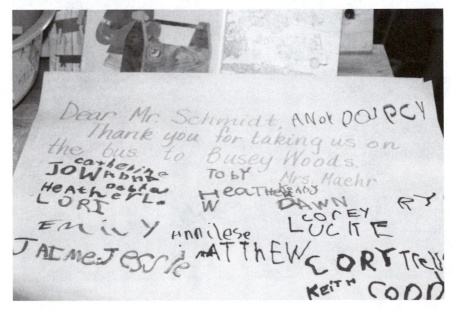

to read the line and simultaneously moves his or her arm from left to right. The children then agree on a title for the story.

The children read and reread the story many times and work on reading skills appropriate to each child's developmental level. These skills can include rhyming words and identifying words with the same meaning, words with opposite meaning, words that sound the same but have different meaning, and vocabulary words. The chart is displayed where children can read it on their own. Copies of the story can also be duplicated for children to take home.

The individual experience story is similar to the group experience story. A child may be more interested in the individual experience story because of personal involvement. Any language experience story is personally meaningful to children because they are the authors. They use their own experiences and their own language to communicate their thoughts in written language.

In a writing program for young children, many children will learn to write their names and others will go beyond that. Pushing children who do not have the skill needed to write discourages them and develops poor writing habits which are later difficult to overcome (Lamme, 1983).

Barbe and Lucas (1974) suggest there should be handwriting readiness programs that cover prerequisite skill areas:

> *Small muscle development.* Many young children cannot hold a pencil adequately because they lack the small muscle control. Small muscle skills can be developed through manipulative tasks such as completing jigsaw puzzles.

> *Eye–hand coordination.* One has to have the muscle control to have the hand do what the eye and brain want it to do. Most small muscle activities also develop eye–hand coordination.

> *Holding utensils or tools.* Children enjoy playing with writing materials. Before young children write, they need many experiences with drawing; in painting with paint brushes, markers, sponges, chalk, and crayons; and in writing with pencils. Pencils are very difficult tools to manipulate and should be the last material children learn to hold.

> *Letter perception.* Children should be taught to recognize form, notice likenesses and differences, infer the necessary movement in producing forms, and verbally describe letters.

Marie Clay (1975) also recommends that children learn:

- to attend and orient themselves to written language
- to organize their exploratory investigation of print forms
- to tell left from right
- to visually analyze letters and words

It is important that children see written language as a way to communicate so that they see the importance of handwriting skills. Young children need to be provided with the appropriate opportunities of writing books, greeting cards, or letters.

Children can be
encouraged to read and
reread a story they have
heard.

Skills in written language include determining the difference between print and nonprint, learning specific characteristics of print, learning to write, knowing and understanding the letters of the alphabet, and learning conventions of print including left to right, top to bottom, upper- and lower-case letters, and punctuation. Young children need to learn about the purposes and types of written language and ways to communicate through writing.

SUMMARY

Early childhood language arts programs include learning both receptive and expressive language skills. When children read and listen, they receive communications; when they speak and write, they express communications. These four areas—reading, listening, speaking, and writing—are all important in any language arts program and need to be integrated through a variety of experiences. These experiences include children's literature, poetry, storytelling, puppetry, and creative dramatics.

The emphasis in preschool should be on oral language experiences. Experiences for young children are planned to develop preliminary learnings in the written communication skills, although the more sophisticated reading and writing skills are usually developed after six years of age. A good foundation in oral language helps young children to recognize the relationship between spoken and written words. Then they can learn to read to receive ideas and impressions just as they are able to listen; they can express ideas, impressions, and feelings in writing just as they are able to speak.

REFERENCES

ANDERSON, R. C. (1984). Some reflection on the acquisition of knowledge. *Educational Researcher, 13,* 5–10.

ANDERSON, R. C., AND P. D. Pearson (1984). A schema-theoretical view of basic processes in reading comprehension. In P. D. Pearson (Ed.), *Handbook of reading research,* pp. 255–259. New York: Longman.

BAKER, A. AND E. GREENE (1977). *Storytelling: Art and technique.* New York: R. R. Bowker.

BARBE, W. B. AND V. H. LUCAS (1974). Instruction in handwriting: A new look. *Childhood Education, 50,* 207–209.

CHAMBERS, B. (1983). Counteracting racism and sexism in children's books. In O. N. Saracho and B. Spodek (Eds.), *Understanding the multicultural experience in early childhood education.* Washington, DC: National Association for the Education of Young Children.

CLARK, M. M. (1984). Literacy at home and at school: Insights from a study of young fluent readers. In H. Goelman, A. Oberg, and F. Smith (Eds.), *Awakening to literacy.* Exeter, NH: Heinemann Educational Books.

CLAY, M. M. (1966). *Emergent reading behavior.* Unpublished doctoral dissertation, University of Aukland, New Zealand.

———. (1975). *What did I write?* Aukland, New Zealand: Heinemann Educational Books.

———. (1977). Exploring with a pencil. *Theory into Practice, 16* 334–335.

———. (1979). *Reading: The patterning of complex behavior.* Exeter, NH: Heinemann educational Books.

COODY, B. (1983). *Using literature with young children.* Dubuque, IA: Wm. C. Brown Company.

CULLINAN, B. E. (1989). *Literature and the child.* Washington, DC: Harcourt, Brace, Jovanovich.

DEFORD, D. (1980). Young children and their writing. *Theory into Practice, 19,* 157–162.

DOWNING, J. AND D. THACKERAY (1978). *Reading readiness.* London: Hodder & Stoughton.

DURKIN, D. (1966). *Children who read early.* New York: Teachers College Press.

———. (1987). *Teaching young children to read.* Boston: Allyn and Bacon, Inc.

GALDONE, P. (1962). *The hare and the tortoise.* New York: McGraw-Hill.

GARNER, R. (1987). *Metacognition and reading comprehension.* Norwood, NJ: Ablex.

GOODMAN, Y. (1980). The roots of literacy. In M. Douglas (Ed.), *Claremont Reading Conference forty-fourth yearbook.* Claremont, CA: Claremont Reading Conference.

———. (1986). Children coming to know literacy. In W. H. Teale and E. Sulzby (Eds.), *Emergent literacy: Writing and reading.* Norwood, NJ: Ablex.

GOODMAN, Y., AND B. ALTWERGER (1981). *Print awareness in preschool children: A study of the development of literacy in preschool children* (Occasional Paper 4). Tucson, AZ: University of Arizona, College of Education, Arizona Center for Research and Development.

GRAYSON, M. F. (1962). *Let's do fingerplays,* illustrated by Nancy Weyl. New York: Van Rees Press.

HARSTE, J., V. WOOD AND C. BURKE (1984). *Language stories and literacy lessons.* Exeter, NH: Heinemann Educational Books.

HEATH, S. B. (1980). The function and uses of literacy. *Journal of Communication, 30,* 123–133.

HEINING, R. B. AND L. STILLWELL (1981). *Creative drama for the classroom teacher.* Englewood Cliffs, NJ: Prentice-Hall.

HENNINGS, D. G. (1982). *Communication in action teaching the language arts.* Boston: Houghton Mifflin.

HIEBERT, E. H. (1981). Developmental patterns and interrelationships of preschool children's print awareness. *Reading Research Quarterly, 16,* 236–260.

———. (1986). Using environmental print in beginning reading instruction. In M. R. Sampson (Ed.), *The pursuit of literacy: Early reading and writing.* Dubuque, IA: Kendall/Hunt.

HILDRETH, G. (1936). Developmental sequences in name writing. *Child Development, 7,* 291–303.

HILLERICH, R. L. (1977). *Reading fundamentals for preschool and primary children.* Columbus, OH: Charles E. Merrill.

HOLDAWAY, D. (1979). *The foundations of literacy.* Sydney, Australia: Ashton Scholastic.

HONIG, A. S. (1982). Language environments for young children. *Young Children, 38*(1), 56–67.

HUCK, C. S. (1979). *Children's literature in the elementary school.* New York: Holt, Rinehart & Winston.

JACOBS, L. B. (1955). Children's experiences in literature. In V. E. Herrick and L. B. Jacobs (Eds.), *Children and the language arts,* pp. 192–218. Englewood Cliffs, NJ: Prentice-Hall.

———. (1972). Enjoying poetry with children. In M. D. Cohen (Ed.), *Literature with children,* pp. 32–38. Washington, DC: Association for Childhood Educational International.

JENKINS, P. D. (1981). *The magic of puppetry: A guide for those working with young children.* Englewood Cliffs, NJ: Prentice-Hall.

JEWELL, M., AND M. ZINTZ (1986). *Learning to read naturally.* Dubuque, IA: Kendall/Hunt.

LAMME, L. L. (1983). Handwriting in an early childhood curriculum. In J. F. Brown (Ed.), *Curriculum planning for young children,* pp. 109–116. Washington, DC: National Association for the Education of Young Children.

MASON, G. E. (1981). *Primer on teaching reading: Basic concepts and skills of the early elementary years.* Itasca, IL: F. E. Peacock Publishers.

MASON, J. (1977). *Reading readiness: A definition and skills hierarchy from preschoolers' developing conceptions of print* (Technical Report 59). Urbana, IL: University of Illinois, Center for the Study of Reading.

———. (1980). When do children begin to read: An exploration of four-year-old children's letter and word reading competencies. *Reading Research Quarterly, 15,* 203–227.

———. (1986). Kindergarten reading: A proposal for a problem-solving approach. In B. Spodek (Ed.), *Today's kindergarten: Exploring the knowledge base, expanding the curriculum,* pp. 48–66. New York: Teachers College Press.

MASON, J. AND C. MCCORMICK (1981). *An investigation of pre-reading instruction: A developmental perspective.* (Technical Report 224). Urbana, IL: University of Illinois, Center for the Study of Reading.

MCCASLIN, N. (1990). *Creative dramatics in the classroom* (5th ed.). New York: Longman.

MCNEILL, J. D. (1984). *Reading comprehension: New directions for classroom practice.* Glenview, IL: Scott Foresman & Company.

MORROW, L. M. (1985). Reading stories: A strategy for improving children's comprehension, concept of a story structure and oral language complexity. *Elementary School Journal, 85,* 647–661.

———. (1986). Promoting responses to literature: Children's sense of story structure. Paper presented at the National Reading Conference, Austin, Texas.

———. (1989). *Literacy development in the early years: Helping children read and write.* Englewood Cliffs, NJ: Prentice-Hall.

PETTY, W. T., D. C. PETTY AND R. T. SALZER (1989). *Experiences in language: Tools and techniques for language arts methods.* Boston: Allyn and Bacon.

PFLAUM, S. W. (1986). *The development of language and literacy in young children.* Columbus, OH: Merrill.

ROSS, R. R. (1980). *Storyteller.* Columbus, OH: Charles E. Merrill.

SARACHO, O. N. (1984). Young children's conceptual factors of reading. *Early Child Development and Care, 15*(4), 305–314.

———. (1985a). The impact of young children's print awareness in learning to read. *Early Child Development and Care, 21*(1), 1–10.

———. (1985b). The roots of reading and writing. *New directions in reading research and practice.* 1985 Yearbook of the State of Maryland International Association, 81–87.

———. (1987). Evaluating reading attitudes. *Day Care and Early Education, 14,* 23–25.

———. (1990). Development Sequences in Three-Year-Old Children's Writing. *Early Child Development and Care.*

SENDAK, M. (1963). *Where the wild things are.* New York: Harper & Row.

SMITH, F. (1978). *Psycholinguistics and reading.* New York: Holt, Rinehart & Winston.

SPODEK, B. (1985). *Teaching in the early years* (3rd ed.). Englewood Cliffs, NJ: Prentice Hall.

SPODEK, B., O. N. SARACHO, AND R. C. LEE (1984). *Mainstreaming young children.* Belmont, CA: Wadsworth.

SULZBY, E. (1985). Children's emergent reading of favorite storybooks. *Reading Research Quarterly, 20,* 458–481.

SUTHERLAND, Z., AND M. H. ARBUTHNOT (1986). *Children and books.* Glenview, IL: Scott Foresman & Company.

TEALE, W. (1982). Positive environments for learning to read: What studies of early readers tell us. *Language Arts, 55,* 922–932.

———. (1986). The beginning of reading and writing: Written language development during the preschool and kindergarten years. In M. Sampson (Ed.), *The pursuit of literacy: Early reading and writing.* Dubuque, IA: Kendall/Hunt.

TORREY, J. (1969). Learning to read without a teacher. *Elementary English, 46,* 556–559.

TORVEY, D. R., AND J. E. KERBER (Eds.) (1986). *Roles in literacy learning: A new perspective.* Newark, DE: International Reading Association.

VUKELICH, C., AND J. GOLDEN (1984). Early writing: Developmental teaching strategies. *Young Children, 39*(2), 3–10.

WARD, W. (1957). *Playmaking with children* (2nd ed.). New York: Appleton-Century-Crofts.

WILLIAMSON, P. M. (1981). Literature goals and activities for young children. *Young Children, 36*(4), 24–30.

YADEN, D. (1985). Preschoolers' spontaneous inquiries about print and books. Paper presented at the National Reading Conference, San Diego, California.

SUGGESTED ACTIVITIES

1. Begin a file of language activities for young children using categories such as children's literature, poetry, storytelling, puppetry, creative dramatics, and action plays.

2. Read a story to a three-, four-, and five-year-old child. Describe the changes in the story form as you prepare for different age groups.

3. Record on tape some children's conversations at snack time, story time, play time, or other similar activities. Compare the different types of conversations.

4. Collect a set of poems appropriate for use with young children. Cut pictures from magazines or find other appropriate pictures to be used with the poems.

5. Develop a lesson plan for a week of reading readiness activities for a group of three-year-olds.

6. Observe a teacher of two- to five-year-old children teaching a language experience. Determine whether the teacher is teaching early listening, speaking, reading, or writing.

13

Cognitively Oriented Learning
Science and Mathematics

OBJECTIVES

After completing this chapter on cognitively oriented learning, the student should be able to:

1. Explain the scientific processes of observing, classifying, predicting, and communicating.
2. Describe a developmentally appropriate science program for young children.
3. Describe a developmentally appropriate mathematics program for young children.
4. Identify the goals of nutrition education for young children.
5. Explain the relationship between cognitive development and the science and mathematics curriculum.
6. Discuss why environmental education is an appropriate part of science for young children.

Children are active learners—both in and out of the classroom, by themselves and with others, and with objects and materials of every conceivable size and shape. Physical activity puts children into contact with the world and enables them to develop a sense of the world. Mental activity enables children to understand their world—in their own way and at their own level.

Firsthand, direct experience with real things helps give children a deeper sense of the world. While we all know what a dog is, those who have a dog for a pet or have similar contact with dogs know more about dogs than those who have gained their knowledge of dogs through being told, or being shown a book or a picture, or watching a television program. Both groups may be able to describe a dog, but what they describe—what they know and feel—will be significantly different.

In a very real sense, experience is the basis for children's knowledge, including knowledge about mathematics and science. Young children learn mathematical and scientific concepts as they interact with objects that are a part of their everyday world. Children learn about quantity, size, shape, order, number, classes, and many other concepts through their everyday experiences.

This chapter explores the child's developing cognitive ability and its relationship to the mathematics and science program. It also provides examples of activities to help young children develop science and mathematics concepts.

COGNITIVE THEORY

One of the theories of knowledge upon which many early childhood programs are built is *constructivist theory*. This theory states that humans construct their own understanding of the world by acting on their experiences. Jean Piaget is best known for his constructivist theory. According to Piaget, children develop *schema*, or conceptual systems, through the process of *equilibration* as they construct their knowledge. This process of equilibration is made up of two complementary processes: *assimilation* and *accommodation*. In assimilation children acquire information from the environment and incorporate it into their existing schema or systems of knowledge. Children revise their existing system of knowledge through accommodation when the information they gather cannot fit within the system. The result is a balance of existing and new knowledge: an *equilibrium*.

Assimilation and accommodation complement one another and operate together. A child who knows that a car has four wheels may call every four-wheeled object a car. However, when the child learns that trucks also have four wheels and are different from cars in that they can carry large objects, he or she can assimilate this new information, but he or she must accommodate it into his or her existing knowledge by creating a new category of wheeled vehicles: trucks. Thus a new balance, or equilibrium, is established that will be modified again and again. It is the schema that is modified as the child assimilates and accommodates information. Another way of looking at a schema is as the organized, personalized information system that an individual uses to understand the world.

Piaget, as noted in Chapter 5, theorized that children go through a series of stages in intellectual development relating to how they process information. Most three- to five-year-old children are in the *preoperational* stage. They have not yet developed the ability to think logically or abstractly about the world. Their thinking is unsystematic and intuitive, bound by their perceptions as they focus on one attribute of an object at a time. Children who are playing with colored blocks of different shapes, for example, may focus only on color and not on shape, or only on shape disregarding color, but they can't consider both attributes at the same time.

Children at this stage focus on the beginning or end state of a transformation rather than on the process of transformation itself. Thus, if a child is given two equal-sized balls of clay and then one is rolled out while the other is left alone, the child might say that the rolled-out one is bigger. The child does not keep in mind that initially they were of equal size and that no clay was added or taken away. Similarly, these children are not aware that pouring water from a tall, thin cylinder into a short, fat one does not change the amount of water. In each of these cases, focusing on only one attribute, length or thickness, and being perceptually bound, limits children's understanding.

The ability to conserve develops between five and eight years of age, as children mature, gain experience, and learn from others. The more opportunities children have to play with objects and the more they are confronted with other children's ideas, the sooner they are likely to develop the ability to think logically.

The science and the mathematics programs in an early childhood class should give children firsthand experiences with objects that allow them to observe, manipulate, and describe them. It should also provide opportunities for children to create and test their schema about these objects, and opportunities to interact with other children who are also developing schema, in this way becoming more mature intellectually as they learn about the physical world.

SCIENCE FOR YOUNG CHILDREN

Science is concerned with the physical properties of the world. Science orders properties, identifies relationships among properties, and attempts to establish theories that can be tested to validate the relationships found in these theories. Science may also be seen as a set of organized concepts and generalizations. By organizing information into systematic sets of concepts, knowledge of the world can be scientifically ordered (Spodek, 1985).

Science is a system of knowledge about the physical world. It includes ideas about processes, objects, and the relationship among them. In developing concepts, scientists involve themselves in the process of creating knowledge. The American Association for the Advancement of Science (1967) identified the processes of science as including:

- observing
- using space-time relationships

- using numbers
- measuring
- classifying
- communicating
- predicting
- inferring

Many of these processes are the same ones young children use when they act on the physical world, discovering attributes, organizing schema, and representing the world. Thus, at the early childhood level the science curriculum can provide opportunities to learn some of the processes of science as they observe and describe *attributes* and observe and describe *actions*. Concepts about animals, plants, weather, water, and food are appropriate for young children to develop as a way of learning about science. Children can be helped to organize the information they gather related to these concepts. Creating and testing scientific concepts can become the basis for the science curriculum. In order to do this, children must have access to materials that will help them to understand objects and their actions and interactions in the world.

Science, like other areas of the curriculum, offers teachers a wide choice of topics, materials, and experiences from which to choose. Robert Smith (1988) suggests criteria that teachers can use in selecting science materials. These are presented in Table 13–1.

TABLE 13-1   Criteria for Developmentally Appropriate Science Experiences in the Preschool

Are the materials selected those:
 A. To which children will naturally gravitate for play?
 B. Which provide opportunities for the development of perceptual abilities through total involvement of the senses (perception of color, size, shape, texture, hardness, sound, etc.)?
 C. Which encourage self-directed problem solving and experimentation?
 D. Which children can act upon–cause to move–or which encourage children's observations of changes to take place?

Do the experiences which evolve from children's play with the materials:
 A. Provide opportunities for the teacher to "extend the child's learning by asking questions or making suggestions that stimulate children's thinking" (NAEYC, 1986, p. 10)?
 B. Allow for additional materials to be introduced gradually to extend children's explorations and discoveries?
 C. Allow for differences in ability, development, and style?
 D. Allow children to freely interact with children and adults?
 E. Encourage children to observe, compare, classify, predict, communicate, make simple quantitative measurements, and use space-time relationships (AAAS, 1967)?
 F. Allow for the integration of other curriculum areas?

R. F. Smith, "Wheels and Things: Developing Preschool Science Learning Centers." *Dimensions, 17*(1), 1988, 10–11.

TOPICS FOR EARLY CHILDHOOD SCIENCE

There are many science topics that will interest most young children. Plants, animals, sound, light, water, seasons, and simple machines are all a part of the young child's experiences and are topics that can be approached first-hand. Topics that are particularly appropriate for young children—physics, animals, plants, weather, nutrition, and ecology—are discussed here.

Physics

Young children can approach physics in relation to what is called physical knowledge: knowledge of the physical attributes of things. They learn about objects by acting on them and observing reactions.

Constance Kamii and Rheta DeVries (1978a) suggest that two kinds of activities are important for generating physical knowledge in young children. The first involves the movement of objects where the action is primary and the role of observation is secondary. In the second kind, the role of observation is primary and the child's action is secondary because the object observed actually changes. Kamii and DeVries suggest the following criteria for selecting phenomena involving the movement of objects:

1. The child must be able to produce the movement by his or her own action.
2. The child must be able to vary the action.
3. The reaction of the object must be observable.
4. The reaction of the object must be immediate. (p. 8–9)

These criteria reflect the importance of equilibration in the child's construction of knowledge of the physical world. As children deal with objects within their experience, the actions they perform are based on what they already know. As they vary their actions and observe the changing reactions, they not only assimilate new information, but they must accommodate into their existing cognitive structures the information they gather.

Constance Kamii and Lucinda Lee-Katz (1979) offer a number of suggestions for activities that enable children to actually move an object. Table 13–2 describes some of these activities.

Activities for children that involve objects changing their status include:

- Melting ice.
- Juicing an orange.
- Boiling water to make steam.
- Making applesauce out of real apples.
- Cooking raw potatoes and mashing them.
- Leaving wax to melt in the hot sun.
- Painting with plain water, then allowing it to evaporate.

TABLE 13-2   Physics Activities For Young Children That Stress Movement

Rolling on rollers. Place a board on a set of rolling cylinders and use it to move objects or children across the room.

Jumping. Use a cylinder and plank to make a teeterboard. When someone jumps on one end, an object can be propelled into the air.

Tilting. Place a ball bearing in a maze and then tilt the maze to allow the ball to roll freely.

Dropping. Objects such as clothespins or buttons are dropped into a plastic bottle. The child stands up straight and attempts to drop the object into the bottle.

Blowing. Use a straw to blow on an object and propel it toward a goal.

Sucking. Use a straw to lift an object such as a piece of paper and move it from one box to another.

Pulling. Have children run around the play area while holding up streamers.

Swinging. Let the children swing a pendulum and attempt to hit a stationary object with it.

C. Kamii and L. Lee-Katz, "Physics in Preschool Education: A Piagetian Approach," *Young Children, 34*(4), 1979, 4–9.

Children can see the changes take place. They can then describe these changes, discuss them with others, and record them in a picture or an experience chart.

Animals

Living things in the classroom seem to provide children with a feeling of wonder and excitement that cannot be generated by inanimate objects. Things that grow, breathe, move, change, and need care cause children not only to sharpen their observation skills but also to ask questions, generate hypotheses,

Fish make fine classroom pets.

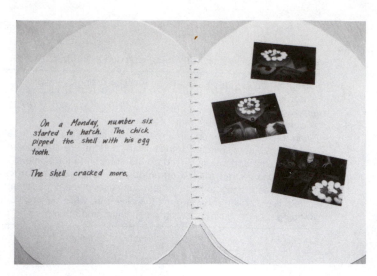

On a Monday, number six started to hatch. The chick pipped the shell with his egg tooth.

The shell cracked more.

The children carefully watched chicken eggs hatch.

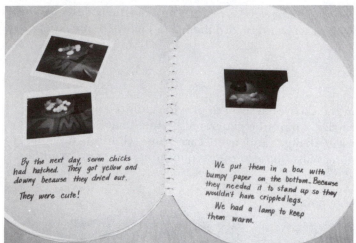

By the next day, seven chicks had hatched. They got yellow and downy because they dried out.

They were cute!

We put them in a box with bumpy paper on the bottom. Because they needed it to stand up so they wouldn't have crippled legs.

We had a lamp to keep them warm.

They regularly took pictures of the process with an instant camera. Along with their verbal descriptions, these made an excellent "egg book."

After a few days they got feathers and lost their egg tooth. They got faster!

We sent them to Cory Douglas' farm. But before they went, we took their pictures.

record data, and solve problems. Caring for plants and animals helps to give children a sense of responsibility as well.

Among the concepts that children can learn from animals are:

- Animals are living things.
- Animals need appropriate food.
- Animals need water.
- Animals need safe places to sleep and live.
- Animals may bite when hurt or frightened.
- Animals need activity and rest.

These concepts are not generated in a single experience but evolve out of experiences over a long period of time with classroom pets.

Baby chicks, ducks, guinea pigs, hamsters, rabbits, fish, turtles, snakes, worms, and ants can all be classroom pets if proper care is taken. In each case an appropriate environment, such as a cage, box, or ant farm, must be provided. Additionally, the pet must have adequate food, a source of water, and opportunities to exercise.

Before choosing a classroom pet, the teacher should review different animals that are available. Once an animal is selected, the teacher should be willing to accept the responsibility that comes with bringing a living thing into the classroom. Although children should share this responsibility, the final obligation is the teacher's. In addition to providing a proper home, food, and water, the teacher must see that the cage is cleaned at regular intervals, that new bedding is provided, and that children learn how to care for and treat the animal.

The children must learn that animals are living and feeling creatures, not toys. They must learn about the animal's behavior patterns, what it eats, and how it acts. They must also learn that there are limits on when, how, and where the pet should be handled. Instruction should be given in proper methods of handling animals.

Activities that can be generated from interactions with classroom animals include weighing, measuring, and recording growth, discussions about comparisons of animals, observing the animal and keeping a log of daily habits, and learning adjectives that describe the animal's behavior, coat, and temperament.

Even when pets are not kept in the room, children can benefit from animal visitors. Their home pets—cats, dogs, sheep, or goats—can be brought into school for a short time as guests. Children take pride in sharing their pets with others, and the class benefits from the comparisons that are made and the language that is generated.

Plants

Although plants are not as cuddly as a rabbit or hamster, they do provide children with a living thing in the classroom. The growth of roots, leaves, stems,

Experiments with vegetables from home provide opportunities
for observation, description, and discussion.

and flowers provides many opportunities to observe, describe, classify, measure, and communicate.

Plants require little care and very little expense compared with animals. Also their death or destruction causes less trauma. Often vegetables from home can start a plant collection. An onion placed in a clear glass of water will let children observe white roots growing out of the bottom and green leaves out of the top. A sweet potato in a jar of water placed in the sunlight will also put out roots and stems. Carrot tops, seed potatoes and many other vegetables work well, too.

Cuttings, pieces of big plants that have stems and leaves but no roots, can also be started in water. Place the cutting in water and watch the roots grow over time. When the root system is large enough, the cutting can be planted in soil. Sometimes a root hormone is helpful to promote growth.

Children can grow grass, flowers, and some vegetables in the classroom using topsoil or potting soil. A flower pot, a pie pan, or a milk carton can be filled with soil, then seeds planted, watered, and placed in the sun to grow. Children can measure the plant weekly and record its growth on a wall chart. Flowers grown in this way make fine Mother's Day gifts, especially if children have decorated the homemade planter.

Schools with large, grassy play areas should consider putting in a garden. A section of the yard that gets enough sun can be set aside and fenced off. Once the soil is turned over, the children can rake, make rows, plant seeds, weed, and record the growth of plants. Leaf lettuce, radishes, and beans are all vegetables that grow in a reasonably short time. Children can eat the vegetables they have grown as part of their lunch or snack. The garden can also serve as a springboard to a unit on cooking, nutrition, or ecology.

A word of caution: plants need to be watered regularly, but they can be destroyed by overwatering. Adequate sunlight is also necessary once the seedlings have started to grow.

Weather

Weather is a good example of a science topic that is related to children's everyday world. Children experience the temperature changes and may be caught in the rain without any protection. They know that the clothes they wear change according to the seasons and that the weather affects plants and animals. Studying weather enables children to make sense of a part of their world that is constantly changing.

In many classes, a discussion of the weather is held at the beginning of each morning. The teacher asks questions such as, "Is it sunny or cloudy?" "Do you think it might rain?" or "Did you need a jacket this morning?" The children's responses may be recorded on a weather chart or written as part of a language experience chart. As information on the weather is accumulated, children may see patterns and begin to generate hypotheses about why certain things occur.

Children are fascinated by many weather related phenomena. Frost on a window, icicles hanging from a ledge, and steam from our breath, all cause children to wonder and to question. An alert teacher can build on that interest and provide opportunities for observation and discussion. Each weather activity enables children to increase their knowledge of the physical world and helps them to expand their vocabulary as they describe what they have observed.

Figure 13-1 describes a variety of weather-related experiences that are appropriate for young children.

FIGURE 13-1   Experiences with Weather

I. MAJOR CONCEPTS

    A. A thermometer measures temperature.
    B. There are many kinds of weather: snow, rain, frost, ice, storms, and wind.
    C. Different seasons bring different weather.
    D. Weather is always changing.

II. DEVELOPMENT OF CONCEPTS

    A. Thermometer

        1. Important Concepts:
          a. A thermometer measures temperature.
          b. When air is warm, colored mercury line is high, when air is cold, colored mercury line is low.
          c. A thermometer helps us know what clothes to wear.

        2. Activities:
          a. Have one large thermometer in classroom and one outside; observe relative position of mercury on thermometer and keep record for as long as children seem interested.

(Continued)

FIGURE 13-1 *(Continued)*

　　　b. Place thermometer in very cold water and then in warm water to notice the change in position of mercury.
　　　c. Experiment with a variety of thermometers—candy, meat, science, etc., in melting, heating, and freezing liquids.

B. Weather is always changing

　1. Activities:
　　　a. Keep a record on the calendar of each day's weather as long as children are interested—use symbols (e.g. umbrella, snowman).
　　　b. Observe daily temperature and record on graph.

C. Different seasons bring different kinds of weather.
　1. Autumn:
　　　a. Cooler days.
　　　b. Need for sweaters and jackets.
　　　c. Frost.
　　　d. Activities:
　　　　1. Observe white crystals on grass; see how quickly sun melts them—use hand lens.
　　　　2. Breathe on window on a very cold day to see the frost form.
　　　　3. Walk on grass with frost, hear "brunching" sound, observe footprints.

　2. Winter:
　　　a. Heavier clothing needed.
　　　b. Colder temperatures.
　　　c. Melting and freezing.
　　　d. Varied weather.
　　　e. Ice characteristics:
　　　　1. Ice is frozen water.
　　　　2. Ice forms on very cold days.
　　　f. Activities:
　　　　1. Experiment with freezing and melting in as many ways as possible.
　　　　2. Observe frozen pond, lake, or river.
　　　　3. Put container of water outside and observe freezing process and temperature.
　　　　4. Make ice cream in a hand-turned freezer.
　　　　5. Observe icicles outside; bring one in and watch it drip.

　3. Spring and summer:
　　　a. Warmer temperatures.
　　　b. Lighter clothing.
　　　c. Varied weather.

D. Snow

　1. Characteristics:
　　　a. Snow is frozen moisture dropping from clouds.
　　　b. Snow turns to water when it melts.
　　　c. Snow can be molded into snowmen, snowballs, etc., when very moist.
　　　d. Each snow flake is different.

2. Activities:
   a. Walk in snow as it falls if possible.
   b. Catch snowflakes on black paper, dark mittens or snowsuit and look at flakes with hand lens.
   c. Fill a bowl with snow, bring it indoors and watch it melt.
   d. Make a snowman.
   e. Take a sleigh ride in snow.
   f. Make snow ice cream.
   g. Feed the birds.

E. Rain

1. Characteristics:
   a. Sometimes it rains hard, sometimes gently.
   b. Rain is moisture falling from clouds.

2. Activities:
   a. Walk in a gentle rain, feel rain on face, hear rain on the umbrella.
   b. Watch a heavy rain from inside; talk about suitable clothing for a rainy day.

F. Wind

1. Concepts:
   a. Wind is simply air in motion.
   b. It moves things around.
   c. It can be gentle or strong.
   d. We do not see wind; we feel it and see its effect on things.
   e. A weathervane tells which way wind is blowing.

2. Activities:
   a. Walk in wind, feel it, watch it blow things—leaves, paper, etc.
   b. Toss soap bubbles in the wind. If the wind is gentle it will carry bubbles; if strong, it will break the bubbles.
   c. Watch wind blow smoke as it comes from the chimney.
   d. Fasten silk scarves (or pieces of old parachute, dyed) with strings at corners (like play parachute) to large clipboard clips. Hang on fence to watch wind's effect.

G. Storms

1. Concepts:
   a. We can do away with fear of storms.
   b. We can learn safety habits in storms.

2. Activities:
   a. Watch a storm from inside.
   b. Watch patterns made by lightning, sometimes straight, sometimes zigzag.
   c. Listen to thunder. Sometimes sounds like rolling rumbling, sometimes crackling and banging.
   d. Observe which comes first, lightning or thunder.
   e. Blow up paper bag and pop it; thunder is something like this, results from sudden pushing of air.

Nutrition

Good nutrition is essential for good health and proper growth. Children can be helped to understand that they should eat a variety of foods. They can learn to appreciate different foods and to make wise choices in selecting what to eat. Breakfast, lunch, and snacks are part of many early childhood programs. Teachers can use these opportunities to help children learn about good nutrition.

In planning a unit on nutrition, teachers must be sensitive to the family patterns and cultural backgrounds of the children. Not all families eat the same kinds of food, although their meals may be highly nutritious. Other families may not practice good nutrition. Criticizing a family's practices can make a child angry or defensive.

Herr and Morse (1982) use 10 categories of foods to help children select a well-balanced diet. They feel that teaching the four basic food groups—milk, protein, bread and cereal, and vegetables and fruit—requires children to make difficult generalizations in regards to food selection. The food and nutrition concepts Herr and Morse have identified are presented in Table 13–3. These catego-

TABLE 13-3   Food and Nutrition Concepts For Young Children

1. There is a wide variety of food.
2. Plants and animals are sources of food.
3. Foods vary in color, flavor, texture, smell, size, shape, and sound.
4. A food may be prepared and eaten in many different ways—raw, cooked, dried, frozen, or canned.
5. Good foods are important to health, growth, and energy.
6. Nutrition is how our bodies use the foods we eat for health, growth, and energy.
7. Food may be classified according to the following categories:

a. milk	f. vegetables
b. meat	g. breads
c. dried peas and beans	h. pastas
d. eggs	i. cereals, grains, and seeds
e. fruits	j. nuts

8. A good diet includes a wide variety of foods from each of the food categories.
9. There are many factors that influence eating:
   a. attractiveness of food
   b. method of preparation
   c. cleanliness/manners
   d. environment/atmosphere
   e. celebrations
10. We choose the foods we eat for many reasons:
    a. availability and cost
    b. family and individual habits
    c. aesthetics
    d. social and cultural customs
    e. mass media influence

J. Heer, and W. Morse, "Food for Thought: Nutrition Education for Young Children." *Young Children, 38*(1), 1982, 5–6.

ries are not taught directly to children, but underlie the food-related activities that teachers provide.

Cooking is an enjoyable and useful activity to include as part of a nutrition unit. Cooking can support language development, help children develop mathematics and science concepts, and assist them in gaining social knowledge. Children can follow recipes using basic ingredients and can go through the process of food preparation, watching the ingredients blend, change their appearance, and finally emerge as a tasty snack.

In planning a cooking experience, teachers should make sure that there are enough utensils and enough ingredients for the number of children who will participate. Cooking experiences are best done with small groups. Care should be taken that the cooking activity is a safe one. If a heat source is to be used, such as an oven or a hot plate, the children should be aware of the dangers of being burned and adequate insulated pads and pot holders should be available. Electric appliances must be treated with respect. Children should be expected to wash and dry their hands before preparing food and to treat ingredients with care. Aprons are helpful in protecting clothing.

It is a good idea to write the recipe on a chart. Pictures as well as words can be used to designate ingredients and amounts. The recipe can be discussed at the beginning, then referred to regularly as the group follows each step in sequence. The teacher can ask the children to describe what is taking place, what changes they see happening, what ingredients they are using, or any thoughts they may have as the activity evolves.

Children should help clean up the area after cooking is done, washing the surfaces of tables, sweeping the floor, and scrubbing the utensils. Whatever is cooked may be eaten by the group itself or by the entire class. Eating can be a social occasion, one in which the activity is discussed and the experience is shared.

There are a number of foods that can be prepared without a heat source. The following are suggestions for cooking experiences that do not require heat:

- Make butter either by churning the cream or shaking it in a jar. The children can then spread the butter with tongue depressors on crackers or bread.
- Make ice cream with a hand-cranked freezer.
- Prepare fresh fruit—apples can be cored and sliced, oranges peeled and sectioned.
- Squeeze oranges or lemons to make a juice drink; add water and sugar if necessary.
- Peel carrots or cucumbers with a hand-peeler; slice for snack.
- Make applesauce by putting peeled and cored apples through a food mill or potato ricer.

Both in cooking and in serving meals and snacks, good nutrition practices should be followed. Snacks need not be high in sugar and salt. Fruits, vegetables, and other snacks that are high in protein, fiber, and complex carbohydrates serve nutritional needs better. Teachers might wish to have "tasting parties" for children to try out different foods. Various raw fruits and vegetables can be of-

Children can be encouraged to share nutritious snacks brought from home.

fered in small quantities, including those foods that children might not normally encounter. The children might also be offered the same foods in different forms:

- A fresh pineapple and cans of pineapple could be put out one day to be examined by children and to build interest. All preparation, such as cutting the fresh pineapple, should be done in front of the children. Serve the fresh pineapple one day, the canned pineapple another.
- On another day, let the children have a choice of sliced pineapple or crushed pineapple. The crushed pineapple can be spread on crackers for ease in eating. Encourage the children to say what they want. On another day, serve pineapple juice.
- Serve raw apples, canned apple slices, applesauce, apple butter on crackers, and apple juice.
- For variety, cut the apples crosswise to show the "star" in the center. Another time, give each child a choice of an apple with a red skin or a yellow skin. Draw attention to the shape, smell, and texture or "crunch" of the apple.
- Different varieties and colors of grapes can be eaten. (Be careful with seeds.)
- Other possibilities are fresh peas, peas in a can, and frozen peas; fresh carrots and canned carrots; fresh tomatoes, canned tomatoes, and tomato juice.

Nutrition education helps open up children to new eating patterns that will lead them to a healthy life. It is a part of the curriculum that can be integrated into the daily lives of the class.

ECOLOGY AND THE ENVIRONMENT

One purpose of science for young children is to teach them the importance of conserving natural resources and taking care of the environment. Young children may not be old enough to understand why they should be concerned with environmental neglect, but they are old enough to appreciate the beauty of the world and to begin developing good habits.

They can learn simple rules like these:

- Do not pull leaves off trees, break branches, or otherwise harm plant life.
- Do not dirty the air, the water, or the earth.
- Respect the lives of animals and humans alike.
- Do not take more than you need of anything. Do not be wasteful.
- Actively work to improve the environment by leaving food for birds and animals, planting flowers, and picking up trash.

They can also be involved in class activities that help them learn the proper uses of the environment. For example, the class could be taken on a trip to a local park to pick up trash and deposit it into trash containers. Simple bird or animal feeders can be made to be placed in the playground in the winter. Peanut butter spread on pine cones and hung on a tree or spread on an ear of corn nailed to a board and left on the ground can attract winter birds and squirrels. Different birds and different climates and terrains have their particular requirements. Often local park employees can be invited to the school to talk with children about ecology and to suggest projects that children can do and that serve a real purpose in the community.

Concern for the environment should not just be a special project, however. Teachers should continuously model good environmental habits for chil-

A trip to local ecological center is followed by the opportunity for each child to categorize his or her personal sensory experiences.

dren. Regular attention to conservation is most likely to help children develop a positive environmental orientation.

MATERIALS AND EXPERIENCES
FOR EARLY CHILDHOOD SCIENCE

Children need to be provided with adequate tools and opportunities to "do science" to get the most out of the science curriculum. The materials of science include such things as animals, plants, stones, seeds, leaves, sand, water, snow, and other things from the world at large. While children are familiar with these, they may never have carefully studied them. Children can observe these materials singly and together to generate hypotheses and make predictions. Placing seeds in dirt and in sand may generate ideas about whether the seeds will grow better in one or the other. Similarly, adding water to one pot of planted seeds and not to the other, or putting one pot on a windowsill and the other in a closet, can lead to similar predictions. Placing live plants alongside artificial ones may lead to comparisons of likeness and differences.

Many times teachers overlook existing activity areas around the classroom when they plan for science. Sand, water, and woodworking are three centers that offer opportunities for learning scientific concepts. Sand can be loaded, dumped, dug, and tunneled. Children can sit on it, pat it, make pies out of it, and run it through their fingers. Sand can also be sifted and wet sand can be compared to dry sand. A thermometer can be used to compare the temperature of surface sand with that deep in the sand pile.

Children at the water table can wash doll clothes, paint with water, and experiment with objects that sink or float. They can pour water from one container into another, use tubes to make siphons, and use egg beaters to make the water churn. When children become bored with water play, the teacher can add food coloring or dish detergent to the water table to stimulate interest.

Woodworking is a third area that offers children a source of scientific knowledge. Children learn about rough and smooth and hard and soft. They use four of their senses—smell, touch, hearing, and sight—when they work with wood. Most important, children make choices and solve problems, processes that are an integral part of learning about science.

The tools for science include magnifying glasses, simple microscopes, tweezers, magnets, pan balances, timers, basins, funnels, cups, clear plastic hoses, collection boxes, eye droppers, clear plastic containers with covers, sieves, pulleys, ramps, rollers, boards, wheels, and labels. Such tools help children to act on the materials of science and make their observations. Different stones can be placed on the two pans of a balance to compare weights. Magnifying glasses or simple microscopes allow for closer observation of objects. But children should also use direct observation, seeing, hearing, and touching things around them.

The materials and tools of science should be kept together and be kept accessible by children. There should be open shelves for storage and a display area for ongoing projects. Plants should be placed in an area of the room that gets adequate sunlight. The kinds of materials and tools available should be changed periodically to keep children's interest high.

MATHEMATICS FOR YOUNG CHILDREN

Mathematics is an area that many adults shy away from because they feel it is too difficult. Part of the reason that some adults react this way is that they do not have an understanding of basic mathematical principles. They were taught to memorize facts and processes and were rewarded for solving problems quickly and correctly. However, they did not learn why and how mathematics worked.

Recently there has been a great deal of research done on how young children learn mathematical concepts. These findings help to explain how children develop an understanding of the underlying principles of mathematics.

Mathematics is oriented toward concept development and is rooted in the concrete experiences that children have on a daily basis. Topics such as patterning, classifying, observing, seriating, graphing, measurement, comparing, and contrasting assist children in developing the concepts that will eventually enable them to compute with understanding (Wolfinger, 1989).

As children develop logico-mathematical knowledge, they organize and make sense of information that is abstracted from activities. Classifying, seriating, quantifying, and placing things in time and space relationships are examples of how logico-mathematical knowledge is developed. In helping young children learn mathematics, the teacher can focus on classification, seriation, and number. For instance, if children are given three balls, they can learn to recognize the relationship of "three" among the balls. In classifying, children can sort objects by some common attribute, such as shape or color. A child might place crayons in order from the shortest to the longest to seriate them.

The way young children develop logico-mathematical knowledge is through activity with the quantitative qualities of objects. Many areas of the early childhood classroom provide opportunities for grouping and counting objects. Counting blocks, buttons, beads, and dolls and sorting pegs, dress-up clothes, stones, and leaves can give children practice in understanding quantity.

Arthur J. Baroody (1987) stresses the importance of cognitive theory in explaining how children develop mathematical understanding. According to Baroody, cognitive theory suggests that knowledge acquisition entails more than accumulating vast amounts of information. Genuine learning involves changing a child's thought patterns. It is particularly important to note that children construct their mathematical understandings slowly, insight by insight. Mathematical knowledge cannot be imposed on a passive learner.

Gary Glen Price (1989) reports on research that provides insight into how teachers can assist children in learning mathematical concepts. For example, children who have a lot of experience counting will learn numerals more easily. Familiarity with counting by tens will help kindergarten children to understand place values and two-digit numbers. Price points out that counting practice can take many different, meaningful forms without becoming a formal drill. Children can count chairs, brown-eyed children, the number of children who have pets, or the number of windows in the room, to name just a few things. The key to helping children learn mathematics is to understand that they must be encouraged to think about what they are doing (Williams & Kamii, 1986). As children act on objects physically they should also be acting on them mentally. Williams and Kamii (1986) offer three suggestions to help encourage children's thinking:

1. Use or create situations that are personally meaningful to children.
2. Provide opportunities for children to make decisions.
3. Provide opportunities for children to exchange viewpoints with peers. (p. 24)

A good mathematics program is one in which children collect information, learn the appropriate terms to describe the new information, and learn to apply the information in problem-solving situations.

TOPICS FOR EARLY CHILDHOOD MATHEMATICS

There are a great many topics that can be part of a mathematics program for young children and that build on their daily experiences. Jean Shaw (1981) suggests that these activities include:

- Describing—noticing one or more characteristics of an object.
- Ordering—arranging objects in order according to some quality such as length, shade of color, or weight.
- Classifying—putting objects in sets or groups according to a characteristic such as color, texture, or shape.
- Patterning—creating, reproducing, varying, and describing arrangements of objects.
- Comparing—making direct side-by-side comparisons; using one-to-one correspondence to see if sets are equivalent.
- Joining and separating sets—making larger or smaller sets by adding or taking away members.
- Equalizing—making sets have the same number of objects; teaching equality by using one-to-one correspondence.
- Experiencing symbols and concepts—tallying and graphing information; recognizing and writing numerals.
- Experiencing geometry—understanding concepts such as open and closed, inside and outside, flat and solid geometric shapes.

These activities can become part of the daily classroom routine. Teachers should recognize their potential to generate mathematic concepts and to help children learn the appropriate language to describe their learning. Included here are suggestions for presenting three mathematics concepts to young children: number, seriation, and set.

Counting

Counting provides the basis for learning a variety of mathematical concepts. The most important aspect of helping children learn to count is practice. They need many opportunities to count familiar objects each day. Children can count aloud, use counting rhymes and songs, use finger games requiring counting, bounce balls and chant numbers, count the steps of a slide, count children by touching heads, or count cups, cookies, or forks. The list of things that can be counted is limited only by the teacher's imagination.

Price (1989) presents three principles that children must apply in order to count accurately. First, the child must use as many counting words as there are objects to be counted. For example, if there are four objects, each one must be tagged with a word. At this point, having a tag for each object is more important than using the correct word. Second, the list of words the child uses must have a stable order and should meet social conventions. Each time the child counts, the same tags should be used in the same order. The first object will always be tagged "one," the second object will always be tagged "two," and so on. The third principle connects the process of counting with the concept of number. When a child is asked how many objects there are in a set that he or she has just counted, the child responds with the last word said during the counting sequence. Children will not learn these counting principles immediately. They will learn them through repeated practice over time.

Number

Number is the synthesis of two kinds of relationships that children create: ordering and class inclusion (Kamii & DeVries, 1978b). Because a number is an abstract idea, children need many experiences with related activities that help them to move toward the conservation of conversation. To *conserve* number is to realize that the quantity remains the same even when the spatial arrangement of the objects has been changed (Kamii, 1982).

Some experiences that are appropriate before counting are:

- Making complimentary sets—set of dolls to set of dresses; set of napkins to set of children; pencil for each child.
- Matching one-to-one correspondence—matching objects that are not usually found together: flower petals to plants; bottle caps to sticks.
- Ordering elements in a set of physical objects (copying a pattern)—arranging a set of objects such as knife, fork, spoon from left to right and then reverse order; doll clothes; colored beads; geometric shapes.
- Ordering sets of objects in which a relation has been imposed—shortest to tallest; lightest to darkest; fattest to thinnest.

After the child has such experiences, it is helpful to provide counting opportunities throughout the day.

Children can be provided with materials to develop the idea of more than one, such as counting cubes, hundred's boards, number rods with lines in-

Concrete manipulative materials allow children to explore
number concepts.

dented, Cuisenaire rods, abacus, and charts on which objects can be placed.
Kamii and DeVries (1978b) suggest the following situations that are conducive to
the development of the concept of number: distributing materials, dividing objects, collecting things, keeping records, cleanup tasks, voting, group games,
board games, hiding games, music, movement, and art.

Teachers should teach number concepts when these are useful and meaningful to the child. Children should be encouraged to think about numbers when
they feel a need and interest. Teachers also need to figure out how children think.
It is more important to learn why an error was made than to correct it.

Seriation

In seriation a relationship is formed when two or more separate objects
are arranged, one before the other, on the basis of one distinguishable characteristic. The child is asked to compare one object with another in arranging a group
of objects.

According to Piaget there are generally three phases a child passes
through in developing the concept of seriation.

1. The child succeeds in constructing fragments of a series in terms of isolated
   pairs.
2. Then the child can form a series through a trial-and-error process, picking ran-
   domly one object at a time.
3. Finally, either the shortest or tallest object is chosen to start and the rest of the
   series is built systematically.

Table 13–4 presents a list of activities for developing seriation.

TABLE 13-4   Seriation Activities For Young Children

1. Ordering objects in a series according to one property:
   a. Arranging materials from roughest to smoothest.
   b. Arranging objects or materials from hardest to softest—styrofoam, erasers, rocks, pencils, cloth, rubber, cotton, sponges.
   c. Seritating shades in color from lightest to darkest—shaded wood grains, homemade color cards.
   d. Arranging groups of miscellaneous objects from smallest to largest.
   e. Arranging things from shortest to tallest (or longest)—making a Family Graph, using an abacus with removable seriated rods, using a hundred board and seriating by number of blocks in a column, using counting blocks, counting rods or other objects (twigs, combs, pencils, dowel rods, etc.). Arranging things from thinnest to thickest—counting blocks, dowel rods, etc.
   f. Ordering a set of Cuisenaire rods from the shortest to the longest.
   g. Ordering boxed sets of beads or objects (ranged from a set of 1 to a set of 5).
   h. Seriating objects on the basis of weight.
   i. Nesting toys, ordering on the basis of base area.
   j. Pink Tower (Montessori), ordering on the basis of size.
   k. Ordering sounds on the basis of pitch (lowest to highest) and intensity (softest to loudest).
2. Ordering objects in two series inversely related to one another. Referring to the activities in 1 above, take the last item of a completed series and ask the child to use that item as the first in a series.
3. Using pictoral representation in seriation. The flannel board may be used with flannel pieces ranging in size (height, length, width) and color (shades) to help the children order pictures of objects.
4. Seriation of geometric shapes. Ordering two-dimensional figures on the basis of number of sides and three-dimensional shapes on the basis of number of faces. Ordering a group of like shapes (for example, all squares) varying in area.

Sets

Organizing things into sets is a basic part of a child's activity with objects. A set is a well-defined collection of objects, ideas, or symbols. In order to recognize a set, a child must know what things are its elements or members. Children can compare two sets either visibly or by counting the elements. The teacher's role in developing the concept of sets is to provide children with opportunities for manipulating objects into sets, to supply vocabulary at appropriate times, and to structure needed learning experiences for individual and small groups. Table 13–5 presents activities that are appropriate for learning sets.

MATERIALS FOR EARLY CHILDHOOD MATHEMATICS

Manipulative materials are commonly found in early childhood classes. These materials can be acted on by children using their own hands and their own imaginations.

Both Froebel and Montessori made wide use of manipulative materials in their programs, but they used them in different ways than we do now. Today we have a more sophisticated understanding of what children learn when they manipulate objects and how their actions lead to learning.

TABLE 13-5 Activities For Learning Sets

PLAY AND MANIPULATION

Many things can be put into sets:

dishes	flowers in a vase
silverware	clothespins in a bag
clothes	pins in a pin cushion
family (dolls, doll clothes)	tongue depressor sticks in juice cans
crayons	balls
books	cooking equipment (spoons, utensils, cookie
checkers	cutters, pans, beaters)

Display on the mathematics table "sets" that are not usual to classroom. Talk informally with individuals about these:

A set of golf clubs in a bag
A can of tennis balls
The objects in a pocketbook
Coins in a coin purse

Introduce new types of materials for making sets. Display them and watch what children do with them. Talk informally with the children about them:

keys	shoes and socks
coins	buttons
beads	matching cards
rocks	bottle caps
clothespins (colored)	spools (different sizes)
balls	bolts, washers
bowls	boxes (different sizes)

Containers for sets:	
muffin tins	jars
ice cube trays	pie pans (various sizes)
divided boxes	paper cups (assorted sizes)
milk cartons with tops cut off	egg cartons

Display sets that are pairs of objects:

A pair of shoes, boots, rubbers
a pair of gloves, mittens
a pair of socks
a pair of earrings
pictures—a pair of eyes, ears, feet, hands
walk in pairs

Make sets (and subsets) of objects collected on nature walks:

seeds	rocks
leaves	shells
acorns	feathers
nuts	

Provide models (miniature toys) and pictures for arranging sets. Talk with children about what they are doing, their reasons for grouping the materials into sets.

Provide hoops (embroidery hoops, wire hoops, hula hoops) and strips of yarn for children to use in defining sets.

Provide children with objects that can be ordered (buttons, leaves, counting cubes, beads). Watch for seriation.

TABLE 13-5 *(Continued)*

COMPARISON

Use day-to-day activities. Children discover "not enough" crackers, straws, etc.

Have children make comparisons in play—enough cups for the saucers, carriages or chairs for the dolls, etc.

Look for comparison in room equipment—lockers to children, etc.

Snack time presents opportunities for matching:
    cups on a tray, cups per person (one-to-one)
    cookies on a plate, crackers per person (many-to-one)
    napkins, straws (one-to-one)
    other snack items—pieces of fruit, sandwich, etc. (one-to-one or many-to-one)

Structure problems of correspondence (equivalent, greater than, less than) for individuals or small groups:
    flowers to vases
    paint brushes to cans
    dresses to dolls or paper dolls
    miniature cups to saucers, etc.
    egges to egg carton holes
    shoes to socks

Provide more astract problems—sets of objects to put into one-to-one correspondence:
    cubes to cubes
    sticks to sticks of another color or size
    cubes to sticks
    rocks to cubes

Provide games that use one-to-one correspondence:
    cherries to holes
    lotto card pictures to cover other pictures
    bingo-type games
    parquetry blocks and design cubes to two-dimensional patterns
    simple card games

Many things can be manipulated to develop mathematical understanding. Beads, buttons, blocks, geo boards, zipping frames, sewing cards, Lincoln Logs, and Cuisenaire rods are examples of good manipulated materials. The characteristics of worthy manipulative materials are:

- The materials should be easy to use and familiar to the children.
- The materials should be brightly colored and pleasing to the eye.
- It should be possible to classify the materials in more than one way. For example, a bead can be classified as wooden, round, or red.
- The materials should be of varied sizes, shapes, and textures.
- The materials should be safe for children to use.

These materials should be available on an open shelf so that children can easily make choices.

USING EVERYDAY EVENTS TO TEACH ABOUT MATHEMATICS

The daily activity of the early childhood class is full of opportunities to teach children about mathematics. Children can help record attendance, matching a mark or symbol to each boy or girl who comes. Preparing for the snack allows children to match one cup or one napkin to one child and to count how many are needed for each table. Music, dance, and games all offer children opportunities to count. Dramatic play, where children might, for example, play "supermarket" or "bus driver," allows children to use play money, count, and measure. Work in the block-building area and at the woodwork bench also provides children with the chance to develop a sense of mathematics.

One way to enhance mathematics learning is through the use of books. There are many children's books that focus on counting, measuring, comparing, contrasting and other concepts that are a part of the mathematics curriculum. Teachers should choose books that are developmentally appropriate and that reflect children's interests. Ann Harsh (1987) suggests the following criteria for choosing math-oriented books for children:

1. Book illustrations and written text should be accurate and portray mathematical ideas correctly.
2. Book illustrations should be attractive and appealing to young children.
3. Book illustrations should be appropriate in size and detail, in keeping with developmental characteristics of the young child.
4. Written text of the books should be easily understood and interesting to young children. (pp. 24–25)

One way for children to gain an understanding of numbers and the different forms of quantity and space is by measuring. Young children approach measuring simply and intuitively. They first compare things with one another directly; later they learn to compare things to an established standard or unit of measurement.

Young children can be seen dealing with the problem of measuring length as they try to match the height of two sides of a block structure or search for a piece of wood the right size for their wood construction. As they deal with these problems, they learn the words "short," "shorter," "long," "longer," "tall," and "taller." They can soon begin to match the length of objects that are far from one another by making a mark showing the object's length on a piece of paper or cardboard, then taking the paper or cardboard to a second object and comparing its length to the mark, making a judgment from that. Words like "foot" and "inch" can be introduced as kindergarten children use rulers.

Weight is harder for children to perceive than is length. A pound of foam plastic feels lighter than a pound of iron. A simple balance scale can help children see whether one thing is heavier than another. Teachers can make a simple balance scale with a short wooden stick, two pie tins, and some string, being sure that the two tins balance when empty. The children can then compare things around the room, using words like "heavier," "lighter," and "the same weight" to

Learning to read a clock is often an extension of early childhood number work. Discussions and demonstrations can be followed by opportunities for children to practice their developing understanding.

describe their comparisons. Later a teacher might provide different kinds of scales along with standard weights for the balance scale.

Time is much more difficult for children to measure and understand. We cannot see time, and our perception of the passage of time is influenced by many things. We measure time indirectly using what seem to be arbitrary units. What passes for learning to "tell" time is more a matter of learning to read instruments for measuring or keeping track of time: clocks and calendars. Kindergarten children can learn to read an analog clock, understanding the meaning of the hands and the numerals on its face. They can learn to mark a calendar and read it as they read numerals. Using a clock and calendar in the classroom gives children a better sense of the passage of time and the weekly order of the days.

Baroody (1987) offers six suggestions for teachers to consider when planning and implementing a mathematics curriculum for young children:

1. Focus on the learning of relationships.
2. Focus on helping children to see connections and change perspectives.
3. Plan for meaningful learning to take a long time.
4. Encourage and build upon children's self-invented mathematics.
5. Consider individual readiness.
6. Exploit children's natural interest in play.
   (Reprinted by permission of the publisher from Baroody, Arthur J., *Children's Mathematical Thinking.* (New York: Teachers College Press, © 1987 by Teachers College, Columbia University. All rights reserved, page 16.)

Baroody's ideas reflect an integrated approach to mathematics education that is embedded in the total program.

Using everyday occurrences helps children see that mathematics is not an abstract, isolated subject but a way of thinking about elements in our actual life. As a result, mathematics can become a much more meaningful and less fearful subject.

SUMMARY

Children must construct their own understanding of the world. Mathematics and science are learned as young children create their understandings. This understanding is based on physical knowledge and on the construction of logical-mathematical knowledge.

The science curriculum should be built around the active involvement of children with their world. The approach should stress children's learning more about the physical world while developing a positive value orientation toward the environment.

A good program should offer mathematics and science experiences in a variety of contexts. Many kinds of materials should be used to present the concepts and many opportunities provided to practice their use. Each child's understanding and progress in mathematics and science should be recorded by the teacher. Open-ended questions should be used to extend children's learning.

If teachers have a clear understanding of what they wish children to learn, and if a rich environment is provided in an open setting, exciting discoveries can be made by children who are relating to the physical world. This is the stuff of which science and mathematics are made.

REFERENCES

AMERICAN ASSOCIATION FOR THE ADVANCEMENT OF SCIENCE (1967), *Description of program—Science: A process approach.* New York: Xerox Educational Division.

BAROODY, A. J. (1987). *Children's mathematical thinking: A developmental framework for preschool, primary and special education teachers.* New York: Teachers College Press.

HARSH, A. (1987). Teaching mathematics with children's literature. *Young children, 42*(6), 24–29.

HERR, J., AND W. MORSE (1982). Food for thought: Nutrition education for young children. *Young Children, 38*(1), 3–11.

KAMII, C. (1982). *Number in preschool and kindergarten: Educational implementation of Piaget's theory.* Washington, DC: National Association for the Education of Young Children.

KAMII, C., AND R. DEVRIES (1978a). *Physical knowledge in preschool education.* Englewood Cliffs, NJ: Prentice-Hall.

———. (1978b). *Piaget, children, and number.* Washington, DC: National Association for the Education of Young Children.

KAMII, C., AND L. LEE-KATZ (1979). Physics in preschool education: A Piagetian approach. *Young Children, 34*(4), 4–9.

NORWOOD, G. R. (1984). Schools need of parent power in the 80's. *Dimensions, 12*(4), 4–5.

PRICE, G. G. (1989). Mathematics in early childhood. *Young Children, 44*(4), 53–58.

SHAW, J. M. (1981). IDEAS: Math for young children. *Dimensions, 10*(1), 15–16.

SMITH, R. F. (1988). Wheels and things: Developing preschool science learning centers. *Dimensions, 17*(1), 10–12.

SPODEK, B. (1985). *Teaching in the early years* (3rd ed.). Englewood Cliffs, NJ: Prentice-Hall.

WILLIAMS, C. K., AND C. KAMII (1986). How do children learn by handling objects? *Young Children, 42*(1), 23–26.

WOLFINGER, D. M. (1989). Mathematics in the pre-school-kindergarten. *Dimensions, 18*(1), 5–7.

SUGGESTED ACTIVITIES

1. Collect a set of buttons, beads, bottle caps, and other things that can be sorted, ordered, weighed, or otherwise manipulated.

2. Start a recipe collection for young children. Pay particular attention to the nutritional value of the foods, avoiding those that have empty calories.

3. Design, develop, and implement a no-heat cooking experience for a group of young children. At the end of the experience make a list of concepts in various content areas (social studies, mathematics, science, etc.) that evolved from the activity.

4. Interview a teacher of young children about the mathematics and science programs in his or her class. Pay particular attention to any suggestions about methods or materials.

14

Social-Personal Learning

The Social Studies and Beyond

After completing this chapter on social-personal learning, the students should be able to:

1. Define physical knowledge, social knowledge, logico-mathematical knowledge, school-appropriate behavior, prosocial behavior, and multi-cultural education.
2. Identify the difference between content, social skills, and socialization in a social studies program for young children.
3. Identify the attributes of a good social studies program for young children.
4. Describe the three elements in planning for a field trip.
5. Explain why mapping activities are appropriate for young children.
6. Discuss how representational activities allow children to refine what they know.

No single subject in early childhood education encompasses more of the child's day than do the social studies. Social studies is both a content area that can be studied separately and a set of skills, knowledge, and values that pervade all other activities in the early childhood classroom.

Over the history of early childhood education, educators have been concerned with three areas of social-personal learning: (1) helping children learn social skills or behaviors that are appropriate and desirable in their interactions with peers and adults; (2) helping to develop children's moral character; and (3) helping children construct concepts about social rules and roles as well as about political, economic, and social aspects of society (Bloch, 1986). The first of these, which include social skills and social cognition or understandings, helps a child learn how to work with others within the intimate environment of the school and the larger environment of the community. Children without adequate social skills have trouble interacting with peers and adults. Because of this they may not participate fully in the learning opportunities offered. The second area reflects the socialization of the child into the culture and the understanding and assimilation of moral values and behavior. The last area has been expanded to include aspects of all of the social sciences, including elements from the scholarly fields of history, geography, economics, political science, anthropology, sociology, philosophy, and psychology.

The social studies help children to understand the world and to understand themselves. They learn to make sense of the world as known through personal experience and action. Children also come to know about themselves and to develop a self-concept that is strong, confident, and supportive of trying new things.

The social studies can also be used as an organizer for the other areas of curriculum. The themes, activities, skills, knowledge, values, and materials that are part of any good social studies program can serve as the basis for all of the subjects that are presented in a classroom for young children.

This chapter presents the social studies as an integral part of the young child's day. It offers ideas relating to social studies content as well as to concerns about socialization.

DEVELOPING AND UNDERSTANDING THE SOCIAL WORLD

All of the goals of early childhood education have also been the goals for social studies education. Because of the concern of social studies for both the child's world and the child herself or himself, the goals for a social studies program should be closely related to the overall goals of early childhood education. That is not always the case, however.

There is a lack of agreement among educators on the definition and priorities of social studies education. R. D. Barr, T. L. Barth, and S. S. Shermis (cited in Price, 1982) suggest that three contending views of social studies exist: (1) citizenship transmission, (2) age-appropriate exposure to the methods used by the social sciences, and (3) an exposure to reflective inquiry that will help children to arrive at reasoned decisions. Most current early childhood social studies programs tend to emphasize the development of social skills and socially desirable behavior. This approach is a mixture of concern for citizenship transmission and reflective inquiry.

One of the best ways to come to understand what appropriate social studies programs are possible for young children is to look back at two experts, Patty Smith Hill and Lucy Sprague Mitchell. Each was a pioneer in early childhood education who many years ago developed innovative approaches to teaching social studies. Hill (1913) suggested that the child's social experience was the basis for knowledge and that themes reflected in child's play should be the basis for a social studies program. Children tended to play out what they knew best, and their experiences with family, peers, and community provided them with a wealth of information that could be replicated, refined, and understood.

Mitchell (1971), who wrote originally in 1934, believed that the "here and now" approach to social studies was the most appropriate for young children. Concrete, familiar, everyday experiences should provide the basis for social studies. Mitchell took children on field trips into the community to help them understand the neighborhood and their relationship to it. According to Bernard Spodek (1974), children who use the "here and now" approach act as laboratory scientists, abstracting information from what they know and applying it with new information to solve new problems. Although Mitchell initially provided children with concrete materials and activities, she felt that older children could function with more abstract, theoretical information.

Both Hill and Mitchell believed in using the real experiences of children to help them develop social studies concepts. While Hill focused on social activity and Mitchell on the social environment, both recognized the importance of beginning with what was real and accessible to children. Both Hill and Mitchell seem quite contemporary in their ideas about social studies education. Social studies programs with similar intellectual goals can be developed in early childhood classes and can serve to integrate the curriculum (Spodek, 1974).

Jean Piaget has posited that children develop three types of knowledge as they come to understand their world: physical knowledge, social knowledge, and logico-mathematical knowledge. Children act on their world and abstract information from it. *Physical knowledge* is knowledge of the physical attributes of things. Through field trips, observations, and interviews children experience firsthand how things smell, feel, look, and taste and, in general, what the world is about. Physical knowledge is directly derived from these experiences. The child's senses are important in gathering the bases for this knowledge.

Social knowledge is knowledge of social rules, conventions, symbols, and values. Social knowledge tells children what things are called. It helps children to understand appropriate and inappropriate social behavior. Social knowledge is arbitrary; it is validated by authority. Unlike physical knowledge, social knowledge cannot be discovered. It must be taught to children, either directly or indirectly.

Logico-mathematical knowledge is the intellectual processes that are used to organize and make sense of information that children are abstracting from activities. Classifying, ordering, quantifying, and putting things in space and time relationships are examples of logico-mathematical knowledge. These are internal processes that are developed through self-regulation.

All three forms of knowledge are present in the social studies and all three need to be acquired by young children. Physical knowledge of places and things can be discovered by children and social knowledge can be told to them. Logico-mathematical knowledge requires that children act on the information they receive to make sense of it.

A fourth element in social learning is that children need to represent what they know. In early childhood programs, children represent things through dramatic play, stories, paintings, block buildings, or other constructions. These activities help children refine their understanding of newly learned information.

When we substitute secondhand and thirdhand information for real experiences from the children's world, we deny them the opportunity to gain a variety of forms of knowledge. Children become "information receivers" rather than "information generators." We have limited their opportunities to know.

Cynthia Sunal (1989) suggests using a developmental framework to determine the appropriate social studies program for young children. The very youngest children should be engaged in social exploration to explore social relationships and facilitate their introduction into the social world. Somewhat older children should be provided with an experientially oriented program to allow them to develop process skills and build a body of knowledge consisting of facts, concepts and generalizations. Such a program would help children discover patterns in the social world. As children mature further, the social studies program would focus on concept attainment, in which children would use observations and inference to gain social studies concepts through induction. In fact, all three approaches should be contained in any developmentally appropriate program of social studies education during the early childhood years.

An appropriate approach to social studies should (1) reflect the child's real experiences, (2) show a concern for children's gaining physical knowledge, social knowledge, and logico-mathematical knowledge, and (3) value a child's efforts at representing what he or she knows. It should also be inquiry oriented. In an inquiry program children gather social data, organize that data, interpret it, and represent what they come to know (Spodek, Saracho, & Lee, 1984). An inquiry approach views the child as both the receiver and generator of knowledge. Such an approach can be related to social science content and to the development of socialization skills by young children.

A SOCIAL STUDIES PROGRAM FOR YOUNG CHILDREN: CONTENT

A good social studies program should reflect the following goals:

- Children should learn social studies concepts and knowledge.
- Children should have an opportunity to apply that knowledge to problems.

- Children should learn physical knowledge from the real world.
- Children should learn to understand the world and their relationship to it.
- Children should be able to learn social science concepts as long as they are presented in a developmentally appropriate manner and are arranged so that children can reflect and act on their learning.
- Children should have access to a wealth of materials.
- Children should have an opportunity to represent their knowledge in many and varied ways.
- Children should become socialized into both the school and community. This socialization requires that children understand their own roles and the roles of others, develop role-appropriate behavior, learn to interact with others, develop their own self-awareness, and become aware of the values of their community.
- Children should become aware of their own culture and the culture of others.

All children come to school with some knowledge of the social world. They know about their family and they know about their immediate surroundings. It's important to remember, however, that each child's understanding of the world is unique. No two children have had the same set of experiences and, unless there are siblings in a class, they have not grown up with the same set of family values.

Initially, the teacher's role is to provide children with opportunities to share ideas and to learn from each other. As children discuss their families, pets, homes, and neighborhoods, the teacher learns about their perceptions of the world. When children play together, they hear other views and begin to incorporate new vocabulary and ideas into their previous conception of the world. Dramatic play is a particularly rich vehicle in which children learn from others.

After teachers develop an understanding of what their children already know, they can begin to present new ideas to enhance the children's understanding of the social world. Social studies activities can be organized around significant social studies concepts acquired through personal experiences in acting on physical and social information.

Concepts

A concept helps children to establish a framework upon which to understand and process information. Huber Walsh (1980) refers to a concept as a word or short phrase that represents a key idea.

He suggests three points to consider in choosing concepts:

1. A high priority should be given to concepts like helping, sharing, rules, values, family, safety, and home, and these concepts should be repeated throughout the social studies program.
2. Concepts need to be carefully screened so that they are appropriate for children and not intellectually confusing.
3. In selecting concepts, preference should be given to those that can be learned through the use of concrete materials.

Young children's concepts include such things as *family, dog, car, store,* and *home.* Children who have learned the concept of car can construct a class of objects which have the attributes of a car, such as wheels, engine, and passenger compartment. Those who have not learned the concept may assign the label "car" to trucks, buses, vans, or campers, vehicles that have some but not all of the attributes of "cars." Concepts lead to efficient use of new information. A child who knows that *McDonald's* is a "restaurant" will have little problem putting other fast-food places in the same category. It is important that teachers be aware of which concepts are developmentally appropriate for young children and which might be beyond their ability to grasp.

There are two levels of meaning that children develop in understanding concepts. The first is the *classification* level, where a child decides which object or event fits into a given category. The second level is *association.* At the association level the child is developing a set of understandings about a given concept (Walsh, 1980). When a child categorizes a chair as a type of furniture, she or he operates on the classification level. When she or he explains that furniture is generally found in homes and makes living more comfortable, she or he is dealing with association.

Concepts are not learned in an all-or-none fashion. They are developed slowly through experiences with examples of the concept as well as with non-examples. Language is important in labeling concepts, but the word cannot stand for the class of objects initially. Concepts are built through experiences that provide children with information. The most vivid experiences are provided in real-life settings. Some experiences can also be provided in the classroom through contact with people and with objects or artifacts. The best experiences from which young children can build concepts are the most direct. When these first-hand experiences cannot be provided, then books, pictures, films, filmstrips, and videotapes can be used to provide information.

Children build concepts as they abstract information from these experiences and mentally operate upon them, categorizing, seriating, and quantifying them, and putting them into the context of space and time. In seeking relationships among these bits of information, children symbolize and act upon the information, representing it in stories and pictures as well as in play activities. Both the search for information and the mental activity through play and other representational activities are necessary for young children to make sense of these experiences and build meaningful social science concepts.

Field Trips

Field trips are one of the best ways for children to begin to acquire new social studies concepts. A field trip enables a child to learn firsthand what a neighborhood, a post office, a grocery store, a gas station, or a firehouse is like. Many children have never walked through their own neighborhood or visited a firehouse. Time constraints may not allow some families to take children on errands and, as a result, they do not have firsthand knowledge of their own immediate community. Even when they do have the experience, the child's perceptions may not have focused on critical elements. Teachers should approach each field trip as if it is a new and unique experience for each of the children.

Field trips do not have to be big productions, such as trips to the zoo,

Field trips can often be walks around the neighborhood.

circus, or other major attractions. Often important trips are simple, such as a walk through the neighborhood, or to a store to shop in preparation for a cooking activity. Even taking repeated trips to the same place can provide children with new learnings each time.

Many field trips fail because of a lack of preparation. Teachers must focus on three distinct elements as they prepare for a trip. First, they have to decide how to get the children ready for a trip. Talking about the destination, reading books, generating questions to be answered or hypotheses about what will be seen are all ways to set the stage. A pretrip visit to the site is a good way for the teacher to learn about any safety concerns or other problems that may take special arrangements.

Second, the teacher must decide what types of activities will be provided on the trip. It is impossible to take a group of young children anywhere without prior thought of what they will do while there. Giving children things to look for, questions to answer, discussing what has been seen, and taking pictures while on the trip will help children to focus their attention and keep them involved during the trip.

Finally, after the trip children need opportunities to discuss what they have seen and to work through new ideas in their play. For instance, simple still photographs can be used for stimulating discussions as well as for providing information. They should be large enough so that they can be seen by a group of children and be relatively free of clutter. Projected slides can work well, too. Pictures taken on the trip can provide a good way to review. This is the time when children begin to make sense of the new concepts. Do not expect all children to learn the same thing while on a field trip. Each will focus on the aspects of the experience that most interest them (Spodek, 1968).

As a follow-up to a field trip, an exhibit can be set up in the room. It could include pictures, props, and photographs from the trip presented in an aesthetically pleasing way. As children explore the exhibit, new concepts are further reinforced. Other follow-ups can be putting on a play, dictating a group story, or any activity that will allow children to recall and reflect on their experience. Figure 14-1 presents an example of plans for a field trip to the supermarket.

Resource Persons

In many early childhood programs resource persons are invited to the class to provide firsthand information similar to what can be gained in a field trip. Fathers, mothers, siblings, community members, and retirees are all good

FIGURE 14-1   A Field Trip to the Supermarket

I. Preparation
  A. Supermarket
    1. Contact the manager requesting permission to visit and set a date.
    2. a. Make a pretrip visit, noting special areas that you particularly want the children to see.
       b. Pay particular attention to any safety hazards and any barriers that may inhibit a handicapped child, if one is in your class.
    3. Discuss the trip with the store manager. Explain what the children are like, how many there will be in the group, and how long you will stay.
  B. Children
    1. Arrange for transportation, extra adults, and parental permission.
    2. Bring books, filmstrips, props, and other materials related to the grocery store into class. Set up a grocery display.
    3. Discuss with children what they think they will see on the field trip. This is a good time to generate questions that can be answered on the trip.
    4. The day before the trip and again on the day of the trip, remind children about appropriate behavior and the rules they must follow.

II. At the supermarket
  A. Use the questions generated in class as a way for children to learn about the store. Tell children particular things to look for.
  B. Make sure each child has an opportunity to see everything.
  C. Take photographs of the experience.
  D. Purchase some foods that can be used to make a soup or salad back at school
  E. Periodically check that children are not lost.

III. After the trip
  A. Prepare a snack with the ingredients purchased on the trip. Discuss the trip in the process.
  B. Review the questions that the children asked on the trip.
  C. Set-up a "supermarket" in the dramatic play area of the room.
  D. Display pictures taken on the supermarket trip. Children may want to discuss or write about their pictures. A class book can be made of the stories.
  E. Additional books, filmstrips, and recipes can be used as appropriate.
  F. Write a thank you note to the grocery store manager. Have all the children sign their names as best they can.

resources for social studies. Inviting a police officer to the classroom allows children to interact with a new figure and to understand better what police officers are like. Anyone who can tell a story, play an instrument, cook a special dish, do arts and crafts, perform a dance, or simply be with the children can provide new, real information.

Planning for having a resource person in class is similar to planning for a field trip. Thought must be given to preparation, the visit itself, and the follow-up. It is important to contact the visitor and to discuss your expectations prior to the visit. The visitor needs to know how many children will be present and what their ages are, how the visit fits into the program and how much time there will be for the visit. The children should have an opportunity to generate questions they want to ask and to review the rules for behavior before the visitor arrives.

During the visit it is important to allow each child to talk and ask questions. There should be a two-way interaction between children and guest. Opportunities for dramatic play as well as for writing language experience stories, painting, viewing pictures, and otherwise representing what has been learned should follow the visit. These can continue until the children begin to lose interest.

Artifacts

Many times artifacts can be interesting and informative. Items from other cultures or from another era, such as toys, clothes, shoes, eating and cooking utensils, and musical instruments, allow children to make comparisons with what they know from their own experiences and can begin to understand that different people see the world in different ways.

Children need to try on, feel, and smell objects in order to learn about them. The artifacts provided should be those that can be handled. Fragile, priceless, or dangerous artifacts have no place in a classroom.

One good way to present artifacts is to show and discuss them in a large group. They can then be placed on a display table for children to handle and explore on their own. Ideally, the artifacts should be on display long enough for all children to explore. They can also be used as parts of learning centers. Old clothes or jewelry can be placed in the housekeeping corner. Beaters, bowls, spoons, cups, and other utensils can be used in cooking. Musical instruments can be played. The use of artifacts is limited only by the teacher's willingness to incorporate them into the classroom experiences.

Audiovisual Materials

A number of audiovisual materials can be used to provide children with information about their world. Picture sets can be obtained from many libraries and are available for purchase. Picture sets on families, pets, transportation, holidays, careers, and many other subjects that are developmentally appropriate provide children with the opportunity to increase their knowledge through careful observation and discussion. They can be particularly useful as discussion starters before or after field trips.

Sound filmstrips and films are also available on a wide range of social studies topics. The sound and action in a film are particularly attractive to children, but a sound filmstrip has the advantage of allowing frame-by-frame discussions. Many local libraries have catalogs of available films and filmstrips that can be obtained either free or for a small fee.

Portable videocassette recorders can be used to record day-to-day classroom experiences as well as field trips and presentations by resource people. Young children (or adults) love to see themselves and their friends on television. Videotape can also convey to children the excitement and involvement of classroom experiences.

A particularly useful machine is the audiocassette recorder. Many of them can be operated by children and can be used to record stories, neighborhood sounds, rhymes, and anything else that intrigues children.

While media can provide children with a wealth of information, teachers must choose wisely and use only those things that are appropriate for children. Of particular concern is selecting appropriate television programs for children. Teachers should select programs according to the developmental appropriateness of the material for young children and to its relation to the instructional program. Television should not be used to fill time that could be used for other kinds of learning.

Acting on Acquired Knowledge

The first step in a social studies program is providing children with information to generate new knowledge. The second is allowing them to act on the knowledge, play with it, refine it, and come to understand it fully.

Children apply their newly acquired information through the use of sand, water, blocks, the housekeeping area, dramatic play materials, art, and dance. For example, after a trip to the firehouse the teacher can add fire hats and trucks, a length of hose, and some small ladders to the block area. These additional props will motivate the children to "play firehouse" and to build structures and play out themes that are representative of what they have learned.

While the class is studying about cars, traffic signs can be placed on the outdoor wheel toy path so children can stop, go, and practice their knowledge of cars in other ways. They may also build superhighways in the block area or act out the mechanic repairing a car in a service station. In these ways they will refine their understanding of cars and rules relating to cars.

A grocery store can be set up with workers and shoppers so the children can experiment with different roles. Stocking shelves, checking groceries, making decisions on food, purchasing groceries, and ultimately bringing the parcels home to the housekeeping area are all valuable learning experiences that enable children to represent their knowledge about grocery stores. Additionally, while children play grocery they are refining their logico-mathematical knowledge by sorting, classifying, organizing, and comparing the items in the store.

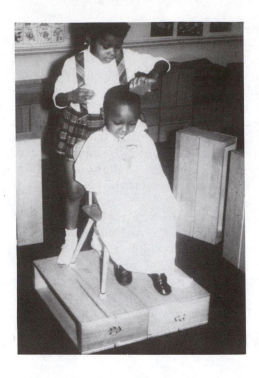

A field trip to a barber shop is followed up by the children's playing barber in the classroom.

Tempera paint, fingerpaint, clay, collage, junk sculpture, chalk, and crayons are media that children can use to represent knowledge. Often a child will draw many different pictures of a trip, each one a further refinement of a new concept. As the drawings are completed and discussed, the teacher gains insight into the child's thinking and understanding.

Children play through the new information they receive in the dress-up area also. Items from the real world support children's play as a way to advance their understanding. For example, after a visit to the post office a prop box containing stamps, envelopes, junk mail, a scale, mailbag, shirts, rubber stamps, and other postal artifacts could be set up in the classroom. A limited number of children can use the props to play post office and refine what they've learned.

Materials are a critical part of the social studies program. They provide both new information and an opportunity to refine knowledge that was previously acquired. Materials are an extension of the teacher in that they become significant in the framework of goal-oriented activities. Their worth is in how well they advance a child's understanding of a concept (Spodek, 1968).

Mapping

Many young children have experiences with maps before they learn anything about map keys, distance, or direction. Children may lay out streets with blocks, pretend to read a road map in dramatic play, or talk about the shortest way to get to a friend's house. These represent a good introduction to mapping.

Young children can do maps (or floor plans) of their classroom, of their school center, of their bedroom at home, or of the playground. At first these maps may be no more than lines drawn on a page; later they will become representations that attempt to show objects in relation to one another. Children may have all the furniture strung out on the bottom edge, or they may show a table with legs sticking out in all four directions. These are all good beginnings.

A good way to begin mapping is to place an outline of the classroom on the floor and let children place blocks or boxes on the outline to indicate the position of desks, tables, or activity centers. The same process can be used to present the playground or a child's bedroom. Using familiar places helps the child refer to reality as the representation is developed.

Later activities can be based on maps of the neighborhood, a local store, or the route from school to home. Children can walk around these areas before representing them. The process allows the child to move from real objects in space to three-dimensional representations to two-dimensional representations.

The best mapping experiences are those that children choose to do. Once they have the basic idea that a map indicates how to get somewhere, they can work on their own maps. The important element that children will learn is that the maps are representations of places in the children's world and that these representations show distance, direction, and the relation of elements to one another.

The inquiry approach to social studies enables children to generate information, act on it, and represent the information in a reasonable way. Children are both consumers and producers of knowledge.

A SOCIAL STUDIES PROGRAM FOR YOUNG CHILDREN: SOCIALIZATION

The second part of a social studies program for young children relates to socialization. Socialization refers to children becoming functioning members of a community, such as the school or the classroom. Children must obey rules, following directions and accepting the fact that sharing, taking turns, and assertive, but not aggressive, behavior is suitable. They also learn that they fit into a role which is related to other roles in the community. In social studies, socialization also refers to children learning the rules, values, history, and expectations of the community at large.

In socializing it is necessary for children to develop a sense of school and community expectations. They must also develop a sense of what they are like. Their self-image, social behavior, value system, and cultural view are all variables that affect the way they respond to socialization efforts.

This section will focus on socialization and ways to socialize children to school and community expectations.

Learning School and Community Roles

As children study topics such as the neighborhood, the grocery store, or community helpers, they begin to understand how society is organized and how each person contributes to the well-being of a community. While knowledge of society is important, perhaps more important is the fact that children learn to value the way society works. Such a value is based not on a sophisticated understanding, but rather on the child's modeling of values that are important to adults.

Children also become socialized to the larger community through listening to stories about historic figures, participating in holiday celebrations, singing traditional songs, learning traditional dances, and interacting with special guests. As children hear about and participate in the traditions of society, they learn to enjoy them and to value them, accepting the traditions of the community as their own.

Holidays are particularly important to children. Celebrations are fun and help to transmit traditions. They are also social events that help form a special bond between child, family, and community. Teachers must plan holiday celebrations that reflect the cultural backgrounds and experiences of the children. Hanukkah, Christmas, and similar holidays can be celebrated during the winter holiday season. Children should understand the significance of the holiday symbols and learn the games, stories, and foods related to the celebrations.

New Year's Day is widely celebrated throughout the world, but not always on January 1. A New Year's unit should help children to learn about the different ways and times of the year that the day is celebrated. For example, the Jewish New Year, Rosh Hashanah, is a two-day fall celebration (in September or October), whereas the Chinese New Year s celebrated on the full moon sometime between January 21 and February 19. UNICEF's *Festival Book*, published by the U.S. Committee for UNICEF, is a useful resource.

It is seldom easy to socialize children to the rules, expectations, values and appropriate behaviors that ensure smooth functioning in the classroom environment so they can become successful learners. Children differ in their developmental readiness and their willingness to work for the good of others. Teachers must begin with the needs of the individual child before proceeding to the needs of the group. Further discussion of ways to help children learn to function appropriately in school, develop positive social skills, and show increased prosocial behavior is presented in Chapter 7.

Developing School-Appropriate Behavior

When children first enter school at any level, teachers must help them understand what behaviors are appropriate for school. Many have learned the proper way to behave at home and believe this is the way they should behave at school. However, while fighting may be acceptable at home, it is out of place in a classroom. In this instance, children must learn how to influence other children in a nonaggressive manner that avoids the use of force.

Children need opportunities to develop social competence in school.

There are a number of school-appropriate behaviors that children must learn. Independence, assertiveness, sensitivity to others, and the willingness to participate in social problem solving are traits that help a child have successful social experiences (Walsh, 1980). Children who are prosocial, who show a degree of sociableness, and who are socially competent are more likely to have positive social experiences (Price, 1982). *Prosocial* behavior refers to helping others without anticipation of a personal reward. *Sociableness* is willingness to be part of a group and interacting with others rather than being an isolate and working and playing alone. A *socially competent* child is one whose behavior and thought processes result in effective interpersonal relationships. Asa Hilliard III (1978) has generated a list of nine social competencies he considers to be appropriate for young children (see Table 14–1). The competencies are based on the child's internal processes rather than on external norms.

Skills that lead to social competence can be taught either directly or indirectly (Price, 1982). In direct teaching the teacher tells or shows children how to behave. A teacher might explain the importance of taking turns or sharing, then demonstrate sharing or organize a method of taking turns. Three indirect ways of teaching can be successfully used to teach social skills: modeling, shaping, and planning (Ladd, 1984). In *modeling*, teachers demonstrate pro-social behaviors as they interact with children. Teachers *shape* behavior by helping children achieve a series of successive approximations toward proper behavior. They need to reward acceptable behavior so these behaviors will be shown more frequently. In *planning,* teachers structure both the interpersonal and physical environments to enhance children's social interaction and allow them to develop relationships

TABLE 14-1 Social Competencies For Young Children

1. One of the domains for assessment of social competence should be the child's attitude. A healthy learning pattern that produces healthy development is dependent upon a set of attitudes in the child which lead that child toward less fear of the environment and interest in and willingness to take risks with the personal and physical environment.

2. Every child, at every stage of life, has a world view that is the product of his or her own unique interaction with the world. That world view has an integrity and can be understood only as a reflection of that child's special environment. The socially competent child's view of the world has a contextual integrity.

3. Social competence would be reflected by the child's increasing acquisition of social skills and school skills. Social competencies have been assessed primarily in relation to "school skills." These are an important element of social competence but only a fraction of the total. The child's relationship to adults and other children, and the ability to negotiate successfully in those relationships, is another aspect of social competence.

4. In order for a child to be successful socially, it is necessary to have an appropriate amount of socially and contextually relevant information. That information is specific to the environment within which the child is growing and learning.

5. The socially competent child is an active learner, displaying a curiosity to use and transform experiences.

6. The socially competent child accurately perceives his or her environment. Distortion and perception of the environment will be reflected in inappropriate responses to that environment.

7. The socially competent child experiences a sense of continuity in growth.

8. The socially competent child has a growing sense of personal and group identity.

9. The child beomes more socially competent when the range of objects and experiences encountered expands at a rapid rate.

A. G. Hilliard, "How Should We Assess Children's Social Competence?" *Young Children, 33*(5), 1978, 12–13.

with others. Most teachers use all four approaches—direct teaching, modeling, shaping, and planning—as they assist children in developing social competence.

Building Self-Awareness

To some extent, socialization is a function of getting individual children to conform to the expectation of the group. However, children first need to be ready to work with others, and part of that readiness is having a positive self-image. Children need to be aware of themselves and feel good about who they are, what they are, and how they interact with others. Many children come to school feeling inadequate. Supportive teachers can help them feel more adequate by reflecting positively to the child and increasing each child's competency.

Teachers should be positive and caring. They can compliment children on new and attractive clothes. They can welcome children when they return after a sickness or after a trip. They can praise children for completing a block structure. They can hug children or simply sit and talk with them, affirming each child's worth as an individual. Teachers can also provide opportunities to explore new materials and to participate in problem-solving situations. The completion of a task leads to feelings of accomplishment and self-worth.

These opportunities for children to learn more about themselves are critical. It is helpful to provide mirrors for children to see themselves in and oppor-tunities to discuss what they see, or to outline the child's body on butcher paper and color it in, or to place photographs of children in the classroom; however, these activities provide limited meaning. It is more important for teachers to provide activities that offer feedback to children relating to their worth and that increases a child's understanding of self as viewed by others.

While the concern for children's self-awareness should be reflected in the entire curriculum, sometimes it is helpful to use a special program to help children focus on their own personal and social development. Such programs as *My Friends and Me* (Davis, 1988) or *DUSO-Revised: Developing an Understanding of Self and Others* (Dinkmeyer and Dinkmeyer, 1982) can help teachers work on their children's personal and social development. These kits contain materials such as pictures, storybooks, dolls, and puppets, as well as teacher's manuals to help guide the program. While providing activities for children, such programs also provide teachers with a form of in-service training that can make them more sensitive to the needs of their children and more capable of flexibly dealing with children's self-awareness in other parts of the program.

As children interact successfully with others and with the physical world, their self-image will improve. Teachers must carefully structure initial attempts at group activities. All children should come away from such activities feeling successful and having positive feelings about school. A child who is bullied, belit-tled, or ignored in a social situation will most likely develop a negative self-image.

Young Children and Values

Values are inherent in everything we say or do. When we make a decision to attend a concert rather than go to a move, we are valuing the concert over the movie at that time. Teachers demonstrate their values in the classroom decisions they make and in the way they govern their lives. Either intentionally or not, teachers transmit their values to children. While teachers have a right to their personal values, they need to be aware of the impact these values might have on children and how they relate to family and community values.

Huber Walsh (1980) defines a value as a principle or standard that is made a part of a person's code for living. Transmitting values is a critical part of the socialization process. It helps a person learn how to act in any given situation. According to Bernard Spodek, Olivia N. Saracho, and Richard C. Lee (1984), val-ues that are basic to early childhood education include the worth of the individ-ual, concepts of freedom and responsibility, the importance of democratic deci-sion making, and concern for the safety of persons and property. While young children would not be expected to understand each of these values or their sources, they would be expected to make them a part of their "code of living."

Teachers can help children to develop values by modeling appropriate values, by using role playing and creative dramatics to clarify and transmit values, by using stories that present value dilemmas, or by reading unfinished stories that require children to provide an ending to a difficult situation. Carolyn Pope Edwards, Mary Ellen Logue, and Anna Sargent Russell (1983) suggest providing three kinds of learning encounters to expose children to social ideas. First, a dramatic skit can be presented to a group of children and the teacher can then allow children to offer opinions on ways to resolve the situations. Through the discussions, children begin to realize there is more than one way to solve a problem. The second type of learning encounter is the "thinking game," in which individuals or small groups of children have a private conversation with the teacher. The thinking game is an open-ended interview about the same problem that was used in the dramatic skit. A third encounter consists of spontaneous discussions as a way to understand further what the child is thinking and why.

Edwards, Logue, and Russell (1983) offer five rules for teachers who are interviewing children:

1. Do not assume too soon that you understand what the child is saying.
2. Never ask rhetorical or leading questions.
3. Do not reinforce children's answers with evaluative terms like "good" or "that's right."
4. Do not race ahead of yourself in your pacing of the discussion.
5. Phrase questions simply. Avoid hypothetical questions with younger children. (pp.17–18)

These five rules can help teachers to talk with children about value-laden situations without influencing their answers.

Levels of Moral Thought

Every teacher who has taught young children has run into problems such as lying and stealing. There is no situation that is more difficult to handle than a child's being accused of taking someone else's toy. While the teacher has to see that the rightful owner receives his or her toy back, the action of "stealing" also requires a response.

Young children do not act out of a sense of what is morally right. Rather, they tend to make judgments on a much more pragmatic basis. Lawrence Kohlberg, building on the work of Piaget, has developed an approach to the study of moral thought and action that can help to explain how children base their moral decisions (Turiel, 1973). Kohlberg views moral development as moving through a universal sequence of stages which represent ways of thinking and interacting with the environment. There are six stages to Kohlberg's theory of moral development (see Figure 14-2). Each stage represents a way of making moral judgments that is the result of an individual's actions in the social world.

When children arrive at preschool, most are at stage 1 or 2. For stage 1 children, those with a punishment and obedience orientation, the physical consequence of an action determines whether it is good or bad. A child in this stage does the right thing because of a fear of punishment. In stage 2, the instrumental-relativist orientation, right action consists of behavior that satisfies one's own needs and occasionally those of the other child. A stage 2 child will do the right thing to earn an ice cream cone or a ride on a pony.

FIGURE 14–2   Definitions of Stages of Moral Development

Stage 1: *The punishment and obedience orientation.* The physical consequences of action determine its goodness or badness. Avoidance of punishment and unquestioning deference to power are valued in their own right.

Stage 2: *The instrumental-relativist orientation.* Right action consists of that which instrumentally satisfies one's own needs and occasionally the needs of others.

Stage 3: *The interpersonal concordance or "good boy—nice girl" orientation.* Good behavior is that which pleases or helps others and is approved by them. Behavior is frequently judged by intention—"he means well" becomes important for the first time. One earns approval by being "nice."

Stage 4: *Authority and social order maintaining orientation.* There is orientation toward authority, fixed rules, and the maintenance of the social order. Right behavior consists of doing one's duty, showing respect for authority, and maintaining the given social order for its own sake.

Stage 5: *The social-contract legalistic orientation.* Right action tends to be defined in terms of general individual rights and standards (laws), which have been critically examined and agreed upon by society.

Stage 6: *The universal ethical principle orientation.* Right is defined by a decision of conscience in accord with self-chosen *ethical principles.* These principles are abstract and ethical; they are not concrete moral rules like the Ten Commandments.

E. Turiel, "Stage Transitions in Moral Development." In R. M. W. Travers (Ed.), *Second Handbook of Research on Teaching* (Chicago: Rand McNally, 1973), pp. 732–758.

Kohlberg has demonstrated that children's thinking about right and wrong and their ways of making moral decisions form organized patterns that vary as the child develops. His studies indicate that children generate their values and conceptions out of efforts to understand the world around them and to organize their social experiences.

Young children can come to grips with moral dilemmas that are much the same as those that adults experience. However, children view these dilemmas and cope with them differently. They are not able to understand adult morality, nor can they understand reasoning more than two stages above their own.

Children need the opportunity to explore moral dilemmas, to hear ethical reasoning different from their own, and to decide on the relative worth of various solutions. The use of unfinished stories, filmstrips, small debates, and discussion groups can give children an opportunity to grow when topics are both relevant and developmentally appropriate. With most groups of young children, however, the teacher does not need to look far to find situations that present moral dilemmas. Not sharing toys, breaking rules, lying, taking the property of others, and telling on others are everyday occurrences. The sensitive teacher can use these situations as opportunities for learning.

If lying becomes a problem, a group discussion can be used to talk about why people tell the truth and why they lie, who is hurt by lies, and who is helped. Children can learn from each other's reasoning in these discussions. The teachers should be careful to see that no child becomes the focus of a dilemma discussion. The purpose is not to punish someone, but to help children learn through reasoning.

Susan Stengel (1982) suggests that there are a number of ways for teachers to facilitate moral development. The first is to create a moral atmosphere in the classroom so children can see examples of fair treatment with everyone getting a chance and everyone sharing materials. The second is to have a limited number of meaningful rules that are enforced. Reasoning with children to help them understand the importance of the rules should be part of the enforcement process and is the third suggestion.

These suggestions are consistent with those offered by Stefan Aufenanger (1987) for creating a just community in the kindergarten. Teachers can help young children develop a sense of justice through the rules they use in the games played. As teachers offer rules, their purposes and implementation should be explained to children. The teacher should then be careful to follow through in a consistent manner. Teachers need to provide real and valid explanations of these rules to children in ways they can understand. Children can also be encouraged to developing their own rules.

Teachers who understand that values and moral reasoning are part of the developmental process are in a position to plan for the inclusion of values clarification activities as a part of the social studies curriculum.

Developing Cultural Awareness: Multicultural Education

Patricia Ramsey (1987) identified the purposes of multicultural education as follows:

1. To help children develop positive gender, racial, cultural, class, and individual identities and to recognize and accept their membership in many different groups.
2. To enable children to see themselves as part of the larger society; to identify, empathize, and relate with individuals from other groups.
3. To foster respect and appreciation for the diverse ways in which other people live.
4. To encourage in young children's earliest social relationships an openness and interest in others, a willingness to include others, and a desire to cooperate.
5. To promote the development of a realistic awareness of contemporary society, a sense of social responsibility, and an active concern that extends beyond one's immediate family or group.
6. To empower children to become autonomous and critical analysts and activists in their social environment.
7. To support the development of educational and social skills needed for children to become full participants in the larger society in ways that are most appropriate to individual styles, cultural orientations, and linguistic backgrounds.
8. To promote effective and reciprocal relations between schools and families. (pp. 3-5)

Multicultural education is not something that is only added to the program during the celebration of winter and spring holidays. Rather, it should represent a point of view that permeates all of the program and is reflected in the books that are read to children, the songs that are sung, and the art projects that are prepared for the class. It is a way of introducing children to diverse cultures in the community, the nation and the world.

For many children the move to school represents a major break from the home. The values, culture, language patterns, and forms of social interactions may all be different. Children who are forced to use a new language and style of behaving may have difficulty accommodating to the school. The school may reject the child's language and culture, leaving the child feeling strange and bewildered. When a child does succeed in accommodating to the school values, there is a price that is paid in feelings of self-worth and the valuing of traditions (Saracho & Spodek, 1983).

Most communities (and most classrooms) include people from a wide range of cultural, social, ethnic and religious backgrounds. It is easy for teachers to lose sight of the rich heritage children bring to school. Cultural awareness can help a classroom reflect the values and heritage of everyone in the class. Differences among people can be accepted and valued rather than ignored.

Teaching that everyone is the same is denying children the right to be proud of who they are. It is difficult to build a positive image of one's culture if that is denied or demeaned. Teachers who prize the differences in children are those who reinforce a feeling of self-worth.

Cultural awareness should be concerned with more than cultural differences. Patricia G. Ramsey (1982) points out that there are three common misconceptions about multicultural education: (1) such programs should focus only on information about other countries and cultures and not on our own, (2) that it

Children learn about another culture as the librarian tells a story using a Japanese *Kamishibaye*, or picture story box.

is relevant only in classrooms that contain students who are members of the racial or cultural group to be studied rather than for all classrooms, and (3) that there should be a unified set of goals and a standard curriculum for multicultural education. In order to design effective multicultural programs, teachers must first understand the backgrounds of the children in the classroom. The foundation should be the children and not a preconceived notion of content. Further, multicultural education should not be a set of activities added to the program but should be a value that is pervasive in all parts of the curriculum.

From a social studies perspective, cultural awareness requires teachers to present an accurate, honest presentation of events, groups, or people (Walsh, 1980). It also demands that teachers be open to differences, reject stereotypes, and be aware of any personal prejudices.

In developing cultural awareness in children, teachers need to provide children with an understanding not only of their own culture, but also of cultures other than their own. Teachers also need to work toward eliminating bias in the way that social knowledge is presented to young children. One way of doing this is to select materials that are bias free. Resources such as the *Guidelines for Bias-free Textbooks and Storybooks,* issued by the Council on Interracial Books for Children (1980), can help in the selection of materials.

Louise Derman-Sparks (1989) takes the process a step further by suggesting that teachers of young children create an anti-bias curriculum in their classroom. Such an approach is more proactive than one that provides multicultural awareness. Such a curriculum would pervade the classroom so that books, dolls, art materials, and all other resources would be selected to reflect children and adults of different cultures, genders, ages and races in nonstereotypic situations. Such a curriculum would involve the parents as well as the children in the program.

Many cultures have contributed to the American heritage. We should praise and celebrate the contributions of each and build upon the varied backgrounds children bring to the school. The multicultural life of children should enrich rather than diminish the curriculum. Cultural awareness is a prerequisite for a truly humanistic approach to the needs of the children, parents, and community. Social studies should reflect who children are rather than to try to make them into someone else.

SUMMARY

A good early childhood social studies program is both a separate subject area and a subject that is intertwined with all other areas of the curriculum. It focuses both on content and socialization. It can provide a framework for instruction in math, science, and language arts and it can provide children with the social skills necessary to be successful in school and in the community. It can serve as the center of the educational program.

Each new day brings many opportunities for providing children with real experiences within the classroom. Taking care of animals, cooking, planting gardens, experimenting with water and sand, playing musical instruments, working with others or alone, and just being a member of a group enable children to acquire a wealth of new information.

These experiences are just the first step. Children must have opportunities to represent what they have learned, to apply their developing understandings, and to refine their understanding. Caring for classroom animals, for example, can generate a wide range of information for children. Children can (1) discuss their experience with the teacher, (2) write about their experience, (3) listen to stories about similar or other animals, (4) tell their parents about what they have learned, (5) collect data on the animal's growth and graph it, or (6) begin to study other living things. The activities help children to make the best possible use of the real experiences.

REFERENCES

AUFENANGER, S. (1987). Who will be first? Creating a just community in the kindergarten. Paper pressented at the annual meeting of the American Education Research Association. Washington, DC.

BLOCH, M. N. (1986). Social education of young children. In C. Cornbleth (Ed.), *An invitation to research in social education.* Washington, DC: National Council for the Social Studies.

COUNCIL ON INTERRACIAL BOOKS FOR CHILDREN (1980). *Guidelines for selecting bias-free textbooks and storybooks.* New York: The Council.

DAVIS, D. E. (1988). *My friends and me.* Circle Pines, MN: American Guidance Service.

DERMAN-SPARKS, L. (1989). *Anti-bias curriculum: Tools to empowering young children.* Washington, DC: National Association for the Education of Young Children.

DINKMEYER, D., SR., AND D. DINKMEYER, JR. (1982). *DUSO-Revised: Developing an understanding of self and others.* Circle Pines, MN: American Guidance Service.

EDWARDS, C. P., M. E. LOGUE, AND A. S. RUSSELL (1983). Talking with young children about social ideas. *Young Children, 39*(1), 12-20.

HILL, P. S. (1913). Second report. In Committee of Nineteen, *The Kindergarten.* Boston: Houghton Mifflin.

HILLIARD, A. G. (1978). How should we assess children's social competence? *Young Children, 33*(5), 12-13.

LADD, G. W. (1984). Promoting children's prosocial behavior and peer relations in early childhood classrooms: A look at four teacher roles. *Dimensions, 12*(4), 6-10.

MITCHELL, L. S. (1971). *Young geographers.* New York: Agathon Press (originally issued in 1934).

PRICE, G. G. (1982). Cognitive learning in early childhood education: Mathematics, science and social studies. In B. Spodek (Ed.), *Handbook of research in early childhood education,* pp. 264-294. New York: Free Press.

RAMSEY, P. G. (1982). Multicultural education in early childhood. *Young Children, 37*(2), 13-23.

RAMSEY, P. G. (1987). *Teaching and learning in a diverse world: Multicultural education for young children.* New York: Teachers College Press.

SARACHO, O. N., AND B. SPODEK (1983). *Understanding the multicultural experience in early childhood education.* Washington, DC: National Association for the Education of Young Children.

SPODEK, B. (1968). *The role of materials in teaching social studies to young children.* Paper presented at a conference for teachers on the child and the real world. University of British Columbia, Vancouver, B. C., October 4-5, 1968.

————. (1974). Social studies for young children: Identifying intellectual goals. *Social Education, 38*(1), 40-45.

————. (1985). *Teaching in the early years* (3rd ed.). Englewood Cliffs, NJ: Prentice-Hall.

SPODEK, B., O. N. SARACHO, AND R. C. LEE (1984). *Mainstreaming young children.* Belmont, CA: Wadsworth.

STENGEL, S. R. (1982). Moral education for young children. *Young Children, 37*(6), 23-31.

SUNAL, C. S. (1989). *Early childhood studies.* Columbus, OH: Merrill.

TURIEL, E. (1973). Stage transitions in moral development. In R. M. W. Travers (Ed.), *Second handbook of research on teaching,* pp. 732-758. Chicago: Rand McNally.

WALSH, H. M. (1980). *Introducing the young child to the social world.* New York: Macmillan.

SUGGESTED ACTIVITIES

1. Develop a teaching unit with a holiday theme lasting at least four or five days and containing at least one cooking activity.

2. Plan and implement a mapping activity for a small group of young children. Be sure to focus the activity on an area the children know.

3. Plan a post office field trip for a group of fifteen four-year-old children. Describe what you would do at each of the three stages of taking a field trip.

4. Visit your local resource center and review/preview audiovisual materials that are designed to advance moral development. Start a file of those that are appropriate for young children.

5. Begin a file of books, songs, poetry, and the like that have multicultural themes. Be sure to include materials that reflect the geographic area where you hope to teach.

15

Toward Professionalism

OBJECTIVES

After completing this chapter on professionalism, the student should be able to:

1. Describe ways that teachers can pursue their professional development.
2. Identify and describe several types of in-service programs.
3. List the important professional associations in early childhood education.
4. Compare the different professional organizations and journals in early childhood education.
5. Identify several resources that provide information on various topics in early childhood education.

The previous chapters have focused on providing the foundation knowledge for becoming an early childhood teacher. It included knowledge of the history of the field, its institutions, the range of practitioners that work in the field, and the child itself. This knowledge must be integrated with conceptions of curriculum, methods of organizing the physical and social resources, and methods of teaching. Ways of evaluating the program and working with parents are also important.

This text has presented foundational knowledge, just the beginning of what anyone should know to be a good teacher of young children. Just as in building a home, a foundation is important but it is not sufficient in itself. There is more that must be built upon that foundation. Preparing to teach at any level is a long-term process that should extend over a person's entire career. Continued professional development is critical for early childhood teachers.

Even though early childhood teachers have a major impact on young children's lives, they do not enjoy high status as professionals (Spodek & Saracho, 1988). There is considerable concern today that teaching standards need to be raised. If perceptions of teachers are to change, teachers themselves need to assume responsibility for becoming better prepared (Saracho, 1984; Saracho & Spodek, 1983). Teacher preparation that includes both personal development and professional development can be meaningful and practical.

TEACHERS' PERSONAL DEVELOPMENT

What teachers do and what they think about what they do are affected by their own values, attitudes, and perspectives. Teachers with low self-concepts might feel threatened and attempt to control children to show their superiority. Teachers with positive self-concepts are able to share their concerns for their classroom children and transcend their personal needs.

According to Arthur Combs (1965), effective teachers have positive attitudes toward themselves and others. Similarly, research shows that teachers who have positive attitudes toward themselves foster a positive classroom environment; in contrast, teachers who have negative attitudes toward themselves foster negative feelings among their classroom students (Hart, Allen, Buell, Harris, & Wolf, 1964). Teachers with favorable attitudes toward themselves are better able to develop a supportive learning atmosphere. Teachers who feel inferior may put others down to make themselves look better. A child who constantly seeks a teacher's approval usually satisfies the teacher's nurturant instincts, but those actions may prevent the child from becoming independent.

Self-knowledge is important. It helps teachers sense when their own needs and concerns affect their judgment. Teachers need to be able to control their reactions toward their children in relation to their own personal needs and their own emotional structure. Self-understanding can guide teachers in reacting positively to their children and lead to understanding of others.

TEACHERS' PROFESSIONAL DEVELOPMENT

Teachers need a considerable amount of practical knowledge to function well in a classroom. This is usually gained through some form of systematic preparation. All teachers possess strengths and weaknesses. Strengths can be built upon, and weaknesses can be overcome through professional development.

Often beginning teachers discover that there is much they still need to learn. They often express the need to learn more about discipline, curriculum ideas, learning centers, early literacy training, language development, and dealing with transitions.

> Ms. Rocha discovered that one of her classroom children was mentally retarded. While Ms. Rocha had learned something about special education, she did not know enough to work on a day-to-day basis with a mentally retarded child. She felt the need to gain new knowledge. She visited with the resource room teacher in the local elementary school who served as a consultant to her.

The professional development of the entire staff (including teachers, aides, cooks, and others) can improve the children's educational program. Schools should invest a portion of their resources in some form of staff development. Some schools organize their own in-service training program; others rely on professional organizations that provide conferences and publications. Some

Teachers need to seek out many sources of information to extend their knowledge and skills.

schools require their teachers to enroll in college or community courses; others leave teachers to their own resources. Whether schools provide the means for staff development or not, teachers ultimately must become responsible for their own professional improvement. Teachers can engage in in-service training, continue their formal education, participate in professional organizations, or independently use the range of educational resources available.

In-Service Programs

In-service programs may include workshops to deal with resource materials, viewing films or videotapes, attending lectures, classes, or study groups, or observing other teachers.

In-service meetings should be based on what teachers feel they need to know. Teachers can assess their strengths and needs, then develop their own in-service remedial activities. Specialists might be called in to identify the resources that could be used to meet those needs.

> Mr. Slater was uncomfortable with transitions in his class. After reading about strategies for transitions in an early childhood textbook, he decided it would be helpful to observe good transitions being implemented. He arranged to observe a teacher who was good at transitions. He also had the school director observe his performance during transitions. They then jointly worked out new strategies to be used in transitions.

Each school differs in its educational needs. It is essential to match particular in-service programs to the staff's needs and interests. Early childhood staff members who have the maturity to discuss problems openly and to provide helpful feedback to each other are developing competence and creating a more productive school. Continual feedback and evaluation of the in-service training can provide insightful information to administrators so that future in-service training will meet the teachers' needs and make their attendance worthwhile.

Teacher-Directed In-Service.   Some early childhood schools do not provide in-service teacher training. In such situations, a meaningful and systematic in-service program can still be developed by teachers themselves using a team approach. If teachers and aides have a good relationship, they can share ideas and coordinate activities. An in-service program that is jointly planned and implemented has the capacity to develop *esprit de corps* in a center as well as help the teachers grow. The major goal of such meetings is to create an environment where staff members can share and learn together and allow teachers to assume responsibility for their own professional development.

> Ms. Klein was concerned that her arts-and-crafts projects were quite limited. She felt that she was using the same material in the same way over and over again. After talking with her colleagues in the school, she realized that her concerns were shared by others. Ms. Klein invited teachers from two neighboring centers for a series of Saturday morning sessions in which each teacher would share favorite activities. The group also began searching through activities books in the local library for other projects to share.

It is best to excuse from the program individuals who have strong reservations. If there is a core of teachers who have an interest in their own professional development as well as that of their fellow teachers, other teachers will join the in-service activities when they are ready. Those who benefit from these sessions will spread the word to other teachers, who will become interested and join in.

Teacher-directed in-service education is based on the belief that a group can provide support for individual efforts in exploring new ideas and testing a variety of teaching strategies. Teachers who isolate themselves professionally do not benefit from the sharing of ideas, the encouragement, and the support that a group offers. Teachers can share and learn from each other if they are motivated to exchange ideas.

Teacher Study Group.   Individuals who participate in a teacher study group should work on one small manageable set of problems (such as transitions, flexibility, or short-term planning) at a time. Once the group is established, the participants identify an area of study, assess themselves in the area, develop specific learning plans to improve themselves, and establish a system for acquiring feedback.

Mr. Oliver and his colleagues in the child care center were beginning to feel that the knowledge of child development they had gained in their preservice training was not enough to help them understand the characteristics and behavior of the children in their classes. They arranged to have a local community college loan them a series of videotapes on child growth and development. The college also loaned them a videotape player and small television set. The teachers would gather once a week during the rest period to view and discuss the tapes while a teacher's aide supervised the children.

Teachers' study groups can work on common problems.

A teacher study group serves the interests of the members of the group. Together teachers study, discuss, share, and acquire knowledge that is particularly relevant to each individual. Participants may view videotapes, focusing on questioning techniques or pacing skills, or they can observe other teachers' practices. Participants in the group will remain involved as long as they are satisfied. Once teachers have lost interest, the group will fall apart.

A study group promotes objectivity in the individual's own behavior by sharing it with others. Teacher study groups also offer their members emotional support. Like any in-service program, these groups must be regularly evaluated to determine their worth.

Observing Other Teachers.   Teachers can observe other teachers as a way of improving their own teaching. They will gain a more objective view of teacher behavior and its effects on children. When teachers are actively engaged in their own teaching, they are so involved in responding and managing the class that it is hard to be aware of many classroom events and behaviors around them.

There are a variety of ways that observations can be scheduled. Two teachers can be paired to observe each other, or teachers can visit another school. Some teachers are fearful of being observed. They may become anxious about what others might think about them. They may be concerned that an observer does not share the same educational philosophy and that they will be demeaned. Visiting teachers can be helpful, however. They can share their view of incidents that the classroom teacher may not have noticed. At the same time visitors can learn new instructional techniques, expanding their repertoire of teaching skills.

A teacher and an aide in the same class can also observe each other. This pairing may be unbalanced, because the aide is usually not as qualified as the teacher. However, since the two work together as a team, they know their classroom situation and may share a similar educational philosophy. They should be able to provide each other with useful feedback. A teaching team can schedule occasional observations where the teacher (or aide) only observes and is freed from other responsibilities for a short period, possibly only fifteen or twenty minutes. The teacher can observe the class more intensely, thereby obtaining important information about individual children that can guide the teacher to respond to their unique developmental levels instead of to some stereotyped characteristics or group norms.

Teachers and aides may not be aware of everything they do or of their influence on their class. Their expectations about children and their ideas about the way specific lessons should be taught may influence what they see. Thus, seeing the classroom from the observer's point of view can be useful in eliminating some of the personal biases we all have.

Mentoring and Networking.   Mentoring and networking are two informal but important techniques teachers use to improve their knowledge of practice. Often a new teacher hired in a school is taken under the wing of a more experienced teacher. Standard procedures will be shown, help will be given in organizing the room, and information will be shared about the staff, the children, the parents, and the community. In addition the senior teacher will often share accumulated knowledge of practice, providing support for the novice teacher who might feel somewhat unsure of what is happening or why.

This help, or *mentoring,* may continue for a while. It eases the transition into the profession and is important for the development of both the novice and the experienced teacher. As a matter of fact, being able to serve as a mentor is an indication of personal maturity, as is noted in Eric Erikson's stages of development (see Chapter 5).

When teachers leave college and move into professional positions, they often promise to keep in touch with their fellow students. Usually one loses touch with those students who do not enter the profession or who move some distance away. However, others can develop a *network* of relationships, communicating with one another, sharing ideas, and providing emotional support when it is needed. Teachers find that networking serves many purposes in their professional development. They also seek or establish new networks as their maturity leads them to find new challenges and accept new roles.

Using Technology.   Recent developments in communications technology have provided other means to promote teachers' professional development. Video recordings are being used more widely for in-service training, evaluating teachers, and conducting research. Teachers can use video cameras and videocassette recorders to observe themselves. Self-viewing can provide teachers with information for self-improvement. Not all teachers accept self-viewing, however.

College teachers can serve as consultants beyond the classroom.

Many are concerned that their spontaneity will suffer or that their rights might be violated. Nevertheless, teachers are learning to use these techniques and precautions are being taken to protect teachers' rights. Teachers' permission should be received before their videotapes are made available to anyone. The teacher should also have the right to limit the viewing of the tape and to request that the videotape be erased. The use of videotapes to analyze teachers' classroom instruction will probably not be accepted until teachers are fully protected and do not feel threatened.

College or University Courses. Another alternative to in-service training is college or university courses. Some institutions offer programs leading to various certificates or advanced degrees. For many early childhood programs, teachers are required to take college courses regularly as a way to keep abreast of the field. Tuition might be paid or salaries adjusted to the amount of advanced education a teacher has. Schools may modify a teachers' work schedule to facilitate college or university attendance.

Professional Organizations

Professional organizations provide many resources to help teachers' self-development. A brief description of some of the major professional organizations in early childhood education follows.

National Association for the Education of Young Children (NAEYC). 1834 Connecticut Avenue N.W., Washington, DC, 20009. In 1926 a Committee on Nursery Education met, and the predecessor to NAEYC, the National Association for Nursery Education, was established. It has become one of the strongest and largest organizations in early childhood education, with more than 70,000 members in almost 300 affiliate groups. Membership is open to those who are concerned with the education and well-being of children. The major goal of NAEYC is to facilitate the advancement and development of early childhood education. NAEYC provides professional development opportunities to early childhood educators to help them improve the quality of services for children ages birth to eight. NAEYC publishes a journal, *Young Children,* along with other publications, and organizes an annual conference. Its affiliates also hold conferences and workshops and publish and distribute a range of printed material.

Association for Childhood International (ACEI). 11141 Georgia Avenue, Suite 200, Wheaton, MD 20902. This organization grew out of the International Kindergarten Union and works for children's education, fostering appropriate educational conditions, programs, and practices through the elementary grades. It is concerned with teachers' professional growth and shares information with the public about school programs. ACEI is composed of individuals, local affiliate groups, and state and provincial associations. It publishes a journal, *Childhood Education,* as well as other publications, and holds an annual conference.

World Organization for Early Childhood Education (OMEP). OMEP, Organisation Mondial pour l'Education Prescolaire (French), was founded in 1948. Its major goals are to foster the study and education of young children and assist all of those working with young children to become aware of young children's needs. It shares information among early childhood educators throughout the world on education, development, health and nutrition, playgrounds, and toys. OMEP holds an international assembly every second year. OMEP and UNESCO have combined their efforts to work on projects of mutual concern. OMEP publishes a journal titled *The International Journal of Early Childhood Education.* There is an active U.S. Committee for OMEP.

Other Professional Organizations. Other organizations related to the education of young children include the following:

American Montessori Society, Inc. 150 Fifth Avenue, New York, NY 10010.

Child Welfare League of America, Inc. 67 Irving Place, New York, NY 10010.

Council for Early Childhood Professional Recognition. 1718 Connecticut Avenue, N.W., Suite 500, Washington, D.C. 20009.

Council for Exceptional Children. 1920 Association Drive, Reston, VA 22091.

Head Start Bureau. Department of Health and Human Services, P.O. Box 1182, Washington, D. C. 20013.

National Committee on Education of Migrant Children. 1501 Broadway, New York, NY 10016.

National Education Association (NEA). 1201 16th Street, N.W., Washington, DC 20036.

OMEP National Committee. 1718 Connecticut Avenue, N.W., Washington, DC 20009.

Parent Cooperative Preschool International. 9111 Alton Parkway, Silver Spring, MD 20910.

Southern Association for Children Under Six (SACUS). Box 5403 Brady Station, Little Rock, AR 72205.

Organizations Concerned with Children and Families

A number of national organizations should be of interest to early childhood educators. These organizations can provide a range of information to those working with young children and their families that is beyond what is normally available within the education community. These information sources are especially important to teachers who go beyond their classroom roles to participate in community activities and in child and family advocacy activities. Among these are:

Action for Children's Television
(ACT)
20 University Rd.
Cambridge, MA 02138

American Academy of Pediatrics
141 Northwest Point Blvd.
Elk Grove, IL 60009

American Bar Association
The National Legal Resource Center
for Child Advocacy and Protection
1800 "M" Street NW
Washington, DC 20036

Center for Law and Social Policy
1616 "P" Street NW
Washington, DC 20036

Child Welfare League of America
440 First Street NW
Washington, DC 20001

Children's Defense Fund
122 "C" Street NW
Washington, DC 20001

League of Women Voters
1730 "M" Street NW
Washington, DC 20036

National Black Child Development
Institute
1436 Rhode Island Avenue, NW
Washington, DC 20005

National Council of Jewish Women
53 W. 23rd Street
New York, NY 10010

National PTA
700 Rush Street
Chicago, IL 60611

National Urban League
500 E. 62nd Street
New York, NY 10021

ERIC Clearinghouses

Teachers can also promote their own professional development by obtaining information from a variety of sources. The most widely available sources are the Educational Resources Information Centers (ERIC). This resource, funded by the Office of Educational Research and Improvement, U. S. Department of Education, provides information upon request on various educational topics. There are different ERIC Clearinghouses on different topics, including

Adult, Career, and Vocational Education
Counseling and Personnel Services
Early Childhood and Elementary Education
Educational Management
Handicapped and Gifted Children
Higher Education
Information Resources
Junior Colleges
Language and Linguistics
Reading and Communication Skills
Rural Education and Small Schools
Science, Mathematics and Environmental Education
Social Studies/Social Science Education
Teacher Education
Tests, Measurements, and Evaluation
Urban Education

The address for the ERIC Clearinghouse on Elementary and Early Childhood Education is

ERIC/EECE
College of Education
University of Illinois
805 W. Pennsylvania
Urbana, IL 61801

Each Clearinghouse surveys a variety of written materials in their fields. Those documents that are considered of educational interest are converted to microfiche and placed in the ERIC collection. This collection is available in libraries throughout the United States and in a number of other countries. Abstracts of these documents are made so that individuals can read short descriptions of each document to determine whether it would be worthwhile to read in its entirety.

Searches of the ERIC system for relevant resources have become more convenient with the availability of the entire collection of abstracts on CD-ROM (Compact Disk-Random Access Memory). These disks, much like the compact disks on which music is recorded, can be accessed by computer and are available in many public and university libraries throughout the country. After reading the abstracts on the computer or from a printout, readers can select the documents most relevant to their needs and read these from microfiche or have them printed out for later reference. Using this easily accessible data base makes an ERIC search quite convenient for teachers to use.

In addition to these abstracts and documents, ERIC prepares separate publications on a variety of topics, ERIC DIGESTS, which are brief discussions on current issues, ANNOTATED RESOURCE LISTS, which include recent ERIC document citations on specific topics, and READYSEARCHES, which are recent computer searches of ERIC, including citations of ERIC documents and journal articles. The entire database can be searched for relevant information.

Journals

Publications are available from a number of organizations and agencies that are concerned with the education and well-being of young children. Private publishers also issue journals related to early childhood education. These include:

American Education. Superintendent of Documents, U.S. Government Printing Office, Washington, DC 20402.

Child Care Information Exchange. C-44, Redmond, WA 98052.

Child Care Quarterly. Human Sciences Press, 72 Fifth Avenue, New York, NY 10011.

Child Development, Child Development Abstracts, and *Child Development Monographs.* Society for Research and Child Development, University of Chicago Press, Chicago, IL 60637.

Early childhood educational journals offer much useful information for teachers.

Child Welfare. Child Welfare League of America, Inc., 44 East 23rd Street, New York, NY 10010.

Childhood Education. Association for Childhood Education International, 11141 Georgia Avenue, Suite 200, Wheaton, MD. Bulletins, leaflets and books are also published.

Children Today. Office of Human Development Services, Department of Health and Human Services, Room 356-G, 200 Independence Ave., S.W., Washington, DC 20201.

Day Care and Early Education. Human Sciences Press, 72 Fifth Avenue, New York, NY 10011.

Dimensions. Southern Association for Children Under Six, Box 5403, Brady Station, Little Rock, AR 72215.

Early Years. Allen Raymond, Inc., P.O. Box 1266, Darien, CT 06826.

Exceptional Children. Council for Exceptional Children, 1920 Association Drive, Reston, VA 22091.

Instructor. Scholastic, 730 Broadway, New York, NY 10003.

Journal of Home Economics. American Home Economics Association, 2010 Massachusetts Avenue, N.W., Washington, DC 20036.

Learning. Education Today Company, Inc., 530 University Avenue, Palo Alto, CA 94301.

National Parent-Teacher. National Congress of Parents and Teachers, 700 North Rush Street, Chicago, IL 60511. Study guides are also available.

Parents. Parents Magazine Enterprises, Inc., 80 New Bridge Road, Bergenfield, NJ 07621.

Pre-K Today. Scholastic, 730 Broadway, New York, NY 10003.

Position Statements

Position statements on developmentally appropriate practices in early childhood education have been developed by several groups relating to early childhood education. Foremost among these is the National Association for the Education of Young Children (NAEYC). In July 1984, the NAEYC Governing Board established a commission to develop a position statement on appropriate education for four- and five-year-olds. The commission, chaired by Bernard Spodek, worked for about a year on this task.

Drawing on the report of the commission (Spodek, 1985) and on a discussion at the 1985 Affiliate Leadership Conference, NAEYC developed a broader statement describing developmentally appropriate practice in programs serving children from birth through age eight (Bredekamp, 1987). This statement provides a framework from which appropriate practice in specific settings may be derived. As of this writing, NAEYC and the Association of Early Childhood Specialists in State Departments of Education are drafting a further position paper dealing with early childhood program content.

Other groups have also attempted to develop position statements to encourage developmentally appropriate practices in early childhood settings, including the Association for Childhood Education International, the Southern Association for Children Under Six, and many local and state associations and educational agencies. A position statement on early literacy, *Literacy development and pre-first grade: A joint statement of concerns about preset practices in pre-first grade reading instruction and recommendations for improvement* was developed by the Early Childhood and Literacy Development Committee of the International Reading Association (IRA). It was adopted by the IRA in 1985 as well as by the Association for Childhood Education International, the Association for Supervision and Curriculum Development, the National Association for the Education of Young Children, the National Association of Elementary School Principals, and the National Council of Teachers of English. This statement is available from each of these associations.

Such position statements should prove useful to teachers as they evaluate their own classroom practices. As teachers take on increased professional responsibility, they should also participate in the process of creating such position papers and of influencing school policies and practices beyond their classroom. Vander Ven (1988) considers such activities beyond the classroom as reflecting a teacher's maturing to higher levels of professionalism.

SUMMARY

There are a variety of ways that teachers can learn more about themselves and their teaching. Staff meetings can be used to upgrade the quality of teaching. Speakers can be invited, films shown, or workshops held. Teachers can also share craft activities, songs, or action plays.

Teachers who are interested in improving themselves professionally can do so in several ways. They can learn through their own experience, from the experiences of their fellow teachers, and from a number of resources outside the school. Some schools support staff members' attendance at community workshops, at local, regional, and national conferences, and in college and university courses, so they may keep abreast in the field.

A number of professional associations also provide resources. Staff members may belong to one or more of these professional organizations, may attend conferences, workshops, and meetings, and may read early childhood publications and resource materials to keep up-to-date in the early childhood field. Professional journals are also helpful.

Early childhood education is growing rapidly. Educators must continue their self-education throughout their careers.

REFERENCES

BREDEKAMP, S. (Ed.). (1987). *Developmentally appropriate practice in early childhood programs serving children from birth through age eight.* Washington, DC: National Association for the Education of Young Children.

COMBS, A. W. (1965). *The professional education of teachers: A perceptual view of teacher preparation.* Boston: Allyn & Bacon.

HART, B. M., K. E. ALLEN, J. S. BUELL, J. R. HARRIS, AND M. M. WOLF (1964). Effects of social reinforcement on operant crying. *Journal of Experimental Child Psychology, 1,* 145–153.

SARACHO, O. N. (1984). Perception of the teaching process in early childhood education through role analysis. *Journal of the Association for the Study of Perception, 19* (1), 26–39.

SARACHO, O. N. AND B. SPODEK (1983). Preparing teachers for multicultural classrooms. In O. N. Saracho and B. Spodek (Eds.), *Understanding the multicultural experience in early childhood education,* pp. 125–146. Washington, DC: National Association for the Education of Young Children.

SPODEK, B. (1985). Goals and purposes of educational programs for 4- & 5-year-old children. Final report of the Commission on Appropriate Education. Washington, DC: National Association for the Education of Young Children.

SPODEK, AND O. N. SARACHO (1988). Professionalism in early childhood education. In B. Spodek, O. N. Saracho, and D. L. Peters (Eds.), *Professionalism and the early childhood practitioner,* pp. 59–74. New York: Teachers College Press.

VANDER VEN, K. (1988). Pathways to professional effectiveness for early childhood educators. In B. Spodek, O. N. Saracho, and D. L. Peters (Eds.), *Professionalism and the early childhood practitioner,* pp. 137–160. New York: Teachers College Press.

SUGGESTED ACTIVITIES

1. Interview a successful teacher to find out the aspects of teaching that are most challenging and least challenging. Ask the teacher for advice to those considering the teaching profession.

2. Review issues of *Young Children,* the journal of the National Association for the Education of Young Children, for a recent six-month period of publication. Report the main themes and points of view evident in these issues. Do the same for *Childhood Education,* the publication of the Associa-

tion of Childhood Education International. Share the reports with a small group or the whole class.

3. Attend a professional conference, meeting, or workshop for teachers of young children.

4. Interview a local officer of a professional organization. If possible, invite the officer to speak to the class on the way the organization improves the teachers' personal and professional development.

Index

Page numbers in italics indicate bibliographic entries.

ABC Bunny, The (Gag), 252
Academically oriented materials, 208
Accessibility, 49
Accommodation, 187, 285
Accompanying instruments, 235
Accreditation, 48–49
Achievement tests, 162
Action for Children's Television (ACT), 344
Action stories, 269–270
Activities
  evaluating, 173, 174
  scheduling, 116–119
  See also Creative activities; Play
Activity centers, 109–111, 242–244, 300
Administration for Children, Youth and Families, 5
Adventure Playground movement, 195–196
Advisory groups, parent, 149
Aesthetic climate of classroom, 107
Aid for Dependent Children (AFDC), 34
Aides, teacher, 56, 137, 340
Alexander, N. L., 58, *71*
Allen, K. E., 148, 154, *159*, 336, *348*
Allen, P. S., 88, *98*, *180*
Almy, M. C., 37, 41, *50*, 55, *71*, 166
Alphabet books, 251–252
Altwerger, B., 273, *281*
American Academy of Pediatrics, 344
American Association for the Advancement of Science, 286

American Bar Association, 344
American Education (journal), 345
American Federation of Teachers, 41
American Montessori Society (AMS), 26, 65, 343
American Society of Personnel Administration, 44
Anastasi, A., 168, 169, *180*
Andersen, Hans Christian, 262
Anderson, R. C., 274, *281*
Anecdotal records, 162–163, 165–166
Animals, teaching about, 289–291
Animal stories, 253
Anti-bias curriculum, 332
Applied behavior analysis theory, 127–128
Appropriateness of furniture and equipment, 112
Arbuthnot, M. H., 249, 250, 259, *283*
Art experiences, 216–228
  craft activities, 226–228
  three-dimensional, 221–226
  two-dimensional, 216–221
Artifacts, 320
Artistic development, stages of, 216
Art of the Storyteller, The (Shedlock), 262
Assimilation, 186–187, 285
Assistance from children, 126
Assistant teacher, 56, 59, 137
Associate teacher, 59–60
Association, 317

Association for Childhood Education International, 113, 347
Association for Childhood International (ACEI), 342–343
Association for Library Services to Children of the American Library Association, 253
Association for Supervision and Curriculum Development, 347
Association Montessori Internationale (AMI), 26, 65
Association of Early Childhood Specialists in State Departments of Education, 347
Associative play, 189
At-risk children, programs for, 11, 39–41
Attitudes
    development of, 92
    teacher, 336
Audiocassette recorder, 321
Audiovisual materials, 320–321
Aufenanger, S., 330, *333*

Bailey, C. S., 261
Baker, A., 260, 262, *281*
Baker, E. L., 167, *180*
Baker, S. M., *97, 180*
Banzet, Sarah, 17
Barbe, W. B., 279, *281*
Barnett, W. S., 8, *12*
Baroody, A. J., 301, *310*
Barr, R. D., 313
Barth, T. L., 313
Bates, L. B., *97, 180*
Bauer, C. F., 262
Bayless, K. M., 235, *245*
Beatty, J. J., 166
Becher, R. M., *211*
Bee, H. L., 9, *13*
Behavior
    cognitive, of three- to five-year-olds, 85–86
    prosocial, 134, 325
    school-appropriate, developing, 324–326
Behavior modification, 127–128
Behavior problems, managing, 131–133
Bender, J., 205, *211*
Bentzen, W. R., 166
Bergen, D., 189–190, *211*
Berger, K. S., 87, *97*
Berk, R. A., *180*
Berndt, T. J., 91, *97*
Berrueta-Clement, J. R., 8, *12*
Big Ones, Little Ones (Hoban), 252
Blake, H. E., 109, *121*
Blended families, 144
Blishen, E., 259
Bloch, M. N., *333*

Block Book, The (Hirsch), 203
Block building, 200–204, 221–223
Bloom, B., 5, 8, *12*
Blow, Susan, 22
Body puppets, 263, 264
Boehm, A. E., 166
Boehm Test of Basic Concepts, 168
Bogdanoff, R. F., 198–199, *211*
Book of Nursery and Mother Goose Rhymes, 251
Books, mathematics learning and, 308. *See also* Literature, children's; Reading
Bredekamp, S., *12,* 38, *50,* 347, *348*
Bretherton, I., 91, *97*
Brian Wildsmith's Puzzles (Wildsmith), 254–255
Bricker, D. D., *12*
Bricker, W. A., *12*
Briggs, B. A., 144, *159*
Brittain, W. L., 216, 224, *245*
Brown, M., 252, 253
Buck, P. S., 262
Budding, B. J., 90, *97, 180*
Buell, J. S., 336, *348*
Building blocks, 200–204, 221–223
Building structures, 195–196
Burke, C., 273, *281*
Burton, E. C., 242–243, *245*
Burton, V. L., 253
Burud, S. L., 44, *50*

Caldwell, B. M., *30,* 34, 35, *50*
Calendar, teaching about, 309
Calhoun, J. A., 41, *50*
Campbell, D. M., 66, *71*
Cardboard blocks, 200
Careers, alternative, 62–63. *See also* Practitioner, early childhood
Caregivers
    long-term effects of, 8–9
    role of, 56
Carew, J. V., 8, *12*
Carle, E., 252
Carney, C. C., 91, *98, 180*
Cartwright, C. A., 63, *72,* 167
Cartwright, G. P., 167
Cartwright, S., 223, *245*
Casa Dei Bambini, 24
Cataldo, C., 56, *71*
Cattermole, J., 153, *159*
Cauce, A. M., 91, *97*
Center director, 54
Center for Law and Social Policy, 344
Certification, 65–68
Chalk, colored, 218
Chambers, B., 257, *281*

Changed Lives (Berrueta-Clement, Schweinhart, Barnett, Epstein, & Weikart), 8
Charles, C. M., 127, *140*
Chatlin-McNichols, J. P., *50*
Checklists, 165, 166
Check sheets, 179
Child abuse and neglect, 46, 68
Child care, extended, 49
Child care centers, 4–5, 34–35
    caregiver role in, 56
    development of, 23–24
    quality of, 35
    types of programs, 35
    work-site, 7, 44–45
    during World War II, 29
Child Care Center Standards (Virginia), 57
Child Care Information Exchange (journal), 345
Child Care Quarterly (journal), 345
Child development, 74–99
    characteristics of three- to five-year-olds, 85–86
    cognitive, 82–84, 87–88, 93, 104
    creativity and, 215–216
    emotional, 90–91, 104
    guidelines for choosing games by stage of, 198–199
    language, 88–90, 187, 210
    nature and nurture in, 84
    physical, 84–87, 240–244
    program needs and implications and, 237–239
    regularities and irregularities in, 92–96
    social, 91, 104
    stages in play development and, 188–189
    theories and theorists of, 75–84
    values, development of, 92
Child Development Abstracts (journal), 345
Child Development Associate (CDA) credential, 60, 65–68
Child Development Associate Consortium, 66
Child Development Associate Professional Preparation Program, 66
Child Development (journal), 345
Child Development Monographs (journal), 345
Child enrollment information, 102, 103
Childhood Education (journal), 343, 345
Children's Defense Fund, 344
Children Today (journal), 345
Child study movement, 22, 75–76
Child Welfare (journal), 345
Child Welfare League of America, Inc., 343, 344
Christensen, D., 146, *159*
Christie, J. F., 188, *211*
Church-related programs, 43–44

Cinderella (Brown), 253
Clark, M. M., 273, *281*
Class, N., *50*
Classification, 317
Classroom environment. *See* Physical environment
Classroom management, 126–136
    behavior modification, 127–128
    guiding children's behavior, 130–131
    models of, 127–130
    play intervention, 134–136, 193–194
    positive social interaction, teaching, 133–134
    problem behavior, managing, 131–133
    redirection, 130, 134–136, 193
    setting limits, 126–127
    supporting prosocial behavior, 134
Classroom pet, 291
Classroom settings, evaluating, 172–176. *See also* Physical environment
Clay, 223–225
Clay, M. M., 272, 274, 275, 277, 278, 279, *281*
Clearinghouses, ERIC, 344–345
Clements, B. S., 106, *121*
Climbing equipment, 194–195
Clock, teaching about, 309
Cober, A. E., 255
Coconut shell clappers, 235–236
Code of Ethical Conduct, 68
Coelen, C., 104, *121*
Cognitive development, 87–88
    behavior of three- to five-year-olds, 85–86
    "domain-specific" sets of cognitive skills, 93
    materials and equipment for, 104
    Piaget's stages of, 82–84
Cognitively oriented learning, 284–311
    mathematics, 301–310
        everyday events to teach, 308–310
        materials for, 305–307
        topics for, 302–305
    science, 286–301
        animals, 289–291
        ecology and environment, 298–300
        materials and experiences, 300–301
        nutrition, 296–298
        physics, 287–289
        plants, 291–293
        weather, 293–295
Cognitive theory, 285–286
Cohen, D., 167
Cohen, S., *12, 91, 97*
Cole, P. M., 90, *97*
Collage, 219–220
College courses, taking, 342
Collins, M., 233, *245*

Collins, R. C., *30*, 41, 44, 47, 48, *50*
Colonial America, educating young children in, 16
Colored chalk, 218
Colored sand, 220
Colwell, E., 262
Combs, A. W., 57, *71*, 336, *348*
Communication
  of evaluation results, 177–179
  with parents, 153–158
Community resources, working with, 138–139
Community roles, learning, 324
Comparison activities, 307
Competence motivation, theory of, 187
Competencies
  CDA, 66–67
  social, 325, 326
Complete Nonsense Book, The (Lear), 259
Comprehensive child care, 35
Concept books, 252
Concepts, social studies, 316–317
Conceptual thought, 87–88
Concrete operational stage, games for, 199
Conditioning, operant, 81–82
Conferences, parent, 154–155, 178–179
Consortium on Longitudinal Studies, 8, 30
Construction sets, 207. *See also* Building blocks
Constructive play, 189
Constructivist theory, 285
  of play, 186–187
Consumer Product Safety Commission, 115
Content words, 248
Conversation as play intervention, 134–136
Coody, B., 250, 258, 259, 260, *281*
Cooking, 297
Cooper, M., 40, *50*
Cooperation, 91
Cooperative play, 189
Cooperative Preschool Inventory, 168
Coordinating movement activities, 241–244
Copple, C., 237, *245*
Cornstarch clay, 225, 226
Corrigan, R., 88, 97
Cost of furniture and equipment, 112
Council for Early Childhood Professional Recognition, 64, 343
Council for Exceptional Children, 343
Council on Interracial Books for Children, 257, 332
Counting, 303–304
Counting books, 252
Craft activities, 226–228
Crayons, 218–219
Creative activities, 213–246
  art experiences, 216–228

  craft activities, 226–228
    three-dimensional, 221–226
    two-dimensional, 216–221
  movement education, 237–244
    creative, 240
    for physical development, 240–244
  music activities, 228–237
    musical instruments, 234–237
    rhythmic, 229–231
    singing, 231–234
  play and, 210
  self-expression and, 214–216
Creative dramatics, 266–267, 268
Creative movement, 240
Creativity
  age-related developmental characteristics, 215–216
  materials and equipment for development of, 104
Crèche, French, 23
Credentialing, 60, 65–68
Criterion-referenced tests, 167
Croft, D. J., 145, 146, *159*
Crow Boy (Yashima), 253
Cryer, D., 157, *159*
Cullinan, B. E., 249, 250, 262, *281*
Cultural awareness, developing, 330–332
Cultural differences, 92–93
Cultural pluralism, 92
Culture, defined, 92
Culver, C., 90–91, *98, 180*
Curious George (Rey), 253
Curriculum
  anti-bias, 332
  play and early childhood, 208–210
Custodial care, 35

Dance, 241. *See also* Movement education
Dauer, V. P., 239, 240, *245*
Davis, D. E., 327, *333*
Davis, J., 38, *50*
Davis, M. D., 38, *50*, 57, 58, 64, *71, 72*
Day care, employer interest in, 44–45
Day Care and Early Education (journal), 345
Day care homes, family, 35–38, 43, 56
Day care program, schedule for, 119
Day nurseries, 23–24. *See also* Child care centers
Dear Garbage Man (Zion), 222
Deasey, D., 17, *30*
Decisions, types of, 105
Decker, C. A., 33, 40, 46, *50*, 178, *180*
Decker, J. R., 33, 40, 46, *50*, 178, *180*
DeFord, D., 277, *281*
Demonstration, 134–136

Demos, V., 90, *97*
Department of Health, Education and Welfare, 5
Department of Labor, 57
Depression (1930s), 28
Derman-Sparks, L., 332, *333*
Desists, 128
Developmental care, 35
Developmental theories and theorists, 75–84. *See also* Child development
Devine-Hawkins, P., 44, *50*
DeVries, R., 287, 303, 304, *311*
Dewey, John, 76
Dickerson, M. G., 114, *121*
Dictionary of Occupational Titles (Department of Labor), 57
Diet, teaching about, 296–298
Dietz, B. W., 232
Dimensions (journal), 345
Dinkmeyer, D., Jr., 327, *333*
Dinkmeyer, D., Sr., 327, *333*
Director, center, 54
Direct teaching, 325, 326
Discipline, 126–127
  Dreikurs' model of, 129–130
Dolch, E. T., 198–199, *211*
Domain-referenced tests, 167
"Domain-specific" sets of cognitive skills, 93
Downing, J., 270, *281*
Dramatic play, 189
  indoor, 204–206
  outdoor, 197–198
Dramatics, creative, 266–267, 268
Dreikurs, R., 129–130, *140*
Drum, 236
Dunn, L., 66, *72*
Durability of furniture and equipment, 112–113
Durkin, D., 248, 273, *281*
DUSO-Revised: Developing an Understanding of Self and Others (Dinkmeyer & Dinkmeyer), 327

Early Childhood and Literacy Development Committee of the International Reading Association (IRA), 347
Early childhood education
  contemporary developments in, 29–30
  defined, 2–3
  development of, 17–28
  federal involvement in, 28–29
  forces affecting field of, 7–9
  institutions. *See* Institutions and programs, early childhood

  long-term effects of, 8–9
  trends in, 9–11
Early Childhood Educator at Work, The (Almy), 71
Early Childhood Task Force of National Association of State Boards of Education, 42
Early Years (journal), 345
Eason, R. L., 241, *245*
Eastenson, A., 91, *97, 180*
Easy-to-read books, 254
Ecology and environment, 298–300
Education
  multicultural, 330–332
  parent, 145, 149–153
  teacher, 64–65, 70, 338–342
Educational Resources Information Centers (ERIC) Clearinghouses, 344–345
Education of All Handicapped Children Act (P.L. 94-142), 10
Education of the Handicapped Act, Amendments of 1986 (P.L. 99-457), 10, 39
Education play, 189–190
Edwards, C. P., 327–328, *333*
Effectiveness of program, evaluating, 171
Ego, 78
Electrical outlets, location of, 107
Elkind, D., 38, *50*
Ellis, M. J., 187, *211*
Emergent literacy, 272–274
Emmer, E. T., 106, *121*
Emotional development, 90–91, 104
Employer-supported child care, 44–45
England, nursery school movement in, 27–28
Enrollment information, child, 102, 103
Environment, ecology and, 298–300
Environment, evaluating classroom, 172–176. *See also* Physical environment; Social environment
Epstein, A. S., 8, *12*
Equilibration, 82, 285, 288
Equilibrium, 187, 285
Equipment, 111–113
  activity center, 109, 111
  relationship between developmental areas and, 104
  selecting outdoor, 115–116
  See also Materials
Equipment and supplies: Guidelines for administrators and teachers in child development centers, 113
Equipment manufacturers, careers with, 62
ERIC Clearinghouses, 344–345
Erikson, Erik, 79–81, *97*
Ershler, J. J., 189, *211*

Evaluation in early childhood programs,
161–182
basis for, 171–172
classroom settings, 172–176
formative, 172
information gathering methods, 162–170
informal tests, 169–170
observations, 162–167
standardized tests, 167–169
recording and communicating results of,
177–179
responsive, 171
screening of exceptional children, 176–177
summative, 172
Evans, E. D., 89, *98, 181*
Evertson, C. M., 106, *121*
Evolutionary development theory, 75
Exceptional children, 96
screening, 176–177
See also Handicapped, early education of the
Exceptional Children (journal), 345
Exercises in Practical Life (Montessori program), 26
Expressive language, 89, 248
Extended child care, 49
Extended families, 144

Families
forces affecting, 158
nutrition lesson and, 296
organizations concerned with, 343–344
types of, 143–145
See also Parents
Family-based programs, 152
Family day care homes, 35–38, 43, 56
Family grouping, 125
Family planning, 8
Fastening frames, 207
Federal government, involvement of, 28–29, 49
Federal Interagency Day Care Regulations
(1968), 47
Feedback, 172
Feedforward, 172
Feeney, S., 113, 146, *159*
Fee-supported programs, 44
Fein, G. G., 185, *211*
Feldman, D., 93, *97*
Field trips, 138–139, 317–319
Filmstrips and films, sound, 321
Fingerpaint, 219
Finger plays, 267–269
First grade, program planning for, 238–239
Fisher Act of 1918 (England), 28
Flake-Hobson, C., *97,* 144, *160*
Flexibility of equipment, 113

Floor plan, 109, 110
Follow-Through Parent Education Program
Model, 143
Foods, teaching about, 296–298
Forest, I., 23, *30*
Formal communication techniques, 154–158
Formative evaluation, 172
For-profit programs, 43
Foster parent families, 144
Four-year-old children, programs for,
41–42
Fowke, E., 232
Freud, Anna, 80
Freud, Sigmund, 76, 77–79, 80, 81, 186
Freyer, M., *30, 35, 50*
Friedman, D., 44, 45, *50*
Friendships, 91, 134
Froebel, Freidrich, 19–22, 24, 305
Frost, J. L., 114, 115–116, *121*
Functional play, 189
Function words, 248
Furniture, 111–113

Gag, W., 252, 253, 262
Galdone, P., 269, *281*
Galinsky, E., 44, *50,* 70, *71,* 155, 156, *159*
Games, 189
indoor, 208
outdoor, 198–200
for physical development, 240–241
thinking, 328
Gardner, D. B., 87, *97*
Gardner, H., 93, *97*
Garner, A. P., 223, *245*
Garner, R., 274, *281*
Gender differences in play, 188
Genishi, C., 166
Gentile, L. M., 210, *211*
Gerber, L., 233, *245*
Gesell, Arnold, 76–77, *97*
Gilmore, J. B., 185, *211*
Glantz, F., 104, *121*
Glazer, T., 232
Goals
of language arts program, 248–49
planning physical environment to support,
102
for social studies education, 313–316
using play to achieve educational, 189–190
Golden, J., 277–278, *283*
Goodman, Y., 273, *281*
Goodspeed, J., 222
Goodwin, L. D., 167–168, *180*
Goodwin, W., 167–168, *180*
Gordon, I. J., 143, *159*

Grasshopper on the Road (Lobel), 254
Grayson, M. F., 269, *281*
Great Society, 33
Greene, E., 260, 262, *281*
Greenfield, P. M., 93, *97*
Grey, L., 129, *140*
Gronlund, N. E., 168, 169, *180*
Grouping, 123–125
  group size, 9, 104–105, 124
Group meetings, parent, 152
Group singing, 231–232
Gruneberg, M. M., 93, *98*
Guidelines for Selecting Bias-Free Textbooks and Storybooks, 257, 332
Guilding children's behavior, 130–131
Guiding play, 192–194
Guralnick, M. J., *12*
Gymnastics, 241

Haan, N., 91, *98, 180*
Hailstones and Halibut Bones (O'Neill), 259
Haines, E., 233, *245*
Hall, G. Stanley, 75–76, *97*
Hall, J. S., 146, 152, *159*
Handbook of Storytellers (Bauer), 262
Handicapped, early education of the, 10, 96
  Head Start and, 41
  Montessori method and, 24–26
  organizing classroom for, 107
  preschool, 39–40
  screening, 176–177
Hand puppets, 263, 264
Hand shaker, 236
Handwriting readiness programs, 279
Hanley, P. E., 158, *159*
Hare and the Tortoise, The (Galdone), 269
Harms, T. O., 157, *159*, 173, *180*
Harris, J. R., 336, *348*
Harrison, J. F. C., 18, *30*
Harsh, A., 308, *311*
Harste, J., 273, *281*
Hart, B., 148, 154, *159*, 336, *348*
Harter, S., 90, *97, 98, 180*
Hartup, W. W., 91, *97, 180*
Hawkins, D., 209, *211*
Head puppets, 263, 264
Head Start, 5–6, 29, 30, 33, 40–41, 49, 68,
  113
  integration of handicapped and nonhandicapped children, 10
  parent involvement in, 9, 95, 143, 149, 152
Head Start Bureau, 343
Health care, career alternatives in, 63
Heasley, C. A., 63, *72*
Heath, S. B., 273, *281*

Heining, R. B., 267, *281*
Heinz, R. S., 143, 146, *159*
Helms, D. B., 86, 87, 88, 89, *97, 180*
Hembree, E. A., 90, *97, 180*
Hennings, D. G., 263, *281*
Herr, J., 296, *311*
Hess, R., 8, *13*
Hey Bug! and Other Poems about Little Things
  (Itse), 259
Hickox, R. F., 44, *50*
Hicks, M., 44, 45, *50*
Hiebert, E. H., 273, *281*
High/Scope report, 8
Hildreth, G., 277, *282*
Hill, P. S., 314, *333*
Hill, Patty Smith, 22
Hillerich, R. L., 271, *282*
Hilliard, A. G., 325, 326, *333*
Hirsch, E. S., 117, *121*, 202, 203, *211*
Historical traditions, 15–31
  child care center, development of, 23–24
  in colonial America, 16
  contemporary developments, 29–30
  federal involvement, 28–29
  infant school, 17–19
  kindergarten, 19–23
    beginning of, 19–22
    reform in, 22–23
  Montessori method, 24–26, 30
  nursery school, 27–28, 30
  Oberlin school, 17
Hoban, T., 252
Hodges, W., 40, *50*
Hofferth, S. L., 33, 48, *50*, 70, 71
Hoffnung, R. J., 87, *98*
Holdaway, D., 272–273, *282*
Holidays, 324
Hollow blocks, 200–201
Home Start, 41
Home visits, 156
Honig, A. S., 151, 152, *160*, 248, *282*
Hoot, J. L., 210, *211*
Horning, M., 189, *211*
Horton Hatches the Egg (Seuss), 253
Hostetler, L., 57, 62, *72*
Hubbell, V. R., 8, *13*
Huck, C. S., 249, *282*
Huebner, R. R., 90, *97, 180*
Humorous and nonsense books, 253
Hunt, J. McV., 5, 8, *13, 95, 97, 180*
Hymes, J. L., Jr., 64, *72*

Id, 78
Ilg, F. L., *97, 180*
Indirect teaching, 325–326

Individual conferences with parents, 178–179
Individualized Family Service Plan, 40
Indoor play, 192, 200–210
   block building, 200–204, 221–223
   dramatic play, 204–206
   table activities, 206–208
Infant emotional development, 90
Infant school, 17–19
Informal communication techniques, 154
Informal reports, 178
Informal tests, 169–170
Information books, 255
Information gathering methods, 162–170
   informal tests, 169–170
   observations, 162–167
   standardized tests, 167–169
Information processing, play as form of, 187
Inner speech, 89
In-service programs, 338–342
Institute for the Formation of Character, 18
Institutional sponsorship, 42–45
Institutions and programs, early childhood, 3–7, 34–42
   for at-risk children, 11, 39–41
   family day care homes, 35–38, 43, 56
   for four-year-olds, 41–42
   issues related to, 46–49
      accessibility, 49
      accreditation, 48–49
      licensing, 46–48
   sponsorship, of, 42–45
   See also Child care centers; Handicapped, early education of the; Head Start; Kindergarten
Instruction
   organizing for, 106–113
   as play intervention, 134–136
Instructor (journal), 345
Instrumental learning, 82
Instruments, musical, 234–237
Intellectual development. *See* Cognitive development
Interactive decisions, 105
International Journal of Early Childhood Education, The, 343
International Kindergarten Union, 342
International Reading Association (IRA), 347
Interpersonal environment, evaluating, 173, 174
Intervention, play, 134–136, 193–194
Intuitive thought, stage of, 88
Itse, E. M., 259
Izard, C. E., 90, *97, 180*

Jaccard, J., 91, *98*
Jacobs, L. B., 250, 258, *282*
Jalongo, M. R., 233, *245*
Jenkins, E., 232
Jenkins, P. D., 262, *282*
Jewell, M., 273, *282*
Joan, B., 233, *245*
Johnson, H., 201, *211*
Johnson, J. E., 188, 189, *211*
Johnson, Lyndon, 33
Journal of Home Economics, 345
Journals, 345–346
Joy to the World (Sawyer), 262
Justice, developing sense of, 330

Kagan, J., 88, *97, 180*
Kamii, C., 287, 288, 289, 302, 303, 304, *311*
Katz, L. G., 68, *72*
Kerber, J. E., 274, *283*
Kessen, W., 75, *97, 180*
Kettlekamp, L., 255
Keyserling, M., *13*
Kim, Y., 134, *140*
Kindergarten, 3, 6–7, 19–23, 33, 38–39
   beginning of, 19–22
   contemporary developments in, 29
   developmentally appropriate programs in, 38
   expansion of, 11
   program planning for, 238–239
   reform in, 22–23
   schedule for, 118–120
Kites (Kettlekamp), 255
Klausmeier, H. J., 88, *98, 180*
Klein, B. L., 114, *121*
Klugman, E., 57, *72*
Knowledge
   acting on acquired, 321–322
   types of, 314–315
Kohlberg, L., 328–329
Kortz, N., 145, 153, 154, *160*
Kounin, J. S., 128–129, *140*

Laban, R., 240, *245*
Labeling, 96
Ladd, G. W., 325, *333*
Lamme, L. L., 279, *282*
Landeck, B., 232
Landesman, S., 91, *98*
Lang, M. E., 41, *51*
Langer, J., 78, *98, 180*
Langstaff, J., 232
Langstaff, N., 232
Language arts programs, 248–270
   action stories, 269–270

Language arts programs (*cont.*)
  children's literature, 249–257, 267
  creative dramatics, 266–267, 268
  finger plays, 267–269
  goals of, 248–249
  poetry, 257–260
  puppetry, 262–266
  storytelling, 260–262
Language development, 88–90, 248
  materials and equipment for, 104
  play and, 187, 210
Language differences, 93–95
Language experience approach, 278–279
Lanham Act, 29
Large-motor activity, 194–195
Larson, J. M., 9, *13*
Lasky, L., 214, *245*
Laursen, B., 91, *97, 180*
Lave, J., 93, *97*
Lazar, I., 8, *13*
League of Women Voters, 344
Lear, E., 259
Learning
  instrumental, 82
  play and curriculum for, 208–10
  See also Cognitively oriented learning; Social-
    ization; Social studies program
Learning (journal), 345
Lee, R. C., 10, *13*, 96, *98*, 151, 156, *160*, 241, *245*,
    248, 275, *283*, 315, 327, *334*
Lee-Katz, L., 288, 289, *311*
Leeper, S. H., 55, *72*
Let's Do Fingerplays (Grayson), 269
Let's Go Watch a Building Going Up (Goodspeed),
    222
Let's Look Under the City (Schneider &
    Schneider), 222
Letters, report, 179
Levenstein, P., 9, *13*
Lewis, M., 90, 91, *98, 180*
Lewis, S., 255
Librarians, school, 62
Library area, 255–256
Licensing, 46–48
Life experiences, reading as result of, 273
Ligon, E. M., 215, *245*
Lilley, I., 20, *30*
Limits, setting, 126–127
Lindauer, S. L. K., 26, *30*
Lindner, E. W., 43, *50*
Literacy, emergent, 272–274
Literacy program, evaluating, 172
Literature, children's, 249–257, 267
Little Bear's Visit (Miniarik), 254
Little Engine That Could, The (Piper), 252

Lobel, A., 254
Locking devices, 207
Logical consequences, 129–130
Logico-mathematical knowledge, 301, 314–315
Logue, M. E., 327–328, *333*
Lombardi, J., 41, *51*
Lowenfeld, V., 216, 224, *245*
Lowenthal, B., 40, *50*
Lubeck, S., 41, *50*
Lucas, V. H., 279, *281*
Lying, dealing with, 328, 329–330

McAfee, O. D., 146, 149, *160*
McCandless, B. R., 87, 89, *98, 181*
McCaslin, N., 266–267, *282*
McCormick, C., 273, *282*
MacDonald, D. T., 229–232, *245*
Macdonald, J., 9, *13*
Machines personified, books on,
    252–253
McMillan, Margaret, 27–28, *30*
McMillan, Rachel, 27–28
McNeill, J. D., 274, *282*
Magid, R. Y., *13*
Maier, H. W., 80, *98, 180*
Mainstreaming, 10, 96
Mainstreaming Young Children (Spodek, Saracho,
    & Lee), 96
Maintenance as play intervention, 134–136
Maioni, T. L., 189, *211*
Malatesta, C. Z., 90–91, *97, 98, 180*
Males in early childhood education, 68–70
Malina, R. M., 86, *98, 180*
Manipulative materials, 305–307
Mann, M., 9, *13*
Mapping, 322–323
Margarick, M., 113
Marion, M., 126, *140*
Marx, F., 11, *13*, 42, *50*
Masden, C. H., Jr., *140*
Masden, C. K., *140*
Mason, G. E., *282*
Mason, J., 273, 274, 275, *282*
Materials
  activity center, 109, 111
  audiovisual, 320–321
  criteria for judging educational toys,
    175–176
  free and inexpensive, 113
  manipulative, 305–307
  for mathematics, 305–307
  outdoor, selection of, 115–116
  relationship between developmental areas
    and, 104

Materials (*cont.*)
  for science, 300–301
  See also Creative activities
Mathematics, 301–310
  everyday events to teach, 308–310
  materials for, 305–307
  play and, 209–210
  topics for, 302–305
Matsumoto, D., 91, *98, 180*
Mattick, I., 173, *181*
Maturational view of development, 77
May, D., 16, *30*
Measuring activities, 308–309
Medical assistance, 46
Meetings
  in-service, 338
  parent, 156, 157
Meisels, S. J., 169, *181*
Melody instruments, 235
Mentoring, 340–341
Merro, J., *50*
Merry Tales for Children (Bailey), 261
Metacognition, 274
Metalinguistic knowledge, 276
Metropolitan Readiness Tests, 168
Michaelson, L., 90, 91, *98, 180*
Mike Mulligan and His Steam Shovel (Burton), 253
Millions of Cats (Gag), 253
Miniarik, E. H., 254
Mitchell, A., 11, *13,* 34, 35, 42, *50*
Mitchell, L. S., 314, *333*
Modeling, 92, 131, 134, 325
Montessori, Maria, 24–26, *31*
Montessori Credential, 65
Montessori method, 24–26, 30, 184, 305
Moomaw, S., 228, 235, *245*
Moore, L., 252
Moore, S., 134, *140*
Morado, C., 41, *50*
Moral thought, levels of, 328–330
Moravcik, E., 146, *159*
Morgan, E. L., *160*
Morgan, G., 49, *50*
Morris, P. E., 93, *98*
Morrow, L. M., 250, 257, 272, 273, 275, 276, *282*
Morse, W., 296, *311*
Mother Goose stories, 251
Mothers, working, 7
Motor development, 87
Movement, physics activities stressing, 289
Movement education, 237–244
  creative, 240
  for physical development, 240–244
Mukerji, R., 214, *245*

Multi-age grouping, 125
Multicultural education, 330–332
Murals, 220
Murphy-Durrell Reading Readiness Analysis, 168
Murray, H., 8, *13*
Music activities, 228–237
  musical instruments, 234–237
  rhythmic, 229–231
  singing, 231–234
My First Counting Book (Moore), 252
My Friends and Me (Davis), 327
Myller, R., 252

National Academy of Early Childhood Programs, 48, 149
National Association for Nursery Education, 342
National Association for the Education of Young Children (NAEYC), 44, 57, 149, 150, 342
  accreditation program, 48–49
  code of ethics, 68, 69
  on licensing, 47
  position statement, 347
  on professional path, 62–65
National Association of Elementary School Principals, 347
National Association of State Boards of Education, 41
National Black Child Development Institute, 344
National Committee on Education of Migrant Children, 343
National Council of Churches, 43
National Council of Jewish Women, 344
National Council of Teachers of English, 347
National Day Care Home Study, 38
National Day Care Study, 35, 48, 104
National Education Association, 343
National Parent-Teacher (journal), 345
National PTA, 344
National Teacher Examination, 65
National Urban League, 344
Nation Prepared: Teachers for the 21st Century, A (Carnegie Forum on Education and the Economy), 64
Nature and nurture, child development and, 84
Nedler, S. E., 146, 149, *160*
Networking, 340–341
Neugebauer, R., 43, *51*
Neumann, E. A., 184, *211*
New Deal, 28
New Harmony, settlement at, 18
Newsletters, 157–158

New York Nursery and Child's Hospital, 23
Noneducational play, 189
Norm-referenced tests, 167
Norwood, G. R., 143, *311*
Not-for-profit programs, 43
Nuclear families, 144
Number concepts, 303–304
Nursery school, 3–4
    contemporary developments in, 29
    development of, 27–28, 30
    federal involvement in, 28
    program planning for, 237–238
    schedule for, 118–120
Nurture and nature, child development and, 84
Nutrition education, 296–298

Oberlin, Jean Frederick, 17
Oberlin, Madeleine, 17
Oberlin school, 17
Observations, 162–167
    of teachers, 340
O'Connell, J. C., 38, *51*
Olmstead, P. P., 143, *159*
OMEP National Committee, 343
O'Neill, M., 259
One-to-one interactions, 125
Open grouping, 124
Operant conditioning, 81–82
Operants, 82
Organisation Mondial pour l'Education Pre-
    scolaire (French), 343
Organization
    of adults, 136–139
    of children, 123–126
    for instruction, 106–113
Organizations
    concerned with children and families, 343–
        344
    professional, 342–343
Orientation meeting for parents, 148
Orton, R., *50*
Outdoor play, 191, 194–200
    building structures, 195–196
    designing areas for, 114–116
    dramatic play, 197–198
    games, 198–200
    large-motor activity, 194–195
    sand and water, 196–197, 300
    wheel toys, 195
Overdwelling, 129
Owen, Robert, 17–19
Oxford Book of Poetry for Children (Blishen), 259

Paired grouping, 124–125
Pangrazi, R. P., 239, 240, *245*
Papier-maché, 225
Parallel play, 188, 189
Paraprofessionals, working with, 137
Parent conferences, 154–155, 178–179
Parent-cooperative nursery schools, 4
Parent Cooperative Preschool International,
    343
Parent meetings, 156, 157
Parents, 142–160
    advisory groups, 149
    communication with, 152–158
    conferences, 154–155, 178–179
    criteria for teacher-parent interaction,
        149–150
    education of, 145, 149–153
    involvement of, 9, 22, 95, 143, 145, 146–148,
        149, 152
    long-term effects of, 8–9
    policy councils, 149
    reporting to, 178–179
    as volunteers, 137, 151–152
    working successfully with, 158–159
"Parents Bill of Rights," 151
Parents (journal), 345
Park Book, The (Zolotow), 222
Parke, R., Jr., *13*
Parks, T. C., 232
Parsons, S. A., 39, *51*
Parten, M. B., 188–189, *211*
Participation as play intervention, 134–136
Participation books, 254–255
Pay for teachers, 70
Peabody, Elizabeth, 22
Pearson, P. D., *281*
Pellegrini, A. D., 210, *211*
Perceptual development, 87
Perceptual-motor behaviors of three- to five-
    year-olds, 85–86
Perkins, F. J., 173, *181*
Perrault, J., 152, *160*
Persistence of preschool effects (Lazar, Hubbell,
    Murray, Rosche, & Royce), 8
Personal development of teachers, 336
Personality development
    physical development and, 87
    psychoanalytic theory of, 77–79
Personal-social learning. *See* Socialization; So-
    cial studies program
Pet, classroom, 291
Peter Piper's Alphabet (Brown), 252
Peters, D. L., 57, 58, *72*
Petty, D. C., 262, *282*
Petty, W. T., 262, *282*

Pflaum, S. W., 248, *282*
Phonology, 248
Phyfe-Perkins, E., 175, *181*
Physical development, 84–87
  materials and equipment for, 104
  movement activities for, 240–244
Physical environment, 100–121
  evaluating, 173, 174
  organizing for instruction, 106–113
    activity centers, 109–111
    free and inexpensive materials, 113
    furniture and equipment, 111–113
  outdoor play areas, designing, 114–115
  planning, 101–106, 136
  scheduling activities, 116–120
Physical guidance, 131
Physical knowledge, 314
Physics, 287–289
Piaget, Jean, 82–84, *98*, 186, 189, *211*, 285, 304,
  314, 328
Picture books, 253
Picture sets, 320–321
Piper, W., 252
Planning, 325
  characteristics, interests and needs impor-
    tant in, 237–239
  of field trip, 318
  for having resource person, 320
  for parent involvement, 146–147
  of physical environment, 101–106, 136
Plants, teaching about, 291–293
Plasticine, 225
Play, 183–212
  to achieve educational goals, 189–190
  curriculum and, 208–210
  defining, 184–185
  developing activities, 190–194
  gender differences in, 188
  indoor, 192, 200–210
  initiating activities, 192
  language development and, 187, 210
  moving play along, 192–194
  outdoor, 191, 194–200
  patterns of, 134
  stages in development of, 188–189
  theories explaining, 185–187
Play dough, 225
Playgrounds, designing, 114–116
Play intervention, 134–136, 193–194
Pluralism, cultural, 92
Poetry, 257–260
Policy councils, parent, 149
Position statements, 346–347
Positive social interactions, teaching, 133–134

Poverty
  federal government involvement and, 29
  Head Start and, 40–41
  Home Start and, 41
  kindergarten development and, 22
  Montessori method and, 24
  nursery school development and, 27–28
Powell, D. R., 66, *72*
Powell, J., 44, 45, *50*
Practicality of program, evaluating, 171
Practice play, 189
Practitioner, early childhood, 52–73
  preparing to be, 64–70
  roles, 54–56
  See also Professionalism
Pragmatics, 248
Praise as play intervention, 134–136
Preactive decisions, 105
Preconceptual thought, 88
Preexercise theory of play, 186
Prekindergarten programs, 11
Pre-K Today (journal), 345
Preoperational stage, 198–199, 286
Preparation programs for practitioners, 64–65
Preschematic stage, 216
Preschool, program planning for, 237–238
Preschool handicapped, 39–40
Prescott, E., 174, *181*
Price, G. G., 301, 303, *311,* 313, 325, *333*
Prime Time program, 9
Private programs, 43
Problem behavior, managing, 131–133
Problem-solving, teacher-parent, 155–156
Professionalism, 56–63, 335–349
  alternative careers, 62–63
  ERIC Clearinghouses, 344–345
  in-service programs, 338–342
  journals, 345–346
  organizations concerned with families and
    children, 343–344
  position statements, 346–347
  professional organizations, 342–343
  professional path, 59–62
  standards and, 57–58
Professional materials for storytelling, 262
Professional organizations, 342–343
Program evaluation. *See* Evaluation in early
  childhood programs
Programs. *See* Institutions and programs, early
  childhood
Progressive education movement, 22–23
Project Head Start. *See* Head Start
Prop boxes, 205–206
Proprietary centers, 43
Prosocial behavior, 134, 325

Psychoanalytic theory of personality develop-
    ment, 77–79
Psychodynamic theory of play, 186
Psychological services, 46
Psychologists, school, 62
Psychosexual stages, 79
Psychosocial development theory, 79–81
Public Action Coalition on Toys, 112
Publications, 345–346
Public Law 94-142 (Education of All Handi-
    capped Children Act), 10
Public Law 99-457 (Education of the Handi-
    capped Act, Amendments 1986), 10, 39
Public programs, 43
Public School Early Childhood Study, 42
Public schools, 3, 11, 42, 49
Publishers, careers with, 62
Puppetry, 262–266
Purchase of service, 45
Puzzles, 206–207

Quality of furniture and equipment, 112–113
Quiet area, 109–111

Ramsey, M. E., 235, *245*
Ramsey, P. G., 330, 331–332, *333*
Ranzoni, P. S., *160*
Rating scales, 164, 166
Reading, 270–275
    to children, 273–274
    designing reading readiness program,
        270–272
    emergent literacy, 272–274
    relationship between writing and, 275–277
    schema theory and, 274–275
Real Mother Goose, The (Wright), 251
Recapitulation theory, 75
    of play, 185, 186
Receptive language, 89, 248
Reciprocity, 91
Recording of evaluation results, 177–179
Records, anecdotal, 162–163, 165–166
Redirection, 130, 134–136, 193
Reed, I. B., 66, *71*
Reflective decisions, 105
Reform
    in kindergarten, 22–23
    teacher-education, 64–65, 70
Reid, M., 91, *98*
Reinforcement, 81–82
Relaxation theory of play, 185, 186
Repetitive songs, 230
Report letters, 179
Representation skills, 274
Resource persons for social studies, 319–320

Resources, community, 138–139
Responsive evaluation, 171
Rey, H. A., 253
Rhythm blocks, 236
Rhythmic activities, 229–231
Rhythm instruments, 235
Ribovich, J. K., 124, *140*
Right from the Start, 42
Rights of parents, 151
Ripple effect, 128
Robinson, B. E., *97,* 144, *160*
Robinson, C. C., 9, *13*
Robinson, N., 153, *159*
Roles
    learning school and community, 324
    practitioner, 54–56
Rome Association for Good Building, 24
Room arrangement. *See* Physical environment
Roosevelt, Franklin D., 28
Rootabaga Stories (Sandburg), 262
Rosche, M., 8, *13*
Ross, R. R., *282*
Rothenberg, M. B., 86, *98*
Roup, R., 104, *121*
Royce, J., 8, *13*
Rubin, K. H., 185, 189, *211*
Rubin, R. I., 143, *159*
Russell, A. S., 327–328, *333*

Safety
    of furniture and equipment, 112
    of outdoor play areas, 115–116
Salzer, R. T., 262, *282*
Sand
    as art material, 225
    colored, 220
    and water, 196–197, 300
Sandburg, C., 262
Sanders, T. S., 210, *212*
Sandford, J. P., 106, *121*
Saracho, O. N., 10, *13,* 57, 64, *72, 98,* 151,
        156, *160,* 162, 166, 171, 172, *181,* 190,
        211, 241, *245,* 248, 273, 274, 275, 276,
        282, 283, 315, 327, 331, *333, 334,* 336,
        348
Saunders, R., 237, *245*
Sawdust and wheat paste, 225
Sawyer, R., 262
Sayers, F. C., 262
Scheduling activities, 116–119
    evaluating, 173, 174
    managing problem behavior and, 132
Schema theory, 274–275, 285
Scheppler, Louise, 17
Schmidt, R., 86, *98*

Schmidt, W. H. O., *98*
Schneider, H., 222
Schneider, N., 222
School-appropriate behavior, developing, 324–326
School librarians, 62
School psychologists, 62
School roles, learning, 324
Schultz, T., 41, *51*
Schurz, Margarethe, 22
Schwartz, J. I., 89, *98*
Schwartzman, H. B., 184, *211*
Schweinhart, L. J., 8, *12*, 41, *51*
Science, 286–301
   animals, 289–291
   ecology and environment, 298–300
   materials and experiences, 300–301
   nutrition, 296–298
   physics, 287–289
   plants, 291–293
   play and, 209
   weather, 293–295
Screening of exceptional children, 176–177
Scribbling stage, 216
Scribner, S., 93, *98*
Scriven, M., 172, *181*
Seaver, J. W., 63, *72*
Secular programs, 43–44
Seeger, R. C., 232
Seifert, K., 69–70, *72*, 87, *98*
Selecting educational equipment for school and home, 113
Self-awareness, 326–327, 336
Self-communication, 89
Self-concept of teacher, 336
Self-control, development of, 126, 127, 133
Self-expression, 214–216. *See also* Creative activities
Self-worth, cultural awareness and, 331
Seligson, M., 11, *13*, 42, *50*
Semantic differential scales, 164–165, 166
Semantics, 248
Semmes, M., *12*
Sendak, M., 233, 249, 254, *283*
Sensorimotor development, 88
Sensory awareness, 87
Sequin, Edouard, 24
Seriation, 304–305
Set, organizing things into, 305
Seuss, Dr., 253
Sex education, 68
Shaping, 325
Shapiro, M. S., 22, *31*
Shaw, J. M., 302, *311*
Shedlock, M. L., 262

Shepard, B., 90–91, *98, 180*
Shermis, S. S., 313
Shipman, V., 8, *13*
Shortage of qualified personnel, 70
Sigel, I., 237, *245*
Singer, J. L., 187, *211*
Singing with young children, 231–234
Single-parent families, 144
Skeen, P., *97*, 144, *160*, 223, *245*
Skinner, B. F., 81–82
Skinner box, 81–82
Smilansky, S., 189, *211*
Smith, F., 274, *283*
Smith, M. M., 49, *51*
Smith, R. F., 287, 288, *311*
Smith, S. C., 259
Smith, T. L., 241, *245*
Snacks, 297–298
Snyder, A., 55, *71*
Sociableness, 325
Social class differences, 95
Social competencies, 325, 326
Social development, 91, 104, 209. *See also* Socialization; Social studies program
Social environment, 122–141
   classroom management, 126–136
   grouping, 9, 104–105, 123–125
   one-to-one interactions, 125
   organizing adults, 136–139
   organizing children, 123–126
Social interactions, teaching positive, 133–134
Socialization, 91, 133–134, 323–332
   cultural awareness, developing, 330–332
   defined, 323
   levels of moral thought, 328–330
   school and community roles, learning, 324
   school-appropriate behavior, developing, 324–326
   self-awareness, building, 326–327
   values, 92, 327–328, 330
   See also Social studies program
Social knowledge, 314
Social Security Act of 1975, Title XX of, 47
Social service agencies, relationships with, 45–46
Social studies program, 315–332
   acting on acquired knowledge, 321–322
   artifacts, 320
   audiovisual materials, 320–321
   concepts, 316–317
   content, 315–323
   field trips, 138–139, 317–319
   goals of, 313–316
   mapping, 322–323

Social studies program (*cont.*)
  resource persons, 319–320
  See also Socialization
Social workers, 62
Socioemotional behavior of three- to five-year-
    olds, 85–86. *See also* Emotional develop-
    ment
Sock puppets, 264–265
Solitary play, 188, 189
Solomon, P., 38, *50*
Songbooks, 232–233
Southern Association for Children under Six,
    343, 347
Space requirements, 8, 104, 111. *See also* Phys-
    ical environment
Specialist, early childhood, 61
Speech, language vs., 89
Spidell, R. A., 135, *140*, 193, *211*
Spock, B. J., 86, *98*
Spodek, B., 7, 10, *13*, 23, *31*, 57, 64, *72*, 96, *98*,
    124, 132, *140*, 148, 151, 156, 158, *160*,
    171, 172, *181*, 189, 190, *211*, 232, 241,
    245, 248, 275, *283*, 286, *311*, 314, 315,
    318, 322, 327, 331, *333*, *334*, 336, 347,
    348
Sponsorship, institutional, 42–45
Spratt, J. E., *98*
Stacking and nesting toys, 206
Staff/child ratio, 104–105
Staffing crisis, 70
Staffing patterns, 136–139
Stake, R. E., 171, *181*
Standardized tests, 167–169
Standards
  ethics and, 68, 69
  professionalization and, 57–58
Stanford Early School Achievement Test, 168
Steig, W., 253
Steinfels, M. O., *31*
Stengel, S. R., 330, *334*
Stepfamilies, 144
Stereotypes in children's literature, 256–257
Stern, V., 167
Stevens, J. H., Jr., 37, 38, *51*, 134, *140*, 158, *160*
Stewart, M. I., 91, *97*, *180*
Stigler, J. W., 93, *98*
Stillwell, L., 267, *281*
Stinard, T. A., 39, *51*
Storage, organizing, 107–108
Stories for Little Children (Buck), 262
Storytelling, 260–262
Storytelling: Art and Technique (Baker & Greene),
    262
Streissguth, A. P., 9, *13*
Study group, teacher, 339–340

Substance abuse, 68
Sulzby, E., 273, *283*
Summative evaluation, 172
Sunal, C. S., 315, *334*
Superego, 78
Surplus energy theory of play, 185, 186
Sutherland, Z., 249, 259, *283*
Swick, K. J., 158, *160*
Sylvester and the Magic Pebble (Steig), 253
Symbolic functioning, 88
Symbolic learning in play, 210
Symbolic play, 189
Symbols (Myller), 252
Syntactics, 248

Table activities, 206–208
Tales from Grimm (Gag), 262
Tax-supported programs, 44
Teacher, 60–61
  assistant, 56, 59, 137
  associate, 59–60
  male, 68–70
  as model, 92, 131, 134, 325
  pay for, 70
  personal characteristics of, 55
  personal development of, 336
  professional development of, 337–347
  role of, 54–55
  types of decisions made by, 105
  visiting, 62
Teacher aides, 56, 137, 340
Teacher education, 64–65, 70
  in-service programs, 338–342
  See also Professionalism
*Teacher Education Guidelines for Four- and Five-
    Year Programs* (NAEYC), 60–61
Teacher-education reform movement, 64–65,
    70
Teacher study group, 339–340
Teaching
  direct, 325, 326
  indirect, 325–326
Teaching certificate, 65–68
Teaching credential, 65–68
Teale, W., 272, 276, *283*
Technology, professional development using,
    341–342
Teen-agers, children born to, 153
Tell Me a Story (Colwell), 262
Tempera paint, 216–217
Temple, Alice, 22
Tesman, J. R., 90–91, *98*, *180*
Tests, 162
  informal, 169–170
  standardized, 167–169

Tests of Basic Experience, 168
Texture drawings, 219
Thackeray, D., 270, *281*
Theodorou, P., 91, *98, 180*
Thinking game, 328
Thompson, G. G., *98*
Thought
  conceptual, 87–88
  intuitive, 88
  moral, levels of, 328–330
  play and development of, 187
  preconceptual, 88
  See also Cognitive development; Cognitively
    oriented learning
Three-dimensional art, 221–225
Time, teaching about, 309
Time allocation, 116–119
Tissue paper collage, 220
Title XX of the Social Security Act of 1975, 47
Tomorrow's Teachers: A Report of the Holmes Group,
  64
Torrance, E. P., 215, *245*
Torrey, J., *283*
Torvey, D. R., 274, *283*
Toys, criteria for judging educational, 175–
  176. *See also* Play
Traffic, organizing for movement of, 106
Transition time, difficulties around, 117–118
Travers, J., 104, *121*
Travis, N. E., 152, *160*
Treder, R., 91, *98*
Trends in early childhood education, 9–11
Tresselt, A., 222
Trotter, R. J., 87, *98, 181*
True, J. H., 143, *159*
Turiel, E., 328, 329, *334*
Turner, J. S., 86, 87, 88, 89, *97, 180*
Tweedy, M., 93, *98*
Two-dimensional art, 216–221

U.S. Bureau of the Census, 37, 153
Unit blocks, 201, 221
University courses, taking, 342
Unmarried mothers, programs for, 153

Values, 92, 327–328, 330
Vandenberg, B., 185, *211*
Vander Ven, K., 347, *348*
Variation in teaching, 129
Vartuli, S., 105, *121*
Verbal guidance, 131
Very Hungry Caterpillar, The (Carle), 252
Videocassette recorders, 321
Vinovskis, M. A., 16, *30*
Visiting teachers, 62

Volunteers, working with, 137–138, 151–152
Vukelich, C., 277–278, *283*
Vygotsky, L. S., 187, *212*

Wadsworth, B. J., 88, *98*
Wagner, D., *98*
Wake Up City (Tresselt), 222
Walsh, H. M., 172, *181,* 316, 317, 325, 327, 332,
  334
Walters, C. M., 144, *159*
Ward, C. B., 63, *72*
Ward, W., 260, *283*
Washtub bass, 236
Waters, E., 91, *97*
Water table, 300
Waxed drawings, 219
Way of the Storyteller, The (Sawyer), 262
Weather, teaching about, 293–295
Weber, E., *13, 23, 31*
Weber, L., 55, *72*
Weight, measuring, 308–309
Weikart, D. P., 8, *12,* 41, *51*
Weinberg, R. A., 166
Weiss, R. S., 144, *160*
Werner, P., 115, *121*
Westhoff, C. R., *13*
Wheel toys, 195
Where the Wild Things Are (Sendak), 249
Whipple, G., 23, *31*
White, F. M., 255
White, R. F., 187, *212*
Whitesell, N. R., 90, *98*
Wildsmith, B., 254, 259
Williams, C. K., 302, *311*
Willamson, P. M., 250, *283*
Wills, T. A., 91, *97*
Wilson, R. M., 124, *140*
Winn, M., 233
Withitness, concept of, 128–129
Wolf, M. M., 336, *348*
Wolfgang, C. H., 210, *211, 212*
Wolfinger, D. M., 301, *311*
Women, working, 7
Wood, V., 273, *281*
Wooden blocks, 200
Woodworking, 223, 300
Woodworking for Young Children (Skeen, Garner,
  & Cartwright), 223
Work-site child care centers, 7
World Organization for Early Childhood Edu-
  cation (OMEP), 343
World War II, 28–29
Worsham, M. E., 106, *121*
Wortham, S. C., 115–116, *121*
Worth of program, evaluating, 171

Wright, B. F., 250
Writing
   relationship between reading and, 275–277
   stages of evolution, 276–277
Written language, teaching about, 277–280

Yabrove, G., 91, *98, 180*
Yaden, D., 273, *283*

Yashima, T., 253
Yawkey, T. D., 188, *211*
Young Children (journal), 342
Your Friend, the Tree (White), 255

Zigler, E. F., *13,* 41, *51,* 65
Zintz, M., 273, *282*
Zion, G., 222
Zoo City (Lewis), 255